The Grave of
Alice B. Toklas

·OTTO FRIEDRICH·

The Grave of
Alice B. Toklas

AND OTHER REPORTS FROM THE PAST

HENRY HOLT AND COMPANY

NEW YORK

Published by Henry Holt and Company, Inc.,
115 West 18th Street, New York, New York 10011.
Published in Canada by Fitzhenry & Whiteside Limited,
195 Allstate Parkway, Markham, Ontario L3R 4T8.

Library of Congress Cataloging-in-Publication Data
Friedrich, Otto, 1929–
The grave of Alice B. Toklas / by Otto Friedrich. —1st ed.
p. cm.
ISBN: 0-8050-0903-5
I. Title.
PS3556.R5659G74   1989
813'.54—dc19   88-23058
                                                                      CIP

"The Grave of Alice B. Toklas" appeared in Esquire (December 1967); "How to Be a War Correspondent" appeared in
The Yale Review (Spring 1959); "On Watching Parsifal
with Molly" appeared in Esquire (May 1970); "A Little Tour
with Henry James" appeared in The American Scholar (Autumn 1975); "The Lion on the Mountain" appeared in
Smithsonian (April 1987); "The Trial of Sergeant Walker" appeared in American Heritage (February 1988); "There Are
OO Trees in Russia" appeared in Harper's (October 1964);
"Reunion in Concord" appeared in Harper's (May 1971).

Henry Holt books are available at special discounts for
bulk purchases for sales promotions, premiums, fund raising,
or educational use. Special editions or book excerpts can
also be created to specification.

For details, contact:

Special Sales Director
Henry Holt and Company, Inc.
115 West 18th Street
New York, New York 10011

First Edition

DESIGNED BY CLAIRE M. NAYLON
Printed in the United States of America
1 3 5 7 9 10 8 6 4 2

To Priscilla

CONTENTS

PREFACE

I should like to be able to announce at the beginning that this book has some underlying theme, some stout thread that almost invisibly ties together all these diverse stories and transforms them into a unified historical work. Unfortunately, it is not so. What unifying theme could possibly connect the bleak grave of Alice B. Toklas with the rituals of Wagner's *Parsifal,* or the romances of the Empress Galla Placidia with the execution of a Civil War sergeant for demanding that black soldiers get equal pay?

Perhaps only the fact that they are all reports from the past, that ever-expanding territory in which all choices have already been made, all actions taken, a territory now a field for reflection, for remembering or forgetting what cannot be changed. This applies just as well to my own past as to that of the human race. When one is young, one speeds nervously along in a kind of perpetual present, but as one gets older, one acquires a clearer view of the shapes of what has already evolved. In some of these stories, I am the main character, in some a minor one, in some a mere shadow in the background. Still, I write about Scarlatti because I love to play his music, and about Monte Cassino because the sight of it moved me. You can hardly avoid guessing that one of my great-grandfathers was a German judge, but another one was an officer in a New York artillery regiment that fought with Grant at Spotsylvania and the Wilderness. Their lives are also mine.

Though I have written several works of history—notably *Before the Deluge* and *The End of the World*—I am not a historian, at least not in the academic sense. I am a storyteller. I have never given a lecture to a roomful of young students—or rather, I only once made the attempt and then decided never to attempt it again—and I dislike the whole apparatus of "scholarship," the footnotes and the waspish euphemisms and the perpetual caution. I have worked most of my life as a journalist, for institutions as different as *The Stars and Stripes* and *The Saturday Evening Post*, the *New York Daily News* and *Time*, but I think that history, journalism, and autobiography are all part of the same process of storytelling, of revelation and self-revelation, of bearing witness. It is the process of the Ancient Mariner clutching at the wedding guest and insisting on his story. " 'There was a ship,' quoth he."

These stories not only are about the past but emerge from the past in which they were written. This involves a period of nearly thirty years. The only two that are really not stories are also the two earliest, and they deal with the methods by which stories come to be told. "How to Be a War Correspondent" (1959) derives from my sense of guilt about "covering" the Vietnam War without getting within a thousand miles of it, for an audience that hardly knew or cared that the war existed. "There Are 00 Trees in Russia" (1964) deals with the newsmagazines' none-too-successful efforts to remedy such shortcomings. When I wrote it, after ending five years at *Newsweek*, I never expected to write for a newsmagazine again; when I went to work at *Time* a decade later, I found that my confessions were now required reading for all new researchers, a chronicle of legends about the bad old days, of malpractices now forbidden.

Not long afterwards, I wrote a story about French politics, and I quoted a few factual details from an article by André Fontaine of *Le Monde*, a man who knew as much about French politics as anyone alive. Under *Time*'s perfectionist rules, even the smallest of such details had to be verified by the Time-Life News Service, and so, since the new Paris bureau chief hadn't answered my researcher's cable on this point, she telephoned Paris late on the night of the magazine's closing to make absolutely sure that Fontaine's parliamentary statistics were accurate. "Just a minute," said the bureau

chief over the telephone from Paris, "I'll ask my wife. She's French."
Plus ça change . . .

Because these stories all come out of the past, I see no point in trying to update them. So although it may seem odd for an account of newsmagazine journalism to begin with the late Senator Henry Cabot Lodge campaigning for the Republican presidential nomination of 1964, a report on the Dukakis-Bush campaign would probably not be wildly different. The secret war that the French were waging in Algeria at the start of "How to Be a War Correspondent" has now become the secret war that the United States is waging in Central America. And so on. Despite the chronic agitation of the press, most things change very little from year to year. Much of the France that Henry James toured in 1882 is still there today, and even though Monte Cassino keeps being destroyed by barbarians, it keeps being rebuilt. *Pax.*

There are a number of cases, though, in which the past simply will not stay past. The legendary island of Iona, for example, was offered up for sale several years after I visited it, and I could scarcely leave that unmentioned. Well, let the event and its consequences be offered as a footnote. Mozart presents a more difficult problem. I wrote what I originally intended as a short book about the last year of his life before anyone had ever seen or even heard of Peter Shaffer's *Amadeus.* I then watched with dismay as Shaffer's essentially false version of that last year became not only a worldwide success but the only version that most people would ever know. Like Shaffer himself, who rewrote his theatrical *Amadeus* into a quite different film of the same name, I broke my own rules and rewrote my version of the story.

As I have generally been unwilling to "update" the past, I have been equally unwilling to correct it. I have undoubtedly made a few errors—no book has ever been wholly free of them—but most are inconsequential. Only two are important and need to be mentioned here, one an error of fact and one of judgment.

When I read in the newspapers that Alice B. Toklas had been buried next to Gertrude Stein, I went to Père-Lachaise and found the scene exactly as I later described it: the rather prim grave marked as that of Gertrude Stein and next to it a grave-size area of rubble and debris. My sense of loss and guilt and desolation at that sight was also exactly as I described it. Only after my story was published in *Esquire* in 1967, with a color photograph of the two adjacent sites, did I learn of what an all-too-jocular *Esquire* editor called my "grave error." When the newspapers spoke of Miss Toklas being buried "next to" Miss Stein, they did not mean "in an adjacent grave," they meant *next to* Miss Stein. Her grave itself had been dug open, and in it, by her side, they had buried her lifelong friend. The adjacent site remained, as far as I know, empty. So, like Henry James reflecting on the Battle of Poitiers while gazing devoutly in the wrong direction, I had felt those powerful emotions of loss while contemplating an empty grave. Well, since no corrections are really corrective, so be it.

The other error was less specific. It derived from my having been raised in the home of a self-exiled German who loathed Wagner almost as much as he loathed Hitler. Bach and Beethoven, that was the only true German art. He worked at Bach's suites on his cello every Sunday morning, and when I got old enough to master the piano part, we struggled through the Beethoven cello sonatas together. We are all too much taught how to approach art; we hear and see what we are taught to hear and see. And so, as I had long listened to Bach with reverence, I first heard Wagner with suspicion and disapproval.

That suspicion and disapproval lasted for about forty years, as recounted in "On Watching *Parsifal* with Molly." And then, in 1983, on watching the Boulez/Chereau production of the *Ring*—on television, where the subtitles enabled me for the first time to understand what all those characters were singing as they were singing it—I was overwhelmed. The *Ring,* I was finally forced to realize, is a great masterpiece, and Wagner a great composer. Does that mean that I should suppress my earlier account of my experience with Wagner, or that I should add a footnote saying that I was all wrong? No, the story is what it is.

Let us not, finally, be too monumentally serious. Although many of my stories are sad, even tragic, there are also many funny details along the way, touches of irony, absurdities. That mixture is what good stories are, for the most part; at least, it is what my stories are. Almost any one of these could have been a book in itself, with a little huffing and puffing to give it bookish dimensions and a bookish tone. But the best stories almost tell themselves, at a length of their own choosing, and that length is apt to be modest. Combined between hard covers, they offer not unity but diversity, a variety of time and place, of subject and idea. Let that be pleasure enough.

August 1988

The Grave of
Alice B. Toklas

The Grave of Alice B. Toklas

▪ AT THE ENTRANCE TO THE CEMETERY OF PÈRE-LACHAISE, ON the boulevard de Ménilmontant in northeastern Paris, stands a yellowish wall of masonry, about fifteen feet high. On one side of the entry, the wall bears the motto *Spes illorum immortalitate plena est*. On the other side is a quotation from St. John: *Qui credit in me etiam si mortuus fuerit vivet*. Behind this entrance, one sunny afternoon last spring, I knocked at the glass door of what appeared to be a custodian's lodge. Inside, there was a gendarme, tightly imprisoned within his blue uniform, and with that gendarme look of a strong man who has never done a day's hard work. The place itself had the musty smell of the gendarmerie, where burly men in uniforms spend their time filling out forms, and the windows are never opened.

I begged his pardon and asked him whether he had a map of the cemetery or whether he could tell a visitor how to find a certain grave. *"Bien sûr,"* he said, reaching to his right and bringing forth a printed map of the graveyard. He picked up a blue pencil from his desk, marked an *x* at the site of his own lodge, and asked me what grave I was looking for. "Gertrude Stein," I said. The blank, stolid face almost frowned. "She was an American writer," I added. "She died about twenty years ago." *"Je regrette, Monsieur,"* he said equably, *"mais je ne connais pas ce nom."* He was not bothered or even concerned. He was simply stating a fact.

"Mais voyons," he said. *"Vous êtes içi."* Then, with his blue pen-

1

cil, he began to trace the proper route for a tourist to follow. Here, he said, was where the composers were buried—Chopin, Cherubini, Bellini, *"et les autres."* Here, the blue pencil moved on, I would find the grave of Edith Piaf. He paused and then wrote on the edge of the map: "E. Piaf." He looked up at me to see whether I appreciated the importance of this revelation. I apparently disappointed him. He made a new effort. Here, he went on, was the grave of Balzac, and he bent down to mark the spot with his blue pencil: "H.B." And here—he didn't seem to care about my reaction to Balzac—were the graves of Héloïse and Abelard. Once again, he wrote on the margin of the map: "E. AB." He looked up at me triumphantly, and I apparently disappointed him again, for he added, "But this name that you ask I do not know."

I thanked him once more and asked him how I might find the grave of Gertrude Stein, so he directed me to an administration building, on the first pathway to the right, and then *"tout droit, tout droit."* I asked him whether I might take along the map that he had illustrated for me, and he eagerly pushed it toward me. *"Entendu,"* he added, "that the guards of the cemetery would appreciate a contribution." I took out a one-franc coin, about twenty-five cents, and plunked it down on his desk. He looked at it with some surprise, as though he had never expected anything of the kind, and I could not guess whether it was too much or too little, but I thanked him once again and walked out of the gloomy office into the April sunshine.

At the administration building, the lady behind the grillwork was less solemn but equally unfamiliar with the name of Gertrude Stein. She looked past me into space for a minute, wondering whether it was some celebrity that she ought to recognize, and then a young man at another desk tried to help. *"Ah, oui, Gertrude Stein, oui,"* he said, "it's 1946 or 1947, I think." The lady went back to a long row of filing cabinets and began to search. In a few minutes, she came back with a satisfied smile and handed me a small printed form entitled *"Situation de sépulture."* The details were clear. *Nom: Stein Gertrude. Date de l'inhumation: 22-10-1946. 94 division. 1 ligne 77. Numéro 12-97.* On the back of the paper was another map, a smaller version of the one for which I had paid a contribution to the guards of the cemetery, and the lady showed me the location of division

94, at the opposite end of the graveyard, and then she took a ball-point pen and marked an *x* at the approximate site of the grave.

In the hot April sun, through the chestnut trees that were just bursting into white flowers, I began climbing the avenue Casimir-Périer, past the carrefour du Grand-Rond, and on up the avenue des Acacias. *Cemetery* is not really the right word for Père-Lachaise, and neither is *graveyard*. It is a burial ground. It is filled not simply with graves but with tombs, stone buildings with the dimensions and the quality of outhouses, built of granite rather than clapboard, asserting a proprietary sense of privacy, and yet crumbling, dilapidated. Clustered together, only a few inches apart, they bear the names of the French bourgeoisie of a century ago, commonplace and unknown names like Verroux and Duvallier. Many of them bear money's warning against the threat of the progress that plows up old graves: *"Concession en perpétuité."* It was in the same spirit that the tombs were built of stone and iron, but many of the stones have fallen in, and the iron is rusted, and there are cobwebs in the corners, and the ivy that once was planted as a memorial now climbs the walls like a strangling weed.

On the avenue des Acacias, the flowering trees grow thickly, and the afternoon sun flickers through the branches. Birds nest here, and the dark asphalt path is whitened with their droppings. Down the hill, at the carrefour du Grand-Rond, there were nurses wheeling babies in carriages on a spring walk, but here there is no one. There is no sense of grief either, nor even of sadness, just tombs and gravestones crowded next to one another in a kind of slum, the tenement rows of French respectability lying in state, forgotten.

I look at my map and risk a shortcut, abandoning the asphalt driveway and turning onto a gravel path. Amid the graves, I meet a lady of about fifty, confused, and wearing too much rouge. She wants to talk to me, but I know that I cannot help her. *"Pardon, Monsieur,"* she says, in an accent that I cannot identify. I shrug at her, indicating that I am as lost as she. *"Pardon,"* she insists, "can you tell me where—where I can find the grave of Sarah Bernhardt?" "I'm sorry," I answer. *"Je suis perdu moi-même."* She smiles and wanders on through the thousands of graves in the setting sun.

I look up and see a sign, and my map shows me that this path will lead to the Ninety-fourth Division, where Gertrude Stein was buried. But I am not really looking for the grave of Gertrude Stein, whom I never met. I am looking for the much newer grave that the newspapers said would be next to hers, the grave of Alice B. Toklas.

World War II, when I was growing up, was a war between where we were and where we came from, who we were and who our ancestors had been. My father had come from Germany as a student and met my mother at Rockford College in Illinois, and he decided in 1933 or 1934 that he could not endure living in his own country. During the thirties, he spent much of his time making speeches against the Nazis, pleading for Allied intervention against Hitler, but on the first of September, 1939, he sat in tears in the pink-walled living room of our farm in Vermont, listening to the shrieking voice of Berlin on the shortwave radio and predicting that the RAF would destroy Germany in thirty days. Finally, we were at war against our-selves.

In the seventh grade, we heard the teachers whispering in the halls about the German attack on Narvik, but in a social studies class my older brother stubbornly denied that the Germans had also started World War I, and he was made to stay after school for disobedience. I, more diplomatic, kept quiet. At home, I filled a scrapbook with battle maps clipped from *Life*, with arrows showing offensives and pincer movements on one side or the other. In high school, we gathered in the assembly hall to hear President Roose-velt denounce the date that would live in infamy, and we aided the war effort by collecting scrap metal and buying defense stamps, and we cheered Robert Taylor as he fired his machine gun against the Japanese who surrounded him in the closing scene of the movie *Bataan*. Still, it was a great day for my father when he got a three-month-old letter from his mother through the Red Cross in Switzerland, bringing news of his brothers, the businessman, the clergyman, and the journalist. And then, walking through the pi-geons on the Boston Common on a sunny spring afternoon in 1944,

I saw the newsboys at the Park Street station waving extras of the *Boston Globe* with gigantic headlines that said: WE TAKE ROME. It was almost over.

Going to Europe in 1946, on a Turkish freighter called the *Bakir,* which took twenty-nine days to get from New York to Marseilles, was like going behind what we had been taught to consider enemy lines. In the war maps in *Life,* all of Europe was a battlefield, and it was hard to imagine what might be left intact. The destruction was appalling. The great cities of Germany were now heaps of rubble, literally mountains of broken brick and stone, suffused with the awful smell of hidden but still unburied bodies. What was equally surprising was that so much had survived, not just the Alps or the River Rhône, not just Chartres or Santa Croce, but a whole civilization, stunned and terribly wounded but nonetheless alive. "As a lone ant from a broken ant-hill / from the wreckage of Europe, ego scriptor," Ezra Pound wrote in the *Pisan Cantos.* "The rain has fallen, the wind coming down / out of the mountain / Lucca, Forti dei Marmi, Berchtold after the other one . . . / parts reassembled." Ezra Pound was then confined in a cage in Pisa, waiting to be sent back to the United States to stand trial for treason, and in Wiesbaden I heard the celebrated Walter Gieseking, who was generally regarded as a Nazi sympathizer, play the piano at the home of an American colonel. He accompanied an untalented singer in Strauss's *Voices of Spring.* Most of the colonel's guests had never heard of Gieseking, and they clinked the ice in their highball glasses throughout the recital. I asked what the pianist would be paid for such a performance, and I was told, "Oh, a couple of cartons of cigarettes."

For almost ten years, Europe had really been a battlefield, as battered as the fields outside Verdun, where the ground still heaves with the scars of shells fired a half century ago, but the amazing discovery of 1946 was that the dead of Europe were still alive. My seventy-three-year-old grandmother, for example, had survived all the bombings of Munich and still smoked two packs of cigarettes a day, and gave away all the clothes that my father sent her to the *"Flüchtlinge"* pouring in from the east. And so, with that outrageous self-confidence of the seventeen-year-old, I began a systematic campaign of barging in on that whole generation of living monuments who had survived the war. It was on the dimly lit lakefront terrace of the Grand Hotel at Lausanne that I accosted the bent and white-haired figure of Richard Strauss and asked him to look at the opening pages of a piano concerto I was trying to write. He shrugged and turned his back, and tugged his cape tighter around his shoulders, and the elderly lady accompanying him angrily waved me off. I didn't mind. I was a tourist, collecting a generation, and, at seventeen, one has no sense of propriety, and no rebuff matters.

Nor is one always rebuffed. The old are sometimes fascinated by young intruders, or too polite or too weary to resist them. So, over the next few years, I knocked on the door of André Gide's apartment and collected an inscribed copy of his new book on Chopin; so I invited myself to tea and cucumber sandwiches with Sir Max and Lady Beerbohm on the sunny terrace of their villa at Rapallo; so I called on George Santayana, reclining in striped pajamas on his bed at the Convent of the Blue Nuns in Rome; so I had dinner with Harold Laski, and paid a visit to Karl Jaspers, and took piano lessons with Georg Pembauer, who was said to be a pupil of Liszt, and, on leaving Munich for Paris, got the elegant and tea-brown old man to write me a letter of introduction that began *"Sehr geehrter Meister Cortot . . ."*

I was in Geneva when I heard that Gertrude Stein had died, Gertrude Stein, whom my mother had greatly admired, because she thought of her as a friend of Hemingway, whom she even more greatly admired, Gertrude Stein, who had lived all those years on the other side of the front, quite peacefully, and then graphically described the arrival of the first Americans, Brewsie and Willie, Gertrude Stein had died, and I thought, in the cold-blooded way of the seventeen-year-old: "Well, now I'll never get to meet Gertrude Stein."

I do not remember how this peculiar form of tourism and monument viewing brought me to Alice B. Toklas. I remember only that, one early evening in the gray Parisian winter of 1948, I found myself pressing the buzzer at 5, rue Christine, passing through the large and empty courtyard, and then walking up the shallow steps to the second floor. Walking beside me was a friend called David Hersey. Perhaps it was his idea; perhaps he had made the arrangements. In any case, he was an actor, and enough of a gentleman to be carrying an armful of lilacs, which he had brought as an offering. We heard the doorbell ring, then the shuffling of steps. A pudgy, red-cheeked woman opened the heavy door, listened to our names, and then turned to shuffle back down the hallway. This was Gabrielle, who never smiled, never showed any interest or surprise. She led us through the hallway, which was full of small paintings, and into the gigantic living room, which was cold and dark, and, despite the extravagant furnishings, austere. While Gabrielle went to fetch "Madame," we stood in a kind of embarrassed awe.

It is hard to remember a first impression of a room that later becomes familiar, but my recollection of that impression was the recollection of a shrine. This must have been the way everything was when Gertrude Stein lived here, and it must have remained unchanged. The paintings, of course, were overwhelming, not just because of what they were but because of the way they were hung, familiarly, crowded. Above the fireplace, casually superimposed on top of a large mirror, was Picasso's *Femme Nue sur Fond Rose,* and on another wall hung an equally impressive work, *Jeune Fille aux Fleurs.* (Janet Flanner, of *The New Yorker,* described this in an obituary note on Miss Toklas as "the famous nude girl holding a basket of flowers—her [Gertrude Stein's] first purchase, with her brother, Leo. Miss Stein thought the figure's legs badly painted, so the Montmartre art merchant said, 'Oh, cut them off if you don't like them—the artist won't mind anything if you'll only buy.' ") To the left of the fireplace was a Picasso painting of a Spanish town, which Gertrude Stein had described, in *The Autobiography of Alice B. Toklas,* as "the beginning of Cubism." On the other side hung a Cézanne apple, and on either side there were three or four rather odd Picasso "African" drawings of men with banana-shaped heads. But I did not really take much note, because I do not see paintings the way lovers of paintings see them. I saw an astonishing horsehair sofa, and a standing screen of flowers done in petit point, and a tiny, hunched old woman creeping toward us, accompanied by a giant poodle with yellowing hair and a rather stupid face.

Miss Toklas was puzzled. Who were we and what did we want? A guided tour of the pictures? Recollections of Gertrude Stein? She was still a little puzzled two years later, when she described it in a letter as "our first meeting when he and you blew in that evening." My friend Hersey was a cultivated young man who could speak easily of Picasso and Braque, which I could not. He had read Gertrude Stein, which I had not, and also such people as Ezra Pound and Ford Madox Ford and Virginia Woolf. While they conversed, I sat in silence, trying to make friends with the poodle, Basket, whom I didn't really like, and observing this newest monument that I had discovered. Miss Toklas was incredibly ugly, uglier than almost anyone I had ever met. A thin, withered creature, she sat hunched in her chair, in her heavy tweed suit and her thick lisle stockings, impregnable and indifferent. She had a huge nose, a dark mustache, and her dark-dyed hair was combed into absurd bangs over her forehead.

When she was young, this ugliness must have tormented her, and there are many photographs of her hovering behind Gertrude Stein on some arrival or departure, taking care of the suitcases. She was usually in the background in those days. Gertrude Stein quotes her in the *Autobiography* as saying, "The geniuses came and talked to Gertrude Stein and the wives sat with me ... I have sat with wives who were not wives, of geniuses who were real geniuses. I have sat with real wives of geniuses who were not real geniuses. I have sat with wives of geniuses, of near geniuses, of would be geniuses, in short I have sat very often and very long with many wives and wives of many geniuses." But in a curious way, the ugliness of Alice Toklas was such that the whole practice of judging people by their appearance became irrelevant. Someone who had been a great beauty at twenty might present an appalling spectacle of self-hatred at seventy, but Alice Toklas, though puzzled by her visitors, was calm and cheerful at seventy-one. I began to notice the qualities that never appear in photographs—the shrewdness of the large, dark eyes, the cultivated and slightly grainy quality of her voice, the warmth of her malicious laughter. Unlike many old people, she was not the least bit resigned to anything. She knew what she admired, and what she despised, and she saw the two in perpetual combat, and she was quite fierce about which side she was on.

My friend Hersey did not interest her. He was nice enough, but he was an actor, and she wasn't interested in actors. She was interested in writers, and so she eventually turned to me, still sitting silently on the horsehair sofa and communing with the unlovable Basket, and began to interrogate me. What was I writing? A novel. Was this my first novel? No, it was my third. Would I show them to her? No, they were not worth it. Would I show her the new one? Not until it was finished. What was it about? About Germany. Then she asked an odd question that I had never really thought about before. "Who," she asked, "are your influences?"

I thought for a minute and said I didn't know.

"Faulkner, I guess."

"Good," she said.

"And Hemingway," I said.

"Not so good," she said. "Not Hemingway."

"And Kafka," I said.

"Really?" she said.

"And Henry James," I said.

"That's good, that's very good," she said. "But you don't sound like someone who would be influenced by Hemingway."

At nineteen, it is hard to have the courage of one's convictions, because one has no convictions, and I did not dare confront this fierce old lady with a defense of Hemingway. Perhaps he did not influence me after all. Perhaps I was influenced mainly by the fact that my mother, who had gone to the same high school in Glen Ellyn, Illinois, thought he was the world's greatest writer. Nothing I actually wrote bore any resemblance to anything by Hemingway, and it was really Franz Kafka who exerted an almost suffocating influence, even more than Dostoyevsky, whom I had not wanted to mention at all, but I was not sure that she approved of Kafka either. "Let me see what you've written," she said, quite commandingly. "I'd really be interested."

Hersey stayed in Paris that whole winter, and we celebrated New Year's Eve in a dingy, empty bar, and I wrote ten pages every day, good day or bad, good pages or bad, and by the time Hersey went back to America I had finished the new novel, which I pretentiously entitled *Angels' Laughter*. I went to the rue Christine with another large bundle of lilacs, and the manuscript in a black snap-on folder. I also brought an earlier novel, a sort of fable called *The Little Wizened Man.*

"Look, don't bring me flowers," Miss Toklas said. "It's silly and expensive and I don't need them. Where's the novel?"

"Which one?" I asked, partly as a joke, but not entirely. It was already a game of the young and the old.

"Well, how many have you brought? The new one?"

"Here." I handed her the fat black folder.

"Good," she said. "What's that one?"

"That's another one," I said. "It's an early work. But it might give you more of an idea."

"An early work," she repeated. "When did you write that?"

"Last summer," I said. That was also partly a joke, but she liked it. In fact, she recounted the whole scene to me almost twenty years later, laughing. "An early work that you'd written the previous summer."

"That's good," she said then. "Come along now, in here." She had opened the door herself, apologizing for the illness of Gabrielle, and she shuffled down the dark corridor, leading me into the living room, clutching the black folder under her arm. "Sit down here. I'll be right back."

I sat on the horsehair sofa, in the great silence of what I still considered a museum. I knew the paintings by now, but dutifully stared at them, not interested.

There were certain rituals at the rue Christine, and one of them was Armagnac, a drink I had never had before, didn't like, and still don't, but that was what Miss Toklas served, always in the same cut-glass decanter, on a tray, with a small glass. She came creeping in with the tray but just deposited it on the long table. "Help yourself." She sank back in a chair next to the fireplace and began the cigarette ritual. On a slender antique table next to her chair stood a silver donkey wagon, a gift, as I recall, from Carl Van Vechten, filled with cigarettes. Next to it was a large box of kitchen matches. Miss Toklas would extract a cigarette from the elegant silver wagon, then pick up the box of kitchen matches, take out one long match, and then begin a conversation, the unlit cigarette between her lips, the unlit match hovering over the cigarette.

"What kind of a book is it?" she asked, watching me, not lighting the cigarette. "The new one, I mean."

All writers want to talk about their books, and young writers want very badly to talk about their books, and a young writer who has just finished a book wants so desperately to talk about it that a welcome almost silences him. Then he begins to make excuses for his work. *The Little Wizened Man,* the "early work," was not to be taken seriously. I had written it in three days, really, three days, as a kind of exercise. Nor could *Angels' Laughter*—Hersey's title, a citation from some Shakespearean play that he knew and I did not—be judged by itself, because it was going to be part of a tetralogy, a series of four novels about Germany, the destruction that it had caused and the destruction that I had seen there. There was really no way of describing it to someone who had not seen it and thought about it. But I had also been reading the Bible, for various obscure reasons, and I had been wondering for some time what it must have been like for the Egyptians in the time of Exodus to live through the plagues that God inflicted on them. The first plague was the miracle that "all the waters that were in the river were turned into blood. And the fish that was in the river died; and the river stank, and the Egyptians could not drink of the water of the river; and there was blood throughout all the land of Egypt." Trying to imagine the reality of such disasters, I wrote an account of these same mysterious plagues striking the Germany that I had seen in 1947, starting with the morning when the bathroom faucets started to spout blood. It was told in a simple narrative, and that was not enough to describe the Germany of 1947, so I had also written my own version of Faust, told in stream of consciousness by Faust himself, and then I had constructed the novel by interspersing one chapter on each plague with one chapter of Faust, convinced he can conquer the Devil but, for that very reason, being conquered himself.

"Just a minute," Miss Toklas said, having finally lighted her cigarette and now lifting herself out of the chair by the fireplace and moving over to the tall windows that gave onto a roof. She opened the latch, and the familiar yellowish figure of Basket padded into the room, guiltily asking, as dogs always do in such circumstances, to be patted and reassured. Miss Toklas helped the animal to nest grumpily by the sofa, where he looked up at me without recognition. "Help yourself," Miss Toklas said, waving at the Armagnac. "And go on. I'm interested."

This novel couldn't really be judged by itself, I said again, because it was just the first volume of the four in the series. As a matter of fact, I had already begun the next one, called *Dies Irae,* which was going to be a story of the war crimes trials. Like *Angels' Laughter,* this would also be two different stories, told in alternating chapters. The first would be the story of the judges and the prosecutors, who had to punish the guilty for crimes that no judge or prosecutor could understand; the second would be the memories of one of the guilty, who accepted his punishment for crimes that he himself could not understand.

Then the third novel would be based on the life of Hans Frank, the Nazi governor general of Poland, who presided over the occupation that included Auschwitz, who played Chopin for his guests at state dinners, and who finally became a Catholic convert during the Nuremberg trials. He had begged to be punished for his crimes, and was duly hanged. And then the fourth novel would be a love story, in which an official in the American occupation would encounter a German girl who was involved with the Nazis, and they would try to love each other, but neither one would understand what was happening. "You see?" I said. For I had worked it all out. The first book showed the failure of the people, both collectively and individually. The second would show the failure of the idea of justice. The third would show, through the perversion of power, the failure of power. The fourth would show, finally, the failure even of love.

Basket rose discontentedly from his nest and went over to Miss Toklas's chair to have his ears scratched. I seemed, she observed, to have started on a rather ambitious project. Yes, but I had all that worked out too. I wrote ten pages every day, so I could finish the first draft of a novel in a month. Miss Toklas went on scratching Basket's ears. Then I edited twenty pages a day, so that the whole novel was finished in two months. Then I took a week off before starting the next novel. This was the way I had written *Angels' Laugh-*

ter—a much more reflective work, after all, than the three-day adventure of *The Little Wizened Man*—and even at this modest pace, I confidently predicted that I could finish the whole cycle of four novels before my twenty-first birthday, almost a year away. Having said all that, I said I would leave her to judge the results so far, and, fortified by more Armagnac than I had ever drunk before, I carefully let myself be shown to the door, and carefully inched my way down the dark stairs of the building, one hand touching the walls, then a hand groping ahead of me through the dark courtyard, then a hand fumbling for the button that would buzz and make the heavy old doors burst open onto the street.

Time passed. At the dingy hotel where I had a dingy room, on the rue Servandoni, just barely out of reach of the Luxembourg Gardens, I worked away at the new novel about the concentration camps and wondered what had become of the last one. Finally, after several weeks, there came a postcard. On one side was a brownish photograph of a banderillero stabbing his dart into the neck of a charging bull. On the other side was a tiny, spidery script that I came to know well. Without any salutation, it began: "Unfortunately I've been very busy and have not yet completely read *Angels' Laughter*. Could you come in Saturday evening at about half after eight? Don't bother to answer if this suits you. Of course I like your book a lot. It would have been an enormous disappointment if I hadn't. Cordially, A. B. Toklas."

That Saturday, all the rituals were the same, starting with the lonely wait in that awesome living room, with the famous paintings that really didn't interest me, so that I no longer even looked at them, and then the Armagnac, which Gabrielle, by now recovered, automatically produced, and then one of those high doors creaking open and Miss Toklas suddenly appearing, this time with hand outstretched.

"You're good, you know," she said, without any sort of introduction. "I haven't quite finished the little book, but now I've finished the other one, *Angels' Laughter*. It's quite fascinating. It really is."

Somewhere Gertrude Stein had written that writers don't need literary criticism, they need praise. In my first visit to Alice Toklas,

I had been a tourist. In my second, I had been an applicant apprentice. Now, in my third, I might still be a tourist and an apprentice, but this extraordinary old woman who had known and judged Picasso and Hemingway and Matisse and Pound and Fitzgerald and just about everybody else had read two of my amateurish novels and was giving me the one thing that matters more to a young writer than agents, publishers, or royalties. Praise.

"I was born in San Francisco, California," begins *The Autobiography of Alice B. Toklas*. "I have in consequence always preferred living in a temperate climate but it is difficult, on the continent of Europe or even in America, to find a temperate climate and live in it." We are told of her Polish patriotic ancestry, and then: "I myself have had no liking for violence and have always enjoyed the pleasures of needlework and gardening. I am fond of paintings, furniture, tapestry, houses and flowers, and even vegetables and fruit-trees. I like a view but I like to sit with my back turned to it.

"I led in my childhood and youth the gently bred existence of my class and kind," she goes on. "I had some intellectual adventures at this period but very quiet ones. When I was about nineteen years of age I was a great admirer of Henry James. I felt that *The Awkward Age* would make a very remarkable play and I wrote to Henry James suggesting that I dramatise it. I had from him a delightful letter on the subject and then, when I felt my inadequacy, rather blushed for myself and did not keep the letter."

In keeping with the gently bred existence of her class and kind, the young Miss Toklas met another San Franciscan, Leo Stein, newly returned from Paris with "three little Matisse paintings, the first modern things to cross the Atlantic." In the same spirit, she decided to visit Paris, and there she inevitably met Leo Stein's sister Gertrude. "I was impressed by the coral brooch she wore and by her voice," she remembered. "I may say that only three times in my life have I met a genius and each time a bell within me rang and I was not mistaken, and I may say in each case it was before there was any general recognition of the quality of genius in them. The three geniuses of whom I speak are Gertrude Stein, Pablo Picasso, and Alfred

Whitehead. . . . In no one of the three cases have I been mistaken. In this way my new full life began."

This opening section of the *Autobiography*, entitled "Before I Came to Paris," consists of only two and a half pages, whereas the later chapter "Gertrude Stein before She Came to Paris" totals almost twenty. Since the whole work bore the byline of Gertrude Stein, the general assumption has always been that Miss Stein was writing her own autobiography, with a technique that various critics have described, depending on their hostility to Miss Stein, as comic at best, and at worst cutely disingenuous. Thirty years after the publication of the *Autobiography*, for example, one substantial reference work called *The Reader's Encyclopedia of American Literature* snappishly refers to Miss Toklas as Miss Stein's "nurse, secretary, chef, confidant, and in her later years the suppositious author of *The Autobiography of Alice B. Toklas*, actually a book by Gertrude Stein about Gertrude Stein."

I only began reading the *Autobiography* after I met Miss Toklas, and I accepted the general verdict, not as a sign of Miss Stein's megalomania, but of her much-underestimated talent for comedy. I was startled, then, during one of those many evenings on the horsehair sofa, next to the tray with the decanter of Armagnac, to hear Miss Toklas tell one of her many anti-Hemingway stories—this time the one about Hemingway saying that his talent was a small flame which had to be turned down and turned down until it exploded—and to realize that she was quoting almost verbatim from the book that had been written almost two decades earlier. And then I began to realize, as I came to know her better, not only that her own autobiography would inevitably have contained ten times as much material about Gertrude Stein as about herself, but that all the malicious stories and all the acerbic judgments were not Gertrude Stein's but her own.

The relationship to Hemingway is particularly interesting. He is introduced at the age of twenty-three as "rather foreign-looking, with passionately interested, rather than interesting eyes. He sat in front of Gertrude Stein and listened and looked." He is portrayed as a sycophantic but pleasantly helpless youth. Miss Toklas was a godparent to his first child, and "I embroidered a little chair and I knitted a gay coloured garment for the god-child. In the meantime the god-child's father was very earnestly at work making himself a writer." She adds that "he heard about bullfighting from me." Hemingway apparently got Ford Madox Ford to publish a section of Miss Stein's *The Making of Americans* in his magazine, the *Transatlantic,* and Hemingway joined Miss Toklas in recopying the manuscript for publication. Miss Stein "remembered with gratitude" Hemingway's role in this, and said, "Yes sure I have a weakness for Hemingway," but Miss Toklas mistrusted Hemingway's role. "I have never known what the story is but I have always been certain that there was some other story behind it all. That is the way I feel about it."

Then she went on to say the unkindest thing of all, declaring that Gertrude Stein and Sherwood Anderson "were endlessly amusing" in discussing the young man they both considered their pupil. "They admitted that Hemingway was yellow. . . . But what a book, they both agreed, would be the real story of Hemingway, not those he writes but the confessions of the real Ernest Hemingway. . . . And then they both agreed that they have a weakness for Hemingway because he is such a good pupil. He is a rotten pupil, I protested." Miss Toklas never changed her mind. "Don't you come home with Hemingway on your arm, I used to say when she went out for a walk. Sure enough one day she did come back bringing him with her. They sat and talked a long time. Finally I heard her say, Hemingway, after all you are ninety percent Rotarian. Can't you, he said, make it eighty percent. No, she said regretfully, I can't."

The appearance of the *Autobiography* in 1933 created, understandably, an uproar. *Transition,* the magazine of the expatriate literary establishment, published a special issue devoted to the rebuttals of the many distinguished figures who considered themselves libeled. Matisse, for example, complained bitterly about the allegation that he had painted portraits of his horse-faced wife. His wife, he declared, was not horse-faced at all. Braque was even more vehement. "Miss Stein," he wrote, "understood nothing of what went on around her." Another contributor, who was unhappy at having been portrayed in a state of drunkenness, complained that "we were all young at that time and had no thought of possible later echoes of our actions. I am not angry but I think Gertrude Stein went too far when she made all these things public." The most angry man of all was naturally Ernest Hemingway, who used his next book, *Green Hills of Africa,* to deny that Gertrude Stein had ever taught him anything, and to accuse her of everything from literary incompetence to sexual peculiarity.

What none of the critics seemed to realize was that the *Autobiography* was exactly what it said it was. "I am a pretty good housekeeper," says the last page, "and a pretty good gardener and a pretty good needlewoman . . . and a pretty good vet for dogs and I have to do them all at once and I found it difficult to add being a pretty good author.

"About six weeks ago Gertrude Stein said, it does not look to me as if you were ever going to write that autobiography. You know what I am going to do. I am going to write it for you. I am going to write it as simply as Defoe did the autobiography of Robinson Crusoe. And so she has and this is it."

It is a comic ending, but it is also a statement of fact. The *Autobiography* is not a cute version of Gertrude Stein's autobiography but literally the judgments, the views, the language, the tone, and the quality of mind of Alice B. Toklas herself. As such, as the recreation of someone else's personality, it is not only Miss Stein's best work but one of the minor masterpieces of this century. But this was not why I was here. I had read very little of Gertrude Stein, and I had not liked what I had read. I would begin a story like "As a Wife Has a Cow"—"Nearly all of it to be as a wife has a cow, a love story. All of it to be as a wife has a cow, all of it to be as a wife has a cow, a love story. As to be all of it as to be a wife as a wife has a cow, a love story, all of it as to be all of it as a wife all of it as to be as a wife has a cow a love story, all of it as a wife has a cow as a wife has a cow a love story"—and I could see a mind at work, struggling with an intractable theory, but I was not interested or impressed with either the theory or the results. And the subject never came up. It was assumed that I was a respectful admirer, or

I would not be there, but I never asked about Gertrude Stein, and so it must also have been assumed that my respectful admiration was a matter of deference.

Like any twenty-year-old, I was interested mainly in myself, and so we talked not about Gertrude Stein but about me, who I was, and what I thought, and what I was reading and writing. At about that time, somebody had invented the theory of highbrow-middle-brow-lowbrow, and *Life* magazine devoted several pages to illustrated charts on highbrow-lowbrow tastes in everything from food to music. According to the charts, as I recall them, highbrows listened to Beethoven and lowbrows ate coleslaw—both of which seemed acceptable, the game being, apparently, not to get trapped in any category that could be associated with the newly named species: middlebrow.

I told Miss Toklas about this new game, one evening by the fireplace, with Basket padding discontentedly around as usual, and we puzzled over the definitive categorization of writers. Henry James, we soon agreed, was the perfect writer for highbrows, and I don't remember whom we selected as the perfect middlebrow, but our real problem lay in discovering the perfect lowbrow. It was a problem because this elegant old lady had only one bookcase—not even a bookcase, really, but a large cupboard containing shelves—and there she kept one beautiful white set of the New York edition of the collected works of Henry James, and only one shelf of miscellaneous new things that people sent her, which she read or didn't read, and gave to me or threw away.

"James M. Cain," I suggested, after some thought, but that was not the solution. "I know the name," she said, "but I've never read any of his books. What has he written?"

"Oh, thrillers," I said, "but good thrillers. *Double Indemnity. The Postman Always Rings Twice.*"

"No, I don't know him."

Thinking some more, I offered the name of someone who was then considered a commercially successful young novelist: "Gore Vidal." The answer was much the same as before: "Who?" I was ready to give up, but Miss Toklas had also been searching for the name of the perfect lowbrow writer.

"I have it," she said at last, grinning. "I know just the man."

"Who?" I asked.

Triumphantly, she brought forth the name: "Osbert Sitwell."

The old and the young play all kinds of games, parlor games, power games, flirtations, games of intrigue. To be twenty is to be ambitious, energetic, heedless, and almost totally lacking in charity or compassion or common sense; to be seventy-one is to be a survivor, sometimes as narrow and self-centered as any youth, but sometimes shrewd and amused, capable of a disinterested affection that nobody of twenty can understand. To be twenty is to want success fiercely and to be ready to fight for it; to be seventy-one is to watch other people fight.

Miss Toklas wanted to help. She invited me to have tea with Carl Van Vechten, and then Thornton Wilder, and I listened to the latter expound an extraordinary plan to write a whole book about one page of Joyce's *Finnegans Wake*, but by now I was beginning to emerge from my monument-collecting period, and I had nothing to say to these dignified old gentlemen, nor they to me. But Miss Toklas was nothing if not practical. She introduced me to Gertrude Stein's London literary agent, a magnificently mustachioed figure called David Higham, and he undertook (without success, as it turned out) to sell my various novels in England. Miss Toklas also understood the value of publicity, and she arranged for me to meet a Paris correspondent of the *New York Times*. I didn't make much of an impression on him, nor did he on me, but I had just written a ferocious denunciation of Thomas Mann, about whom I knew little but felt strongly, in a new magazine called *Zero,* and since New York's middle-aged publishers are chronically obsessed with the question of what young people are thinking about, this seemed a natural subject for the *Times*'s correspondent.

"It was *Zero,*" he wrote, "that published recently a giant-killing review of Thomas Mann's 'Doctor Faustus' by a 22-year-old American novelaster (four unpublished novels) and Paris resident named Otto Friedrich. Thomas Mann's theory of great art, writes Friedrich, 'as devil-ridden disease, is a theory which is utterly alien to almost every real practitioner of great art. . . .' " Writers are rarely content, of course, and they are never content with anything written about them. Why did he have to make such a point of my novels being unpublished? Isn't it an insult to be called a "novelaster"? Why did he say I was twenty-two when I was barely twenty? Can't the *New York Times* get anything right? Still, no writer is immune to the intoxication of publicity and the sight of his name in print. By what rational standard would I be entitled to say anything at all about Thomas Mann, and by what rational standard did my jeremiad deserve mention in the *New York Times*?

Writers' recollections tend to be literary, a vindictive chronicle of one's own achievements honored and one's enemies dishonored, but writers are also human, and my greatest problem in the spring of 1950 was that I had an abscessed tooth. I asked Miss Toklas if she knew a good dentist, and she said she did. There were two sisters who had an office on the boulevard Montparnasse. "But I must warn you," she added. "Try to get the better-looking one, because she's also a better dentist. The other one is all right, but she's not as good."

"Can't I ask for the better one by name?"

"No, they don't allow that," she said. "Besides, I can't remember which is which. They only use their first initials, and the initials are almost the same, something like E.B. and E.H."

"But how will I tell which one I want?"

"Well, you'll just know," she said cheerfully. "You'll know as soon as you see them."

I telephoned the sisters' office the following morning and made an appointment for that afternoon. I was welcomed by a small, bent old lady who ushered me into her dental chair and began to probe with her instruments. I have always hated going to the dentist, and one of the first fruits of being old enough to leave home was that I stopped going. Now I sat and twitched every time the pick touched a tooth. *"Oh, qu'il est nerveux!"* the old lady scolded each time I shuddered. "Why are you so nervous, *monsieur?*" I could scarcely tell her that I was wondering whether her sister looked better or worse than she did, so I just said that I was afraid of dentists. *"Ça se voit,"* she said amiably, poking further.

After she had inspected the problem, she excused herself for a few moments, and then returned with a stately lady with a rich head of white hair. *"Ma soeur,"* said the crookbacked one, and I realized, as Miss Toklas had said I would, that I was in the hands of the wrong sister. The "better-looking" one also inspected the problem, and I vaguely hoped that she might take charge, in view of the gravity of the case, but then they both drew back and announced their verdict. The tooth would have to come out, but they did not perform extractions. It required too much strength. For such operations, they called in their brother, who lived in the country, and who was strong. But I was in luck. The brother would be in town the following day, and they would ask him if he could help.

I accepted their prescription for Veganine pills, to kill the pain, and returned the next day to meet their brother. He was a heavyset man with a coarse red face and crew-cut white hair. *"Très mauvais,"* he said brusquely as he pulled back my upper lip and jabbed in the first shot of Novocain. Then, as we waited for it to take effect, he told me his problem. He hated dentistry. He had had a munificent practice on the rue de la Paix, but he couldn't stand it. Dentistry was boring, the same problems day after day. He was an artist, he said, not a dentist. He had moved to the country so that he could paint. See, there? He had painted those two pictures on the wall, one a landscape, the other a view of his country house. Both were impressionistically messy, in ugly pastel colors. Did I not think they were beautiful? Yes, they certainly were, I said, waiting for my jaw to grow numb, poking at it with my tongue, wondering whether this landscape painter had injected the needle in the right place, yes, very beautiful. And here, look at this. He strode over to a side wall, unhooked a large painting, and carried it over in front of the dental chair. "These are my two dogs, Alsatians," he said proudly. The two large animals, malformed by the incompetence of their creator, stared balefully out at me. "Very good," I said. "Very beautiful."

"Eh, bien," the painter finally announced the moment of decision, holding up his clawlike pliers. Having a tooth extracted is a disgusting operation, disgusting particularly for that crunching sound of the thing being torn out, but it really doesn't hurt, and I was surprised that it was over so quickly, and the dentist cried, *"Voilà!"*

and triumphantly held up the bloody object while his sisters gibbered their praise of his strength and artistry. They told me to go to a café and have two cognacs, then shook my hand, wished me well, and sent me wandering dazedly out into the rushing traffic of the boulevard Montparnasse. By the time I felt well enough to visit Miss Toklas again, I told her the story as a funny story, and she laughed. "Well, at least it's over with," she said, "thank heavens."

I had other occupations that winter and spring. I had finished the concentration camp novel, *Dies Irae,* and started yet another one. This was to be the fourth novel in the tetralogy about Germany, the love story, which I then called *Lilacs Out of the Dead Land.* Through the good offices of Jimmy Baldwin, who was then a charming and virtually unknown young novelist, I had acquired a literary agent, Helen Strauss, of the William Morris Agency, who began sending these manuscripts to various publishers, but she and they all agreed that I was writing too much and too fast. People in Paris said the same thing. Even Miss Toklas was somewhat less enthusiastic about *Dies Irae* than she had been about the previous books. Lionel Abel, the poet and critic, who was then living in Paris, argued vehemently that *Dies Irae* showed not improvement but decline, that most of it should be discarded, and that only one section of it was fit to be published. With his help, I edited that section into a novella about a concentration camp guard and sent it off to New York to join the orbiting collection of manuscripts. But I liked writing too much and too fast. Once, as a kind of game, or test, or challenge, I wrote a whole book in a day. I got the idea late one evening and began writing at midnight. By about ten o'clock the following night, I had finished a 120-page collection of about twenty-five stories, and that, too, was shipped off to New York.

In the midst of all this, I had met a girl whom I was determined to marry, Priscilla Boughton, and I pursued her back to New York to persuade her to marry me. She was not easily persuaded, and since I had limited the trip to six weeks, we spent six weeks arguing. During those same six weeks, I finally met Miss Strauss, and the wheels of publication finally came into gear. The various novels were all at Little, Brown, in Boston, and though they had misgivings about all of them, they signed a contract for the new novel, the love story, and they provided a modest advance. Miss Strauss also got me an advance from *Life* magazine to go to Rome to write a profile of George Santayana. And James Laughlin accepted the novella about the concentration camp guard for his annual anthology, *New Directions*.

Priscilla also agreed to come to Paris and marry me there in April. For good measure, I retyped a section of a novel she was writing, and I took that to Helen Strauss, and she got Dial Press to sign a contract for it. Just after my twenty-first birthday, in February of 1950, I sailed back to France. I had failed to finish the tetralogy on schedule, I told Miss Toklas, but otherwise everything seemed to be working out very well. I had a pretty regular job translating movie scripts from French into English; I had sold a novel and a novella, and the advance from *Life* would pay for a honeymoon in Rome right after the wedding in April. I showed her photographs I had taken of Priscilla, and she admired them. "Very good," she said. "She looks immensely civilized."

Within three months after my return to Paris, almost everything I was counting on had collapsed. The movie people, during my absence, had found other translators who could do the work as well as I, and at lower rates, so I was out of work. *Life* rejected my article on Santayana. I had hurried through the novel for Little, Brown, since the contract called for more payments when the manuscript was finished, but now they delayed their decision. I looked for jobs in Paris but found nothing. The money gurgled away until there was nothing left. I borrowed a hundred dollars from reluctant friends, and, without saying good-bye to anyone, without taking more than one suitcase and a typewriter, fled with Priscilla to look for some kind of work in Germany.

We found a cheap hotel room in Frankfurt, overlooking a heap of rubble, and settled down to living on a daily ration of ten cigarettes and two meals of bread, cheese, and tomatoes. There were jobs available, working for the army or the HICOG occupation authorities, but they all required security clearance, and the security clearers were all so busy during these Korean War days that it took three months to clear anyone for anything. After about two weeks of increasing hunger (and fear), I finally found a job so lowly that nobody cared about security. It was also so lowly that I was not "authorized" to have a wife, and so we had to find shelter in one room in a German widow's house, and I commuted to work on a bicycle through the cobblestoned streets of a heavily bombed town called Darmstadt. Only then could I write to Miss Toklas and tell her what had become of me. For sixty dollars a week, I was now a copy editor on the sports desk of *The Stars and Stripes.*

"You have at last explained your silence," she wrote back from a summer place near Bourges. "It is a relief to know that you are both all right. You will by now have received my p.c. re Rinehart's desire to hear from you. You fortunately stayed in Paris to be mentioned as a writer there. . . . Let me know if there is anything I can do for you. Best to you both, and the novels. *Chaude poignée de patte de Basket.*" Her letter mystified me until someone else sent me the *New York Times* Sunday book section of that August 6, and there I saw on the front page an essay entitled "They Who Came to Paris to Write," by Alice B. Toklas. It was, as far as I know, the first thing she had ever written for publication, and it was very much like her, a rather wandering and gossipy recollection of Sherwood Anderson and Scott Fitzgerald, Pound and Eliot. "Of the young American writers in Paris today," she went on, "there are the G.I.'s with their Bill of Rights and their second novel on the way who are taking a course at the Sorbonne called French Civilization, for which at the end of the year they will be given a certificate of attendance. And there are the more serious Fulbright scholars who are writing tomes for their doctorate. There is a young, a very young man named Otto Friedrich who is now working on his fourth novel and who may easily become the important young man of the future."

It was very flattering, of course, for a sports department copy editor, marking the capitals and the commas in Associated Press stories about the Philadelphia Phillies, to be so extravagantly saluted in the *New York Times,* and I think Miss Toklas, too, was a little pleased and amused at the way the publishing industry snapped to attention. She had, after all, known the long, long years of struggling to get Gertrude Stein's early work published, by any publisher at any price. Now Rinehart wrote to ask where those four Friedrich novels were, and so did Knopf, and Harcourt, Brace, and then she wrote me: "This time it is Random House that is pursuing you. A letter from no less than Bennett himself asking for your address and did I advise Random House 'signing' you. Your address has been sent. I begged to be excused from giving advice but said it would surprise me greatly if you didn't make your way and go a considerable distance. A short biographical notice of your past precocity, your fecundity and gifts. . . . Best always."

It was a pleasant ritual of flirtation, but it was all too late. I had already begun to drop out of the "promising young writer" sweepstakes. Little, Brown had finally decided to buy the love story, which I had renamed *The Poor in Spirit*, and they sent the rest of the advance, which I spent on a defective used car, vintage 1938, made by a locomotive company called Hanomag, so that I could sell my bicycle before winter set in. But they said nobody could understand the ending of the novel and they wanted revisions, which I didn't want to provide. I was busy trying to write a new novel called *Child of Scorn*, about a Harvard student who commits a murder at random, and is never caught, because a random murderer would be almost impossible to catch, and because a Harvard student wouldn't even be suspected. But everything I wrote now was bad. I knew it myself, even though I doggedly went on writing.

Something had gone wrong in Paris, in that brief three-month period when the great golden daydream was evaporating before my eyes. Through a failure of nerve, or simply a sense of survival, I had all too quickly come to realize that I wasn't going to make it, and, like someone perched on a magnificent cliff that suddenly starts crumbling, I had leaped for my life. I had survived, but it is jarring to fail, suddenly and badly. It is jarring to have to flee from one country to another, a refugee, and all the more so when it means fleeing from a country you love to a country you hate. It is jarring, as a refugee, to have to change from doing work you care about to work you despise. But there I was in Darmstadt, and I was being paid to write headlines that said things like "Phils Nip Cubs, 2-0." I was also paid to cover the local competitions between various military teams. As summer turned into fall and the Heidelberg Hawks won the GI World Series, I was writing stories that began like this:

"The hotly contested championship of the 1st Inf Div Conference will finally be decided at Soldiers Field in Nurnberg, when the 16th Inf Rangers and the 18th Inf Vanguards clash in a playoff game that will close this year's chapter of their rivalry. . . ."

The only good thing that happened was that Priscilla became pregnant. She was determined to have a boy, and, for reasons I have never understood, she was determined to call him Inigo. "I liked your letters and its news," Miss Toklas wrote from Paris. "Priscilla and you must be very pleased. Inigo or Inogine as the case may be. During the next few days I'll be getting some wool to crochet a cover which you may remember is an evening's occupation of mine. They are all in white but if Priscilla fancies a colored border perhaps she should say which one she prefers. . . . What has come over Little Brown to account for their behavior to you? Is the frayed excuse of Korea enough? Does that excuse such inexcusably bad manners?"

Miss Toklas was intrigued by the name Inigo, partly because the only man who had ever borne it was Inigo Jones, the seventeenth-century English architect, of whom Ben Jonson had said, "Whenever I see a rascall, I always call him Inigo." She wrote: "In Bennett Cerf's dictionary I came across the possibility of Inigo being Ignatius so I asked Max White—whom you may or may not remember but who remembers you pleasantly—and who is the one person here now who knows Spain well—He says that Inigo is the Basque for Ignatius—How does this affect Priscilla—And now it is imperative that I discover how the only other Inigo I've ever heard of came to receive his name—Did he have a Basque grandmother or did his mother Priscilla just like the sound of it . . . ? The baby blanket is unlikely to be done for March but tell Priscilla she will have it in time."

I still wanted to call the boy Max, and we had agreed that this would at least be his middle name. "Max is a splendid name and goes admirably with Inigo . . . ," Miss Toklas wrote. "But what happens if the baby is a girl? The result of such criminal neglect as yours produced a Billie-Anne. And be warned that in France the father within twenty-four hours after the birth is required by law to register it at the nearest city hall and to sign the name of the baby. And you may not name a girl Nancy because it is the name of a town."

We had talked of driving to Chamonix to have the baby there, so that he would not suffer the disgrace of being born in Germany, but we had no money, and the baby was late, and everything was uncertain, and Miss Toklas wrote anxiously from the Riviera: "You may count me a fussed and aged parent. Priscilla and you are exaggerating the nonchalance of modern parenthood—a bit more determination and Inigo would have been amongst us long ago—Of course he may happily have arrived several days ago now for the mail is slow in being forwarded, and it's already a week since I've been pleasantly installed here with friends in an ancient house in this still more ancient little town in the hills above Cannes. . . . You do well to avoid the American newspapers. The country can't be as desperately stupid as they make it out—possibly as solemn but surely not as stupid. Did you read the Senate investigation of General MacArthur day by day—it was rich, like the old Congressional Records that fascinated me when I was young. . . . The Chinese Communists are a lot livelier than all this. Basket is asking to go out—so this will be dropped at the P.O. Do give me some good news soon. Best of good wishes . . ."

The baby was finally born after more than twenty-four hours of labor, sleep, and more labor, during which we played *The Abduction from the Seraglio* from end to end and I read through all of *Swann's Way*, which is all the Proust I have ever read or ever want to read, and it was, of course, a girl, whom we named Liesel. I described it all to Miss Toklas, and she replied with some excitement. "If you haven't yet heard—what a relief Liesel's eventual arrival—accompanied by Mozart and Proust—certain to correct each other's influence—was—don't take the time to think it wasn't the greatest *soulagement*, and though one has the utmost confidence in Priscilla's coming up to scratch she did keep me frightfully nervy—One kept asking oneself what is she up to? Well nothing else than what one had been hoping indeed expecting. By now the daughter is doubtless sitting up taking notice and asking for a sensible book. Is there anything else she wants or either of you want for her that is not to be achieved at your PX or commissary? Let me know if there is anything I can send you." She went on, then, about Paris, and Gide, and a French adaptation of *The Turn of the Screw,* and an American publisher she disliked, but she did not forget what was essential between us. "When is your book coming out? Has the date been fixed? Would you like me to say something about it? Would you like to tell me what you would like said? Don't hesitate, unless conscience is a stumbling block."

All that had happened was that I had finally agreed to do some revision on *The Poor in Spirit,* and that the revised version had been formally accepted for publication at some unspecified date. In the meantime, the sports editor had quit and the new sports editor was a tyrant who disliked me as much as I disliked him. Within three days, we both agreed that I should move to the general news desk. To mark the commas in non-sports copy required a security clearance, so I had to remain officially a member of the sports department until the government's detectives checked my references, one of whom was Miss Toklas. "You were quite right to use my name as reference for anything they may foolishly be investigating," she wrote. "Alas no one has turned up for my verbal recommendations, for it would have been a rare pleasure to have told him all the things there are to say concerning your political opinions and private life—of which naturally I know nothing and care even less—in the course of such a declaration there were perceptions and appreciations which would have been touched upon which might have been useful for him to know but the principal person hasn't appeared. It is too late to hope he still may." She also sent a neatly crocheted white blanket, which was wrapped around the baby.

And in due time, I was granted security clearance, and now, instead of checking box scores, I could check middle initials. It was a rule of *The Stars and Stripes* copy desk that every officer's name in every story must be verified in the fat, brown *Army Directory,* including the middle initial. As for the novel *Child of Scorn,* I had given up after a hundred pages, and I sent the manuscript to New York to see what the publishers would make of it. After a decent interval of anguished reflection, Little, Brown's editor in chief, Angus Cameron, wrote to my agent, Helen Strauss, that the manuscript was so bad that a more cynical editor could only consider it an "option-breaker"—in other words, something written solely for the purpose of provoking a rejection—but that he considered both Miss Strauss and me too honorable to engage in such tricks, and so he would prefer to think that the manuscript had never been submitted. Miss Strauss forwarded that message and said that she also thought it was pretty bad. I wrote back to say that I agreed, and that she might as well throw the manuscript in the wastebasket.

After a year and a half at *The Stars and Stripes,* I got a telephone call from a friend who had escaped from the sports department to a job with the United Press in Paris, and who told me there was a job open at the UP in London. It would mean a cut in pay from ninety dollars a week to eighty-five, but he wondered whether I was interested. On my next day off, I took a plane to London, got the job for seventy-five a week, flew back to Germany, quit *The Stars and Stripes,* sold the old Hanomag to a sergeant who promised to send me fifty dollars a month, and loaded my pregnant wife and year-old daughter on the train for Hook of Holland and Dover. The UP was a strange but interesting place, where you were judged primarily on whether you got the news out one minute ahead of the AP or one minute later. Shortly after I got to London, King George VI died, and the new Queen Elizabeth flew back from a hunting expedition in Kenya, and there was a coronation, and our man wrote a complete description of the event the day before it happened, all marked "hold for release." On coronation day, our reporters were strung out along the route of the march, unable to get to telephones, and the president of the United Press watched it all from a window in Claridge's Hotel, but our bureau manager sat by the office television set and shouted periodic "flashes" that served to release another one of the "new leads" that had been sent out the day before. As far as I know, nobody who actually saw the coronation contributed anything whatever to the stories that described the event in vivid detail.

These were also the last days before the publication of *The Poor in Spirit.* Everything followed Murphy's law: "Everything that can go wrong will go wrong." After the original arguments about revision, there had been internal upheavals at Little, Brown. The editor in chief disappeared, and I received a mysterious document, printed on very expensive paper, stating categorically to the general public that Little, Brown was a distinguished publishing firm and had never been under leftist influences. More specifically, I got a frantic cable asking what I had done with the galley proofs, and saying that the publication date would have to be delayed if they weren't found within forty-eight hours. I had already returned the galleys to the printing plant, as instructed, but that was somehow a mistake, and they had gone astray. On the actual publication date, when it ultimately arrived, in May of 1952, I got a cable of good wishes from the publisher, which was a pleasant gesture, but that was all that happened. My "first novel" was finally appearing, an event I had been looking forward to for almost five years, but whatever might be happening was all happening far away. In London that day, the sun rose as usual, there were no choruses of angelic trumpets, and I worked my usual shift among the clattering Teletypes of the United Press.

The only one to sound a trumpet was Miss Toklas, who wrote in hyperbole beyond any expectation of even the most egotistical young writer. "Let me at once say— *Félicitations, monsieur.* I take off my hat to you. Very definitely you are the important young man of the prediction, and more, for *The Poor in Spirit* marks the beginning of the second half of the century. . . . It has an unobtrusive flawlessness, like Juan Gris. What more would you have me say? So thank you for having written it. . . ."

That was very flattering, but the printed reviews that began trickling in were less intoxicating. *The New Yorker* called the book "sensible, thoughtful, kind, and frequently clever," but also "slight" and too long. The review, buried among a miscellany of other short notices, said all it had to say in thirteen lines of type. The *New York Times* offered praises like "he can write beautifully, he has tension, and at moments suggests the moral pregnancy of Camus," but it went on to say that this was "the material of a short story dragged out into a novel." And the *Times* limited its comments to four short paragraphs. The *Saturday Review* didn't like the novel, and, as far as

I know, the *Herald Tribune, Time,* and *Newsweek* never mentioned it. So it was stillborn, dead.

The sales figures were correspondingly funereal. According to my last blackened royalty statement from Little, Brown, I had been advanced $1,000, and the book earned $95.94, leaving what the accountants called a "debit balance" of $904.06. I estimate this to mean that less than three hundred copies were sold. It is customary for writers to blame their publishers for such disasters, alleging that aggressive advertising might have created a best-seller. But I was dismayed and ashamed rather than angry, dismayed because I had disappointed everyone, because everyone considered the novel second-rate, because I considered myself in disgrace with my publisher, my agent, and with everyone else who had shown any confidence in me. To this day, I have never reread the book.

Day by day, I took the Tube down to Fleet Street and put in my working hours at the United Press, and the only one who refused to be dismayed at my failure was Miss Toklas. In a letter from Seville, after a brief visit with the historian Bernard Faÿ, she offered unqualified support: "Before coming to Spain I spent three happy days with Bernard. I took him your novel. He has a very vivid memory of you as a child with your father and his happiness with you. I haven't heard from him since seeing him but will let you know as soon as he writes about your book, which I reread on the voyage to where he is, and found nothing to revise after my first reading of it. . . . It is a sadness that it hasn't made a great stir. The only consolation I can offer you is that that is proof not only of its distinction but its originality, which are the two bugbears of our compatriots. Isn't it that which makes them so prosperous and so dull? You are, I hope, trying to get another book published—by anyone who will. Don't— let me beg you—be too fussy. The important thing is to get them published and not hope to earn your living with them yet."

I was, of course, trying exactly that. By this time, everything I had written before *The Poor in Spirit* had been junked, but I had barely settled down in London before I began writing a novel called *The Summer Soldiers,* about *The Stars and Stripes,* about the way the news was twisted and suppressed to conform to the dictates of Cold War propaganda, about the self-corruption that poisoned all the people who took part in this propaganda. The oddity was that, after five finished novels and two unfinished ones, this was the first book in which, having grown up a bit, I knew what I was talking about. Unfortunately, what I was talking about was what I hated, and the publishers' readers soon began to send back reports saying things like "Mr. Friedrich has talent but he despises his subject," and "This novel is interesting, but there is no character with whom the reader can sympathize." And so, reading these reports, and accepting them, I began planning what I conceived to be a counterattack, a book of literary criticism, essays, which would explain why I wrote the way I did, why novels did not need sympathetic characters, why novels could and should be written in hatred, why, in short, I thought that the two most important events of the twentieth century were Auschwitz and Hiroshima, why many great novels had anticipated those two disasters and why any novel written after them had to be written under their influence. It was called, from the start, *The Dark Tradition*.

The United Press, however, judged things from minute to minute. One day in July of 1953, the vice president of the European division came to London to find a replacement for the Paris bureau, called me into his office, questioned me in broken French, and decided I would do. With a pregnant wife, and, by now, two babies, I boarded the boat train for Dover. It was marvelous, at first, to come back to the Paris from which I had fled. I had fled penniless, but now I had a job and an employer and a small but regular income. Besides, it was Bastille Day, and, from the second-floor balcony of the hotel where the UP had installed us, we could look out at the bands playing at the crossroads of the boulevards du Montparnasse and Raspail, both avenues closed off so that people could dance in the street under chains of lights strung from the trees. We soon left the babies in charge of a chambermaid and came down into the streets and wandered through the *quartier*, listening to the bands at every street corner, and feeling that this whole city was ours again, that we had come back and recaptured our place in it.

But the Paris of 1950 had disappeared forever, and the Paris of 1953 was quite different, because the city where you live alone is quite different from the city where you have a job and three children. Just as inevitably, the city in which I could walk a few blocks to Miss Toklas's apartment to drink Armagnac in the evening, bearing a new novel under my arm, was quite different from the city in which I had to be invited to lunch. In the three years I had known Miss Toklas, and known her rather well, I had never been invited to a meal. I had been invited for drinks, and for tea, and even, on one occasion, for dessert—an exquisite *crème de marrons* that was just being served as I arrived. Now, finally, after much negotiation about the appropriate day and time, we were ushered in—Gabrielle was still on duty—to the familiar living room.

Miss Toklas looked as magical as ever, bright, shrewd, lively, bustling about with her preparations for lunch. She seemed delighted to see me, and I was delighted to see her, and delighted to bring Priscilla into this ménage, and we all talked about Paris, and books, and the pleasures of being reunited. We talked about Ivy Compton-Burnett, whom Priscilla and Miss Toklas both admired. Miss Toklas liked to quote Miss Compton-Burnett's complaint: "I don't understand why I am not a best-seller, don't I write about the scandalous subjects people love to read—adultery, incest, embezzlement?" While we lived in London, I had persuaded my wife to adopt my traditional tactic and ask Miss Compton-Burnett for an interview, and Miss Compton-Burnett had been considerably less hospitable than Miss Toklas. She had pretended to believe various bizarre theories of her own invention, declaring, at one point: "Of course, I realize that you Americans have all your food sent from the chemists." Priscilla had fled in confusion, and now the story of the encounter amused Miss Toklas. But her mind was on the lunch, and she would glance at her watch and stare into space and look quizzically toward the dining-room door, until she decreed it the moment to start serving. Then she led us through the tall doors and seated us in two very high straight-backed chairs, around a dark and equally high Spanish dining table, and under the fetid influence of several giant paintings by Sir Francis Rose, while she scuttled off to the kitchen to see what was happening.

Three years ago, I had sometimes felt slighted at Miss Toklas's failure to invite me to dinner, but in retrospect that failure seems a kind of honor, a sign that she and I had more important concerns that could never be advanced at the dinner table. For now that we had been honored with an invitation to lunch, Priscilla and I sat alone, waiting, looking at one another, glancing at the forbidding paintings, and wondering what had become of Miss Toklas. After about ten minutes in the kitchen, she came scuttling in, followed by Gabrielle, bearing little plates of shrimp appetizers. We began to eat, and Miss Toklas asked a few questions, but before she had finished her own shrimp, she was off to the kitchen again, leaving us to contemplate the works of Sir Francis Rose. Then she returned with a chicken, with Gabrielle lurking behind with a plate of zucchini. Miss Toklas jabbed at the chicken with a large fork and then began sawing away at one of its legs. Gabrielle stood watching for a while, concerned, and then set down the plate of zucchini and retreated to the kitchen. . . .

Miss Toklas carved with skill, but she was so tiny that she could barely reach across the high table to get at the animal, like a bullfighter lunging forward for the kill. Once she had served three helpings, she vanished again, and we sat in silence for several minutes until she returned with the orange sauce. Once again, desultory questions, compliments on the sauce, gossip about a new novel, and then Miss Toklas slipped out of her high chair again and was off to supervise the dessert, a complicated custard. The dessert was delicious, but it was a relief to have the struggle ended, the meal over with, and, with coffee served in the living room, the conversation was never as easy as it had once been during the long evenings that involved no social gestures more complicated than a carafe of Armagnac.

Paris, with three children, on a salary of eighty-five dollars a week, and a six-day workweek, soon proved to be intolerable. The third child, Nicholas, was born there, and brought home from the hospital to sleep on cashmere sweaters in a suitcase until we finally found an apartment near the Trocadéro, where the rent was more than we could afford to pay, where the neighbors complained about the children's noise, and where we reached a kind of dead end. On my day off, I worked on the chapter on Henry Adams for *The Dark Tradition,* but, in writing my commentary on his evaluation of Chartres,

I couldn't afford to go the fifty miles to Chartres. And as I joined the Parisian office workers rushing down the steps to the Métro at seven in the morning, six days a week, to work an eight- or nine-hour shift writing stories about war in Vietnam and rebellion in Morocco and winegrowers' strikes in Burgundy and the new fashion shows and some new crisis at NATO headquarters, none of which I had ever seen, or ever expected to see, or ever wanted to see, I suddenly had a sense of self-recognition, like recognizing a lined and unfamiliar face in the mirror, a realization that this wasn't why I came to Europe, and this wasn't what I wanted.

It then took only an insulting telephone call from the UP bureau chief, denouncing a story I had just written as dull and incompetent and "not what we're paying you for," plus another complaint from the noise-hating neighbors to the police, which I had to answer in person at the local commissariat, to convince me to give up on Europe, the only place I have ever enjoyed living, and go home. I carried out my last assignment, covering the presidential election at Versailles, and then I quit. "Life," Fitzgerald had written in *The Crack-Up*, "was something you dominated if you were any good." It is a childish doctrine, but most of us are children, and I believed in it as fiercely as Fitzgerald himself did, and now I had to confront the fact that, twice in three years, the city of Paris had defeated me, the idea of living and writing in Paris had defeated me. I even had to appeal to my parents and my in-laws for the boat fare back to New York. I must have seen Alice Toklas before I left. I must have gone to the rue Christine for a last visit and a last drink of Armagnac, must have told her that I was leaving and why I was leaving, and that it would be many years before I would ever see her again. But I have no recollection of it whatever.

That was 1954, and the years began to pass with increasing speed. Back in New York, in the middle of a recession, I applied for work at almost a hundred places—first at respectable places, the *Times* and *Herald Tribune*, then *Time* and *Newsweek* and a new magazine known as *Muscles*, which eventually became *Sports Illustrated*, then advertising agencies and public relations offices, and *Supermarket Weekly* and *Electronics Monthly* and even comic-book publishers—until, by a wild stroke of luck, after three months of increasing desperation, I got a job as a rewrite man at the *New York Daily News*.

And three more years began to drift past. And another child was born. By now we had four children under the age of three, all screeching and scrabbling through a tiny cottage on the south shore of Long Island. I labored away on *The Dark Tradition,* still manically trying to explain to people why I wrote the kind of novel that I was no longer writing. I had finished Melville in London, Henry Adams and Jonathan Edwards in Paris, and now I was explaining Hemingway and Mark Twain and Ambrose Bierce. I also collaborated with my wife on some children's books, which were moderately successful, but I had committed myself mainly to literary criticism, which is an almost certain route to bankruptcy. Six months' work resulted, if I was lucky, in a check for $75. The grocery bills, meanwhile, were paid by the weekly check for $134, which rewarded me for writing about the trials of Dr. Sam Sheppard and the marriages of Marilyn Monroe.

After three years, I moved to *Newsweek,* and made a last try at writing a novel—this one, I determined, would be a commercial success. It was again about a crime, a kidnapping, and about the responsibility of a newspaper for breaking the story before the kidnapped baby could be recovered (all this had happened at the *News*). It was rejected by eight publishers and even by two agents before I put it away in a drawer. As for *The Dark Tradition,* I was still struggling with it, but no less than eighteen publishers rejected it. What was there to write to Miss Toklas except a long series of failures and exasperations? I wrote her those from time to time but less and less often. "Send me your *good* news," she said in ending one of her letters.

The books that were actually being published, in these years, were those of Miss Toklas herself. In 1954, she brought out *The Alice B. Toklas Cook Book,* a charming collection of reminiscences and recipes, which Miss Toklas described to her editor at Harper's as her own autobiography, or the nearest to it that she ever expected to write. In 1958, she published a somewhat less authentic cookbook called *Aromas and Flavors of Past and Present,* with an introduction and miscellaneous commentaries by Poppy Cannon. Finally, in 1963, came the autobiography itself, *What Is Remembered.* Curiously enough, it began almost exactly as Gertrude Stein had begun the original autobiography: "I was born and raised in California, where my maternal grandfather had been a pioneer before the state was admitted to the Union." Gertrude Stein appears on page 23, and from there on, the pattern is much the same as before. But there is one closing scene that is unforgettable, Gertrude Stein lying in the hospital, so near death that most of the doctors refused to operate. One surgeon finally agreed to try. "By this time Gertrude Stein was in a sad state of indecision and worry. I sat next to her and she said to me early in the afternoon, 'What is the answer?' I was silent. 'In that case,' she said, 'what is the question?' Then the whole afternoon was troubled, confused, and very uncertain, and later in the afternoon they took her away on a wheeled stretcher to the operating room and I never saw her again."

In her early eighties, Miss Toklas began to fail, slowly, reluctantly, inexorably. It annoyed her, but she was stoical. "I am writing close to a strong lamp with the paper eight inches from my eyes," she reported in a letter from Rome, where she was spending the winter of 1960–61 in a convent. The script was larger than it used to be, and much more shaky. "I have renounced half of my only luxury—smoking. These are my woes. *Schwamm drüber.* Otherwise life is very agreeable in the convent and Rome is ravishing—the gardens, the churches, and the shops, the restaurants and the cooking—Spring green peas from the hills are incredible. And the ices are unequalled. California produces more abundantly but with less delicacy." And again that January: "On account of my failing sight writing has become very difficult—accomplished mostly by remembered movements—A great Paris oculist said there was nothing to do about it but to do what I could with what I had. *Basta.* The winter here has been comfortable and happy. The convent is warmed and the two cloistered nuns who I see are good and kind. The Roman winter as you remember is not cold but raining torrentially this year. Added to the failing sight acute arthritis makes going out difficult. Thanks a lot for your card of good wishes. [It was] used as a book mark as long as reading was possible."

The reality was more serious than she ever indicated. There had been a bad fall, which had kept her bedridden for a time, and her hearing, as well as her eyesight, was badly impaired. And during the long convalescence in Rome, a lawsuit by Gertrude Stein's rather distant heirs, who were to inherit the art collection after Miss Toklas's death, argued that Miss Toklas's absence from Paris jeopardized the physical condition of the abandoned paintings. The Tribunal de la Seine reacted by ordering the entire collection, including twenty-two works by Picasso and seven by Juan Gris, stripped from Miss Toklas's apartment and stored in the vaults of the Chase Manhattan Bank.

In January of 1963, I got a chance to go back to Europe for the first time in nine years. The trip would last only two weeks, and I allotted only four days to Paris, but I wrote Miss Toklas to say that I was coming, and that I hoped I could come to pay her a visit. Her answer filled me with foreboding. It was a postcard. Scrawled diagonally across the top of one half was an almost totally undecipherable message. I could make out only a few words. Below that, someone else, a friend, had written a postscript saying that Miss Toklas wanted to see me, and that the friend thought the visit would do Miss Toklas a lot of good. When I got to Paris, I telephoned, and a servant answered. Miss Toklas was asleep, she said, but she had left word that if I called I was to be asked to come for tea at three o'clock the next afternoon.

The same servant opened the heavy door and led me through the hall into the empty living room. "Miss Toklas has been sleeping—she sleeps every afternoon—but she wants very much to see you," she said, and then shut the door behind her. The great room was infinitely bleak. Outside, it was a gray, cold January day, and the light from the tall windows made the whole room look gray. The disappearance of all the familiar paintings, which had once dominated the place, left the walls naked, just faintly marked with the lines that showed where the pictures had been. And it was cold, with only one thin electric heater glowing next to the dead fireplace.

Miss Toklas came creeping in, as always, through the high white doors at the far end of the room. She peered at me for a moment, as though unable to make out my features, and then said, uncertainly, "Otto?" Then she shuffled forward, hands outstretched. We sat down in the familiar places, she in her chair, I on the sofa, and there was the customary exchange of surprises at how long it had been, and how much the same we looked. But she did not look the same—nor, I suppose, did I—for she had aged many, many years in the decade since I had last seen her. She had been very old then, but animated by an iron vitality. The stooped walk was just one of her curious attributes, like the leathery skin and the dyed bangs. Now the once bright eyes were blurred, and the deep voice was feeble, and the hunched back was hunched like that of someone being crushed.

"So, tell me your news," she said. "You're still writing."

"Oh, some." I shrugged. "The job takes just about all my time."

"I don't hear," she said, so I repeated what I had said.

"Have you given up?" she demanded.

"No, I haven't given up. It just goes more slowly. You remember that kidnapping novel, the one I wrote about five years ago? I've just rewritten the whole thing. I threw away the first fifty pages and started on page fifty-one."

"Good, and what's happening to it?"

"The same thing that always happens. It's making the rounds."

She began a long story, then, about the absence of a table that had once been in this room. It involved the local furniture repair shop, and the carpenter's inability to follow instructions, and the excuses he had offered Miss Toklas, and the reprimand Miss Toklas had given him.

"But tell me about yourself. How's Priscilla? How are the children?"

"Oh, they're fine. Liesel's in the sixth grade now . . ."

"Who? I'm sorry, but I don't hear."

"Liesel, the oldest one," I said, louder. "She's in the sixth grade. Doing fine."

"Is Priscilla writing anything?"

"No, she wrote this novel two years ago, but it never got sold, and then the baby came . . ."

Then there was another story. This time, it concerned some paperwork that the American embassy had required, and the number of forms to be filled out, and the absurdity and irrelevance of the questions that the embassy always asked.

"But listen," she suddenly interrupted herself. "I want to see you again. Can you have lunch tomorrow?"

I was sorry, but I really couldn't. I was only in Paris for two more days. "Oh," she said. She was sorry too. "There's a nice place just down the street, where I go sometimes. It's nothing fancy, but the food is good." No, I was awfully sorry, and I'd like to, but I just couldn't. I was not really lying, because I did have lunch dates on both days, but I probably could have made some changes. But I also knew that I didn't want to have lunch with Miss Toklas. Too much time had passed, and too much had happened—or, perhaps more accurately, too little had happened—and we were not what we had been, and the relations between us could never again be what they had been.

The simple fact, I think, is that death was fourteen years closer to both of us, and, to her, it was very close indeed. In that gray, empty room, it invisibly surrounded her, and though she may have accepted its presence, as anyone of eighty-five is bound to do, she could not resist peering out through the mist, and reaching out a hand for someone to hold on to. And I, feeling an irresistible need to escape, could only apologize again—knowing that, for the first and last time, I had hurt her, knowing, too, that she knew what I was doing, pushing the drowning hand away from the gunwale of the lifeboat, and saying, "Sorry." Knowing all this, we said good-bye, and promised to keep in touch, and I walked out.

I resolved to write her, cheerfully and affectionately, not to explain everything but just to provide pleasant gossip and a sense of better things ahead. For a year, I periodically made notes to myself to write to her during the next weekend, or the next vacation, or definitely before the first of the month. And for another year, no longer making notes, I still kept meaning to write. One spring day in 1966, I got a telephone call from the man who had once been a correspondent for the *New York Times*, the one whom I had met in Miss Toklas's apartment, and who had written that foolish blurb about me almost twenty years earlier. I invited him to lunch at Ratazzi's, a noisy but good little restaurant on East Forty-eighth Street. We didn't recognize each other at first, but it was a pleasant lunch, and we talked aimlessly about Paris and the old days and mutual friends. He still saw a lot of Miss Toklas, and so the conversation repeatedly returned to her, and I began to be puzzled by the way he seemed to assume that I knew all the recent details of her life. At one point, I finally said, "I'm afraid I really haven't kept in touch with her, you know. I haven't written to her for ages."

"Are you serious?" he asked.

"Yes, I haven't written to her for several years, three or four years."

"You know, that's funny," he said. "She always talks about you as though you'd written to her just last week."

The obituary was in the *Times* on March 8, 1967. "Alice B. Toklas, the longtime friend of Gertrude Stein, who helped the late writer preside over a celebrated literary salon, died here early today. She was 89 years old and had been ill for several years...." Miss Toklas had become a convert to Catholicism in her last years, and the obituary concluded by saying: "After a funeral mass at St. Christophe's Roman Catholic Church on Friday, Miss Toklas will be buried beside Miss Stein in Pere Lachaise cemetery."

As you climb the hill toward the far end of the cemetery, the jungle of chestnut trees and wood ivy begins to thin out, and you emerge from the nineteenth century into the twentieth. There are only a few of the gray stone tombs. The twentieth century is more functional. Modern tombs lie flat on the ground, great blocks of marble, mostly dark, each inscribed in gold with names and dates and crosses, each within a foot of its neighbor.

The grave of Edith Piaf is an attraction, just as the gendarme had said. It stands waist high, and on top of it, the singer's admirers have installed plaques attesting to their devotion. *"Edith—nous avons prié pour toi à Lourdes,"* says one. *"Nous avons prié à Lisieux,"* says another.

There are seven plaques in all, each bearing witness to prayers recited at a shrine. Alongside the plaques, there are vases of flowers, fifteen of them, fading carnations and daffodils.

This outer ring, the avenue Circulaire, overlooking a series of shabby apartment houses, is wide and public, suitable for public ceremonies. Here stand the bleakly institutional monuments dedicated to the Frenchmen, Jew and Gentile, who died in Nazi concentration camps. One is for Buchenwald. Another commemorates 10,000 who died at Mauthausen. Still another cites 13,800 dead at Neuengamme. Here too, close by, lie the bureaucrats of French Communism. Maurice Thorez. Marcel Cachin. One large tomb appears to be reserved for members of the Communist Central Committee. Three names are listed, with blank spaces reserved for several more.

It is hot, climbing the asphalt pavement in the fading afternoon sun, and my map shows that I am following the wrong path. It says that I should take an avenue Transversale to the avenue Greffulhe and then to a spot that the lady at the central office has marked with an *x*. I follow the instructions, but at the spot marked *x*, there are just tombs and more tombs. There are no celebrities here. The graves are small and orderly, and I thread my way up one row and down the next, reading the unknown name on each stone, like some inventory taker checking the stock in a warehouse. I take off my jacket and wander on, searching.

The grave is suddenly in front of me. It has a square headstone that says: Gertrude Stein. Next to it, where Miss Toklas is supposed to be, there is nothing but a bare patch of ground. I look again, more carefully. To the far left is a small stone building, perhaps some kind of storage shed. Then the square headstone that simply says: Gertrude Stein, and the dates and places of birth and death. It is surrounded by a scraggly border of box hedge, about six inches high. The grave itself is bare earth, with one small vase containing four dead roses. And then to the right there is a large black tomb, shiny, inscribed to the Famille Deuieb, the most recent of whom was interred here in 1964. In between Gertrude Stein and the Famille Deuieb, there is just an empty patch of dirt, slightly humped in the center, and there are two or three shards of broken pottery, and bits of glass, and a piece of brick, the kind of debris that always appears when the earth is dug up and then replaced.

Someday, probably soon, a headstone will stand here, with the name of Alice B. Toklas chiseled into the stone. But I will not have to come back here to see it.

1967

How to Be a War Correspondent

▪ THE WAR NEWS FROM ALGERIA THESE DAYS HAS A CERTAIN uniformity about it. "Eighty Algerian rebels were killed within the last twenty-four hours, the French Army announced today. Some fifty others were wounded and eighteen captured. French losses were not disclosed." Give or take a few dozen corpses, that is the full story that reappears every few days near the bottom of an inside page in many American newspapers. It is basically a filler, just like the little paragraphs about the number of buffalo in Wyoming.

If the French haven't learned how to avoid colonial wars or how to win them, they have apparently learned at least one thing about them—the less said the better. The outside world needs nothing more than a few announcements of enemy casualties and an occasional declaration that the "terrorists" are on the run. What taught the French their lesson, of course, was the disaster at Dien Bien Phu. Was any other war ever lost because of such a strategically insignificant defeat? The only importance of the isolated outpost was that the French had ballyhooed their capture of it as the beginning of a campaign to subjugate the interior of Indochina, and that they had always claimed the "terrorists" did not dare to meet them in open combat. When the Vietminh fought and won, the French lost little more than their mythology, but that was too much for a disgusted public to bear. The war in Indochina was lost by the very fact that it proved to be a war.

Still, the mythical period of French supremacy had a certain fascination for the war correspondents assigned to cover it for the American press. At the start, it had been just a "rebellion." Then came the Korean War, which occupied everyone's attention for a while (though one curious editor eventually printed the same story and the same headline—YANKS SHELL / REDS ON HILL—every day for about a fortnight without attracting a single complaint from his readers). But in the summer of 1953, the Korean armistice was signed. As an amputee is said to feel that his severed arm is still there, American editors apparently felt an instinctive need for war stories, and they turned to that long-ignored struggle in Indochina. It wasn't worth the money to send reporters there, but the wire services were expected to do the job.

For that job, they had one basic source of news, the French army communiqués. And since Agence France Presse relayed the communiqués to Paris very soon after they were issued in Hanoi, it was very economical for an American agency to depend on its Paris bureau, rather than on a Hanoi correspondent, to write the three or four daily war stories that were needed in New York or Chicago. We had stringers in Hanoi, of course, but such part-time correspondents are rarely worth even the pittance they get. The French provincial journalists who act as stringers are generally blind to what is called news, and those who turned up in Hanoi were even worse than usual. Ours were not really expected to be reporters. They were limited to a few hundred words a week—cable tolls were expensive—and they had to be slapped down periodically for sending long essays about *"les hordes rouges."* Aside from occasional tips, their chief function was to provide a certain legitimacy to our use of their bylines and of the magic dateline: Hanoi. With a byline and a dateline, all we needed was "enthusiasm."

When I was transferred to the Paris bureau that summer of 1953, I was only partly aware of how the war was being covered, and my first stories reflected the drabness of the French communiqués. I had worked on old-fashioned newspapers, where city editors were fussy about what they called "facts," and stories usually began with the name, age, and address of the murder victim. This was the way the rival news agency was covering the war. Its stories usually began: "The French High Command announced today that . . ." But I was soon taken aside by the assistant bureau chief and scolded about what he called "your all-the-news-that's-fit-to-print approach." There was no point in even writing a story that just reported what was happening, he said, because such a story usually ended on some editor's dead spike. That verdict, I soon learned, was perfectly right. The story that got into the papers—and getting into the papers was our reason for existence—was the story that showed "enthusiasm."

What is "enthusiasm"? It consists of writing about something as though it were exciting, even though you know nothing about it, even though you are thousands of miles away, even though it is not exciting at all. The basic technique involves verbs of action, lots of adjectives, a sure grasp of clichés, and a readiness to fill in gaps where the facts are missing. Next to our desk, the AFP ticker announces, for example, that *"des avions ont bombardé les Communistes."* We are not told how many planes, what type, what they dropped, or even where, but enthusiasm translates this into "Waves of American-built Bearcat fighter-bombers zoomed low over cleverly camouflaged Red positions and rained down bombs and fiery napalm. . . ." To the enthusiastic war correspondent, Foreign Legionnaires are never just legionnaires; they are "tough" or "crack." Enthusiastic soldiers never "go" anywhere; they "slog through waist-deep rice paddies," they "wade through turbulent flood-swollen streams," or they "knife through sweltering jungles." If it is an amphibious attack, they "splash ashore in full battle kit" in a "bold three-way land-sea-air attack."

Unlike the Algerian war, which the French describe as an "internal" affair, the Indochinese war was sanctified by the fact that the Communists were leading and equipping the enemy side. And the French made the most of it. When there was an important debate in the National Assembly or an important mission to Washington to ask for more money, the French would coincidentally launch one of their "offensives." The AFP started out with great alarums, which we translated as "armored spearheads crunching through the pre-dawn dark," accompanied by the usual "fighter-bombers zooming low." The noisemaking was usually little more than a training maneuver, for the French "offensives" struck at undefended beaches or wandered through the jungle, but our enthusiasm whetted the appetites of American editors. Instead of our usual three stories a day we had to write five or six about the great battle. But once the game had begun, the AFP's reports often faded into pale daily communiqués about the Communists "fearing an open fight" or "retreating before the massive onslaught." Finally, we would be left with a day or two of complete official silence—and still six new stories a day to write. That was when our enthusiasm became overpowering.

We got out maps of Indochina and tried to find the spot where the AFP had abandoned our intrepid attackers. If it was near a river, for example, we had several alternatives. Our heroes could "fan out along the muddy banks and consolidate their swift gains." They could "establish a precarious bridgehead across the strategic stream." They could "splash through the raging torrent in hot pursuit of the fleeing Reds." For self-protection, we often described these fantasies as "battlefront reports filtering through heavy censorship." Occasionally, we went too far, of course. Then someone else's representative in Hanoi would get the Northern Command to issue an official denial of whatever we were saying, but this caused us little concern. For one thing, the dramatic war story had been printed in a prominent place, and the denial wouldn't rate better than a brief, obscure mention, if that. Besides, the home front trusted us war correspondents, while everyone knew that government denials didn't mean much.

Were we criminal frauds, we war correspondents? Perhaps, if the function of the press is to print the facts and create an enlightened electorate. But if the function of the press is to sell newspapers, you could put our "colorful" stories in the same category with the lovelorn columns, the comics, and the front-page accounts of Marilyn Monroe's love life. God knows we would have stuck to the facts if we had known them, for it is much easier to write a factual story than to make everything up.

What prevented us from knowing the facts? First of all, the French government itself. The American idea that the press represents the public, and that either press or public has a "right" to know anything, is totally alien to French officials. In America, I once telephoned a Nebraska prison during a convict riot and had the state's governor politely answer every question I put to him. In France, I once telephoned a prison simply to ask for the name of the warden, and the request was met with amazement and outrage. It is only natural that most foreign correspondents do most of their reporting by reading the local newspapers.

But if the average official's secrecy was bad, the army's crazed desire for publicity was worse. Its phantom offensives and phantom victories made one wonder how the war had lasted so long. At one point, Gen. Henri Navarre, the supreme commander who repeatedly beat his breast about "carrying the war to the enemy and destroying him," launched another attack that "destroyed" the Vietminh 320th Division, according to the AFP communiqués. A week later, the government-sponsored news agency calmly announced that the 320th had just attacked the French in force. When the Vietminh made their second invasion of Laos and the French retreated from an obviously strategic crossroads town, a "military spokesman" described it as "of no strategic value." When the Vietminh moved out again a week later and the French moved back in, a "military spokesman" said the town had "considerable prestige value." The official habit of either lying or hiding behind a blackout was worsened by the political bias that most French newspapers not only practiced but considered natural. Politicians and officials habitually leaked their side of the story to newspapers on their side, which passed it on to readers who expected to have their prejudices satisfied. A Foreign Office press spokesman consequently summed up the role of the official *porte-parole* as *"Mentir et démentir* (To lie and to deny)."

Such obstacles, according to the old newspaper tradition, should only serve as a challenge to the red-blooded American reporter in search of the facts. But while editors express such worthy sentiments at their conventions, they make only a limited effort to put them into effect. In many American cities, editors depend on local agencies to get the news, not on their own reporters. How many New York City courts are covered at all? At best, local reporting is a hit-or-miss operation. A British editor once complained that in every case where he personally knew the facts he found the newspaper accounts grossly inaccurate, and no other editor answered his hopeful request to be challenged. Beyond city limits, obviously, anything goes. So how much attention is paid to the accuracy of what comes from Indochina?

Blame sloth, blame indifference, blame incompetence, but the basic fact is that it would cost a lot of money to support one of those red-blooded American reporters in Indochina. Figure at least a hundred dollars a week in salary and at least fifty dollars a week in expenses, and is it worth it? It might be, if an American newspaper really wanted to find out what was going on in Indochina. But that would involve finding out the answers to complicated and embarrassing questions: Why were the French fighting? What were they fighting for and what were they fighting against? Why did they prop up Bao Dai as "emperor"? How high did the currency black-marketing scandal go? And what did the Indochinese people think of it all? But this was not what American editors wanted. They wanted stories of good guys fighting Reds, and that was what they got. Aside from the expense and the possibly embarrassing results, the fact-finding American reporter often doesn't live up to his reputation. Our agency once had an American covering the Indochina war and he was out at the beach when the French evacuated a major stronghold. Returning home, he found angry cables from New York demanding explanations and improvements. He went to the French headquarters, I've been told, and was given one of the official fantasies—that French troops had already recaptured the place. So he sent off what should be a classic story: "Fierce, bearded Goumiers, with a song on their lips and murder in their hearts, today stormed back into———." For that kind of thing, it cost the agency and its clients less to have the job done in Paris.

From both ends of the news cycle, then, came pressure for fiction rather than facts. At the source, French officials wanted their mythology spread. At the outlet, American editors wanted melodrama. And in the middle was the news agency, an easy target for blame. But who in that agency actually should be blamed? In New York, where the budgets were made out, and where the executives made speeches about a free and responsible press, only a certain amount of money could be allotted for foreign coverage, if there was to be any foreign coverage at all. It was an utterly inadequate amount, in terms of what could or should be done, not only in Indochina but all over the world, and in the United States too. But the money had to be extracted from editors and publishers, who all basically wanted something for very nearly nothing. When it came to Indochina, the agency executives passed on the responsibility to Paris, where a half dozen underpaid men were expected to cover not only all of France but the whole French Union, battles outside Hanoi, riots in Morocco, the discovery of a coelacanth off Madagascar. I assume the executives knew nothing of the fakery that went on—they didn't want to know. They must have known that the money they were spending could not legitimately provide the "top coverage" they demanded, but they didn't want to know the details.

In Paris, the successive bureau chiefs may each have gone through a crisis of conscience about the situation, but I never saw signs of one. They knew perfectly well that their careers depended on getting the job done without spending any money. When one of them was asked by an outsider why something wasn't done about the farce, he answered that he had tried to get New York to send a reporter to Hanoi but the executives couldn't see any need for it because "we always got the play." Here is the traditional pattern of buck-passing. The top doesn't know, the middle can't do anything, and the bottom only carries out orders. At the bottom, we war correspondents strapped on our helmets, consulted our maps and our day-old French newspapers and our lurid imaginations, and aimed our typewriters at the front page.

It did not really matter who did the dirty work. My predecessor was a charming fellow whom I had met when we were both sportswriters. He started out by going to briefings at the defense ministry in Paris, but it was not long before he found that he could create fantasy as well as the defense ministry could. His greatest achievement came during the first Vietminh invasion of Laos, when it took about a week for the Vietminh to march unopposed to the royal capital of Luang Prabang. Needing a shot of adrenaline to keep the story alive, he produced a wild tale about some kind of prophecy by a Moon God that "superstitious natives" believed would save the capital. It was the kind of thing that nobody could really deny, and it made good headlines, and he was not surprised to see his "prophecy" appear under the bylines of other "reporters" and even in a weekly magazine. But he was almost shocked when the Vietminh mysteriously withdrew without a fight and made his Moon God's prophecy come true. He finally quit and went to work for an advertising agency. Writing advertising copy not only paid him more money but relieved him of that war correspondent's feeling that he was drifting ever further from reality toward schizophrenic hallucination.

I did my tour of duty, then, fired away like the rest of them, and quit in due course—we war correspondents suffered a special kind of shell shock that caused a spectacularly high turnover. But I left my fantasy war in the able hands of a genial young man who carried on the tradition. I had covered the French capture of Dien Bien Phu, and even before I left there were signs of a possible disaster. I wrote stories about the Vietminh buildup in the surrounding jungle, but the French pooh-poohed such things, and editors were not interested in buildups. It was not long after I returned to America that the siege of Dien Bien Phu became front-page news, and I couldn't help thinking that my old agency's accounts of the fighting sounded remarkably authentic, at least from a distance. I wrote to ask my successor whether he had discovered some secret source of information, and he wrote back that before producing his night lead for the morning papers he ate a handsome lunch with a good amount of wine and then headed for the garish carnivals along the Grands Boulevards. "I wander into the shooting galleries on the Faubourg Montmartre," he wrote, "to get inspiration and local color." I got the letter just about the day that the French empire in Asia fell in ruins.

1959

On *Watching* Parsifal *with Molly*

> *Parsifal* is a work of perfidy, of vindictiveness, of
> a secret attempt to poison the presuppositions of
> life—a *bad* work. . . . I despise anyone who does
> not experience *Parsifal* as an attempted assassina-
> tion of basic ethics.
>
> —Friedrich Nietzsche

▪ HURRY UP, MOLLY!

Row G, the little purple tickets say. Seats 18 and 19. We are
assigned to the last row of the dress circle, which means the third
balcony, and the curtain goes up at seven o'clock sharp.

And the Metropolitan Opera of New York defines the term *caveat
emptor* to mean that not even the payment of $10.75 for a seat in
the third balcony entitles you to see the opera unless you get to
your seat before curtain time. If you fail, you are condemned, for
whatever period of time the Metropolitan management deems suitable, to watch the performance on closed-circuit TV in the empty
lobby. The Long Island Rail Road takes a similar view of its duty to
its customers—that is, it declines any obligation to provide the pas-
senger with the services he paid for. So hurry, Molly, because the
train was late, as usual, and we have only fifteen minutes to get from
Pennsylvania Station to Lincoln Center before they raise the draw-
bridges and make us watch the whole first act over the TV.

Molly is my daughter, my second daughter. Molly is eighteen, a
college freshman, home for the Thanksgiving weekend. She is wearing a black velvet dress with short sleeves, and her blonde hair,
which she washed this afternoon, and tied with a ribbon at the back
of her head, flows loosely down over her shoulders, all of which
makes her look rather like the Tenniel drawings of Alice in Won-
derland. And she is hurrying, through the filthy tunnels of the Seventh Avenue subway, through the brighter but no less forbidding

tunnels under Lincoln Center, through endless mazes of white tile and fluorescent light, through turnstiles and swinging doors, up escalators and onto stairways, which change from concrete to marble, and then acquire red carpeting, as we ascend from the subterranean treadmills of the poor to the balconies built for opera audiences.

"You have exactly three minutes to make it," says the uniformed ticket taker, enjoying his brief opportunity to threaten the customers and make them scramble.

"Hurry, Molly!"

We board an elevator to the third balcony, emerging just in time to run through the doors before they close. The theater is already darkening as an usher hands us two programs, and we stumble past a row of unrelenting knees. When we finally reach our seats, Molly decorously stows away the shopping bag that contains our dinner, two ham sandwiches, two apples, and a peanut-butter jar filled with cheap red wine, Gallo Paisano.

And the stately prelude to *Parsifal,* which Richard Wagner, having borrowed fifty musicians from the duke of Meiningen's orchestra, conducted for the first time in the front hall of his own house to awaken his wife Cosima on her birthday on Christmas morning of 1878, begins.

When I was young, I confidently believed that there must be some way to combat the length of Wagner's operas. I acknowledged that the operas were masterpieces, which must somehow be endured, and might even be enjoyed, but I could not understand why they had to be endured (enjoyed) for five or six hours. There could be little aesthetic justification, after all, for any opera lasting twice as long as *Don Giovanni,* or, for that matter, longer than one hundred repetitions of the most beautiful Chopin mazurka. To a large extent, I thought, it was simply a contest of wills between the composer and his audience, a question of whether the former could totally dominate and subjugate the latter, and I did not choose to be subjugated.

The first tactic I devised was the most expensive but also, I think, the best. This happened more than twenty years ago, when I was studying at the University of Geneva, and various touring opera companies would come for weekend performances, Friday and Saturday nights, and then move on to Basel or Zurich. The tickets to Geneva's musty old opera house were quite cheap, so I bought one every week—to Mozart, to Puccini, to Strauss and Smetana, and inevitably to Wagner, whom, because of my parents' intense disapproval of the man, I had never heard before. On learning that *Tristan und Isolde* lasted more than five hours, however, I bought tickets for both nights. On Friday night, I watched the first half and then left Isolde swinging her torch while I went out to have a good Swiss dinner, barley soup and veal cutlets with cheese sauce, or some such thing. On Saturday night, after a slightly earlier but equally fortifying dinner, I returned to the opera house to find Isolde still swinging her torch, and I stayed on until she dropped dead shortly after midnight. (It was Wagner, incidentally, who inflicted the moment of destiny on that marvelously decrepit Geneva opera house a few years later, when the sea-of-fire scene at the end of *Die Walküre* went out of control and gutted the place.)

In some way, then, my early struggle with Wagner was associated with hunger. By staging his marathon operas at a time when most people eat their dinners, Wagner seemed to be trying, like the young Schopenhauer scheduling his lectures at the same time as those of the great Hegel, to compete against the basic instincts of his audience. But perhaps I have it all wrong. Perhaps my association of Wagner and hunger began before I had ever seen one of the operas.

The previous summer, I had decided to attend the annual music festival in Lucerne, and since I had no money, I lived there like a kind of medieval hermit. I ate no meals, and I passed my nights in a sleeping bag in a local forest called the Gütsch. In the mornings, I would get up, often soaking wet from the night's rain, and then spend most of the day wandering through the harvesttime countryside, stopping occasionally to make a fitful effort at a book I was solemnly carrying around with me, Henri Pirenne's gigantic *Histoire de la Philosophie au Moyen Âge*. My wanderings along the southern shore of Lake Lucerne inevitably led me to a beautiful, bright, sunny villa, three stories high, with a superb view across the lake to the wooded hills on the far side.

The villa was named Triebschen, and here, in the spring of 1866,

Richard Wagner had moved in with his celebrated mistress, Franz Liszt's daughter, Cosima von Bülow, and her three daughters, known as Lusch, Boni, and Loldi—the last, Isolde, being an illegitimate child by Wagner. Here the composer found refuge from prosecution as a revolutionary, and from lawsuits accusing him of defaulting on some $10,000 in debts in Munich. Here, in beatific exile, he received a stream of distinguished visitors, including a distant relative of mine— the docile cuckold, Hans von Bülow, the famous conductor and pianist, husband of Cosima, who did his best to suppress the scandal for several months by joining the Triebschen ménage. And here Wagner worked continually at his newest and most joyous opera, *Die Meistersinger,* which was composed largely in this villa by the side of this lake. But I knew nothing of Wagner then. I knew only that Triebschen, now a museum that I couldn't afford to enter, stood in the midst of an apple orchard, and so I wandered in every two or three days and picked quantities of apples to keep me alive throughout the music festival. And went on trying to read Pirenne's *Histoire* on a bench by the side of the orchard.

Whatever the reasons for my association of Wagner and food, I found, when I moved to Paris a few years later, and forced myself to dutiful attendance at the *Ring,* that the long hours of Wagner's music made me ravenous. I also discovered, however, that the Paris opera still (in 1948 and 1949) sold fifth-balcony box seats for fifty francs each. The Paris opera company was thoroughly mediocre, but fifty francs in those days was the equivalent of about fifteen cents, and that made mediocrity quite acceptable. Since a box ordinarily contained six seats, it could be bought in its entirety for less than one dollar. All I needed, then, were five friends willing to pay a share, and one of those five willing to pack a picnic dinner. I forget who took the other four seats, but I knew a very pretty girl who liked both Wagner and picnics, and I still remember the moment in *Die Walküre,* when Siegmund draws the magic sword from the tree, as the moment when six of us tore open a large brown paper bag and began devouring, to the accompaniment of a surge of closing chords, roast chicken.

The fifth balcony, I now realize, was the perfect spot from which to watch Wagner's *Ring.* Since there is virtually no action onstage, we miss nothing by sitting at a distance. On the contrary, looking down from the remote heights of the fifth balcony, we begin, and quite rightly, to regard the descending tiers of silent witnesses as part of the spectacle. We achieve, simply by sitting at a great distance above the stage, Brecht's famous "alienation effect." And this is particularly appropriate to Wagner, as it would not be to a composer like Puccini, for as we regard the stylized drama of gods and heroes, we ourselves acquire, up in the astral fifth balcony, the viewpoint of the gods.

As one gets older, however, it becomes increasingly difficult—increasingly unnatural—to play the role of Bohemian. By the time Kirsten Flagstad emerged from the disgrace of collaboration with the Nazis and returned to Paris for her first postwar appearance, in *Götterdämmerung,* the pretty girl with the roast chicken had long since returned to New York, and I bought two tickets, for my wife and me, in a first-balcony loge. The price of 1,200 francs, a little under four dollars, seemed outrageous, but the loge provided another technique for surviving Wagner. For the master's most celebrated works have always inspired me not only with hunger but with a yearning for sleep (the two responses may, in fact, be related). And a loge at the Paris Opéra includes not only four chairs at the front of the box but a very comfortable sofa at the back. I do not know the original purpose of such sofas—whether designed for a discreet seduction during one of the more tedious operas of Saint-Saëns or simply for intermission visits by the dowagers in the neighboring boxes—but I found this resting place admirably suited to Wagner. During most of the middle of *Götterdämmerung,* I contentedly slept, awakening quite refreshed in time for the final disaster.

Molly sits engrossed. The previous day, she had gone to visit one of her high-school teachers, who had taught a course in culture history, and she had told him of the coming event. "He says *Parsifal* is better than pot," Molly said. "He says it's a complete experience, like getting high."

Molly is very attractive, although she doesn't know it. She has a sexy voice, and a charming laugh, but she doesn't know that either.

"That's what fathers always think," she once said. "That's what fathers *have* to think, but nobody else thinks so."

About ten years ago, when my two older daughters were just children, there came a sudden, violent rainstorm, and two boys knocked on our kitchen door, in search of shelter. The four of them sat in the kitchen, in embarrassed silence, and my oldest daughter said, by way of conversation, "My father is a famous writer." But Molly said, "What are your hobbies?"

A celebrated astrologer once worked out the charts for all the people in our family, and he said that Molly, unlike the rest of us, had been reincarnated many times upon this earth, and therefore she had acquired the stoic wisdom of her many reincarnations. She was, he said, that relatively rare phenomenon known to astrologers as "an old soul."

Being a mediocre amateur pianist, I have always dreamed of having a child who would turn out to be a second Mozart. To have such a dream come true, to have one's child actually be a second Mozart, would undoubtedly be a hideous fate, but that does not make the dream any less real. Of the various curses I have borne through life, therefore, one minor curse is that none of my five children has the slightest musical talent whatever.

I started in the inevitable way, trying to teach my oldest daughters, then six or seven, to play the piano. I soon learned that music is a very strange and difficult language to the unmusical. In trying to teach and explain, I recognized difficulties that I had long forgotten. Any given note, to be specific, must be seen/heard as a certain level of pitch (e.g., three whole tones above middle C), and also as a certain time value (e.g., a quarter note, or one beat in four-four time, though the rules change in six-eight time), and it also has a name (E), and a number (3), indicating which finger should play it. And all these acts of recognition must take place simultaneously, and at high speed.

My daughters, inevitably, began to cheat. While pretending to read the notes, they actually read only the numbers that told the beginner which finger to use on each note. Thus, the number 1 always stood for middle C, and middle C could always be identified by the number 1. After two or three weeks, when the fingering became more complicated, and the number 1 might apply to D or E, the system of cheating broke down. Then there were tears on one side and scoldings on the other, and attempts at guessing the right note, and scornful corrections of mistakes in guessing, and I realized, before too long, that the girls' inability to learn was fully matched by my inability to teach. And so the piano lessons stopped.

The public school system of Long Island, however, refuses to accept the idea that some people are musical and others aren't. Just as it teaches the "new math" by dogmatic and arcane rules that neither teachers nor pupils understand, just as it starts foreign languages at such an early age that the child who used to spend three years failing to learn French presently spends eight years failing to learn French, so, with a flourish of terms like "the learning experience," it now issues orchestral instruments with such enthusiasm that I have, as I write, a seventeen-year-old son honking away upstairs at "Twinkle, Twinkle, Little Star" on a saxophone.

So they handed Molly a violin, and she, who could not play a simple instrument like the piano, was supposed to start learning about first position and double-stops. But the thing that exasperated me the most was that I kept finding the rented violin lying on the ground next to Molly's bicycle under the yew tree in the backyard. To me, a violin, any violin, still implies something of what it implies to Central Europeans—*Kultur*—a symbol to be treasured and cherished on its bed of velvet. To Long Island children, on the other hand, a violin is just another piece of school equipment, easily smashed and just as easily replaced.

For a time, Molly doggedly practiced her violin. In the evenings, after supper, there would come from the second floor, through several closed doors, the unbearable sounds of a violin being sawed at. Scales, little exercises, little songs—by the time each piece was mastered, we were so sick of the screechings and flattenings that we could not appreciate the fact that the piece had been finally mastered, and that new songs and exercises were under way. And I doubt that anyone has ever learned the violin this way, through exercises undertaken in shame and self-consciousness on the second floor, in the knowledge that everyone on the first floor hears and hates each note. No, to learn the violin, one must practice in the living room, at the center of the household, and in the presence of a mother who insatiably listens and tirelessly repeats, "That was fine, Jascha, and now let's hear it again."

For four or five years, we continued these games, and then we moved to a new house on the North Shore, and Molly entered high school, and when it came time to enroll in the volunteer music classes, she didn't enroll.

But she did finally find her way to opera. About two years ago, my wife picked me up at the railroad station one evening and said, "I just want to warn you that when you get home, you'll find Molly absolutely dissolving in tears on the living-room sofa, but it's nothing to worry about."

"Why, what's the matter?" I asked.

"Molly has just discovered *Traviata.*"

"What is *Parsifal* really about?" Molly asked as we rode the Long Island Rail Road train through the darkening warehouses of Queens.

I didn't know the answer—I still don't—but it is difficult for a father to make to his daughter a confession of ignorance. I told her about the legend of Parsifal, and the knights of the Round Table, and the Grail, and the Fisher King in Eliot's *Waste Land.*

"Of course, Wagner didn't follow the legends too closely," I offered as a final gesture, "but that'll give you the general idea."

"Yeah, I see," Molly said, in the tone of someone who finds himself, according to the phrase of a wild Georgian I once knew, up to the eyeballs in a swamp of owl turds.

Well, what *is* the story of *Parsifal?* At the first intermission, after two hours of bewilderment, we consult the programs handed out by the Met's ushers, and the synopsis does not do much to get us out of the swamp. "As the curtain rises on the forest near Monsalvat," it begins, "the knight Gurnemanz rouses two young Esquires who are standing guard with him before the castle. Morning has dawned and Amfortas, their ailing leader, will soon be passing on his way to his bath. Gurnemanz' reverie on the causes of Amfortas' suffering is

interrupted by the arrival of the wildly disheveled Kundry, with bal-
sam from Arabia for Amfortas' bath. Gurnemanz explains that no
one knows of Kundry's origin, that Titurel, father of Amfortas, found
her lying rigid in the forest when he selected this spot for the home
of the Grail and its knights. She comes and goes, apparently under
a curse. . . ."

And so on. Let us try, then, not to synopsize the narrative but
to reduce the story to its essentials. In the temple of Monsalvat,
Amfortas and his knights have undertaken to guard the Holy Grail
and the Holy Spear that once stabbed Christ in the side. Outside, in
a rival fortress, lives the wicked magician Klingsor, who once tried
to become a knight of the Grail but was rejected as unworthy. Klingsor used Kundry to seduce Amfortas. Klingsor thus gained possession
of the sacred spear and inflicted an incurable wound on Amfortas.
This wound can be healed only by a youth of complete innocence,
namely Parsifal. When the youth appears, Klingsor once again uses
Kundry as his seductress, but Parsifal rejects her, recaptures the
sacred spear, destroys Klingsor, cures Amfortas, and becomes the
new leader of the knights of the Grail.

This story, loosely adapted from a thirteenth-century epic by
Wolfram von Eschenbach, has very little relation to reality, of course,
and none of its characters behaves in accordance with what modern
audiences call "motivation." One might wonder, therefore, whether
the plot and narrative, the words, really mean anything at all, particularly when sung in a foreign language over the roar of a one-
hundred-piece orchestra. To Wagner and his followers, the question
itself would be outrageous. The composer considered himself a titan
of both poetry and philosophy, and he regarded this saga as a masterpiece of Christian art. He insisted that it was not an opera at all
but a *"Bühnenweihfestspiel"* (roughly, "sacred festival play"). And
Wagner's critics have always been equally solemn. The first and most
important one, Friedrich Nietzsche, decried the Parsifalian idea of
knightly chastity as a negation of life itself. Even today, one of Wagner's most recent biographers, Robert Gutman, denounces *Parsifal*
as an expression of anti-Semitism, homosexuality, and even Satanism.
He quotes, and apparently agrees with, the statement of Adolf Hitler:

"Whoever wants to understand National Socialist Germany must know Wagner."

It is undeniable that Wagner was an anti-Semite, and perhaps even a bizarre kind of proto-Nazi. It is also undeniable that his operas became, long after his death, the official music of Hitler Germany. But does that loathsome history mean that Wagner's music was not a great artistic achievement? Or that we must damn great art because of either the folly of the creator or the wickedness of his admirers? Wagner's first major English biographer, Ernest Newman, stated the counterargument in a characteristically English way. He remarked that the rejection of *Parsifal* would be "like asking us to give up having breakfast because some horrible murderer or other liked bacon and eggs." As for the opera itself, Newman declared that "its central idea . . . is simply an artist's dream of an ideally innocent world, purged of the lust, the hatred, the cruelty that deface the world we live and groan in."

"Why, of all places, Bayreuth?" wrote the eminent Vienna music critic Eduard Hanslick, back in 1876, on the occasion of Wagner's first festival in that obscure Bavarian town. "Wagner stuck to tiny, out-of-the-way Bayreuth in order that his listeners might not be distracted from his work by urban disturbances. In this he counted upon the festive mood of an audience predisposed in his favor. According to the unanimous statements of numerous festival guests, he appears to have miscalculated. Even yesterday, I saw many who had arrived in the flush of enthusiasm crawling up the hot, dusty streets to the distant Wagner Theater in a considerably more sober frame of mind."

The first Bayreuth festival, dedicated to the *Ring*, was a disaster—rows of empty seats and a deficit of 150,000 marks (about $40,000, which Wagner, characteristically, never paid). For six years, then, the hilltop theater that Wagner had built for himself stood empty, like Frankenstein's castle, until the eventual appearance of *Parsifal*. Wagner had said many years earlier that this would be his last work, and now that the composer was nearing seventy, he seemed to be keeping himself alive solely in order to complete his destiny. One tends to think of him as a large and powerful man, but he was just the opposite—scarcely five feet high, and sickly, afflicted throughout most of his life by a variety of nervous skin diseases. But he forced himself to supervise every detail of this first production of *Parsifal*, and at the end, he even clambered into the orchestra pit, during the third act of the farewell performance, and snatched the baton away from the conductor, Hermann Levi.

"I remained standing next to him because I feared he might make mistakes," said Levi, who was quite familiar with Wagner's incredible eccentricities (the composer had even requested, in vain, that Levi convert to Christianity before conducting *Parsifal* so that he would not "profane" this supposedly Christian drama). "But this was an idle fear; he conducted with . . . certainty. . . . At the end of the work, the public broke into a jubilation defying description. But the master did not show himself, remained sitting among us musicians, and made bad jokes. . . . And now the master (still on the podium) began to speak, first to me and the orchestra . . . and the master spoke with such affection that everyone started to weep. . . ."

In considering such moments of triumph over circumstance, one can feel a certain degree of *Mitleid* for the vainglorious old man. He moved on to Venice the following year, and died there, and was brought back to Bayreuth for burial, and *Parsifal* remained the exclusive property of Bayreuth for the next twenty years. In 1903, however, despite lawsuits by Cosima, the "sacred festival play" was pirated by the Metropolitan Opera of New York, an action that the Wagnerites promptly condemned as *"Der Gralsraub,"* or the theft of the Grail. Ten years later, then, the copyright expired, the work passed into the public domain, and it was soon performed all over the world. But *Parsifal* still lives in, still haunts, the ugly brick Festspielhaus in Bayreuth, not only because Wagner himself conducted it here but because Wagner's most celebrated admirer, Adolf Hitler, came here to pay homage to the master. We have countless photographs of the uniformed tyrant bowing low to kiss the hand of Winifred Wagner, the composer's English daughter-in-law, keeper of the shrine. And of the swastika flag hanging over what was once King Ludwig's royal box.

It took six years after World War II before the general disgust at the behavior of the Wagner family abated sufficiently for the Bayreuth festivals to resume. And there I was, the young reporter, wandering through drab, deserted streets with names like Siegfriedstrasse and Walkürestrasse and Rheingoldstrasse, and finally taking up a position on the Nibelungenstrasse, just outside the Festspielhaus, where I could watch the black Mercedeses and Jaguars stream up to the theater entrance and disgorge their cargoes of Allied generals and diplomats, all looking rather bored and disdainful. And those infinitely repeated figures of German recovery, the man with the wavy gray hair and the gray silk necktie and the pearl stickpin, and the woman with the gray hair in a bun and the gray silk dress that stretches to the floor. As curtain time approached, a platoon of trumpeters marched out onto the balcony of the Festspielhaus and played a fanfare from—of course—*Parsifal*.

The music on that reopening night was not by Wagner, however. No, to reconsecrate the Festspielhaus, which had been used intermittently for USO shows like *Ten Little Indians*, and which, worse, had been used by various bands of mocking American soldiers for unofficial but full-dress burlesques of Wagnerian opera—no, to recreate the atmosphere of the shrine, they had called in Wilhelm Furtwängler, that misguided yea-sayer who had conducted *Die Meistersinger* here during the last Nazi-subsidized wartime Bayreuth festivals of 1943 and 1944. They had called in Furtwängler to conduct the same work that Wagner had conducted at the laying of the cornerstone in 1872, Beethoven's Ninth Symphony. And the old man gave us a furiously melodramatic performance—sighing, singing, storming—and at the end, he stood for fully thirty seconds in deathly silence, his fists clenched, and only when he turned around did the audience rise to its feet to stamp and cheer and cry "Bravo!" Overhead, throughout the concert, several bats flittered to and fro.

So much for ritual and symbolism. On the following night, the first postwar Bayreuth festival really began, with Bayreuth's own opera, *Parsifal*. And now the assembled members of the cult, having survived two decades of political controversy, having survived the approval of the Nazis and the disapproval of the Allies, having gathered once again from all over Europe for the reopening of their temple, found that they had been betrayed by their idol's own grandsons. The creaky machinery that used to roll the elaborate backdrops into place was gone, and so were the dragons and the surging waves of the Rhine, and so was Klingsor's castle. "It used to be," one Englishman complained during an intermission, outside on the balcony, where the sky was still pink, "that when Parsifal pointed the spear and made Klingsor's castle fall in ruins, it really fell in ruins. Now there's nothing but lights going on and off."

It was true. For that opening night in the summer of 1951, Wagner's thirty-four-year-old grandson, Wieland, had revolutionized all the basic ideas of how to stage these operas. All the horned helmets and the sets of armor and the mechanical swans were consigned to history. Now the stage was almost totally bare. Three steps were enough to suggest a wooded hillside, and a switch to red spotlights represented the transformation of Kundry from supplicant into seductress. And this technique, soon applied to the other operas, naturally became known as "the Bayreuth style." Despite the howls of the traditionalists, moreover, various critics found good reasons to support the change. Artistically, the bare sets and the optical illusions seemed modern, a revitalization of Bayreuth's musty tradition. Economically, the new productions cost much less than it would have required to replace all the paraphernalia that the American GIs had "liberated" after the war. And politically, it was a good way of breaking with the past, of demonstrating that Wagner's characters were not primitive demons of German nationalism but symbolic expressions of universal human types. Whatever the reasons, the change was permanent. The *Parsifal* at the Met today is essentially the same one that Wieland Wagner created in Bayreuth twenty years ago.

There was another lesson to be learned at Bayreuth, though, and that is that all states of boredom (representing the presence or absence of pain or pleasure) are relative. I once knew a man, for example, who, in the army, had to sit in one of a row of dental chairs, being worked on by none-too-competent military dentists for six hours of virtually nonstop drilling. "And you know," he said, several years later, when he was a dean at a major university, "after a while, even the most excruciating pain becomes just boring." At the opposite extreme, I once knew a young banker with a beautiful mistress, not just a pretty girl but a really luscious blonde, and this man complained to me that he was bored because—"I mean, every once in a while, I feel I want to get away from her."

On more modest levels, it becomes clearly possible that after six hours of beautiful Wagnerian harmonies, one might begin to long for a toothache. Yet six hours of mere existence in the dusty Bavarian town of Bayreuth can become far more boring than anything that any composer could conceive, and so, after a morning and an afternoon of wandering through dull streets and looking into dull store windows and perhaps paying a visit to the dull little barrow-shaped graves where Wagner and Cosima lie outside their Villa Wahnfried—and perhaps even a trip to the black stone that marks the grave, in the city cemetery, of Franz Liszt—after a day of this, one is prepared to climb the hill to the Festspielhaus and to accept whatever the authorities have to offer. "One leaves oneself at home when one goes to Bayreuth," Nietzsche observed. "One renounces the right to one's own tongue and choice, to one's taste. . . ."

There are no concessions, you understand. For the sake of the acoustics, you sit on folding rattan seats, without armrests, and there is no air-conditioning. And whatever instructions the master left, his descendants carry out. Thus *Rheingold* lasts four hours without an intermission. You learn to accept, to endure, and to realize that compromises in these matters are meaningless. If Marcel Proust wanted to write a novel that required fifteen volumes, then there could have been no point in condensing it to one volume, in the manner of Maxwell Perkins, for the sake of "today's busy reader." If, for that matter, some Egyptian architect designed a pyramid to outlast all of time, there could have been no point in telling him to reduce its size to conform to this year's decreased tax revenues. The madness of art, in other words, decrees its own laws, which the rest of us are free to accept or to reject or to ignore. And if we fail to accept them, I think, the loss is largely our own.

At Bayreuth, therefore, I heard-watched-enjoyed-endured-experienced the entire *Ring of the Nibelungen,* plus *Tristan,* and *Die Meistersinger,* and, of course, *Parsifal.* And then decided that I had done my duty to Wagner, and myself, and never wanted to hear another one of the master's operas as long as I lived. And, for twenty years, never did.

At the end of the first act, at the end of that truly superb chorus of the knights of the Grail, I applauded loudly. Not because I didn't know that applause was considered "disrespectful," but precisely because I did.

"In Germany," I said to Molly, clapping noisily, mostly by myself, "everybody shushes and glares if you applaud at *Parsifal,* because they think it's religious."

"I see," Molly said, once again.

Here, however, there was fitful applause, and only a mild craning of necks at the sources of that applause. For those who did not know the traditions, the Met's program provided the most solemn instructions. "The quiet ending of Act I precludes applause," the program said. "However, Richard Wagner himself wished that after Acts II and III the artists should not be deprived of the audience's appreciation."

I, however, wished that the artists should not be deprived of my appreciation even after Act I. (At the premiere in Bayreuth, as a matter of fact, Wagner had burst into lonely applause at the end of the flower maiden scene and had been loudly shushed by his neighbors.) I also wished, just as in the old days, for my supper, so as soon as the applause faded away, Molly and I took our shopping bag and went to eat. Molly's theory was that we could munch our sandwiches on any bench in the lobby, but I have become too conventional for such an exhibition beneath the crystal chandeliers and the Chagall murals. We went outside to sit in Damrosch Park, right next to the opera. The November winds howled in off Amsterdam Avenue, however, and so we retreated inside again and found seats along a stairway leading down to the basement. Both the ham sandwiches went to me, and so did the peanut-butter jar full of Paisano. Molly, who has the most elegant eighteen-year-old figure imaginable, wouldn't touch such fattening things. She had brought only a small plastic bag containing nuts and raisins.

"Would you believe that I once stood on that same stage where

Parsifal is standing?" I remarked. "And got trapped at the end of a stairway just like this one?"

It had been a moment of primeval, almost bestial panic, and I never enter the Met without remembering it. About a year earlier, I had gone to interview one of the Met's officials, at a time when the opera company was on strike and the huge building was almost entirely deserted. A uniformed attendant had let me in at the stage door and led me across the stage—yes, right across that vast, bare wooden platform where, even in these few years of the new Met, Joan Sutherland had stood and sung to me of the miseries of Norma, and Birgit Nilsson those of Tosca, and Cesare Siepi those of Don Giovanni, and Robert Merrill those of Rigoletto—right across that stage and onto the carpeted corridors of the executive offices on the other side of the building. When my interview was over, I returned to that same stage but stopped before a sign which sternly forbade all access to the stage itself and directed the visitor to a tunnel that passed underneath the stage. Not a very big tunnel either. I had to bow my head as I passed through a long corridor of brightly lit brickwork, and then up a stairway at the far end, and then, following signs that said EXIT, to another corridor, and more stairways, and more white-brick corridors, until I finally reached a door that was chained shut. And then, cursing, retraced my steps, and turned into another corridor of those white building blocks, and down another stairway, following yet another series of signs marked EXIT, and through a series of doors, and another corridor, and ended at another doorway that had also been chained shut. And turned back again, really cursing now. And found that the door behind me had locked by itself.

I was trapped within a coffin of concrete blocks, perhaps thirty feet long, ten feet high, and ten feet wide. The locked door behind me offered no chance of escape back into the maze of subterranean tunnels. The only possibility was the outside door, which, though chained, had a small, thick window, perhaps four by six inches, and this provided a view over a ramp that led down to the Lincoln Center parking garage. The ramp was not exactly a busy sidewalk, but it was not exactly deserted either. Every few minutes, somebody would wander past my prison, and I would shout at him, banging my fists on the thick window and crying, "Help! Help!" And he would wander past, either not hearing, because of the thickness of the door and the roar of traffic, or else pretending not to hear, because this is New York, and the best thing to do, if you hear somebody shouting for help, is to ignore it.

For the first fifteen minutes or so, I thought that this couldn't be happening. It was not possible, I kept telling myself, to become helplessly trapped in a corridor of the Metropolitan Opera, in the catacombs of Lincoln Center, the supposed temple of culture in New York City. But the fact was that it was happening, and that it was nearly five o'clock on a Friday afternoon, and that the skeleton staff manning the strike-bound theater would probably be going home soon, for the weekend. And if nobody had heard me so far, who would hear me in the middle of a Friday night, down there on the dark and deserted ramp to the underground parking lots? I began to wonder what one might eat or drink during a weekend inside a locked corridor of the Metropolitan Opera, and even whether there would be enough air to last until the dawn of Monday morning. . . .

It would be a better story if they had found a skeleton there a month later, when the strike ended, but, of course, someone did finally take note of me—a middle-aged black woman with two children, she said nothing to me but notified some guards that there seemed to be a man causing a disturbance behind a doorway on the ramp—and so, after half an hour of increasing claustrophobia and paranoia, a uniformed doorman came to liberate me. I greeted him with a mixture of relief and rage (that a series of exit signs should lead to such a trap), but he seemed quite indifferent.

"Funny, you know," he said, "somebody else got stuck here the same way about six months ago. You'd never guess who."

"Okay, who?" I said.

"Onassis," the doorman said.

Well, it was a pleasure to think that the millionaire might have felt the same panic I had felt, and might have wondered whether his millions would ever rescue him from this place, or whether he, too, might end as a skeleton clawing at the bottom of the padlocked door. . . .

"Yes, you've told me that story," Molly said, gnawing the last of her nuts and raisins. I drank the dregs of the Gallo Paisano from the peanut-butter jar and then put all the debris back in the shopping bag and stuffed the shopping bag into the handsome silvery cylinder that stands beneath the bulletin board announcing the Met's forthcoming productions of *Elektra* and *Don Pasquale*.

At the time that Wagner began writing *Parsifal,* this hymn to chastity and renunciation, the composer was a virtual prisoner of his own erotic and fetishistic obsessions. Not a prisoner, really, but rather a libertine who had long since given up any attempt to restrain his self-indulgence.

To get himself in the mood for composition, he undertook, apparently as a matter of policy, his last major love affair. Judith Gautier, daughter of the poet, was forty years younger than Wagner, but the old man did his best to impress her by climbing trees and swinging from the branches. And she, a devoted admirer of the modern opera, was fully prepared to be impressed. Cosima Wagner was quite aware of the secret meetings, but she determined not to interfere, determined to cling to her role as the guardian of the artistic household.

Cosima was probably wise to let the aged enfant terrible wander loose, for Judith Gautier eventually returned to Paris. Wagner pursued her with letters asking for various soft materials with which he could have robes made for himself. "Coincidentally with his work on the first act of *Parsifal,*" according to Robert Gutman's biography, "he wrote frankly to his *'douce amie,'* Judith, whom he also called *'geliebtes Weib,'* of certain childish indulgences *('enfantillages')* he wished to permit himself. . . . [He] confessed to Judith the enormous pleasure satin woven of silk gave him. But although he required vast quantities of it, alas, Judith's suppliers seemed unable to come up with *his* shade of 'pale and delicate' pink. . . . And he wanted a yellow silk lampas with embroidered pink flowers, which he would call 'Judith' and use as a cover for his chaise longue. Reclining on 'Judith,' he would be able to conceive music. . . .

"In the late years, with the decay of the senses, his erotic interest in perfumes grew even stronger. He asked Judith to ship limitless amounts of amber, Milk of Iris (he poured half a bottle of it into his daily bath), and Rose de Bengale, and he called for powdered scents to sprinkle over fabrics. . . . His study in Wahnfried was directly over the bath, which he would inundate with rare odors. Seated at his desk and attired in incredible silk and fur outfits douched with sachet, he breathed in the aromatic fumes rising from below and with them memories of Judith's glowing embraces. . . . Amid scenes worthy of Huysmans's Des Esseintes, the first act of the 'religious' drama, *Parsifal*, came into being."

"Have I ever seen *Parsifal*?" My friend Charles B. Chapin echoed the question. "Yes, I have indeed seen *Parsifal*. In fact, something very strange happened to me right in the middle of *Parsifal*, right there in the orchestra of the Metropolitan Opera."

Everyone has his own experiences with Wagner's operas, and those of Charles B. Chapin, a Wall Street executive now in his mid-thirties, are not without relevance to what I am writing. Since Chapin has a certain social eminence, though, it seems appropriate to change his name.

"This was a girl who really turned on to Wagner," said Chapin. "I remember she used to go sunbathing on the roof of her house, with Wagner records playing out on the roof all afternoon. Once she even jumped off the roof while the Wagner was playing, but she survived that."

"So you took her to *Parsifal*," I prompted him.

"Right," said Chapin. "I was at Yale then, and the thing she wanted most was to go to *Parsifal*, so I got the tickets, orchestra seats, at the old Met down on Thirty-ninth Street, and I was in evening clothes, and so was she, and all of a sudden, in the middle of the second act, during that seduction scene, she moved over and sat in my lap."

"This is supposed to be an opera in favor of chastity," I said.

"Right," said Chapin. "And you can imagine the *frowns* we were getting from all sides."

"And then—?" I prompted him again.

"Then—well—I was very uptight in those days," Chapin confessed. "And she berated me all the way home in the taxi. Said I was a square. Said I didn't understand her. Said I didn't understand Wagner."

"The final insult," I said.

Given its first official chance to express "the audience's appreciation," the crowd broke forth at the end of Act II with a wild roar. Helge Brilioth, a young Swede making his New York debut, had just finished the seduction scene with considerable style, and Christa Ludwig was a splendid Kundry, strong and passionate, and for fully five minutes, the Wagnerites clapped and shouted "Bravo!"

"I've never seen anything like *this* before," said Molly, who had seen her first opera the previous spring. "They never clapped this way at *Traviata.*"

It has taken me twenty-five years to overcome—to the extent that one can ever overcome it—the horror of the Nazi regime. I mean that after twenty-five years, I have been able to persuade myself, at least partly, that I am not guilty. And that the fate of being descended from Germans is a fate like any other. And that my sense of hatred and disgust toward everything German does no good either to me or to anyone else. And that I might as well stop trying to escape from my own heritage, or to deny it. That, in fact, I have an obligation to learn more about it, to try to understand it. Thus, Wagner.

My father, who left Germany for good in 1933, represents those survivors who are known, sometimes with a patronizing sneer, as "the Good Germans." Therefore, partly as a matter of conviction, partly as a matter of taste, he loathes Wagner, though I suspect he has not heard a Wagnerian opera in fifty years, if ever. My father even argued once that no intellectually respectable German ever listened to Wagner any more. "Only the French," he said, "still take such things seriously." Unconsciously, he was echoing Nietzsche: "Paris is the real soil for Wagner: the more French music develops according to the needs of the *âme moderne,* the more it will Wagnerize. . . . French romanticism and Richard Wagner belong together most closely. . . . All fanatics of *expression,* great discoverers in the realm of the sublime, also of the ugly and the horrible. . . ."

But there is a contradictory pattern here. In the very words with which a German denies Wagner, he becomes Wagnerian. In the very act of rejecting Wagner as nationalistic, pathological, decadent, or whatever, the German critic succumbs to the temptation of blaming this wholly German phenomenon on the French. No, to deny Wagner is to deny Germany, and, conversely, to try to understand and accept Germany (I mean, of course, the permanent Germany, not Hitler's Germany) means trying to understand and accept Wagner.

So there I was in Berlin last spring, interviewing people for a book about the Weimar Republic, and I suddenly decided to go and see *Die Walküre.* The West Berlin Opera is mediocre, like the Paris Opéra of my youth, but it makes up for its mediocrity in the same way, by being available; in contrast to New York, one can just buy a ticket and go. Besides, isn't mediocrity a kind of blessing when one goes to see *Die Walküre* in Berlin? Mediocrity can wash away some of the inflated pretensions of Bayreuth and reduce even the celebrated *Ring*—"the most characteristic work of the Aryan race," Wagner had called it—to the more congenial level of minor Verdi in some provincial Italian town like Padua or Bologna, to the level of a musical *vin du pays.*

Reverting to my old ways, I arrived about an hour late (the opera started at six) and strolled nonchalantly up to the balcony, arriving just in time for the beautiful love duet between Siegmund and Sieglinde—the one that begins with Siegmund's song *"Winterstürme wichen dem Wonnemond"*—that same scene that I had celebrated in Paris by feasting on roast chicken as soon as the hero got his sword out of the tree. But the circumstances were quite different now. I was forty instead of twenty, for one thing, and I was alone, and I was also sick, with the mild fever that usually accompanies the start of a bad cold. The fever had begun quite suddenly that afternoon, while I was interviewing an aged art historian on the outskirts of the city, and now my face was oozing sweat, and I felt that I might pass out at any minute. And this, I can testify, is the best possible way to hear Wagner.

Sick was the word that Nietzsche used about Wagner's later work, and not without reason, though the accusation sounds odd when it comes from a man who, a few years later, fell unconscious and insane with his arms around a horse he was trying to save from a coachman's whipping. They were all sick, to one degree or another, Wagner and Nietzsche alike, and old Alfred Krupp, who had the aroma of horse manure piped into his bedroom, and poor Robert Schumann, who threw himself into the Rhine to drown the sound of the high A that kept ringing in his ears, and the stately Arthur Schopenhauer, who had to pay sixty talers a year for twenty years to an aged seamstress whom he had pushed down a flight of stairs, and poor old Leopold von Sacher-Masoch, who wrote bad novels that are remembered only because they attached his name to one of the most fundamental of neuroses. The whole latter part of the nineteenth century was sick—perhaps more so in Germany than elsewhere, but perhaps not—sick with a fever of the self, selfishness, self-aggrandizement, self-indulgence, self-gratification. And sitting in that balcony, sweating like a malaria victim, hardly able to breathe, and inundated, in the rustling darkness, by wave after surging wave of Wagner's undulant, blue-green, foam-crested, and dizzyingly beautiful music, I finally understood the sickness in the only way one ever really understands anything, by becoming part of it.

But the opera, like marijuana, is not to be enjoyed alone, and Wagner, above all, demands a sense of community.

If being German is a matter of blood, then my wife is just as German as I am, but her grandparents came to Boston before World War I, and since she didn't have a Germanic name, she could deny and despise all things German, so she solved the Wagner problem by ignoring it. Ever since that night in Paris when I slept through the middle of *Götterdämmerung,* she refused to listen to the master's work. After a great deal of arguing, she reluctantly agreed to go to the Metropolitan's new *Parsifal,* but then, on discovering that I had inadvertently bought tickets for the day before Thanksgiving, she insisted that she had to spend those last hours in stuffing the turkey. That was how I came to be sitting in the balcony with Molly.

"But how much German do you understand?" asked my friend the schoolteacher. He had been born in Germany and fled to England in 1936, at the age of twelve.

"A good deal," I said.

"I mean, how much of Wagner's text do you understand when you hear one of his operas?"

"Almost none," I said, "but I go to the opera for the music, not for the text. Even when I hear an opera sung in English, I can't understand much of the text. And don't care at all."

"Nonetheless," said the schoolteacher, "a German-speaking Wagner audience would say that you weren't really hearing his work at all."

The problem bothered me, and so I took it to another friend, a chemist. He, too, was born in Germany, and he, too, fled to England as a boy in the midthirties. He could remember being taken by his mother to *Parsifal,* the first opera he ever saw.

"But how much of the text did you understand?" I persisted.

"Oh, very little," said the chemist. "But the Germans had a solution to that. Before you were taken to see a Wagner opera, you were presented with the text, and you had to read it through. That way, they said, you *might* understand what was happening."

But do I want to understand what is happening? I have never really understood the plot of *La Forza del destino,* and I believe that the less one understands of *The Magic Flute,* the less its ridiculous plot interferes with one's enjoyment of the music. Am I justified, though, in being so patronizing? Presumably Mozart saw truth and beauty in Schikaneder's absurd tale of pseudo-Masonic ritual— otherwise, he wouldn't have set it to music at all—and he presumably intended that we take the text seriously. As for Wagner, he spoke of himself as the successor not only of Beethoven but of Shakespeare as well. Whoever separates "my songs from my words . . . ," he once wrote, "does me [a great] injustice."

To me, the story of *Parsifal* is ludicrous bombast ("operetta material par excellence," Nietzsche jeered), and when I hear of aged Germans still treating it as a "religious" work, to be played only on Good Friday, I think of them, too, as bombastic and ludicrous. But there are other views of this saga of the Grail, according to which Wagner does have a message that is both important and sinister. During these last years of his life, Wagner's various eccentricities had become almost lunatic. In a series of essays promulgated from his villa in Bayreuth, he held forth on vivisection and vegetarianism, and he sank deeper and deeper into that form of paranoia that expresses itself in anti-Semitism. Thus, although *Parsifal* is not openly a racist work, it easily lends itself to that interpretation. "On its darkest level . . . ," to quote once again and somewhat more fully from Robert Gutman's biography of the composer, *"Parsifal* is an allegory of the Aryan's fall and redemption. The seemingly ruined Grail King, Amfortas . . . contrasts the divine blood of Christ in the Grail with his own sinful blood, corrupted by sexual contact with Kundry, a racial inferior, this criminal miscegenation epitomizing the Aryan dilemma." As for Klingsor, the sorcerer, Gutman quotes Wagner as telling Cosima that he represents The Jew, and "not only the Jew . . . but the Jesuit, too." The biographer concludes: *"Parsifal* is not only un-Christian, it is anti-Christian. . . . With the help of church bells, snippets of the Mass, and the vocabulary of the Passion, he set forth a religion of racism under the cover of Christian legend. Parsifal is an enactment of the Aryan's plight, struggle and hope for redemption. . . . The temple scenes are, in a sense, Black Masses, perverting the symbols of the Eucharist and dedicating them to a sinister god."

And finally, we come back to that inevitable quotation from Adolf Hitler: "Whoever wants to understand National Socialist Germany must know Wagner."

It is true, to a certain extent, but not only for Wagner. Hitler and Mozart were both Germans (both Austrians, if we want to be technical, and so it can be said that the culture that produced *The Magic Flute* also produced Auschwitz. And what are we to make of that?

Some years ago, a young man called me up at my office and said he wanted to talk to me. He had been a pupil of my father, and he wanted to tell me what he had learned. He looked quite neat and conventional, but as he talked on, about some baffling philosophy that he called "Friedrichism," which he described as "the solution to the Cold War," I came to the conclusion that he was mad. And when I later asked my parents about this apparition, my father just shrugged, and my mother said, "Oh, him!"

But I began to wonder about the responsibilities of teachers (also philosophers, preachers, and writers). For if a teacher undertakes to explain to the young and impressionable all problems from the nature of meaning to the meaning of life, doesn't the teacher then have a responsibility (guilt?) even for those who find in his teaching something he never intended?

Thus, is Jesus Christ responsible not only for St. Francis but also for Torquemada? Is Rousseau responsible not just for Jefferson but also for Robespierre? And is Wagner (and then Nietzsche?) responsible for Hitler?

"Well, what's the answer?" Molly asked.

"I don't know the answer," I said. "These things have been bugging me for thirty years and I still can't figure them out. And by this time, I'm not sure whether anybody even cares very much any more, but when I was your age, we all thought that there must be some way to judge everybody who had collaborated with the Nazis. Not just the obvious criminals but every schoolteacher and businessman and every artist too. They had what they called 'denazification courts.' And they brought in Furtwängler, for example, who had been the conductor of the Berlin Philharmonic, and he *said* that he had helped a number of Jews to get out of Germany, and perhaps he had, but on the other hand, he couldn't deny that he had performed for Hitler and generally served as a cultural lion for the Nazi regime, but he *said* that he was just a musician, not a politician, and that it was his function in life to conduct Beethoven, and he couldn't see what was wrong with that. But if there is any meaning in the music of Beethoven, we thought, then Beethoven was on our side, not on the Nazis' side—we even took the Fifth Symphony as part of our battle music, because the first four notes were the same as three dots and a dash, which was the same as the Morse code signal for *V*, as in *Victory*—so anybody who played Beethoven for Hitler was betraying the music itself. Right?"

"Uh-huh," said Molly, which is one step lower than "I see." It wasn't that she was not interested but that all these problems seem infinitely remote to anyone under twenty-five. Ask any average college student to name some of those men who were tried at Nuremberg; I have yet to encounter anyone who knew as many as five.

"And there were lots of others, too," I said. "People we'd once thought were great musicians, and now tainted. I remember some friends of mine in Belgium telling me how Walter Gieseking gave concerts there under the auspices of the German occupation. All he did was to play Mozart and Debussy, just as he always did, but he did play them under the banner of the German occupation. And then there was Alfred Cortot, who was actually some kind of cultural official for the French regime that worked with the Nazis, but all Cortot really did, as far as I know, was to go on playing Chopin. But after the war they banned him from playing in public for two years, and when he appeared for the first time after that, to play a Chopin concerto, the whole orchestra walked off the stage."

"Good," Molly said.

"Okay, but what would you do about Edwin Fischer, who I once thought was a great pianist—used to play Beethoven with great passion, much stamping of the feet and much waving of the long gray hair. He married a rich woman, a Jewish woman, and so he had enough money to hire his own orchestra to accompany him. But then he divorced her, and went on giving concerts in Berlin, all through the Nazi time. And one day—a piano teacher of mine once told me this story—one day a bunch of storm troopers marched into the concert hall and stopped Fischer's concert and said they had a list of Jews playing in the orchestra, and they grabbed a couple of violinists, and maybe a horn player or something, and frog-marched them out of the theater, and then Edwin Fischer went right on with the concert. So what would you do about him?"

"Awful," Molly said.

"But you couldn't do anything to him," I said, "because he was Swiss. So he didn't have to go to Germany at all—unlike a lot of little second violinists who couldn't get out and had nowhere to go—but after the war he was quite safe. He used to teach at the conservatory in Lucerne, and I heard him give lots of concerts. And he was really still pretty good."

"And—?" Molly said.

"And so you have to ask whether there's any connection at all between art and morality, or immorality. I mean, is a pianist who played Beethoven before an audience of Nazi officials during the middle of World War II really fit to play Beethoven at all, ever, to anyone? And if he is, then what do we really get from Beethoven? Just a series of pretty sounds? Or for that matter, is there something basically wrong with Beethoven that made the Nazis like him so, just as much as they liked Wagner?"

"I don't know," Molly said. "What's the answer?"

"I told you, I don't know the answer either."

Perhaps because they are younger, or perhaps simply because they have paid less money, the spectators in the balconies of the opera are less reverent than those in the orchestra. There is more shifting in the seats, more grunting and rustling. There is more coughing, too, and it's louder, less apologetic. There is even talking, mostly men offering sage comments to their wives. For a time, this is tolerated—a sentence or two—but then the shushing starts, for although our eleven-dollar seats are more Bohemian than the eighteen-dollar thrones in the orchestra, eleven dollars entitles one to a reasonable degree of quiet.

But now, as Parsifal sits by a pool, and Kundry washes his feet, and the music floats on and on—we are in the third act, and it is nearly eleven o'clock, and we have been here for four hours—the balcony audience suddenly begins to suffer a kind of psychological disintegration. It is beginning to feel that it can't stand any more, not one more declaration from old Gurnemanz, not one more diminished seventh chord. "Everything is endless," Eduard Hanslick had written after seeing the premiere back in 1882, "everything too long, from the largest to the smallest, from the solemn Holy Communion to Kundry's impossible kiss." In the dress circle, one feels, more and more, a sense of people squirming. The coughing becomes almost constant.

In front of me, a white-haired gentleman with a crew cut says loudly to his wife, "I hear that those clarinetists are getting close to three hundred dollars a week these days." But although we are all beginning to disintegrate, the diehards among us, the fanatics, the Jesuits, the Stalinists, still want to listen to the music, and so one of them finally performs that witchlike ritual of hissing at the old man: "Ssh!" The old man does not stop talking immediately but defiantly adds a few more words before falling silent.

This is called the Transformation Scene. Parsifal has been wandering around and performing various good deeds, and now he is ready to save poor King Amfortas. The music is funereally slow—is there one measure in *Parsifal* that moves faster than *andante,* and is there any other opera, or mass or oratorio, of which that question could be asked?—but exceptionally beautiful, soft, ethereal, and quite narcotic.

Suddenly, the old man in the row before me breaks out again. "I hear the orchestra has to get paid overtime if this goes beyond midnight," he says, and not in a whisper either. Once again, from a different direction, comes the response: "Ssh!" And once again, the old man says a few more words and then falls silent. Is he deaf? Doesn't he realize how loud he is? Doesn't he hear the neighbors asking him to keep quiet?

I was raised to respond to such situations by doing nothing, a brief glare, perhaps, but no more—two wrongs don't make a right, there is no excuse for rudeness, and all the rest of the Boston ethic. And old Gurnemanz goes on singing about Parsifal's great exploits, and I slip back into the narcotic flow of Wagner's music, and then, for the third time, the white-haired old man in the row in front of me loudly addresses his wife: "You sure you remember where we parked the car? I think it was on that little cross street—"

This time, I am the one who volunteers for the leadership of the silent majority, and bend forward toward the old man and hiss into his ear a most vehement and long-drawn-out "Shhhhhh!"

"—behind the restaurant"—the old man goes right on talking. "Not the one with the—"

So I kick him, quite hard, several times—not him, literally, but the back of his seat, and hard enough to jar him rather severely. He does not look around to see who is kicking him, but he does stop talking.

Throughout the great finale, the last Grail scene, in which Parsifal raises his magic lance and cures the stricken Amfortas, I imagined a variety of future conflicts with the old man. The next time he spoke out, I imagined myself summoning an usher and having him ejected from the theater. I imagined myself jabbing him in the shoulder, or shaking him, or even dumping my overcoat on top of his head. I also imagined his retaliations—at the very least, a flailing swing back at my shins, or, more elaborately, a formal complaint to the police, a taking of depositions, and a missing of the last train home. But the old man never said another word, and never looked behind him.

It was only on the train home—lurching out of Penn Station at quarter of one—that I said to Molly, "Did you see me *kick* that old man who kept talking?"

"I sure did," Molly said.

I have never before kicked anyone at an opera, and I began to wonder whether I would have kicked the old man at *The Marriage of Figaro,* or *Trovatore.* Or was this, after all rational arguments have been raised and examined, after we have joked about picnic dinners and various other physical gratifications, the ultimate religion of *Parsifal*?

A night frost has glazed the windshield of the car, and even after I scratch at it with a handkerchief, I can barely see to drive home from the station, but it is two o'clock in the morning, and there is no traffic here at such an hour, so we wobble off onto the road toward home.

"You really liked all that?" I say to Molly. "Better than pot?"

"I *loved* it," says Molly.

"Well, at least you can say you've done it. You've heard all five hours of *Parsifal*, from beginning to end. And just think, you may never see it again in all the rest of your life."

"I guess that's right," Molly says. "Maybe I never will."

1970

A Little Tour of France with Henry James

> I write these lines with the full consciousness of
> having no information whatever to offer. I do not
> pretend to enlighten the reader ... I hold any
> writer sufficiently justified who is himself in love
> with his topic.
>
> —*Portraits of Places*

■ FODOR'S AND FIELDING'S AND FROMMER'S—AND, ABOVE ALL,
Michelin—the fat guidebooks keep offering the traveler to France
their expert opinions on which cathedrals to see, where to eat dinner, and how to get the laundry done. In time, though, these volumes
of authoritative pronouncements can become oppressive. One occasionally wonders how some more fallible voyager might have
viewed a Loire château that he found to be locked, or how he passed
his time when he had just missed his train and all of sunny Provence
was swept by the mistral. Perhaps, then, one might still be guided by
Henry James, who set out in the autumn of 1882 on what he mod-
estly called "a little tour of France."

James's approach was magisterial, as was he himself—a heavily
built figure, nearly bald, with a closely cropped brown beard and
large, penetrating eyes. Ivan Turgenev, whom he visited at Bougival
on the eve of his departure, wrote to a friend that James was ". . . as
amiable as ever. But he has grown enormously fat." He was already
an experienced journalist, of the feuilleton sort, having served several
years as a Paris correspondent for the *New York Tribune* and written
two volumes of travel sketches. More important, his career as a
novelist was finally beginning to flourish. *The Portrait of a Lady* had
just been published in the previous year, with considerable success,
and he wrote in his journal that he could well remember being "an
ingenuous youth . . . passionately eager for what life might bring,"
and that "life has brought . . . a measurable part of what I dreamed

of then." Despite these autumnal reflections, however, he was still only thirty-nine. He had yet to experience the failure of *The Bostonians* and the disaster of *Guy Domville*. And so, since he lived by his writing, he cheerfully boarded a railroad train in Paris and headed south.

I took an old and unread copy of James's *Little Tour* along with me on a recent trip to France, but not until I had landed in the white plastic wilderness of de Gaulle Airport, rented a little Simca, and fought my way through the torrents of Parisian traffic to the Loire Valley did I actually open my century-old guidebook and find that James, too, had started his voyage in Tours. "It is a very agreeable little city," he observed. "Few towns of its size are more ripe, more complete, or, I should suppose, in better humour with themselves. . . . It is truly the capital of its smiling province; a region of easy abundance, of good living, of genial, comfortable, optimistic, rather indolent opinions."

Despite all its amiable fertility, though—its abundance of apple trees and lettuces and mild red wines and all those other riches that grow along the river that James described as "full, tranquil, powerful, bending in large slow curves and sending back half the light of the sky"—despite all this, the Loire Valley, like much of France, still bears the scars and memories of armed conflict. Our hotel in Tours was on the place de la Résistance, and our window overlooked the rue des Fusillés, and these were only the newest memorials to death. James, who was traveling through France less than a century after Robespierre's Reign of Terror, and scarcely more than a decade after Bismarck's triumph over Napoleon III, found it "astonishing" that the Germans had advanced so far as to occupy Tours "during that terrible winter" of 1870–71, and he added: "It is hardly too much to say that, wherever one goes in certain parts of France, one encounters two great historic facts: one is the Revolution; the other is the German invasion."

These great historic facts are more apparent in the provinces than in Paris. Time moves more quickly in the metropolis, for the city is more isolated from the natural cycle of the seasons, and the past is more quickly obliterated. There is a place de la Bastille, of course, but it is little more than a noisy traffic circle, without a

trace of the dungeon that once stood there, and hardly anyone remembers that the place de la Concorde was once the place de la
Révolution, resounding to the clang of the guillotine. The porte de
St.-Cloud, like all the gateways to Paris, implies a walled city, but
there are no longer any walls to impede the traffic flowing out to
the suburbs. Driving through that vanished gateway on the road to
Chartres, one eventually finds in the great cathedral not only the
glowing rose windows that inspired Henry Adams to proclaim that
Mary herself had built this church, but also, in the candlelit Chapel
of the Virgin, long rows of statues with their stone faces smashed
in by the angry revolutionaries of two centuries ago. There is
also new evidence of James's other great historic fact. A few blocks
from the cathedral, an ungainly stone angel grieves for the memory
of Jean Moulin, once a prefect of the Loire, then an organizer of
the Resistance, tortured to death by the Gestapo. But the spirit
of the Virgin, and the demands of commerce, and the passage of
time all join to soften great historic facts. Busloads of pilgrims now
arrive daily from Cologne, Munich, and Berlin, and a sign outside
the cathedral announces guided tours in German. TREFFPUNKT HIER,
it says.

The revolutionaries of 1789 made a passionate attempt to
change the nature of time. Just as they smashed the statues in
Chartres, they abolished the Christian seasons, rebaptizing the
months with names like Ventôse and Pluviôse. They ended the sequence of years A.D. and began again with the year I, a statement
of faith that was ended by Napoleon in the year XII. The seasons
that nurtured the vines and flowers of France remained as before.
High on the walls of Chartres, in the dirt that has accumulated
in the crevices between the stones, a tenacious weed called giro-
flée sauvage brings forth its bright yellow flowers every spring,
among the buttresses and the gargoyles, far beyond the reach of
human hands.

The tourist, too, is making an attempt to stop time. To land
in the futuristic temple of de Gaulle Airport and then to drive to
the Loire is to abandon the contemporary world and enter the domain of Francis I. Almost every castle wall bears his heraldic sal-
amander, or the ermine of Anne of Brittany. Yet although one

thinks of the Loire châteaux as a historic entity, a series of architectural statements that have outlasted their creators, these buildings themselves are as vulnerable to time as the giant trees that surround them.

To the traveler coming from Paris, Blois is the first of the great châteaux to be encountered. It once controlled an important bridgehead, and the counts of Blois ruled an area extending from Chartres to Tours. They claimed the kingdom of Burgundy and fought at the siege of Acre. The surviving château, however, was built mainly by the Valois kings, notably Francis I, and it enchanted James. "As you cross its threshold you step straight into the sunshine and storm of the French Renaissance . . ." he wrote. "In the middle of it, or rather a little to the left, rises the famous winding staircase . . . which even the ages which most misused it must vaguely have admired. . . . This exquisite, this extravagant, this transcendent piece of architecture is the most joyous utterance of the French Renaissance."

The intrepid James entered the courtyard "by jumping over the walls," but such escapades are not permitted today. One stands in line to buy a ticket, then waits in the courtyard for the next tour to begin. The courtyard is filled, as in many of these châteaux, with bored American students, twitching and giggling. Finding themselves on gravel, they begin picking up pebbles and throwing them at each other. The guide disapproves, prissily, but the students do not pay much attention. They shuffle after him from room to room, prisoners of culture.

Because of its very celebrity, Blois was among the first châteaux to be, in James's words, "unsparingly restored." Like many others, it had survived the storm of the Revolution only to be turned into a barracks by Napoleon. "Whitewashed, mutilated, dishonoured," as James put it, "the castle of Blois may be said to have escaped simply with its life." While modern restorers have sought primarily to re-establish what once existed, the nineteenth-century restorers of Blois tried to create a château that fitted their own romantic visions of what a Renaissance palace ought to have been. So the walls that were bare in the times of King Francis, or perhaps hung with tapestries of scenes from the life of Moses, now gleam with brightly painted suns and stars and fleurs-de-lis. "This terrible process," as James called it "[was] a work of great energy and cost [but] the universal freshness is a discord, a false note; it seems to light up the dusky past with an unnatural glare." The guide who now leads us through these Medici bedchambers emphasizes the anachronism, and his own distaste. All the decorations are *"fantaisiste,"* he says. They could, of course, be scraped away, but one suspects that they will not be. Perhaps the French authorities believe that a château once restored had been restored forever. Or perhaps, as with the Baroque facades that both augment and disfigure some of the classical temples of Sicily, there is by now a certain aesthetic interest in observing the nineteenth century's view of the sixteenth century.

One of the most striking aspects of Blois is not architectural but ghostly, for it was here that King Henry III disposed of the challenge of the duke of Guise by having him murdered. "Every spot connected with the murder," James reported, ". . . is pointed out by a small, shrill boy." The uniformed guide still performs the same function, and I particularly savored his recital because I had been raised on a family legend that the duke of Guise was one of my ancestors.

The duke arrived at the château early on the morning of December 23, 1588, after spending the night with one of Catherine de Médicis's ladies-in-waiting. The Estates-General, meeting in Blois that day, were expected to impeach King Henry and depose him in favor of the duke. The duke was eating preserved plums by the fireplace in the council chamber—there, that vast and ornate fireplace over there—when he was notified that the king wanted to see him in his study, on the far side of the royal bedchamber. As the duke passed through the bedchamber, eight of the royal assassins rose and saluted him. As he opened the door to the study, he confronted twelve more assassins awaiting him with drawn swords. Turning back, he saw that the first group had drawn their daggers from their cloaks. Several of the assassins seized the duke's arms and legs, but he was a large and powerful man. He threw off four of them, and then, stabbed over and over again, dragged several more of the clinging attackers to the far end of the room before collapsing at the foot of the king's bed.

The king finally emerged from his study and slapped the dead man in the face. "God, how big he is!" he said. "He looks even bigger dead than alive." He went to tell the good news to his mother, Catherine de Médicis, and then he went to hear mass in the Chapel of St. Calais. "What episode was ever more perfect—looked at as a dramatic occurrence—than the murder of the Duke of Guise?" James wondered. "The insolent prosperity of the victim; the weakness, the vices, the terrors, of the author of the deed; the perfect execution of the plot; the accumulation of horror in what followed it—render it, as a crime, one of the classic things."

No restorers can scrub the bloodstains from the royal châteaux of the Loire. Nor do they try, for bloodshed that is old enough to appear romantic is a valuable item in the tourist traffic. Still, the killing of my supposed ancestor in the royal bedroom at Blois serves as a reminder that much of the destruction in this land came not from foreign invaders but rather from the ferocious civil strife that has repeatedly ravaged France.

Amboise provides another example. It is perhaps the most charming town in the Loire Valley, and the château towering above the river is undoubtedly the most formidable. This, too, fell into use as a barracks and then a prison, and an old lady at James's hotel in Tours described it to him as "very, very dirty, but very curious." James toured the "blank old apartments" and was greatly impressed. "The platforms, the bastions, the terraces, the high-niched windows and balconies, the hanging gardens and dizzy crenellations, of this complicated structure, keep you in perpetual intercourse with an immense horizon. . . . The clustered houses at the base of the rock are like crumbs that have fallen from a well-laden table."

Here, during the brief reign of the sixteen-year-old King Francis II and the semiofficial regency of the duke of Guise, a number of Protestant landowners from Brittany came to demand the right of religious dissent. The château is all refurbished now, filled with Renaissance tapestries and solemn oak chests, but there has been no need to refurbish the iron balcony outside the royal chambers where the Breton Protestants met their fate. Some were tied in sacks and thrown from the heights down into the Loire, while others were left

hanging from the balcony for the entertainment of their executioners. It is said that Catherine de Médicis came after dinner to watch
the spectacle, bringing along her sixteen-year-old daughter-in-law,
Mary Stuart. James discounted such tales as "rumors," but he added
that "there is little doubt that the future Queen of Scots learnt the
first lessons of life at a horrible school."

And Chinon. "We never went to Chinon . . ." James wrote, a
rather disarming confession for a guidebook writer to make. "We
planned it a dozen times; but the weather interfered, or the trains
didn't suit, or one of the party was fatigued with the adventures of
the day before." He tried, nonetheless, to describe it on the basis of
photographs: "The castle of Chinon . . . appears to me as an enormous ruin, a mediaeval fortress of the extent almost of a city. It
covers a hill above the Vienne, and after being impregnable in its
time is indestructible today. . . . To the castle, the lover of the picturesque is earnestly recommended to direct his steps. But one always misses something. . . ."

I should make a similar confession. I never went to Chaumont
(where James, having found the gates locked, could only "trudge up
a hill . . . where, over the paling of a garden, we might obtain an
oblique and surreptitious view of a small portion of the castle walls");
but I did direct my steps to Chinon, for it was here that Joan of Arc
first encountered the dauphin who was to become Charles VII. Here
occurred the famous recognition scene in which the dauphin tested
Joan by hiding behind some courtiers while an impostor installed
himself on the throne. The photographs had misled James, as photographs usually do. The ruin is neither enormous nor indestructible.
It is little more than a hollowed-out shell, and as the troops of young
Americans straggle in through the gate on a warm spring afternoon,
they can find little to amuse them except a pair of peacocks that
wander solemnly around the little courtyard, ready to be photographed. Of the royal council chamber where the dauphin received
Joan there is nothing left but a few stone steps leading up to a
roofless, unwalled floor, open to the sun, with one surviving fireplace
at the far end.

James also noted, from his distance, that Rabelais had honored
Chinon by being born there, but ministries of fine arts are less con-

cerned about such things. I found no official birthplace and no official memorials, only a shopping center with a large sign that said RABELAIS CENTRE COMMERCIAL. What would James have made of that if he had come to Chinon and seen it? About the same, perhaps, as he would have made of the vast conglomeration of concrete and plastic that has arisen near my home in Long Island and calls itself the Walt Whitman Shopping Center. Will there ever be, somewhere near the official birthplace in New York, a Henry James Shopping Center?

The master was not greatly impressed by Poitiers. His hotel was dirty, and "a dirty inn has always seemed to me the dirtiest of human things." He found the old hilltop town "as crooked and straggling as you please; but these advantages are not accompanied with any very salient features or any great wealth of architecture." James declared that "the most charming thing at Poitiers" was Blossac Park, an eighteenth-century public garden with "a beautiful sweep of view over the surrounding country." Here he sat and reflected on what had inspired him to come to Poitiers, the battle in which Edward, the Black Prince of Wales, outnumbered by more than two to one, had defeated and captured King John of France. (The battlefield is not a great public memorial, of course, for very few nations commemorate their defeats; there is no Waterloo Station in Paris, just as there is no Gare d'Austerlitz in Vienna.)

James confessed himself "very much at a loss" as to why "the very name of [Poitiers] had always caused my blood gently to tingle." He said that it would be "carrying the feeling of race to quite inscrutable lengths when a vague American permits himself an emotion because more than five centuries ago, on French soil, one rapacious Frenchman got the better of another. Edward was a Frenchman as well as John, and French were the cries that urged each of the hosts to the fight." Even after these disavowals, however, he added that the Black Prince's victory "was something done, I know not how justly, for England; and what was done in the fourteenth century for England was done also for New York."

In pursuit of this odd view from the ramparts of Poitiers (was it not the French, after all, who helped eject King George's troops from New York?), I made my way to Blossac Park and found it still as charming as it was in James's day. The red and yellow tulips stood in formal parade, as suits the French taste, but modified by gentler beds of pansies and forget-me-nots. A small *jardin zoologique* in one corner boasted a modest collection of wallabies, pheasants, and Senegalese goats. But the view from the ramparts showed only a panorama of the French *banlieux:* gray-white factories, boxlike housing projects, and the orange-tiled roofs of what pass for suburban "villas." On consulting my map, I realized that the vanished battlefield lay well off to the east, and that James had been staring nostalgically in the wrong direction.

It would be possible, I think, to recount a whole tour of France in terms of its gardens, for gardens tell as much as vaulted roofs or tapestried halls about how past generations chose to decorate their surroundings. The most striking aspect of French gardens, of course, is their extreme formality, their constant denial of nature's first law, which is that of uncontrolled growth. At Versailles, all the evergreens bordering on Le Nôtre's great esplanade of fountains are clipped into perfect cones, a series of toy trees marching up and down the slopes like toy soldiers. At Chenonceaux, where the box hedges are all sculpted into the shape of reversed G clefs, the keepers of Diane de Poitiers's "Italian" gardens are so solicitous of their sprouting rosebushes and their beds of daffodils that no visitor is allowed to walk along the flawless diagonal paths. At Nîmes, finally, the designer dispensed with plants almost entirely. Using as his source the gently bubbling spring of Nemausus—"the prettiest thing in the world," James called it—he worked entirely with water, leading it through a series of stone arcades and gravel promenades, and leaving only a small area around the entrance to be planted in that exotic vegetation known as grass.

The most beautiful garden in the Loire Valley could not have been seen by James, however, for it was torn up during the nineteenth century to be replaced by the then fashionable savagery of a freely growing *jardin anglais.* In due time, a Dr. Carvallo acquired this Château de Villandry and tore up the *jardin anglais* to re-create the original sixteenth-century garden. It was, and now again is, built

on three different levels, extending over some fifteen acres. The top
level is all designed in water, a lake, inlets, fountains, waterfalls. The
second level is all hedges, carved into dozens of different designs—
the fleur-de-lis, the cross of Languedoc, and even a series of heart-
shaped patterns devoted to the varieties of love: true love, angry
love, demented love. . . . At the bottom level is the kitchen garden,
where fruits, flowers, and vegetables all grow in alternating beds,
three by three, the strawberry plants neighboring to beans and dai-
sies, according to the appropriate categories of color and size. Standing on the rampart and looking down on these acres of herbal
chivalry, one raises an inevitable question: Who was the inspired Dr.
Carvallo?

"He was a Spaniard"—the guide shrugs—"a physician, although
I don't think he ever practiced medicine."

"And rich? Or how did he get so much money?"

"Rich? No, he was the son of a baker. But he married a millionaire's daughter from Philadelphia."

How Gilbert Osmond would have savored the gardens of Villandry. Or Merton Densher. Or Prince Amerigo.

As James progressed southward, he seemed to become more and
more discontented. He had left behind his "companions" (Fanny
Kemble, the actress, and Mrs. Owen Wister, the mother of the novelist), and so he had nobody to complain to about the untidiness of
provincial inns or the vagaries of the French railroads ("perverse,
capricious, exasperating").

He liked the Huguenot fishing port of La Rochelle because it
was "Dutch and delightful" and "extraordinarily clean" and "a quite
original mixture of brightness and dulness," but the more impressive
city of Bordeaux left him dissatisfied. It is, he said, in words that
remain true today, "a big, rich, handsome, imposing commercial
town, with . . . an air of almost depressing opulence." So on to
Toulouse, where depressing opulence gave way to depressing poverty. He found an Italian quality to the city, but his comparisons
were invidious. "Toulouse . . . has a little of this Italian expression,
but not enough to give a colour to its dark, dirty, crooked streets,

which are irregular without being eccentric. . . . Toulouse has no architecture; the houses . . . have no particular style. . . . The shops are probably better than the Turinese, but the people are not so good. Stunted, shabby, rather vitiated looking, they have none of the personal richness of the sturdy Piedmontese; and I will take this occasion to remark that in the course of a journey of several weeks in the French provinces I rarely encountered a well-dressed male. Can it be possible that republics are unfavourable to a certain attention to one's boots and one's beard?"

The neighboring cities were even worse. James judged Narbonne to be "a *sale petite ville* in all the force of the term." All the hotels were "stuffed with wine-dealers," so he had to spend hours trying to find a room. He finally sat down to dinner with "a hundred hungry marketers, fat, brown, greasy men, with a good deal of the rich soil of Languedoc adhering to their hands. . . . There were swarms of flies; the viands had the strongest odour." Moving on to Montpellier, he found it "charming," for no particular reason, but partly because "I reflected that I had washed my hands of Narbonne." One of his difficulties was that he felt the Revolution had corrupted the French, filling many of them with "a sinister passion for theories." He observed that although the average Frenchman had been "permeated in a high degree by civilization," he was still "untouched by the desire which one finds in the Englishman, in proportion as he rises in the world, to approximate to the figure of the gentleman."

It is easy to mock such snobbery, but it illustrates not only James's limitations in understanding Republican France (he hardly gives us any observations at all on the workings of French politics or society) but also his myopia in regarding the past. Even if one decides that it is the natural function of the tourist to view France almost entirely in terms of its historic buildings, the significance of those buildings may lie not in their architectural details but in the fate of the people who once occupied them. Toulouse today is perhaps even more grimy than it was a century ago, but what James seems hardly to have noticed is that Toulouse is the capital of a conquered land, and that the whole southwest still reverberates, like Wales or Sicily, with the echoes of its lost independence.

"The history of Toulouse is detestable, saturated with blood and perfidy," James writes—but then no more. It is a sentence one might apply to any fallen capital. In fact, Toulouse was once the center of a culture at least as rich as that of France. Its rule extended from the Atlantic to the Rhône; it enjoyed its own language, its own court of troubadours. The cosmopolitan towns of Languedoc and Provence were inclined to tolerate Jews, skeptics, heretics. Thus their downfall. In 1208, a papal legate assigned to preach against heresy was speared by a knight, possibly acting for Count Raymond VI of Toulouse. That was the pretext for the outraged Pope Innocent III to unleash the Albigensian Crusade, a fearful onslaught of north against south, orthodoxy against diversity. It began with the sack of Béziers, in which all the men, women, and children were slaughtered, in accord with the Crusaders' slogan: "Kill them all—God will recognize his own." Some thirty-five years later, a few hundred of the heretics known as Cathars were besieged in their last major stronghold, the mountaintop fortress of Montségur. For nine months they withstood the siege, and then the Crusaders began working their way up the mountain. At the end, the heretics stoically accepted the Crusaders' ultimatum: all who converted would be given short prison sentences by the Inquisition; all the others would be burned.

There is still no road up the mountain, and so one must leave the car at the base and begin climbing upward through the muddy gulleys that rake the slopes. The mountain is about two thousand feet high, almost straight up, an angle of perhaps eighty degrees, and as one claws upward, clinging to twisted outgrowths of shrubbery, the fog thickens. Before long, the ground becomes invisible. At the top, finally, there is an unbelievable stillness. The pentagonal walls—this was once a temple for sun-worshipers, and on Midsummer's Eve, the sun shines directly through the eastern and western windows—stand as witnesses, jagged and roofless. The gates are open. The floor is a sea of mud. The fog swirls around the ramparts. There is nobody here, nobody and nothing, except, on top of the highest wall that looks out over a sea of fog, the spoor of previous tourists: two orange peels. The last 215 heretics were led down from here in chains and burned alive in the field at the foot of the mountain. There a small plaque commemorates them in the lost language:

> *Als Catars*
> *Als Martirs*
> *De Pur Amor*
> *Crestian*
> *16 Mars 1244*

James recorded a few details of the Albigensian Crusade on his arrival in Carcassonne, but he added, a bit disingenuously, "I am not one of those who, as I said just now, have a head for such things." He was fascinated, however, by the walled town itself—founded by the Romans, fortified by the Visigoths, and now the largest preserved fortress in Europe: "We passed along the battlements . . . ascended and descended towers, crawled under arches, peered out of loopholes, lowered ourselves into dungeons, halted in all sorts of tight places while the purpose of something or other was described to us. It was very curious, very interesting; above all it was very pictorial. . . . One vivid challenge, at any rate, it flings down before you: it calls upon you to make up your mind on the matter of restoration. For myself I have no hesitation; I prefer in every case the ruined, however ruined, to the reconstructed, however splendid. . . . The one is history, the other is fiction; and I like the former the better of the two—it is so much more romantic."

I think not. It is the fiction created by reconstruction that is more romantic, if romantic is what one is looking for, as James was. "The restoration of Carcassonne," he said, after a stroll about the ramparts in the moonlight, "is a splendid achievement. . . . There can be nothing better than this . . . a wonderful evocation." And so we come to Eugène-Emmanuel Viollet-le-Duc, who created a considerable part of the medieval France that we now admire. Born in 1814, he became an architect, a student of Greek and Roman relics, an expert in the Gothic. His masterpiece is Notre-Dame de Paris, to which he devoted eleven years, but his hand can be seen all over France, at Narbonne and Amiens, Bordeaux and Avignon. To Viollet-le-Duc, there was no question of falsifying old buildings for the sake of artificial restoration. Ruins remain completely intact only when, as at Montségur, they are far from humanity. Or when, as with the sacked château of the marquis de Sade, which still towers over a haunted stone village in a valley of Provence, humanity remains indifferent. In a place like Carcassonne, Viollet-le-Duc found the moats around the fortifications already filled with slum hovels, and the villagers felt free to tear stones from the crumbling ramparts of the Visigoths to build their garden walls. His only choice, therefore, was to re-create an artificial medieval city or to let its ruins slowly vanish from the earth.

This process of restoration is now continuing all over France (the influence of André Malraux?). At the mountaintop shrine of Rocamadour, where such pilgrims as St. Dominic and St. Bernard, King Philip the Fair and Henry Plantagenet all climbed on their knees up the hundreds of stone stairs to the grave of St. Amadour (said to be the publican Zacheus), the various statues and relics were all destroyed by marauding troops of Englishmen, Protestants, and revolutionaries (the cadaver of St. Amadour refused to burn and finally had to be smashed with a hammer)—here everything has been rebuilt, and the pilgrim who labors up the stairs today (there is an elevator for the less hardy) is greeted at every way station with new offerings of postcards.

On the Riviera, similarly, even such a relatively insignificant town as Eze, which was a jumble of dirt-floored hovels as recently as the 1940s, and remarkable mainly for its view out over the Mediterranean, is now all stone-walled summer villas, expensive restaurants, mosaic sidewalks, and souvenir shops. In St.-Paul, not far away, the same transformation is still under way, almost within sight of the Calders and Giacomettis and Mirós that sprout in the gardens of the Maeght Foundation, a bit higher up in the hills. A tourist who wanders a few blocks away from St.-Paul's rows of boutiques and postcard stands is likely to encounter a squad of grunting Algerians tending the cement mixer that is building a new medieval house before his eyes.

The restoration of Carcassonne began earlier, and so the implications of the process are more fully developed. As the guide leads his flock of tourists along the ramparts, pausing every now and then before a tower of nineteenth-century masonry to give a lecture on the arts of medieval defense and to point out the familiar sluices for the boiling oil, we reach, eventually, the corner of the fortress where this whole stage setting becomes, in fact, a stage setting. Behind the eleventh-century Church of St.-Nazaire there was once a monastery, wrecked during the Revolution, and in 1908, long after both James and Viollet-le-Duc, the restorers decided to build an open-air theater here. After World War II, they refurbished the whole thing, installing some six hundred black bucket seats on the concrete steps of the amphitheater, and now there is a festival every summer, with *son et lumière.* "The Comédie-Française has played here," the guide says proudly. *"Hamlet, Macbeth, La Reine morte . . ."*

As we move backward through time, from the ramps of de Gaulle Airport, to the Renaissance on the Loire, to the Crusades in the southwest, we watch, as on a film in reverse motion, the disintegration of France from a modern nation into a collection of feudal provinces, and so we finally reach, in the Roman ruins of Provence, the spectacle of France as a minor colony. Nîmes, for example, was founded by the Roman legionnaires who had been discharged with grants of land after Octavian's victory over Antony and Cleopatra; hence the heraldic appearance, on city walls, of a crocodile in chains.

James observed the architectural relics of the Roman provinces with the conventional approbation of nineteenth-century aesthetics. The charming city of Nîmes struck him as not being "a town with, as I may say, a general figure," but the arena impressed him as "astounding," and the little temple known as the Maison Carrée appeared "perfectly felicitous." The Roman theater at Arles "seemed to me one of the most charming and touching ruins I had ever beheld." The theater at Orange was "magnificent in its ruin," and the triumphal arch was, "as Roman monuments go . . . remarkably perfect."

Contemplating such things, James enjoyed letting his imagination wander. "There was a certain contagion of antiquity in the air," he wrote of Nîmes, "and among the ruins of baths and temples . . . the picture of a splendid paganism seemed vaguely to glow." Yet there was a quality about the stridently aggressive Romans that must have reminded James of the America he had only recently decided to abandon. He described that quality, as best he could, in describing the celebrated arches of the pont du Gard. "They are unspeakably imposing, and nothing could well be more Roman. The hugeness, the solidity, the unexpectedness, the monumental rectitude of the whole thing leave you nothing to say. . . . I remained there an hour and got a complete impression. . . . It came to pass that . . . I discovered in it a certain stupidity, a vague brutality. That element is rarely absent from great Roman work, which is wanting in the nice adaptation of the means to the end. The means are always exaggerated; the end is so much more than attained."

I myself share many of James's reservations about provincial Roman ruins. The Colosseum in Rome still seems to reverberate to the cries of Christian martyrs, but the arenas in Arles or Nîmes do not echo so richly. One marvels at their state of preservation, and at the fact that this vanished race left such powerful monuments to its presence, but there is a curious impersonality about these various arches and amphitheaters. There is little passion in them. They are, simply, public buildings. Still, one feels a kind of duty to inspect them, and so, arriving in Orange late at night, I determined to visit the Roman theater as soon as it opened the following morning. Its exterior wall, towering more than one hundred feet high in the moonlight, was said to be the best preserved Roman wall in all of Europe, and Louis XIV had described it as "the most beautiful wall in the kingdom." When I arrived there in the morning, however, all the approaches were cordoned off for a parade.

The sky was as "magnificently black" as the one that James had seen over Vaucluse, and a raw wind scraped across the place des Frères-Mounet as the first hard-faced soldiers came marching into position, loudly singing a kind of dirge. Most of them were in khaki, with baggy trousers tucked into their boots, but a good number wore those colorful costumes that have long given the French army a look of absurdity—white kepis, red and green epaulets, blue hats ornamented with plumes of white feathers. *"Halt!"* an officer shouted as each new contingent reached its place in front of the worn old theater. This was, it turned out, the First Cavalry Regiment of the Foreign Legion, which I thought had long ago been disbanded, the last remnant of the German invasions of France. They were celebrating some anniversary of some long-forgotten battle of Camerone (in Mexico, someone said), and the festivities were to last for two days. The celebration would reach its climax, according to the announcement on the wall of a nearby pharmacy, in the election of "Miss Kepi Blanc."

The last oddity in James's little tour is that he never went to the Riviera. Perhaps it was then a less inevitable part of the tourist itinerary than it is today. Cannes, after all, was still a small fishing village in 1834, when Lord Brougham, avoiding Nice because of an outbreak of cholera, stopped at Cannes, found it charming, and built a house there. In any case, James turned north from Provence and concluded his tour, mysteriously, in Dijon.

But I went on to inspect the traffic jams of Nice, and the bathers packed onto the beach at Cap d'Antibes, and the miles of tawdry villas crawling up the mountainside above Monte Carlo. Henry James liked the rich, and he liked the way the rich live, but now that the spread of wealth has brought hundreds of thousands of people swarming to the Riviera, I kept wondering what James would have made of it all. Would he have regarded the rulers of Monaco as yet another pair of his own creations? Would he have gambled his meager royalties at their casino? Would he have taken tea with those elderly ladies who sit on terraces in Menton? Or stripped off his elegant waistcoat and lumbered down to the beach?

On an idle afternoon in Nice, I wandered into the English library, a deserted, subterranean sort of place, tended by a rather taciturn old gentleman in greenish tweeds and filled with bound sets of writers like Somerset Maugham and P. G. Wodehouse. There was, of course, a copy of James's *Little Tour,* and next to it stood an equally obscure work by his friend Edith Wharton. It was entitled *A*

Motor-Flight through France. As I opened it, I saw that Mrs. Wharton had transcended James's difficulties with the French railroads. "The motor-car," she began, with all the enthusiasm of a tourist setting out in 1907, "has restored the romance of travel."

1975

Mozart: The Last Year

■ EMANUEL SCHIKANEDER HAS EARNED A PLACE IN HISTORY BY writing the libretto for Mozart's *Magic Flute*. It is not, unfortunately, a very distinguished place. In the disdainful words of Professor Edward J. Dent, the libretto was "one of the most absurd specimens of that form of literature in which absurdity is regarded as a matter of course." Schikaneder was more than an absurd librettist, however. An actor, singer, and impresario, he had commissioned the debt-ridden composer of *Figaro* and *Don Giovanni* to write a new German opera. While the ailing Constanze Mozart spent much of the summer of 1791 taking the waters at Baden—where, in addition to flirting with other invalids, she gave birth to Mozart's sixth and last child—Schikaneder installed his friend in a tiny wooden cottage near his theater, and there they talked and caroused and argued and courted the impresario's protégés, and finally completed, in the course of that summer, *The Magic Flute*.

Schikaneder was proud, inevitably, of the masterpiece that he considered his own creation. We still have the handbills for the premiere, September 30, 1791, which announce, presumably at the producer's direction, "The Magic Flute, A Grand Opera in Two Acts, by Emanuel Schikaneder." Underneath that, the program lists the entire cast—Sarastro, Herr Gerl; Tamino, Herr Schack . . . and only at the very bottom does it say, "The music is by Herr Wolfgang Amade Mozart." In the following sentence, announcing that the composer will conduct the premiere, his name is misspelled: Mozard.

Having commissioned and written the work, Schikaneder also undertook the role of Papageno, for which the hired composer had written a number of remarkable songs. Of this, too, there is a record an engraving by J. Alberti depicting a rather boyish Schikaneder (he was then a portly forty-three) arrayed in feathers from head to toe. After the premiere, somebody approached the creator and told him that his opera had been a great success. "Yes, it has been a success," said Schikaneder, "but it would have been far more of a success if Mozart had not ruined so much of it."

A little less than two months later, Mozart was dead, at thirty-five, buried in an unmarked grave somewhere in the Vienna cemetery of St. Mark. Schikaneder lived on for another two decades, but in his later years, he became as crazy as Papageno—"A girl has come to live in our house," Dylan Thomas once wrote, "a girl mad as birds"—and he too ended, in 1812, in a pauper's grave.

Mozart's last year was a prodigal year. It was a year of continental upheaval, a year in which King Louis XVI fled from Paris and was recaptured at Varennes, a year in which the new Austrian Emperor Leopold II was preparing to go to war for his sister Marie Antoinette . . .

About Mozart's private life in these last months, there is considerable mystery. About the cause of his death, there has been much speculation, many theories. Poisoning. Adulteries. Conspiracies at the imperial court. This speculation reached a bizarre flowering in the enormous success of Peter Shaffer's *Amadeus*, which is simply wrong about many aspects of Mozart's life and death—not to mention its essentially false portrait of the man himself—but which has nonetheless led many people to think that they now know the basic facts of Mozart's end. Well, we will deal with that later.

The main thing is that Mozart's last year was a year of almost incredible creativity. Across the street from his apartment on the Rauhensteingasse, in the shadow of St. Stephen's Cathedral, he played, as his final public performance, the premiere of the exquisitely serene Piano Concerto in B-flat (K. 595). He wrote, for his friend Anton Stadler, the Clarinet Concerto in A (K. 622). To pay his bills, he undertook every available commission, exploring all the possibilities of such contemporary novelties as the mechanical organ (Fantasia in F Minor, K. 608) and the glass harmonica (Adagio and Rondo, K. 617). And knowing somehow that his career as a piano virtuoso was finished, he finally wrote down two dozen of the cadenzas that he had once improvised for his concerti. He was asked, then, to write a new opera for the coronation of Leopold, and so he finished, in less than three weeks, *La Clemenza di Tito*. And when a mysterious messenger came to commission him to compose an anonymous mass for an anonymous patron, he began sketching the Requiem. *Requiem aeternam dona eis.* . . . In the midst of all this—sick, in debt, and (can it be doubted?) frightened—he wrote *The Magic Flute*.

Where did I first hear *The Magic Flute*? In Boston, I think, in the early 1940s, as performed by a now-disbanded troupe that called itself the San Carlo Opera Company. None of us could then afford the touring Metropolitan, which was always sold out long before it even arrived from New York for its annual two-week appearance, so we used to trek in from the suburbs to see the San Carlo's more modest productions at the moribund Boston Opera House. The San Carlo specialized in novelties like *Rigoletto* and *Aïda*, performed by monumental Italian sopranos who lumbered about the stage in diaphanous gowns and ended by swooning heavily into the arms of their tenors. For Boston's small but determined German minority, the San Carlo also possessed a few blonde wigs so that the same sopranos in the same diaphanous gowns could provide an occasional *Magic Flute*.

And then Paris, where, from a fifteen-cent seat in the fifth gallery, one could witness a collection of equally sturdy sopranos sing Schikaneder in French, *La Flûte Enchantée*. And then, in the 1950s, in Mozart's own Salzburg, where *Die Zauberflöte* was performed outdoors, and Sarastro's white-robed priests marched with flickering torches through the tiers of arcades that had been carved into the hill of rock above the Reiterschule. And then back at the Metropolitan in New York, where the rituals of initiation took place in front of Marc Chagall's rather self-conscious draperies, all twittering birds in pastel colors. "No, the Chagall sets are *great,*" said a dark and dogmatic woman who taught French literature at one of the city colleges. "The Chagall sets made me *see* the opera for the first time as a childlike vision, a fairy tale." But *The Magic Flute* is not a fairy tale, not a childlike vision, not in the sense that fairy tales are charmingly meaningless, not at all.

In the gloomy depths of a Long Island winter, I was listening to a recording of Mozart's Great Mass in C Minor—unfinished, just as the Requiem was to remain unfinished—and I began staring, half-hypnotized, at the cover of the album, the interior of some extravagantly Baroque Austrian cathedral, a jungle of cupids and curlicues and organ pipes—the Dreifaltigkeitkirche, according to the album notes, in Stadl Paura near Lambach in Upper Austria.

"Why don't we go to Vienna," I suddenly said to my wife, "and hear a Mozart mass on Easter morning?"

It was an inspired idea, considering the burdens of maintaining a Long Island household, and so we simply bought two plane tickets and went to that imperial capital that we had never seen before. The Bristol Hotel, across the street from the Opera, proved to be wickedly expensive, but the room had a fireplace, a chaise longue, and steam-heated towel racks in the bathroom, and on Easter morning, as the lilacs were beginning to bud in the Hofgarten, the entire center of Vienna became a kind of religious music festival: Bruckner's E Minor Mass in the Gothic darkness of St. Stephen's Cathedral; Mozart's Coronation Mass in the narrow clutter of the Franziskuskirche; Haydn's Theresienmesse under the chaste vaults of the Augustinerkirche. . . . We went from church to church, not just hearing wonderful music but watching each flock of parishioners, gray-haired women in black hats, streaming toward the altar at the end of the *Agnus Dei* to partake of the communion that the horns and trumpets were celebrating.

On the following day, Monday morning, Vienna seemed almost hung over, a formidable city, gray and imperial, yet wearied by the strains of vanished power. It was time to fly on to the orange groves of Sicily, but Vienna still offered one last ritual to be fulfilled—at the opera that night, *The Magic Flute.* Everything was sold out, except for some standing room in the fifth balcony. In middle age, one becomes self-indulgently accustomed to the view from the red plush orchestra seats at the New York Metropolitan, and one regards, with a kind of pitying complacency, the shabby enthusiasts who stand so expectantly behind the guardrail at the back of the hall. Still, if standing room is all there is, one can, for fifty cents, climb the endless stairways back up into one's youth. In the last row of the topmost gallery sat a group of American students, all outfitted with musical scores and notebooks. Behind them, the only standing room left was off to one side, next to a pair of neatly inconspicuous Japanese.

The view from the side of the fifth gallery is all too real, all artifice exposed. The overture does not billow up from unseen depths, for the orchestra is directly below us, a congregation of elderly employees sawing at their violins, flipping the pages on their music stands, shaking the spit out of the mouthpieces of their horns. Tamino appears, pursued by the giant snake, and then vanishes into a corner of the stage that cannot be seen. The students stand and crane their necks, then slump back in stoical realization that most of this opera will remain invisible to them.

From the left, Papageno enters in his grotesque feathers, an absurd and inherently unbelievable character, and begins his first marvelous song, *"Der Vogelfänger bin ich ja. . . ."* In the seat in front of me, an American girl diligently begins to work at her notebook. I cannot resist looking over her shoulder to see what she has written. It is dutifully matter-of-fact: "Pap. is bird-catcher." At my right, the two Japanese contemplate the half-hidden spectacle with detached curiosity. What must an ambitious young salesman from Yokohama think, I wonder, of a culture in which thousands of people pay large sums of money to watch (partly) a fat German baritone dressed up as a bird?

Tamino was originally said to be a Japanese prince—or perhaps Javanese. The early printed versions differ, and either one may have been a typographical error, since two such exotic places were probably interchangeable to the Viennese of Schikaneder's (or Mozart's) time. Whether Japanese or Javanese, Tamino has the proper attributes of a Viennese opera hero—he sings in a dainty tenor, in German, and he is, like any German Japanese, white.

He has a villainous black-faced rival, however, named Monostatos, the Moor. Monostatos is, from the beginning, that classic caricature, the would-be rapist. His first words resound from offstage: "Ho, slaves! Bring chains!"* Three slaves skitter about in horror. "The maiden has been caught!" says one of them. "See how the relentless devil grasps her by her tender hands—I cannot bear it!" Enter, then, Monostatos, "dragging Pamina in," as the stage directions say. His intentions, even in the Victorian translation of the Schirmer score, are unmistakable: "My dainty lambkin, enter please! . . . Your life is at my mercy! . . . I'll force you to obey me. . . ."

It is the height of Viennese comedy that Pamina, confronting what used to be called a fate worse than death, should be saved by the sudden appearance of Papageno. The bird-man and the Moor regard each other as demons incarnate, each quaintly singing at the other, *"Das ist der Teufel sicherlich* (That is the devil certainly)," each pleading for mercy, each fleeing from the other with cries of "Hu! Hu! Hu!" Papageno goes meandering on, but Monostatos maintains a single-minded dedication to the ravishing of Pamina. A few scenes later, we again encounter him lurking in a garden, where Pamina is asleep under a rosebush. "Hah!" he says, in the Schirmer translation, "here I find the prudish beauty! What man could remain cold and unmoved before such a vision! The fire which burns within me will surely consume me. . . . One little kiss, I should think, could be excused." Instead of kissing her, however, he sails into an aria that is supposed to explain the fire that burns within him. He feels lonely, he says, *"Weil ein Schwarzer hässlich ist! . . ."*

Edward Gibbon, in describing the debaucheries at the court of Elagabalus, liked to lapse into what he called the decent obscurities of a learned language, and so it is permitted, apparently, to speak the unspeakable in German. Imagine the scene: The Metropolitan

---

* Schikaneder's text is not very elegant German—full of "unskillful, childish, vulgar turns of speech," as Alfred Einstein puts it—and it does not improve in translation. The doggerel was seriously intended, however, and so we must judge it with a certain tolerance. I have generally quoted the translation by Ruth and Thomas Martin in the vocal score published by G. Schirmer, Inc., copyright 1941 and 1951.

Opera, temple of high culture in the citadel of high liberalism, filled to overflowing with earnest gray-haired people who feed on *Times* editorials and donate money to worthy causes. With benign indulgence, they watch a darting little man in blackface (no genuine black man, presumably, would accept the role) sing a song that says, indisputably, *"Weil ein Schwarzer hässlich ist!"* The words were too raw for the Schirmer translators, who rendered them as "no one ever looks at me!" But that is not what they mean. They mean "because a black is ugly." The second verse is equally disreputable: *"Eine Weisse nahm mich ein,"* which is translated as "all I do is steal a kiss," but which means, "I catch myself a white woman."

One wonders, in this liberated age, whether Mozart (or Schikaneder) ever actually saw a black, and if so, under what circumstances. It was fashionable, in the eighteenth century, for ladies of high position to be attended by black children in turbans and silk robes. What happened to these young servants when they grew up? Pushkin was partly black, and so was Dumas, but this is not part of our cultural history. The New York public libraries are full of books about black America and black Africa, but black Europe remains rather mysterious. To seek enlightenment, I made one of my periodic visits to the Goethe Haus, a palatial institution on upper Fifth Avenue, filled with volumes on Germanic culture. The door is always locked, however, and when one sounds the buzzer, the nervous guardians of the gate peer out to make sure that the visitor is white and respectable. At the end of the long parquet-floored corridor sits the head librarian, a svelte blonde deeply tanned in (I suppose) Jamaica or Barbados.

"Do you have any sort of history of black people in Europe?" I ask. "Or, more specifically, do you have any book that would tell me whether Mozart ever saw a black man in the Vienna of the eighteenth century?"

"No," says the tanned blonde, a little surprised at such a question. "No, we have nothing here like that."

Whatever bleak thoughts Mozart (or Schikaneder) may have had about blacks, he also had about other people whom we now regard as "ethnic minorities." His letters contain a number of derogatory remarks about Jewish moneylenders, and he despised Italians. As for Vienna's legendary enemies, who had been driven from the gates of the city scarcely a century earlier, the villainous guardian of the *Seraglio* says: "Here we are in Turkey . . . I am your master, you my slave." Blondchen, the object of Osmin's wicked threats, represents the only foreign nationality that Mozart seems to have approved of. "I am an Englishwoman born to freedom," says she, "and I defy anyone who tries to force me to anything."

In that exchange, though, one senses that Mozart rather sympathized with Osmin, for despite the conventional pieties of the *Seraglio*, written at about the time of Mozart's marriage, he was profoundly a misogynist. It is a dismal prejudice, to be sure, but it permeates his operas. Zerlina, for example, has hardly met Don Giovanni before she abandons her fiancé and strolls off hand in hand with "your lordship." When the sworn loyalty of Fiordiligi and Dorabella is put to the test, they fail their oaths almost immediately—the only moral being *"Così fan tutte."* These *tutte* (the feminine pronoun applies only to females) are literally all women, as Leporello lists Don Giovanni's 1,003 conquests "so far" in Spain: "Ill or healthy, poor or wealthy, plain or pretty, dull or witty. . . ." Modern psychology accuses Don Giovanni of sadism, pseudoparricide, repressed homosexuality, and various other sins, but Mozart's view was rather different. Near the beginning of Act II of *The Magic Flute*, two of Sarastro's priests join in singing a beautiful duet on the following text: "Beware of woman's crafty scheming: / This is the Order's first command! / Many a man, of wiles not dreaming, / was tempted and could not withstand. / But then he saw he was mistaken, / The truth he came to know too late. / At last he found himself forsaken. / Death and damnation were his fate."

Mozart's first great love was Aloysia Weber, then fifteen, daughter of an impoverished singer, prompter, and copyist at the court opera in Mannheim. Mozart was a boarder in the Weber household. Aloysia rejected him, recalling years later, "I only thought he was such a *little* man." Mozart soon came to regard Aloysia as "a false, malicious person and a coquette," but he continued living with the Webers and duly fell in love with Aloysia's younger sister, Constanze, whom he described in rather strange terms to his horrified father. He must get married, he said, because "the voice of nature speaks as loud in me as in others, louder perhaps," but he was "too honorably minded to seduce an innocent maiden," and he had "too much dread and fear of disease . . . to fool about with whores." So he declared himself, at twenty-five, still a virgin. "I can swear," he wrote his father, "that I have never had relations of that sort with any woman."

And there were other considerations. "I have never been accustomed to looking after my own effects, clothes, washing, etc.," he wrote. By this time, while he regarded Aloysia as "insincere and ill-disposed," Constanze appeared a paragon of practicality. "One could not call her a beauty," he admitted. "Her whole beauty consists in two little black eyes and a graceful figure. She has no wit, but wholesome common sense enough to fulfill her duties as a wife and mother. She is *not* inclined to extravagance. . . . On the contrary, she is used to being ill-dressed . . . and most of the things that a woman needs she is able to make for herself."

Surviving portraits do not provide an image any more flattering than the one provided by her suitor. A rather plump face, large and shrewd eyes, a handsome nose, and an oddly twisted and sarcastic mouth. One imagines a lively talker, with a sharp sense of humor; one also imagines a lonely young Mozart, a wanderer since the age of five, desperately eager to settle down with anyone who could provide domestic company. Mrs. Weber, with her four young daughters, all professional or nearly professional singers, offered a raffish domesticity of a kind that Mozart had never known before. Once she saw that her boarder was sufficiently involved with her daughter, she took the precaution of persuading him to sign a legal contract promising either to marry Constanze within three years or to pay her 300 florins* a year until someone else married her. Mozart, an honest young man, willingly signed because he was determined to marry her in any case; Constanze, an honest young woman, just as

---

*Translating eighteenth-century Austrian currency into any modern equivalent is an uncertain business. According to H. C. Robbins Landon, a florin or gulden could be valued in 1791 at about 9.5 to the English pound, and a 1791 pound was worth about twenty times today's pound, which, when last checked, was worth about $1.70.

willingly tore up the signed contract. Leopold Mozart refused his consent, despite several pleading letters from his son, and so, on August 4, 1782, they were married without it. He was twenty-six, she nineteen.

There is a tradition of criticizing Constanze as unworthy of her husband, a frivolous girl who got him into debt and never appreciated his genius. If one considers the Mozarts not as a genius and his handmaiden but simply as husband and wife, the tradition is quite unfair. It seems to be true that Constanze thought of her husband as simply another musician, but Mozart was just as improvident as his wife, a spendthrift without any regular income, a restless soul who moved in and out of twelve households during the nine years of the marriage. Constanze was almost constantly pregnant, and the pregnancies led, with dreadful regularity, to the graveyard. The first son, Raimund, was born just ten months after the marriage and died two months later; the second, Karl, was born a year later and survived (a gifted pianist and an Austrian government official, he died, unmarried, in 1858); the third, Johann, was born in October of 1786 and died a month later; the first daughter, Theresia, was born toward the end of 1787 and died the following June; the next daughter, Anna, died on the day of her birth, November 16, 1789; the sixth and last child, Franz Xaver Wolfgang, born in the *Magic Flute* summer of 1791, lived until 1844, also unmarried and childless, a composer of sorts.

It is easy enough to say that such a regimen of doomed births (history does not record the miscarriages) was commonplace in the eighteenth century, as indeed it was, but that cannot have made Constanze's life any easier. The repeated pregnancies afflicted her with various fevers and edemas, lamed her in one knee, made her legs and feet swell, and the doctors' only prescription was to tell her to soak in tubs in which tripe had been boiled. Yet she remained cheerful and flirtatious, perhaps all too much so. Mozart's last letters to her at the resort of Baden appeal to her to have regular bowel movements for the sake of *"votre santé si chère et précieuse à votre époux,"* but also to avoid going on garden walks alone, "both for your *and* my honor."

The warning is rather ominous. Mozart's letters to Constanze are so full of extravagant expressions of love—"Prepare yourself, kisses begin to fly around amazingly... what the devil! I've just caught three—they were delicious!"—that he is often considered to have been the most faithful of husbands. "Mozart's knowledge of women," as Alfred Einstein puts it, "was not derived from any actual success with women." And near the end of the first act of *The Magic Flute,* Mozart wrote a charming duet in praise of marriage: "Wife and man, and man and wife, / Reach the height of godly life...." There is something a little odd, though, in the fact that Pamina sings this duet not with her suitor Tamino but with the bird-man, Papageno.

There is no proof of Mozart's infidelities—why should there be?—but the romantic biography by Marcia Davenport offers some hypotheses. During Mozart's last voyage to Berlin in 1789, for example, she suggests that he had an affair with Henriette Baranius, a soprano who was then singing the role of Blondchen in the *Seraglio.* And during the summer of 1791, alone in Vienna, he entertained himself with the wife of Franz Gerl, he being the original Sarastro and she the original Papagena. There was also the sad case of Franz Hofdemel, an attaché to the imperial court, a brother in Mozart's Masonic lodge, and the husband of one of his pupils. Just a few days after Mozart's death, Hofdemel attacked his pregnant wife, Magdalena, with a razor, slashing her face and throat and then killing himself. Frau Hofdemel recovered and named her son after both Mozart and her husband. As for the missing Constanze, Mrs. Davenport remarks only that "a slight weakness was sufficient excuse" for her to escape from Vienna to Baden, adding that "an officer stationed at Baden ... now seems very plausible cause for her protracted visits there."

This may all be false conjecture, but it is remarkable how Mozart's heroines evolve from the high-flown loyalty of Constanze in the *Seraglio* ("Tortures unabating, unabating / May for me be waiting. / I shall welcome woe and pain ...") to the foxy sophistication of Susanna ("Was ever such delusion? / He'll find to his confusion, / How deep are women's wiles ...") to the wrath of Donna Anna and Donna Elvira ("We come for vengeance / Now he shall pay ..."). It could be argued that these women are all reacting to various forms of male oppression—the Pasha threatening torture, Count Almaviva demanding his *droit de seigneur,* Don Giovanni committing murder in the course of attempted rape. But the indictment continues. Nobody coerced Dorabella and Fiordiligi into betraying their fiancés in *Così,* and it is simply injured vanity that inspires Vitellia to demand that her lover Sextus assassinate the Emperor Titus. One cannot help suspecting that Mozart, who wrote during his bachelor days that "God has not given me my talent that I might dance attendance on a woman," felt some degree of half-suppressed, irrational anger about Constanze's pregnancies and illnesses, about his own confinement and impoverishment—and then guilt about his anger, and more anger about his guilt.

Mozart's misogyny annoys a critic like Brigid Brophy (*Mozart the Dramatist),* who seems unable to believe that anyone who could write such beautiful music could entertain such unpleasant thoughts about women. She therefore interprets *Figaro* as a plea for liberation, *Don Giovanni* as a study in repressed homosexuality, and *Così* as a "tragic satire." The words of *The Magic Flute* do not mean what they say, she argues, because Pamina is given beautiful music to sing and is finally permitted to join Tamino as an equal in undergoing the ritual tests. But the "equality" of Pamina lies mainly in the fact that she is judged by the male priesthood ("These women profane our station . . .") to be, unlike Constanze, a self-sacrificing bride suitable for Prince Tamino.

The female center of gravity in *The Magic Flute* is actually Pamina's ferocious mother, the Queen of the Night (Mozart pretended great affection, in his later years, for the mother-in-law who had once forced him to sign a marriage contract). It is she who assigns Tamino to rescue her daughter Pamina from the wicked Sarastro. (Pamina's origins are not much emphasized, but there is one scene, usually omitted, in which the queen reminds Pamina that she is the widow of Sarastro's predecessor, that she had hoped to inherit his throne, and that she was rejected because "these matters are not accessible to your woman's spirit. Your duty is to submit.")

When Tamino arrives at the temple and is persuaded that Sarastro is a priest of wisdom, the exiled queen is made out to be, like most of the troublesome women of mythology, a kind of witch. She who first appeared as a martyr, singing a lament for her stolen daughter ("In lonely grief I am forsaken, / For my poor child no more I see . . .") reappears near the end as a harridan promising this same daughter to the wicked Monostatos. "Their lives are thine by law and right!" her three attendants sing. Thunder and lightning suddenly break out, and, according to the stage instructions, the queen, Monostatos, and the three attendant ladies all "sink into the earth."

We cherish, perhaps a little sadistically, the image of Mozart dying in poverty and in debt, but it is useful to remember that until the last years, he was an arrogantly successful virtuoso. "This is clavierland," he wrote home from Vienna on his arrival in 1781, and he was the master of the clavier. He had been earning 400 florins a year as a rather dilatory organist for the archbishop of Salzburg, but now he charged 2 florins per lesson, roughly ten times what his father earned for teaching the violin in Salzburg. He preferred to keep his compositions unpublished, to avoid plagiarism, but he could sell them whenever he chose. He frequently performed in the palaces of such nobles as Esterhazy and Galitzin, and he also organized subscription concerts of his own. The receipts of one concert alone brought in 559 florins, more than a year's pay from the archbishop, more than a year's rent on his apartment.

He probably could have continued to earn sums like that, but he preferred to concentrate on composing. The financial rewards for composition, as Elliott Carter could tell Vladimir Horowitz, are considerably lower than those for virtuosity. Mozart nonetheless liked to live well—even when he couldn't pay his bills, he was never without a servant—and Constanze, often ill, was no more frugal than he. Toward the end of the 1780s, he began importuning his friends, and so Michael Puchberg acquires his small place in history. He was a wealthy businessman, an amateur musician, and a fellow Mason. In his honor, Mozart wrote the superb Divertimento in E-flat for violin, viola, and cello (K. 563). Most of their surviving correspondence, however, consists of Mozart's endless pleas for money, and Puchberg's stolid notations that the pleas were answered.

Early June 1788: "Dearest Brother! Your true friendship and brotherly love embolden me to ask a great favor of you. I still owe you eight ducats. Apart from the fact that at the moment I am not in a position to pay you back this sum, my confidence in you is so boundless that I dare to implore you to help me out with a hundred gulden until next week, when my concerts in the Casino are to begin. . . ." [Puchberg's annotation: Sent 100 gulden.]

Mid-June 1788: "Most Honorable Brother of the Order, Dearest, Most Beloved Friend! . . . If you have sufficient regard and friendship for me to assist me for a year or two with one or two thousand gulden, at a suitable rate of interest, you will help me enormously. . . . If you will do me this kindness . . . I can work with a mind more free from care and with a lighter heart, and thus earn more. . . ." [Puchberg's annotation: Sent 200 gulden.]

June 27, 1788: "Most Honorable B.O. [Brother of the Order], Dearest, Most Beloved Friend! . . . I am obliged to tell you frankly that it is impossible for me to pay back soon the money you have lent me and that I must beg you to be patient with me . . . !"

Early July 1788: "Dearest Friend and B.O., Owing to great difficulties and complications my affairs have become so involved that it is of the utmost importance to raise some money on these two pawnbroker's tickets. In the name of our friendship I implore you to do me this favor. . . ."

July 12, 1789: "Dearest, Most Beloved Friend and Most Honorable B.O. Great God! I would not wish my worst enemy to be in my present position. And if you, my most beloved friend and brother, forsake me, we are altogether lost, both my unfortunate and blameless self and my poor sick wife and child. . . . So it all depends, my only friend, upon whether you will or can lend me another 500 gulden. . . . O God!—I can hardly bring myself to dispatch this letter!—and yet I must . . . ! For God's sake, forgive me. . . ."

July 17, 1789: "Dearest, Most Beloved Friend and Most Honorable B.O. I fear you are angry with me, for you do not send me a reply . . . ! I entreat you, if it is quite impossible for you to assist me at this time with such a large sum, to show your friendship and brotherly affection by helping me at once with as much as you can spare, for I am really in very great need. . . ." [Puchberg's annotation: Sent 150 gulden.]

*   *   *

In the spring of 1945—on April 28, to be exact—I found and bought a treasure that nobody else in Harvard Square possessed, a treasure that several other students tried to buy from me at two or three times the price I had paid. I found the treasure in, of all places, a hardware store in Concord, Massachusetts, where we then lived. Hardware stores had a hard time getting supplies in the spring of 1945—steel nails were scarce, rubber tires were rationed, photographic film appeared only once every week or ten days—and so they filled their shelves with whatever they could sell: birthday cards, chewing gum, gramophone records—Frank Sinatra, the Andrews Sisters, Hoagy Carmichael. There I spotted the treasure, a mud-brown album containing Artur Schnabel's recording of Mozart's Twenty-seventh Piano Concerto in B-flat (K. 595). The London Symphony Orchestra, conducted by John Barbirolli. A Victor Musical Masterpiece (DM-240).

I still have the album—obviously, for how else would I know all these details?—even though the first of the four records has broken in about the middle of Schnabel's first solo. It looks as though some great raven had taken a fierce nip out of one edge of a cookie. Most of my old records—I still have more than sixty albums of them—are in similar condition. I rarely play them, but I would never want to give them up, for each album represents hours of work and weeks of saving. At $1.10 per record, it took four of them to capture a Mozart concerto, about twenty-five for *The Marriage of Figaro*, and although we played them with fragile cactus needles that had to be sharpened on sandpaper every hour or so, they nonetheless cracked at the slightest provocation. And no replacements for single records would be available, we were told, until after the war. Now, although the latest Schwann catalogue lists ten different versions of the twenty-seventh concerto, all presumably available at any discount store in your neighborhood, the Schnabel is not among them, and so I still keep mine, with its first and last sides smashed, in a corner of my living room.

I was just discovering the Mozart concerti in those days, and just discovering my own ambition to play them, in public, with an orchestra—an orchestra that would rise, at a signal from the awed conductor, to join in the standing ovation—but I was much too young and ignorant, at sixteen, to appreciate the valedictory beauties of the twenty-seventh. My first favorite was the twenty-first in C Major (K. 467)—the one my children now think of as the theme song for *Elvira Madigan*—because it was brash and assertive, and I could impress people with the speed at which I played the tremolo octaves in the first movement. My favorite of favorites, however, was the twenty-fourth in C Minor (K. 491), because it was dark and passionate, and I impressed myself by the noisy passion with which I played it. The prewar performance by Edwin Fischer was the most beloved of all my Mozart records, and when I first ventured to Europe in 1946, I went as soon as possible to attend Fischer's master classes in Lucerne. I found him to be a rather windblown, white-haired old gentleman who stamped and snorted and made a great many mistakes when he played. As a gesture of reaffirmation, I asked my mother to send me my recording of the C Minor, and it arrived, inevitably, in bits and pieces.

It is not completely clear why Mozart wrote his last concerto. Most of his earlier ones had been written as virtuoso pieces for himself, or his best students, and the last of these, the rather brittle No. 26 in D Major (K. 537), had been finished early in 1788. Mozart took it on tour with him the following year, playing it in Berlin and Dresden, and it eventually acquired its nickname, the Coronation Concerto. The coronation of Leopold II, after the death of Joseph II early in 1790, meant a period of retrenchment both in Hapsburg military ambitions and in the imperial support of the arts. Mozart was not invited to Leopold's coronation in Frankfurt—his great rival, Hofkapellmeister Antonio Salieri, headed the troupe of fifteen court musicians taken to the celebrations—but he rashly decided to make the voyage anyway. In Frankfurt, a surviving playbill records that he joined forces with a castrato, a soprano, and an orchestra to provide an all-Mozart concert featuring two symphonies, three songs, and two concerti "played by Herr Kapellmeister Mozart from his own composition." The assembled dignitaries applauded Mozart's Coronation Concerto, but there were competing attractions that day—showy maneuvers by Hessian troops—and the concert was not a financial success. The great virtuoso, who had been performing in public since childhood, never went on tour again.

Mozart finished his last concerto on January 5, 1791, possibly for a pupil who never performed it, possibly just for himself. It is quite unlike any of his earlier concerti, simple in structure, rather chromatic in harmony, utterly without ostentation, almost unworldly in tone. Such works traditionally inspire commentators to rhetoric. Cuthbert Girdlestone, the author of *Mozart and His Piano Concertos,* professes to see in this work "an evening light, announcing the end of a life." Alfred Einstein is even more lyrical, comparing the rondo to a scene of "blessed children playing in Elysian fields." It is evidently impossible, as Proust and Mann and E. M. Forster have demonstrated all too well, to describe the sound of a piece of music. It can only be evoked by name, thus causing a moment of recognition in a reader who knows the work, or else technically analyzed, thus demonstrating how the composer achieved a certain result. Charles Rosen, for example, in his admirable study *The Classical Style,* not only describes this concerto with the customary phrases like "iridescent chromaticism" and "limitless melancholy" but also cites a specific measure in which the violins descend from a D to a C while the cellos play a D flat: "In this way there is the unplayed but audibly imagined harshness of a minor ninth (D-D-flat) along with the major seventh (D-flat-C), which gives the effect of the most dissonant and most expressive harmony without the harshness of actually playing it."

Do we now understand this work better? Possibly.

The only way to understand a Mozart concerto thoroughly, though, is to sit down at the piano and play it, which I do with this No. 27, humbly, every six months or so. Yes, better my faltering inadequacy than Rosen's easy virtuosity, or even the magic of Schnabel. The main problem is that a piano concerto hardly sounds right without an orchestra, and since I am neither a virtuoso nor a millionaire, I have had to spend years in simply imagining how my version of the *Emperor* or the *Variations symphoniques* would really sound if I were not alone at my out-of-tune piano.

Every vain fantasy eventually inspires some entrepreneur to offer a fulfillment for sale—not a real fulfillment, not Carnegie Hall occupied by a joyous claque, but a sort of cut-rate, do-it-yourself fulfillment. So fantasy gave birth to a little corporation called Music Minus One, whose sixty-four-page catalogue ranged from Twenty Dixieland Classics minus tenor saxophone to the Brandenburg Concerto No. 2 minus violin. That was how I encountered Emil Kahn, who, in case the name is unfamiliar, can be hired for less than ten dollars to conduct a rather nondescript group called the Stuttgart Festival Orchestra in a half-dozen Mozart piano concerti without piano.

How I have raged at Emil Kahn! Not for his tempi, which are rather brisk, or for his interpretations, which are almost nonexistent. The real trouble with Emil Kahn is that he won't cooperate. When I have to turn a page, Emil Kahn never pauses for even half a beat to let me find my place, and when I make a mistake, I cannot get Emil Kahn to rein in his orchestra and go back to the last fortissimo. Once Emil Kahn gets ahead of the soloist, the only solution is to skip five or ten bars and catch up with him at the next tutti.

The only place Emil Kahn ever stops, actually, is during the cadenzas, and there he stops indefinitely. Since the speed and duration of the cadenza are left up to the performer, there is no way for the engineers to plan ahead of time, so they have created a "locked groove," which will hold the needle in place forever. The standard cadenza ends, after much wandering and variation, with a long trill on the dominant seventh, by which the pianist signals to the conductor that his display of virtuosity has finished, and it is time for the orchestra to come crashing in with a few concluding bars. But Emil Kahn never hears his cue, or, if he hears it, he stands with arms paralyzed in his locked groove. After trilling for a while, the pianist has to get up from his piano, go to the record player, and lift its arm into the next groove so that Emil Kahn can resume his beat. Music Minus One never promised more than ten dollars' worth of fantasy, but the mood is never quite the same again.

Mozart, as far as can be discovered, played his twenty-seventh concerto in public only once, on March 4, 1791, two months after its completion. A clarinetist named Joseph Bähr organized a concert at a small hall in the Himmelpfortgasse, announcing, aside from his own performance, a new concerto by Mozart and some songs by Mozart's first love, Aloysia Weber. The audience was apparently small, the financial reward modest. We have only one brief account in the *Wiener Zeitung,* observing merely that Mozart's concerto was admired, as was his performance at the piano. It was the last concert he ever gave.

There is a theory that the enigma of *The Magic Flute* can be resolved in a stone-walled cellar, dank and chilly, deep beneath Vienna's Neuer Markt. There, all stored away in dark metal coffins, lie the unburied Hapsburgs. The largest of these coffins is that of Maria Theresa, plump and enthusiastic, sovereign empress for forty years, mother of sixteen children, who commanded that her leviathan tomb should depict not a sleeping penitent awaiting the trumpets of Judgment Day but a recumbent bride turning expectantly toward her recumbent husband, a portrait of herself as she had once been or as she hoped, under the watching eye of a watching angel, once again to be.

To the court of this matron, Leopold Mozart brought his prodigies, the six-year-old Wolfgang and his sister, Nannerl, then ten. Wolfgang promptly climbed into the empress's lap and kissed her on the cheek. The children then regaled the royal family with duets on the clavier and sonatas for the violin. The Emperor Franz made them do tricks, like playing with one finger. The empress gave them some of her own children's used clothes and invited them to come again. Mozart became particularly fond of one of the empress's younger daughters, Marie Antoinette, who was then seven. According to sentimental tradition, she picked him up when he fell down in a corridor of the Schönbrunn Palace, and he promised to marry her when they both grew up.

The theory about Maria Theresa and *The Magic Flute,* first propagated by a nineteenth-century Mason named Moritz Zille, is that she, the Catholic empress who formally banned the Masonic movement in 1764, is the wicked Queen of the Night. According to this theory, Tamino stands for the more enlightened Emperor Joseph II, and Pamina is a symbol of the Austrian people, while Monostatos speaks for the black-hearted lust and treachery of the Jesuits. It is a theory supported less by evidence than by Masonic fervor, and yet there is something fitting in the idea that Tamino, whom Robert Moberly aptly describes as "a timid prince trying to be brave," should represent Joseph II. He was, during the last ten years of Mozart's life, the figure to whom the composer repeatedly looked for support, and from whom he repeatedly got less than he sought and deserved.

Joseph II had been brought up with music lessons, like all of Maria Theresa's children, and he became a fairly skilled amateur cellist. He appreciated Mozart, warily. He attended, and thus made fashionable, Mozart's piano concerts, as well as his operas, but his imperial judgment on the *Seraglio* was typical of imperial judgments on the arts. "It has," he said, "too many notes in it." Joseph II banned Beaumarchais's *Le Mariage de Figaro* as subversive, but his admiration for the music of Mozart and the libretti of Lorenzo da Ponte was sufficient to persuade him to permit the production of their opera. He pronounced the music of *Don Giovanni* "divine," and he commissioned, shortly before his death, *Così fan tutte*. It was not until 1787, however, after the death of Gluck, that Mozart was appointed to Gluck's court position as a *Kammermusiker*. He was paid only 800 florins a year, compared to Gluck's 2,000. Even though the court finally gave him this official position, it never gave him any specific tasks to perform, and so Mozart once wrote on his tax return: "Too much for what I do; too little for what I could do."

But how supremely unimportant Mozart was to the Hapsburgs, whose rule then extended from Brussels to Florence to Sarajevo. When Joseph II inherited the throne in 1781, he was determined to renovate his entire empire. A student of the French philosophes, he wore a plain frock coat and freely gave audiences to citizens with grievances. He granted religious liberty to all dissenters and freed the Jews of their obligation to wear yellow stripes. He abolished censorship of the press, and police torture, and the death penalty. He founded the world's largest maternity hospital. He made primary education compulsory. Indeed, like many enlightened monarchs, he made his entire enlightenment compulsory, and to carry out the estimated 6,000 decrees of his reign, he began to centralize the police into the force that was to become notorious under Prince

Metternich. In his enthusiasm for education, he abolished all monasteries and convents that were not devoted to teaching or nursing (more than 1,000) and confiscated their property for the benefit of the new reforms. He abolished the autonomy of Hungary, Lombardy, and the Netherlands, and made German the sole official language throughout his realm. He even banned *Lebkuchen* (gingerbread) as bad for the digestion, and outlawed coffins as less efficient than cloth sacks. Only after fervent protests did he issue a new decree rescinding his decree on coffins, informing his subjects that "His Majesty no longer cares how they bury themselves in the future."

It was a fundamental part of the Enlightenment, too, to expand one's power by attacking neighboring states. Just as Frederick the Great had welcomed the accession of Maria Theresa by invading Silesia, so Joseph joined the Prussians and Russians in the first partition of Poland. Most of the emperor's aggressions were less successful. He tried several times to acquire Bavaria in exchange for Belgium; he attacked the city of Belgrade but was beaten off; he joined the Russians, finally, in attacking Turkey. (Mozart, for whatever reasons of nationalism or sycophancy, wrote a contredanse with Turkish battle music entitled "The Siege of Belgrade" [K. 535] as well as a patriotic song, "I would like to be the emperor" [K. 539].) Joseph not only had no talent as a general but ruined his health while maneuvering against the Turks. He returned to Vienna near death from various fevers, coughs, and liver troubles. On his tomb in the Capuchin crypt, he ordered the inscription "Here lies Joseph II, who failed in everything he undertook."

To Mozart, the death of Joseph II meant the death of *Così fan tutte*. Commissioned by the emperor, it had opened with moderate critical success on January 26, 1790, but there were only ten performances before Joseph died on February 20, and then all theaters were closed in mourning. A month later, the childless Joseph's younger brother Leopold arrived from Italy with his wife and fourteen offspring to take charge of the empire. Mozart sent to the palace a "most humble petition . . . to apply for the post of second *Kapellmeister. . . .* Some small renown now accorded me by the world for my performances on the piano-forte encourages me also to beg for the favor of being entrusted with the musical instruction of the Royal Family." The petition was never answered.

Mozart's biographers, writing from a two-century perspective that endows the composer with an importance somewhat greater than that of any Hapsburg, have generally dealt harshly with Leopold II. Marcia Davenport, for example, refers to him as "a stupid, narrow weakling, who neither knew nor cared anything about music." It may well be that all political rulers should be judged not according to the politics of the moment but according to their support of art—does anyone even remember the name of whoever was president of the United States when Melville published *Moby-Dick*? (It was Millard Fillmore.) On the other hand, Leopold II had to deal with problems that he and his ministers undoubtedly considered more important than anything on the Viennese musical scene. He confronted, on his accession to the throne, all the debris of his older brother's political experiments—near rebellion in Belgium and Hungary—as well as intrigues by Prussia and Russia and an increasing danger of involvement in the French Revolution. In late August of 1791, when Mozart went to Prague to supervise the final rehearsals of *La Clemenza di Tito* for Leopold's Bohemian coronation, Leopold himself was conferring in Pillnitz with King Frederick William II of Prussia and warning that the French Revolution had "compromised the honor of all sovereigns and the security of all governments."

Even if Emil Kahn were available to wave his baton next to my piano, the Mozart cadenzas would present problems. He is the only composer who has left us great concerti without any cadenzas at all. Beethoven not only wrote them out but offered alternative versions; Schumann and Brahms prescribed every note. Mozart simply provides a fanfare that leads to a fermata over a six-four chord on the dominant. There he leaves us.

We know that Mozart was a great improvisor. We know that even the published scores are incomplete, partly because Mozart liked to vary each performance ("I always play what occurs to me at the moment," he wrote), partly because he feared plagiarism, so even the orchestral parts were often handed out just before a concert ("One shudders to think," Harold Schonberg has written, "what the accompaniments must have sounded like"). The written piano part, therefore, is sometimes little more than an outline, and the cadenza is a blank.

Improvisation is, of course, a musical tradition that dates back to the drums around the campfire. There are still skillful improvisers today, but outside of jazz, the art of improvisation has become a kind of circus trick. The improviser solicits song tunes from the audience, to prove the honesty of his performance, and then he provides variations in the manner of Chopin or the Beatles. It is a little difficult, however, to imagine even a Serkin or a Brendel arriving at Carnegie Hall to play the Coronation Concerto without any idea of what to do about a cadenza except "what occurs to me at the moment."

Perhaps Mozart was taking pity on us, in the last year of his life, when he wrote down a collection of the cadenzas that he had once improvised (K. 624). Perhaps he simply heard the winged chariot and felt a need to impose a greater permanence on the ephemeral. We have no way of knowing whether these cadenzas are really the ones he used to play, or how widely the cadenzas that he played differed from one performance to another. What is most mysterious of all is that in collecting and writing down and thus ossifying his improvisations, Mozart deliberately did not provide cadenzas for six of his last concerti, five of these being among his very greatest (the two in C major, the C minor, the D minor, and the E-flat). He may have felt some inexplicable reluctance to codify everything, some need to leave part of his past unconfined, or perhaps he simply intended to imply that anyone who could properly play these five concerti was a master of sufficient virtuosity to provide his own cadenzas.

For two centuries, composers and pianists have been trying with varying degrees of failure to fill the void that Mozart left. The Schirmer editions provide cadenzas written by Johann Nepomuk Hummel, the half-forgotten composer who was once, just like Mozart, a child prodigy touring Europe under the aegis of his father. The father became a conductor at the theater of Emanuel Schikaneder, who undertook to introduce the young Hummel to his friend Mozart, who, in turn, took the boy as his pupil for two years (1785–1787). But Hummel's cadenzas are ponderous intrusions of nineteenth-century density, quite out of character for the concerti of the master who was scarcely twenty years his senior. Nowadays, of course, it is even more of an effort for a pianist to assume the Mozart style, but we can hear the recorded attempts of an eclectic like Robert Casadesus, and there are published offerings in the careful creations of Lili Kraus and Paul Badura-Skoda. How laboriously they have all striven to capture those elusive elements of fantasy and summation that Mozart simply improvised according to "what occurs to me at the moment."

The cadenzas by Mozart's heirs all suffer, in different ways, from the most predictable of faults—they are too complicated. Who, on confronting the test of writing a cadenza that is to form part of a Mozart concerto, can escape the fear of being thought inadequate? Who, therefore, can avoid the temptation to include some citation of every theme, to modulate into remote harmonies, and to exhibit displays of virtuosity more ostentatious than anything in the original concerto? Certainly not Beethoven, who was, before his deafness, both a great virtuoso and a great improviser. For the most Beethovenian of all Mozart's concerti, the D minor (K. 466), Beethoven wrote the most Beethovenian of cadenzas. It begins with an aggressive series of rising trills in the right hand and an even more aggressive quotation of the opening theme in the left. After a brief display of virtuosity, Beethoven progresses logically to the second theme, but he treats it first as a canon at the octave and then as a kind of nervous cantilena. After a rather conventional series of runs and scales, he ends with an outburst of trilling that is almost a parody of his standard conclusions. To all of this melodrama, an editor like Lili Kraus adds inspirational instructions—*cantabile, con dolore,* and *molto espressivo* and *deciso ma leggiero*—which are no more an exaggeration of Beethoven's wishes than Beethoven's cadenza is an exaggeration of Mozart's original concerto.

We can never know how Mozart might have performed Liszt's *Études transcendentales*—cautiously, I suspect—but we know how Liszt dealt with Mozart, for he published, in 1843, his extravagant fantasia on *Don Giovanni*. It begins, inevitably, with a thunderous D minor chord, but it soon wanders off into a series of vast arpeggios, storms of octaves, runs in chromatic thirds. The commendatore's proclamation of doom is briefly cited, and then it disappears in a flood of trills and tremolos. The first intimation that *Don Giovanni* was actually written by Mozart, rather than Liszt, comes in an ostentatiously simple statement of "Là ci darem la mano," but that is only the pretext for a prodigious series of variations, *accelerando, stringendo, con bravura, prestissimo, brillante, velocissimo.* . . .

The cadenzas that Mozart wrote down in his last year were quite different. Though they were intended to display the virtuosity of the performer, they also display, unlike the labored creations of Mozart's successors, a reluctance to violate the integrity of the concerto as a whole. The cadenza that Mozart wrote for the marvelously gentle Concerto in A Major (K. 488), for example, leaves all the major themes untouched. It recapitulates, instead, a motif from the development section and then comes to a long, reflective pause. Then a few arpeggios, a long trill, and we are finished. His first-movement cadenza for the last concerto (K. 595) is a bit more fully worked out, but not much. It begins, a typical Mozart touch, not with a restatement of the opening theme but with a continuation of the closing theme. This leads, after a brief and modest series of variations, to a simple presentation of the second theme, first in the major and then in the minor, and then, with only the barest hints of the other main themes, to the run that leads to the closing trill.

The Mozart cadenza, in short, is not a grand fantasia on all the themes and motifs that have gone before. It is not what a great virtuoso, knowing that he was expected to improvise, might compose and memorize and then bring forth as his extravagant inspiration. It is, on the contrary, a very realistic suggestion of what a gifted performer might improvise on the stage. It is short and simple. It is less difficult, both musically and technically, than the work that surrounds it. It is marked, quite understandably, with pauses and hesitations. It expresses virtuosity not in outrageous display but rather in a restrained semblance of display, thus making the final orchestral reentry seem not an anticlimax but a triumphal reassertion. It expresses an eighteenth-century sense of proportion that ended with Napoleon's assumption of the imperial crown. Talleyrand, the great survivor, could only attempt to convey that sense in his warning to his diplomats: *"Surtout, Messieurs, point de zèle."*

Mozart to Puchberg, December 29, 1789: "Most Honorable Friend and B.O. . . . I am to receive from the management next month 200 ducats for my opera [*Così fan tutte*]. If you can and will lend me 400 gulden until then, you will be rescuing your friend from the greatest embarrassment. . . . Beloved friend and brother!—I know only too well how much I owe you! I beg you to be patient a little longer in regard to my old debts. I shall certainly repay you, that I promise on my honor. Once more I beg you, rescue me just this once from my horrible situation. . . ." [Puchberg's annotation: Sent 300 gulden.]

January 20, 1790: "Dearest Friend! . . . I am very much touched by your friendship and kindness. If you can and will send an extra hundred gulden, you will oblige me very greatly. . . ." [Puchberg's annotation: Sent 100 gulden.]

February 20, 1790: "Dearest Friend! . . . I beg you, most beloved friend, to lend me a few ducats just for a few days if you can do so, as I have to settle a matter at once which cannot be postponed. . . ." [Puchberg's annotation: Sent 25 gulden.]

April 8, 1790: [No salutation]: "If you can and will extricate me from a temporary embarrassment, then, for the love of God, do so! Whatever you can easily spare will be welcome. . . . Tomorrow, Friday, Count Hadik has invited me to perform . . . the trio I composed for you [the Divertimento for String Trio, K. 563]." [Puchberg's annotation: Sent 25 gulden.]

April 23, 1790: "Dearest Friend and Brother, If you can send me something, even though it be only the small sum you sent me last time, you will greatly oblige your ever grateful friend and brother. . . ." [Puchberg's annotation: Sent 25 gulden.]

On the day before the dress rehearsal of *The Magic Flute*, scheduled for September 28, Mozart still had not written the overture. The beginning was perfectly clear, a series of fanfares in the majestic key of E-flat, fortissimo—but then what?

Somewhere in the caverns of that extraordinary mind lay the bitter memory of an encounter that had taken place fully ten years earlier. The Italian-born virtuoso Muzio Clementi had been touring Europe with such spectacular success that Joseph II invited him to the imperial palace to engage in a competition with his own favorite, Mozart. "On entering the music room," Clementi later recalled, "I beheld an individual whose elegant attire led me to mistake him for an imperial *valet de chambre*. But we had no sooner entered into conversation than it turned on musical topics, and we soon recognized in each other, with sincere pleasure, brother artists—Mozart and Clementi."

On two imperial pianos, with keys that sometimes stuck, each of the brother artists improvised preludes, then played some original compositions, then sight-read some sonatas by Paisiello; then they were asked to select one of Paisiello's themes and to improvise variations on two pianos. The courtiers' applause left the competition undecided, but most witnesses seem to have thought that Clementi emerged victorious. He was both magnanimous and impressed; his subsequent compositions show a greater sensitivity than can be found in the brittle virtuosity of his earlier work. Mozart, unfortunately, was less gracious. He denounced Clementi's skill at thirds and sixths as that of "a mere *meccanicus*," scorned his compositions as "worthless," and added, for good measure, that "Clementi is a charlatan, like all Italians." Yet one of the works that Clementi had played on that occasion, the Sonata in B-flat (op. 47, no. 2), stayed in Mozart's head. Now, on the eve of the opening of *The Magic Flute*, he simply stole its opening theme (was it Bertolt Brecht who said that minor writers imitate whereas great writers steal?) and began writing the nervous fugato that he himself would conduct when the curtain rose at Schikaneder's theater on the following evening.

Mozart's whole system of composition defies explanation. He never worked out his ideas at a piano, like Chopin or Schumann. He did not fuss over preliminary sketches, like Beethoven, or labor over elaborate revisions, like Brahms. When he started on a wrong course, he soon recognized his error, threw away his draft, and started over again. He did not understand the process himself. "I cannot account for it," he once wrote. "When I am, as it were, completely myself, entirely alone, and of good cheer—say, travelling in a carriage, or walking after a good meal, or during the night when I cannot sleep; it is on such occasions that my ideas flow best and most abundantly. Whence and how they come, I know not; nor can I force them. Those ideas that please me I retain in memory, and am accustomed, as I have been told, to hum them to myself. . . . Provided I am not disturbed, my subject enlarges itself, becomes methodized and defined, and the whole, though it be long, stands almost complete and finished in my mind, so that I can survey it, like a fine picture or a beautiful statue, at a glance. Nor do I hear in my imagination the parts, *successively*, but I hear them, as it were, *gleich alles zusammen*, all at once. What a delight this is, I cannot tell!"

Gleich alles zusammen. His scores bear him out, for the process of composition can actually be seen in the frequent changes to fresh quills and newly thinned ink. He started with the whole idea complete in his head, and then he needed only to follow what Leopold had called *il file* (the thread). In whole sections of symphonies and operas, he wrote out the complete melodic line, for violins or voices, as well as the bass accompaniment, from beginning to end, then went back and filled in the parts for winds and middle voices. No other composer ever worked this way, for no other composer ever heard his music so clearly before it was written down. The last three symphonies, generally considered to be a flowering of almost inconceivable suddenness, were actually composed in a rather leisurely manner. Mozart spent six weeks finishing the three of them during the summer of 1788. The Linz Symphony, by contrast, was completed during a stopover that lasted a mere four days.

Mozart had such confidence in his skill (or such desperation about his finances) that when he was asked in early August, just two months before the premiere of the unfinished *Magic Flute*, to compose a wholly new opera in less than a month, he had no hesitation in accepting. The request came, after all, from the state authorities in Prague, where Leopold II was to accept the Bohemian crown on September 6, and Prague was no ordinary place. This was the city that had gone delirious over *Figaro* after its rather lukewarm reception in Vienna. Prague had commissioned a sequel and rejoiced in the result: *Don Giovanni.* So now Mozart bundled Constanze into a stagecoach, along with his dutiful young pupil, Franz Xaver Süssmayr, and set out for Bohemia.

The libretto assigned to him by the local authorities was entitled *La Clemenza di Tito,* a rather tattered hymn to monarchical magnanimity, originally written in 1734 by Pietro Trapassi, better known as Metastasio, and previously set to official music by Gluck, Galuppi, and half a dozen other composers. For this occasion, the libretto had already been turned over to Caterino Mazzolà, a friend of da Ponte and court poet to the elector of Saxony, who discarded a number of the stationary arias that were traditional to opera seria (the original *Clemenza* consisted of little else) and "modernized" the work by writing in a few duets and trios. Mozart seems to have been satisfied, since he wrote in his own catalogue of his works that *Clemenza* had been "made into a real opera by Signor Mazzolà."

It remains, however, a work of almost paralyzed stasis. Vitellia, indignant over the failure of her hope of marrying the Emperor Titus, demands that Sextus, her suitor and Titus's best friend, murder the emperor. Sextus unhappily agrees. Titus, who originally planned to marry Sextus's sister, Servilia, learns that she is in love with Annius, and therefore changes his mind and decides to marry Vitellia after all. Vitellia tries to stop Sextus from carrying out her assignment, but it is too late. The Capitol has already been set afire, and Sextus stabs a man he takes to be the emperor. It was the wrong man, and the stabbing was not fatal anyway, but Sextus is arrested and threatened with being thrown to the lions. Vitellia confesses her transgression and everyone receives the benefits of Titus's clemency. "I know all," the emperor sings, "forgive everyone and forget everything."

A similar condensation of the plot of *Figaro* or *Don Giovanni* (not to mention *Aïda* or *Tristan*) would probably sound similarly absurd. But Figaro and Don Giovanni are in themselves grand characters, whereas Titus and his entourage never become much more than a collection of walking statues. Their unreality is emphasized by the opera seria tradition of having many male roles sung by castrati, or, in our less demanding age, by women. It must have pleased Leopold II, in a time when his sister was being threatened by the Parisian mobs, to hear the chorus in Prague sing: "Oh, let us render thanks / To the Supreme Creator, / Who in Titus has preserved / The glory of the throne." It may also have pleased him, in a more subtle way, that Titus and the commander of his Praetorian Guard were the only figures onstage who sang with male voices, and that all the voices of conspiracy were those of sopranos. Apart from such political considerations, however, it remains strange to hear both Sextus and Annius played by women. It makes Sextus's love duets with Vitellia sound comradely, while his comradely exchanges with Titus sound like love duets.

Mozart had presumably been humming all the way to Prague. He settled in with his old friends the Duscheks, he a pianist, she a singer, and the quill pen began to fly across the manuscript pages. Mozart liked to scribble away in the midst of after-dinner conversations—everything was complete in his head, after all—and to take breaks for billiards and wine. He assigned Süssmayr to the task of writing the long recitatives between arias, and he himself worked like a man possessed. In just eighteen days, while messenger after messenger came to collect pages for the copyists, the entire opera was finished. (This was not considered as much of a feat in those prolific days as it would be now. Donizetti wrote the marvelous *Don Pasquale* in eleven days, and when someone observed that Rossini had devoted two weeks to the creation of *The Barber of Seville,* Donizetti said, "Rossini was always a slow worker.")

For those who do not like *Clemenza,* the haste of its composition explains its shortcomings. There are indeed longueurs in a mediocre libretto, and the whole tradition of the stately opera seria was an anachronism, made obsolete partly by Mozart himself in such buffo masterpieces as *Figaro.* But *La Clemenza di Tito,* dull on a first hearing, indifferent on a second, mildly interesting on a third, is really full of splendid music. The duets *"Deh prendi"* and *"Ah perdona"* are wholly worthy of the composer of *Figaro,* and Mozart's friendship with Anton Stadler, who was playing in the Prague orchestra, produced two unique arias with a sensuously weaving accompaniment by clarinet and basset horn. In the finale of Act I, too, Mozart produced an extraordinary experiment in a form he had never tried before, a combination of soloists and chorus declaiming on Sextus's treachery before the spectacle of the burning Capitol. Indeed, the entire work is, as Michael Levey aptly describes it in *The Life and Death of Mozart*, "not a sterile story of wooden people but . . . a poignant and terrible story of betrayal. . . . The combination of cosmic stage and small-scale suffering creatures, whose affections must give way before reasons of state, is something Mozart had hardly attempted before, and it gives a resigned, Racinian tone to the whole opera."

For those who admire *Clemenza*, on the other hand, it seems impossible to believe that Mozart could have written it all in eighteen days. There is, in fact, some evidence that he did not. Just as the success of *Figaro* led to the commissioning of *Don Giovanni*, so the success of *Don Giovanni* apparently led the producer, Domenico Guardasoni, at least to discuss the prospects of yet another Mozart work for his Italian opera company in Prague. Mozart wrote to Constanze in 1789 that he was "almost certain to receive 200 crowns" for an unspecified piece called simply "the opera." There may have been plans for some state visit to Prague by Joseph II, an emperor more worthy of Mozart's praises than was Leopold II, but the visit never took place. There are sketches for some numbers from *Clemenza* that seem to antedate 1791, and Madame Duschek gave a concert that spring, before the official commissioning of *Clemenza*, that included a Mozart obbligato for basset horn, which sounds very much like Vitellia's *"Non, più di fiori."*

Even if there was an earlier version of *Clemenza*, however, it cannot have been much more than a few bits and pieces, and we must marvel once again at the genius that, in the middle of *The Magic Flute*, and beginning to hear the somber indictments of the Requiem, could finish such a commission in the Duscheks' living room. Stendhal, for one, marveled; he is said to have wept on first hearing *La Clemenza di Tito*. Goethe was deeply impressed. Shelley wrote a poem, "I arise from dreams of thee," to the music of *"Ah perdona."* *Clemenza* was, in fact, one of Mozart's most popular operas during the first half of the nineteenth century. But the premiere, toward which so much energy had been expended, was a stinging failure. One anonymous critic described the principal castrato, presumably Sextus, as "a curtailed creature whose fleshy mass startled us every time he appeared," and dismissed the prima donna, presumably Vitellia, as someone who "sang more with her hands than her throat." The new Empress Maria Luisa summed up the imperial court's disdain. *La Clemenza di Tito,* she said, was *"una porcheria tedesca,"* a German piggishness.

In Sir George Grove's *Dictionary of Music and Musicians,* the entry on Anton Stadler says that he was apparently born in 1753, and that "little or nothing is known of his early life." He never wrote his memoirs, and whatever letters he may have written, nobody bothered to save. We know that he won an appointment to the imperial court orchestra in 1787, for 400 florins a year, and he seems to have been pensioned off in 1799, but, as Grove's biography concludes, "of Stadler after Mozart's death little is recorded."

Marcia Davenport, apparently relying mainly on her imagination, describes him in her impressionistic biography of Mozart as "the most conspicuous of the leeches ... a wretched lying thief who took every sort of advantage of Wolfgang, [who] shared his house and his pittances with Stadler." The principal evidence for this accusation is that when Mozart died, deep in debt, he was still owed 500 florins by Stadler, who never repaid his borrowings to Mozart's widow. He was, however, Mozart's friend, and apparently a brilliant performer on the clarinet. ("My thanks to thee, brave virtuoso," one ecstatic critic wrote after a Stadler concert in 1785. "Never should I have thought that a clarinet could be capable of imitating a human voice so deceptively as it was imitated by thee. . . .") To this friendship we owe the existence of some of Mozart's most superb woodwind music, the clarinet trio (K. 498), the clarinet quintet (K. 581), which he unfailingly referred to as "Stadler's quintet," and finally the clarinet concerto (K. 622). These were wonderful gifts, and yet Stadler was not purely a recipient. As Mühlfeld later served Brahms, so Stadler taught Mozart what the clarinet could do, taught him all the technical possibilities that Mozart heard sounding only in his inner ear.

The clarinet was still a novelty, at that point, in the rather disorganized evolution of the woodwind instruments. It was "invented" at the beginning of the eighteenth century by a flute maker named

J. C. Denner, whose invention consisted mainly of discovering that a "speaker hole" in the back of the traditional pipe could make it overblow in twelfths. Thus a two-foot instrument could acquire a range of nearly four octaves. The early-eighteenth-century clarinet was still a rather simple instrument, however, and its tone may be deduced from its name, a diminutive of the older and brassier Italian *clarino,* for it was said to "sound from afar like a trumpet." It was used, to that effect, in certain orchestral works by Handel and Vivaldi, and in Rameau's operas *Zoroastre* and *Acanthe et Céphise.* In none of this tooting, however, was there any indication of the richness that the clarinet could provide. That was Stadler's revelation.

He seems to have been a tinkerer. He altered his own clarinet so that it could descend below its bottom E down to a C below middle C. He also experimented with the basset horn, which had been invented in 1770 by an instrument maker named Mayrhofer, and which attempted to duplicate the clarinet's range by bending a thin four-foot tube into a scythe-shaped horn. The basset horn made a dark and lovely sound—Mozart not only wrote his elaborate obbligato for Stadler to play in *Clemenza* but he also gave the basset horn a special prominence in his Requiem—and Brahms, on hearing several of Mozart's arias sung with the accompaniment of basset horns, wrote to Clara Schumann: "I do not think any instrument blends so perfectly with the human voice." Stadler preferred the brilliance of the clarinet, however, and he showed Mozart how its lower tones, the so-called chalumeau register, could produce a sonority unlike that of any other instrument in the orchestra.

I, too, struggled with those beautiful low tones, nearly forty years ago, and what a prolonged and ultimately doomed struggle it was. (Perhaps I should apologize for repeatedly introducing myself into this story, or simply refrain from doing so, but remember that the distinction between amateur musicians and professional virtuosos is a modern perversion, in which the passive audience pays a few highly trained experts to provide entertainment. In Mozart's Vienna, many more people could enjoy playing his music, and simply did so.) After a year in Europe, where I had by now discovered the agonies of working on the Chopin *Études,* I returned home to find that a friend of the family—my godfather, actually, and a composer of minor repute—had left us on loan, for unexplained reasons, a clarinet. How beautiful it looked, all silver and polished wood, lying there in five fragments in its fitted bed of green velvet. I immediately enrolled myself in the Longy School in Cambridge under the tutelage of a young instructor named David Glazer.

We began by taking my godfather's expensive clarinet out of its case and attaching a reed to the mouthpiece, and then the first lesson started. The first lesson was that when you blow into a clarinet, expecting to emit a mellow tone that will sound like Reginald Kell, nothing comes out except the white sound of thin air. The second lesson is that tighter pressure of the lips on the reed and a concentrated effort that feels like the hemorrhaging of a lung will produce a tone that sounds roughly like the skraak of a strangling pigeon. From that nadir, we progressed, slowly, to the first scale, the first arpeggio, and the first little book of songs with titles like "Over the Hill" and "The Rainbow" and "The Skaters."

The trouble was that I did not want to play "The Skaters"; I wanted to play Mozart's clarinet quintet. Mr. Glazer disapproved. He insisted that I learn legato phrasing by practicing "The Skaters," but I, once I had learned to make the clarinet produce its mellifluous sound, bought the Mozart score and secretly practiced nothing but that. At the end of the term, I hoped to surprise Mr. Glazer with my mastery of the Larghetto, but he only regarded me with the dismay of the teacher betrayed, and so, of course, I performed little more than a series of skraaks, and then I went back to dreaming about becoming a piano virtuoso. In the decades that have passed since then, we have all gone our separate ways, but I was only mildly surprised when a friend recently gave me a recording of the clarinet sonatas of Brahms, beautifully played by none other than David Glazer. Now that I am no longer a prospective piano virtuoso, I wonder whether I could ever have learned to play the more exciting parts of Mozart's clarinet concerto.

Mozart started in 1789 to write a concerto for basset horn, but he put it aside after the first two hundred bars and did not take it up again until the summer of 1791, when he transposed it from G to A for Stadler's clarinet. It is, partly because of the tone of the clarinet, the most autumnal of works, the most valedictorian. The orchestral part, lightly scored for strings and woodwinds, is almost translucent. The clarinet, swooping down from the heights of Pamina's sorrowful songs into the depths of Stadlerian invention, resembles nothing so much as an osprey, winging up again with its catch, soaring, forever free.

Mozart's choice of E-flat for *The Magic Flute* was scarcely haphazard—key signatures rarely are—for it represented, to his ear, a kind of magisterial solidity. Its three flats are supposed to have a Masonic meaning, but it seems just as likely that Mozart's Masonism reflected his views about E-flat. Few other composers have liked the key so well. To Bach, who created much of our sense of tonality by the way he used keys in *The Well-Tempered Clavier,* E-flat lacked any single character. He demonstrated its solemnity in the Prelude of Book I and the Fugue of Book II, but the E-flat Prelude of Book II is a pastorale, and the Fugue in Book I is a playful little piece that might just as well have been written in B-flat or F. Beethoven saw heroic possibilities in E-flat, perhaps because it is the relative major of that most heroic of all keys, C minor (the Fifth Symphony), and so he used it for such grand enterprises as the *Eroica* and the *Emperor.* The less heroic Romantics were less attracted to the key. Chopin, for example, hardly ever used it, and when the pattern of key signatures in the *Études* and the Preludes required E-flat, he established it as a point of departure for his wanderings into more exotic harmonies.

Mozart felt no such nervousness. As in his other favorite keys, like C and D major, he seemed to consider the simplicity of tonality as a force for stability. And in E-flat, one of the most stable of keys, he composed a body of work that would have made him celebrated even if he had never written in any other key at all. Aside from *The Magic Flute,* he used it for the first of the three great last symphonies of 1788 (K. 543), for the *Sinfonia concertante* for Violin and Viola (K. 364), and for four of his great piano concerti (K. 271, 365, 449, and 482). He seems to have grown increasingly fond of E-flat as a tonality for chamber music, and so it appears in the third of the Haydn Quartets (K. 428), in the marvelous Quintet for Piano and

Winds (K. 452), in the second Piano Quartet (K. 493), the Clarinet Trio (K. 498), and in two of his last major works for strings, the Divertimento for violin, viola, and cello (K. 563) and the final quintet (K. 614).

Mozart was almost alone among composers in his mastery of the stringed instruments. We have, of course, the displays of a Viotti or a Vieuxtemps, but one always feels that pianists like Schumann and Brahms had to rely on a violin virtuoso like Joachim to explain the fine points of double-stopping. Mozart learned such things in infancy, for his father was not only a professional violinist but the author of a learned treatise on the techniques of playing the instrument. Mozart himself played the violin excellently but preferred the greater richness of the viola, and so, when it came time for him to write string quartets, he wrote quartets that could only have been created by a musician who loved to join in playing them. They are written from the inside.

The occasion for their creation came, however, from the outside. From the series of dances known as serenades and divertimenti, Joseph Haydn had been developing a more concentrated use of the string quartet, treating each instrument as a separate voice and thus creating an ensemble of equals. This development reached a fruition in November of 1781, on the occasion of the visit to Vienna of Grand Duke Paul of Russia, later to become Czar Paul II, when the visitors attended a concert of quartets that Haydn had written in what he called "an entirely new and original manner." The six so-called Russian Quartets were duly published as opus 33 and dedicated to the grand duke, who rewarded the composer with a box studded with diamonds.

From Mozart, there was a more important response, the electric moment of genius encountering genius with what Melville once called "the shock of recognition." Inspired by the Russian Quartets, Mozart wrote, over the course of three years, the six magnificent Haydn Quartets, which he sent to the older man with a touching letter of dedication: "I send my six sons to you, most celebrated and very dear friend. They are, indeed, the fruit of a long and laborious study; but [I hope] that these children may one day prove a source of consolation." On hearing the last three performed at a soirée in

February of 1785, Haydn approached Leopold Mozart and delivered the testimonial that showed that he too knew the shock of recognition. "Before God and as an honest man," he told Leopold, "I tell you that your son is the greatest composer known to me either in person or by name. . . ."

Charles Rosen has shrewdly observed that three times in Mozart's life, after writing a series of quartets, he turned to the string quintet, "as if the experience of composing for only four instruments prompted him to take up the richer medium." After the Haydn Quartets came the great quintets in C major and G minor (K. 515 and 516). The next sequence occurred in 1789, when Mozart voyaged to Berlin in search of concerts and commissions. His welcome was warm but not very lucrative. King Frederick William II, who played the cello, gave him 100 Friedrichsdor and commissioned six quartets, along with six easy piano sonatas for his daughter, and then sent him on his way. Back in Vienna, Mozart wrote only one of the sonatas—K. 576, a splendid work but by no means easy—and three of the quartets (K. 575, 589, and 590). They are admirable, as Mozart's works almost always are, but they betray signs of weariness, of work done conscientiously on assignment. Mozart's mind was on other things, on Constanze's illness, on his debts, and, once again, on the richer possibilities of the quintet.

We do not know the exact circumstances surrounding the composition of the last two quintets, in D major and E-flat (K. 593 and 614). They are said to have been commissioned by a Hungarian merchant named Johann Trost, who was also an amateur violinist and a friend of Haydn. At the same time, the prominence of the cello, particularly in the questioning opening phrases of the D major, suggests that Mozart was still thinking of pleasing the portly king of Prussia. Mozart's farewell to chamber music was, in any case, wholly lacking in the elegiac quality that we have come to expect in his last year. The opening Allegro di molto of the E-flat Quintet starts with an energetic trilling theme that most critics consider an homage to Haydn; it actually sounds more like an anticipation of Beethoven, who, after all, owed his own homage to Haydn. There comes, then, a marvelously eloquent set of variations in andante—an eloquence that strongly reminds us of *The Magic Flute* ensembles that Mozart was soon to undertake—and a rather strenuous minuet and a bustling finale, both echoing the rumbustious spirit that Haydn bequeathed to Beethoven.

But what banalities such statements are! How can one write about a string quintet without sounding like those forlorn people who produce the homilies on the backs of record albums? Operas and religious works have texts that can provide the critic with footholds, sometimes all too much so. Piano music is more abstract, and yet one can speak from one's own experience. But my experience in playing the violin ended when I was about seven. My mother had the misbegotten idea that it would be good for my older brother and me to be in the same class at school, and so, by skipping the second grade, I kept up with him, I fiercely competitive, he haunted by the nipping of a younger equal. Having made this miscalculation, my mother also decided, contradictorily, that my brother and I should in other ways be differentiated. He was to wear red clothes, for example, while I was assigned to blue, and when the music lessons began, he was to play the violin, and I the piano. At her funeral, she said (she being not yet forty), he would play Bach's Air for the G String, and I would play the Moonlight Sonata. I howled for red clothes, of course, and for violin lessons at Longy.

I learned to play a scale, and to shift from the G string to the D, and to luxuriate in the delight of sawing away at two strings at once. But after a few months, my violin teacher decreed that I lacked talent. He kept my brother as his pupil and consigned me back to the purgatory of Czerny's piano studies. My mother herself took up the violin at the age of about forty and got as far as some Beethoven slow movements before returning to the requirements of the kitchen. My father, throughout all this, practiced doggedly, behind closed doors, on Bach's suites for unaccompanied cello. So we never played quartets, and so Mozart's music for strings remains to me a little alien, music of unsurpassable beauty, and yet hard to grasp.

There are, then, the usual alternatives. The first is to be technical. Thus Rosen writes of a beautiful passage in the C Major Quintet, "a simple plagal phrase IV-I . . . is decorated. . . . The F Major starts once again and then is turned into F Minor, and the cadence is lengthened, and made deceptive. . . ." The other alternative is to be sentimentally descriptive. Thus Aldous Huxley on the slow movement of Beethoven's A Minor Quartet: "It was an unimpassioned music, transparent, pure, and crystalline, like a tropical sea, an Alpine lake. Water on water, calm sliding over calm; the according of level horizons and waveless expanses, a counterpoint of serenities." The scene, near the end of *Point Counter Point,* becomes still more maudlin. A character called Spandrell believes that "the music was a proof; God existed." The more worldly Rampion retorts that it is "just a hymn in praise of eunuchism." Spandrell insists that "it's the beatific vision, it's heaven," but he can prove his point only by getting himself shot to death.

No viola player, and Mozart was always a viola player, would ever do or say or even think such things. To a viola player, who sits at the center of things, the richness of a quintet is simply that a second viola provides a greater weight among the inner voices, and a diminished seventh chord, though it may sound like the harmony of doom, is simply a diminished seventh chord. Or as Stephen Crane wrote near the end of *The Red Badge of Courage,* "He had been to touch the great death, and found that, after all, it was but the great death."

In the finale of Act I of *The Magic Flute,* there occurs the only instance ever recorded of a racial clash being halted by a glockenspiel. Papageno is trying to lead Pamina to a reunion with Tamino when they are arrested by the ferocious Monostatos, who cries, "I shall rule by force and cruelty! / Ho, you slaves, bring chains and ropes!" Monostatos's slaves promptly arrive to do his bidding, but Papageno takes out his magic glockenspiel and begins to play a tune of such charm that Monostatos and his troop all begin dancing about. "This jingles so softly, this jingles so clear!" they chorus. "La la ra, la la la la ra, la la la ra. . . ."

It was a scene that Mozart apparently intended as a lyrical allegory, but one that Schikaneder played, to great applause, as farce. So Mozart decided on a trick. He crept backstage one night, and while Schikaneder was tapping on his stage-prop bells, Mozart played an offstage arpeggio of his own. The flustered Schikaneder, author, star, and impresario of *The Magic Flute,* turned toward the wings and cried, "Shut up!" More laughter and applause from the audience. "This joke," Mozart delightedly wrote to Constanze, "taught many of the audience for the first time that Papageno does not play the instrument himself."

By now, the glockenspiel is itself a joke, partly because of its name, partly because we have become accustomed to considering the classical instruments as a stately series of creations all unchanged since time immemorial. But just as the piano was changing from year to year, with different improvements from different manufacturers, so the orchestral instruments were evolving in any number of ways, and nobody was more willing than Mozart to experiment with the newly invented basset horns and clarinets, to compose a bassoon concerto or an oboe quartet. In his last year, as a result of the unsuccessful concert tour to Frankfurt for the coronation of Leopold II, he decided to write anything for anyone who would pay him. Specifically, as he wrote to Constanze, "I have now made up my mind to compose at once the Adagio for the clockmaker and then to slip a few ducats into the hand of my dear little wife."

The clockmaker was Count Josef Deym (his aristocratic lineage is somewhat uncertain), who had to leave Vienna because of a duel and then made himself, in exile, an expert in the molding and display of wax statues of the dead. He returned to Vienna in 1790, under an assumed name, possibly his original name, and presented himself as the owner of the Müller Waxworks on the Stock-im-Eisen Platz. The pièce de résistance was a mausoleum featuring the waxen cadaver of the late Emperor Joseph II, guarded by another tomb for the late Field Marshal Ernst von Laudon. For musical diversion, Deym's waxworks contained a mechanical Pan playing his pipes, a "Bedroom of the Graces" that resounded to the music of flutes, a robot canary, and various clocks that gave concerts on the hour. For one of these clocks, Deym commissioned the impoverished Mozart to provide a suitable composition. "It is the kind of composition which I detest . . ." Mozart wrote to Constanze. "I compose a bit of it every day—but I have to break off now and then as I get bored. . . . But I still hope that I shall be able to force myself gradually to finish it. If it were for a large instrument and the work would sound like an organ piece, then I might get some fun out of it. But as it is, the works consist solely of little pipes, which sound too high-pitched and childish for my taste."

The dark and gloomy Adagio and Allegro in F Minor (K. 594) is hard to imagine on any "childish" mechanical clock. We can hear it recorded only on full-size organs, where it sounds quite worthy of a mausoleum for the wax figures of Joseph II and Marshal Laudon, but it is most readily available, along with its sequel, the Fantasia in F Minor (K. 608), in the volume that contains Mozart's collected works for four-hand piano. It is a volume that provides, to the middle-aged pianist who will never reach Carnegie Hall, more pleasure than all the great concerti. Four-hand music, as Schubert later demonstrated in his four volumes of duets, is the ideal music for amateurs, for the amateur secretly wants an audience, and yet he is all too aware of how his mistakes must sound to dinner guests sitting in stiff embarrassment on his living-room sofa. In four-hand music, the sonorities are the same, but the mistakes are made jointly, and besides, the other four-hand player is often an amiable housewife who sits close on the piano bench.

The four-hand piano believeth all things, hopeth all things, endureth all things, and so it undertakes not only four-hand sonatas, not only transcribed symphonies and string quartets, but also music written for instruments that we shall never hear. G. Henle Verlag in Munich has published the mysterious Andante for a Little Organ (K. 616), the only one of Mozart's late works for Deym's mausoleum clocks that actually did get transferred to a series of mechanical pipes and performed on the hour. On the piano, too, we can hear the Adagio for Glass Harmonica (K. 617A), but here there is also a fanatic named Bruno Hoffmann who has dedicated his life to recreating and recording the sound of one of Mozart's strangest instruments.

The glass harmonica seems to have been invented in London in 1743 by one Richard Puckeridge, who collected a number of glasses of different sizes and filled them with water to various levels to achieve various tones when he rubbed them with his finger. The device became a kind of fad—Gluck himself composed and performed a concerto for it in 1746—and it fascinated Benjamin Franklin, who, in his characteristic way, set out to improve it. He had a series of hemispheric glasses blown, ranging in diameter from three to nine inches, and then he had thirty-seven of them mounted on a spindle, which was mounted in a harpsichord case and connected to a treadle. The performer worked the treadle with his feet, making all the glasses spin, and then played on the rims with his finger. "The advantages of this instrument," Franklin wrote to a friend, "are that its tones are incomparably sweet beyond those of any other; that they may be swelled and softened at pleasure by stronger or weaker pressure of the finger, and continued at any length."

The first virtuoso on this instrument was an Englishwoman named Marianne Davies, who toured Italy and Austria in the 1760s, making a great impression on Gluck and giving lessons to Marie Antoinette. Dr. Franz Anton Mesmer, the hypnotist, made his own version of the instrument, and according to a letter by Leopold Mozart in 1773, "Wolfgang too has played upon it. How I should like to have one!" Mozart produced nothing for the instrument at the time, but his interest was revived in 1791 by the appearance of a new virtuoso, Marianne Kirchgessner, a woman of twenty-one, who was blind. She gave a concert in Vienna that June, which Mozart apparently attended, and, according to her own announcement, "I deem it my duty to respond with all that lies within my power to the exhortation, so flattering to me, to allow myself to be heard on the armonica once more. I shall therefore . . . hold another grand musical concert next week . . . and play on the armonica an entirely new and surpassingly beautiful concert quintet accompanied by wind instruments by Herr Kappellmeister Mozart [This is the eerie Adagio and Rondo, K. 617, for glass harmonica, flute, oboe, viola, and cello] . . . and such pleasing pieces as to persuade every connoisseur of music entirely that the armonica is the noblest of all musical instruments, exciting not sad and melancholy, but rather glad, gentle and elevated feelings."

The Viennese love for strange instruments grew inexorably into a passion for instruments that played themselves. Schikaneder organized a concert performed entirely by robot instruments, and his chief rival organized a counterconcert by scores of mechanical birds, which imitated every sound to be heard in the Vienna Woods. There now appeared on the scene Johann Nepomuk Maelzel, musician, engineer, creator of artificial limbs, and inventor of the metronome that every music student comes to fear and hate. If he had been born two centuries later, he might have created the Moog synthesizer.

Maelzel began his career as an inventor by building mechanical military bands, which played marches for drums, cymbals, and up to sixteen trumpets. He devised an automatic orchestra called the panharmonium, for which Beethoven created a quasi-symphony called the *Battle of Vittoria.* He even combined his mechanical instruments with mechanical people and mechanical weather. In Maelzel's version of Haydn's *Seasons,* according to one chronicler, "in winter, the snow fell, and the shepherds' huts were buried by avalanches; in summer, the rain streamed down, the thunder rumbled. . . ."

Count Deym, alias Müller, who had commissioned Mozart to write music for the mechanical clock organs in his mausoleum, apparently sent an emissary to the Rauhensteingasse during the anarchy that followed Mozart's death. He had a wax impression made of the composer's dead face. He also acquired one of Mozart's suits and created an artificial cadaver to be laid out alongside those of the Emperor Joseph and Marshal Laudon. The addition was evidently not a great success, and the mausoleum moved to the Kohlmarkt a few years later and then went bankrupt. The death mask reverted to Constanze, who, in what was said to be a household accident, smashed it.

Emanuel Schikaneder, for all his feathers and his glockenspiel, was no fool. He was, in fact, an extraordinary example of talent and energy triumphant over circumstance. He was born in Regensburg in 1751, in conditions of poverty far below the threadbare professionalism of the Mozarts. While young Mozart was touring the capitals of Europe as a court prodigy, Schikaneder was scrabbling through the carnivals of southern Germany as an itinerant violinist. In his adolescence, he became an actor, adept in everything from tragic fathers to street-corner buffoons. He was wholly uneducated, but by his midtwenties, he was already the manager of a wandering repertory troupe, and his repertory included *King Lear* and *Hamlet,* Goethe's *Clavigo* and Voltaire's *Sémiramis.*

He specialized in spectacles. Even in Mozart's time, he staged one play with an army in two hundred tents and full-scale cavalry charges. He wrote an operetta that featured a balloonist who was to take off as part of the finale. He presented a "miraculous marvel" named Niklas Roger who came onstage in the costume of a Spanish bullfighter and had himself set afire without apparent harm. In his later years, Schikaneder organized productions in which five hundred infantrymen and fifty cavalrymen wheeled about onstage, and the volleys of gunfire became so noisy that they had to be banned, in 1807, by imperial decree. When reproached for his vulgarities, he is said to have replied, "My sole aim is to work for the box office and to see what is most effective on stage, so as to fill both the house and the cash-box."

Schikaneder's most extravagant years were still ahead of him when he proposed to Mozart, in the spring of 1791, that they collaborate on *The Magic Flute.* The conditions of this collaboration are still disputed. One version is that Schikaneder's little troupe in the suburban Theater-auf-der-Wieden was on the verge of bankruptcy, and he pleaded with Mozart, his fellow Mason, to save him. There is contradictory evidence, however, that Schikaneder had recently achieved a great success with an opera based on *Oberon* and was simply looking for a sequel. It was probably beneath Mozart's dignity as a court composer to write an operetta for a suburban repertory troupe, but on the other hand, Schikaneder's plan for a German vaudeville-opera appealed to Mozart's intermittent nationalism. Besides, Schikaneder's company included Constanze's sister, Josepha Hofer, who was destined to be the first Queen of the Night.

What Schikaneder wanted, in any event, was a fairy-tale spectacle with a major role for himself. He had already found his story, *Lulu, oder die Zauberflöte,* by A. J. Liebeskind, published in 1786 in a collection of Oriental tales entitled *Dschinnistan,* under the editorship of C. M. Wieland. Prince Lulu, in this little drama, wanders near an enchanted castle in the kingdom of Khurasan and encounters the resident fairy, Perifime. She pleads with him to recover her magic sword, which has been stolen by the evil magician Dilseng-buin, who is also courting her daughter Sidi. To help him in his quest, she gives him a magic ring, which enables him to change his appearance, and a magic flute, which charms everyone who hears it. And so on.

The Magic Flute starts out in much the same way, but with some-what more melodrama. Prince Tamino rushes onstage in flight from a large wood-and-canvas serpent ("Help! Help! Or else I am lost!") and then faints dead away. Three veiled ladies appear with silver javelins, kill the serpent, argue protractedly about which of them should remain with the fallen prince, and then drift off again. Pa-pageno the bird-catcher arrives to sing his famous opening song, and then the three ladies reappear to show Tamino a portrait of Pamina, held captive by the wicked Sarastro. *"Ein Bösewicht,"* they call him, a villain. Tamino instantly falls in love with the portrait. The Queen of the Night then enters to lament her daughter's kidnapping by the *Bösewicht* and to promise that if Tamino rescues the girl, "forever then shall she be thine." The three ladies, who serve the Queen of the Night, drift in once again and present Tamino with a magic flute that charms the very beasts of the woods (luring, traditionally, a flock of children out onto the stage in floppy lion costumes). For Pa-pageno, who also serves the Queen of the Night, they provide a glockenspiel.

Toward the end of Act I, however, all becomes confusion. Tam-ino reaches Sarastro's empire and finds it to be a Temple of Wisdom. "My son, you are ensnared in error," an old priest tells him. Tamino echoes the indictment by the Queen of the Night, but the priest expresses surprise that he has believed a mere woman. "A woman does little, talks much," says the priest. "Then all is false as false can be . . ." cries Tamino. "Yes, I will leave, glad and free, never return again." The priest persuades him, however, to remain until "friendship's guiding hand / has led you to the holy band." And so the long process of initiation begins.

This wrenching change in the story has inevitably inspired a considerable amount of critical scrutiny. The traditional explanation is that Schikaneder's strongest rival, Marinelli of the Leopoldstheater, produced on June 8 an operetta also drawn from Wieland's Oriental tales and entitled *The Magic Zither,* thus prompting Schikaneder to scurry around and rewrite his libretto. "Some of the music was already written," according to Dent, "but Schikaneder was not going to have that wasted, so the join was covered up as well as could be managed." Recent scholarship has strongly challenged this tradition, citing evidence not only of the eighteenth-century indifference to plagiarism (the similar title was never changed, after all) but also of Mozart's indifference to Marinelli's novelty. "To cheer myself up, I then went to see the new opera which is making a sensation," he wrote Constanze, "but there is nothing in it at all."

The simplest explanation for the change in direction is that Mozart didn't like what Schikaneder had written and asked him to change it. None of his previous major operas had been so witless as the story of Prince Lulu. *Figaro, Don Giovanni, Così* are all, in their way, statements of political or social purpose. One can imagine, then, the standard arguments between composer and librettist, the composer saying that he has nothing to work with, the librettist saying that what he has written will work well onstage. The arguments were further complicated by the fact that Schikaneder seems to have assigned much of the actual writing to a young member of his troupe, Johann Georg Metzler, called Giesecke, another Freemason, a mineralogist and lawyer of sorts, a stage manager, a member of the chorus (he played the minor role of Monostatos's First Slave). A half century later, Giesecke claimed that Schikaneder had actually produced nothing but his own Papageno scenes, and that he, Giesecke, had written everything else. Perhaps, then, Schikaneder was primarily the chairman and coordinator. In any case, the fairy-tale spectacle that he had originally conceived gradually became a portentously Masonic opera.

Although it is indisputable that some revision of the libretto took place, the contrast between the opening scenes and the rest of the opera is actually less radical than it sometimes seems. Mozart (or Schikaneder, or Giesecke) never tells us explicitly in the opening that Sarastro is really a villain, or that the Queen of the Night is a tragic victim. We simply hear the queen and her ladies make those accusations. Still, the apparent contradictions in *The Magic Flute* have inspired generations of interpreters to seek a unifying thesis. As early as 1794, a pamphlet by Johann Valentin Eybel argued that the Queen of the Night represented the tyranny of Louis XIV, the three ladies represented the three estates, and so on. Moritz Zille, as we have seen, offered in 1866 a more explicitly Austrian political interpretation—Maria Theresa as the Queen of the Night, Tamino as Joseph II, and Pamina as the Austrian people. At about the same time, an anticlerical rationalist named Georg Friedrich Daumier insisted that the Queen of the Night represented Superstition, and therefore her three ladies must represent the three religions, Christianity, Judaism, and Islam.

There was never any doubt that *The Magic Flute* reflects Mozart's involvement in the pseudoreligion of Freemasonry. Mozart had joined the movement in 1784, and the head of his Newly Crowned Hope Lodge was Baron von Gebler, to whose Masonic libretto of *Thamos, King of Egypt* he had already written a series of marches and choruses. He also frequently attended the True Unity Lodge, of which Haydn was a member, and of which the Venerable, or leader, was an eminent scientist, Ignaz von Born, generally considered to be the model for Sarastro. One of the scriptures among the Masons of the eighteenth century was a novel called *Sethos,* said to have been translated from an ancient Greek manuscript by the Abbé Jean Terrasson in 1731, and translated into German in 1732 and again in 1778. It tells of an Egyptian prince's wanderings through Africa and of his initiation into a community of the elect. The description of this initiation, through a series of trials by fire and water, is more or less what Mozart and Schikaneder grafted onto the original tale of Prince Lulu and his magic flute. The grafting was a hasty job, leaving many mysteries. We never discover, for example, who Papageno really is, or why he changes from a servant of the Queen of the Night into Tamino's fellow supplicant. (Robert Moberly offers the interesting conjecture that Papageno might be an illegitimate child of the Queen of the Night, which would account for the chaste love duets he sings with his then half sister Pamina.) We understand even less of the ambiguities in Monostatos, who begins as the would-be attacker of Pamina and then is driven off by the Queen of the Night and yet ends as the queen's choice for Pamina's hand.

All these contradictions are merely challenges to the Masonic exegetes, of whom the most dedicated is Jacques Chailley, professor of the history of music at the Sorbonne and author of *The Magic Flute, Masonic Opera.* To him, every twist of Schikaneder's Viennese clowning masks a hidden Masonic message, and even the most conventional passages in Mozart's music contain a profoundly symbolic significance. He devotes an entire chapter, for example, to the first three chords of the overture, which, because the last two are played twice in succession, he makes out to be five chords, five being the mystic number representing women (as three is the number for men). The fugue theme that Mozart stole from Clementi is, similarly, not a last-minute expedient but rather a musical expression of the Masonic initiate knocking at the temple door.

Chailley's book makes a persuasive argument, as does Brigid Brophy's *Mozart the Dramatist,* that all the apparent nonsense in *The Magic Flute* can be interpreted in terms of Masonic ritual and symbolism. Tamino's wandering through the darkness represents the first stage of initiation, the so-called Trial by Earth, in which an applicant is enclosed in a pitch-black "Cabinet of Reflection" and instructed to write, by candlelight, his "Philosophic Testament." The oath of silence, which requires Tamino not to speak to Pamina, and thus inspires her to sing the quasi-tragic *"Ach, ich fühl's,"* is part of the Trial by Air, and the ritual marches through water and fire at the end of Act II represent the conclusion of the traditional Masonic initiation. "Rejoice! Rejoice! The victory is gained!" the offstage chorus sings.

But to say that the plot of *The Magic Flute* expresses Masonic rituals does not make it any less absurd. The philosophy of the Masonic movement seems to have been nothing but a series of platitudes, a belief in a vaguely pantheistic Creator of the Universe, in a brotherhood of man and a universality of virtue, or, as everyone sings at the end of *The Magic Flute:* "Thus courage has triumphed and virtue will rise / The laurels of wisdom receiving as prize." These views are unexceptionable, but they are not very interesting either, and there is something inherently unattractive about a movement that protects its belief in brotherhood and virtue behind a series of secret tests and rituals, and behind repeated threats of death to anyone who fails to win acceptance.

While there is no reason to doubt the sincerity of Mozart's Freemasonry, or that of Haydn, or, for that matter, George Washington, there is also no reason to believe that he took it quite so seriously as the Masonic interpreters of *The Magic Flute* imply. The Masonic lodges of Vienna in the eighteenth century were also social clubs, where members could eat and drink and gossip and do a bit of business with their lodge brothers. The idea that Freemasonry is something less than a monastic commitment becomes clearer when we listen to Papageno parody the initiation of Tamino. Thus:

SECOND PRIEST (to Papageno): Will you, too, fight for the love of wisdom?

PAPAGENO: Fighting is not exactly in my line. To be truthful, I don't demand any wisdom, either. I'm just a child of nature, who is satisfied with sleep, food, and drink. And if I once could catch a pretty little wife—

In the Masonic interpretation, Papageno simply represents the theatrical tradition that every noble love story requires a parallel romance among the servants. But Papageno is not a minor *doppelgänger*. He is really the main character, not only because Schikaneder created him, wrote his lines, and played the role himself, but because Mozart gave him the best parts to sing. And the emotional climax of the opera is not the solemn final chorus but the penultimate encounter of Papageno and Papagena ("Pa-pa-pa-pa," and so on). While Sarastro and his chorus sing a rather sterile hymn to abstractions ("The sun's radiant glory has vanquished the night"), Papageno and his bride think in more earthy terms of populating the world: "What a joy for us is near when the Gods . . . will send us tiny children dear. . . . First we will have a Papageno. Then we will have a Papagena. Then comes another Papageno. . . ." It is Papageno, in short, who makes it clear that *The Magic Flute* is not about Masonic rituals of virtue but about love, that "wife and man, and man and wife, / Reach the height of godly life."

♪　♪　♪

It is considered mawkish nowadays to devote too much attention to the celebrated specter of "the man in gray," but he did exist, and he did haunt Mozart's last year. His name, which Mozart never learned, was Leutgeb, and he was dressed entirely in gray as a sign of mourning for the recent death of the wife of his employer, Count Franz Walsegg zu Stuppach. This count, who happened to own the house occupied by Mozart's friend Michael Puchberg, was an amateur cellist who nursed vain ambitions of becoming a composer. Instead of actually writing music, he commissioned impoverished composers to provide works that he could claim as his own creations. Since his wife had died that February, he was now contemplating the gratifications of honoring her with a fake requiem mass that he could conduct in the private chapel on his estate. He therefore sent his steward Leutgeb to the Rauhensteingasse with an unsigned letter to Mozart, asking him to compose the mass, in any form or style he chose, and to name his own price for carrying out the commission. It was a weary July day, and Mozart was oppressed with innumerable anxieties. Schikaneder was importuning him to finish *The Magic Flute*, Constanze was off in Baden, in her ninth month of pregnancy, and the unpaid bills were everywhere. Mozart named a price of fifty ducats, the equivalent of perhaps one thousand dollars today. The man in gray nodded his acceptance and departed.

Requiem aeternam dona eis, Domine, et lux perpetua luceat eis. . . . I have heard many masses many times in many places, and yet the familiar words always seem a unique expression of the stone vaults where I first heard them—Bach mourning the grayness of postwar Berlin, Verdi's trombones celebrating a Roman spring. The Mozart Requiem I heard for the first time in the cathedral of Lucerne, during the same festival that featured the piano playing of Edwin Fischer. Being penniless, I slept in the woods every night, in a haunted, rain-soaked forest called the Gütschwald, emerging every morning to take long walks around the lake to the gloomy mountain called Pilatus and to the cottage where Wagner wrote *Die Meistersinger*. The cathedral of Lucerne, standing on a modest hill on the north side of the lake, is a rather undistinguished specimen of Swiss Baroque (1633), but it has its traditions. There once was a Benedictine monastery on this site, founded in 750, when the village of Lucaria was a Christian outpost in the Dark Ages. More recent inhabitants recalled that during the 1930s, Arturo Toscanini, a refugee from Fascism, had conducted a shattering performance of the *Missa solemnis*. In my time, 1946, the conditions were less exalted and the performance more modest. The conductor was Paul Kletzki, taut, acerbic, and very professional, and the audience was, as it so often is in the smaller cities of central Europe, hopeful rather than expectant. The men waited patiently in shabby gray suits, and the women wore their hair in gray buns. Up in the pillared loft, where I sat on a thin wooden bench, two bats flittered tirelessly about under the eaves. The dark and measured tones of the *Introit* seemed to come from very far away. *Requim aeternum dona eis, Domine. . . .*

Mozart sketched in about forty pages, including that dark *Introit* with its mysterious bassoons and basset horns, including the powerful *Kyrie* fugue. Then he had to stop. Guardasoni, the opera producer in Prague, wrote to him that he needed a new opera for the coronation of Emperor Leopold II. As Mozart was about to board the coach for Prague, he was accosted by the mysterious man in gray. The stranger remarked on Mozart's departure and asked when he would produce the Requiem that he had promised. Soon, soon, said Mozart, once he had finished the production of *La Clemenza di Tito*.

Mozart was shaken by this second encounter, and he came to think of the man in gray as a kind of emissary from beyond the grave. "I cannot remove from my eyes the image of the stranger," he wrote to da Ponte (a letter of disputed authenticity). "I see him continually. He begs me, exhorts me, and then commands me to work." Constanze, whose recollections have also been challenged, told a similar story to an interviewer who came to visit her in her old age, in 1829. "Some six months before his death he was possessed with the idea of his being poisoned," Constanze said to Mary Novello. " 'I know I must die,' he exclaimed. 'Someone has given me acqua toffana and has calculated the exact time of my death, for which they have ordered a Requiem. It is for myself I am writing this.' "

Modern scholarship has denied all of this—as scholarship generally does—as romantic melodrama. There is no documentary evidence that Mozart seriously thought he was writing his own Requiem, and yet it is not impossible to suspect that the melodrama may be true. Indeed, the executioner who demanded that Mozart write his own Requiem may well have been, in Mozart's mind, the God to whom the Requiem prayers were addressed. Mozart's God was neither a solemn abstraction to be sought in the Old Testament nor the all-forgiving martyr who currently appears in Broadway musicals. He was infinitely familiar, close, and yet awesome, a force to be both loved and feared, a figure, in fact, very much like Mozart's own father. Leopold Mozart had once been destined to become a priest, and although he never regarded his employment by the archbishop of Salzburg as anything much more sanctified than a career in the National Park Service, he did require his children to attend, regularly and devoutly, all the rituals of the church.

Mozart believed. When Leopold once wrote him a warning not to fail in his religious obligations, the son, then twenty-one, wrote back: "Papa must not worry, for God is ever before my eyes. I realize His omnipotence and I fear His anger; but I also recognize His love, His compassion, and His tenderness toward His creatures. He will never forsake His own. If it is according to His will, so let it be according to mine. Thus all will be well, and I must needs be happy and contented." Five years later, just after his marriage to Constanze, which Leopold strongly opposed, Mozart again wrote reassurances to his father: "For a considerable time before we were married, we had always attended Mass and gone to confession and taken communion together; and I found that I never prayed so fervently or confessed and took communion so devoutly as by her side."

Mozart had written his first religious music, a brief *Kyrie* (K. 33), when he was a boy of ten, but most of his religious work was produced on assignment for the archbishop of Salzburg, Hieronymus Colloredo—fifteen masses, three offertories, four litanies, two vespers, and nearly thirty *kleinere geistliche Gesängwerke*—all finished before he was twenty-five. There is no reason to doubt the sincerity of these early works, but Mozart chafed under the duties and restrictions of the archbishop's service. He loafed and malingered and even lied about his protracted absences until the conflict reached such a crisis of mutual resentments that one of the archbishop's vassals,

Count Karl Arco, achieved his own small place in history by kicking the delinquent composer in the rear end. Once Mozart left Salzburg to pursue his fortunes in Vienna, he virtually ceased writing church music.

The only important exception, before the final Requiem, is the Great Mass in C Minor, which Mozart seems to have written as a gesture of gratitude for his marriage to Constanze. "I made the promise in my heart of hearts and hope to be able to keep it . . ." he wrote to his disapproving father early in 1783. "The score of half a mass, which is still lying here waiting to be finished, is the best proof that I really made the promise." It is a grand work, conceived on a far grander scale than anything he had previously written, and the aria to the text of *Et incarnatus est* is of a sublimity that he never surpassed. Yet he never finished this work, and when it was finally performed in the summer of 1783, with Constanze singing one of the soprano roles, he simply patched together a concluding *Agnus Dei* out of his previous compositions. Why did he never finish this masterpiece? The most practical theory is that nobody paid him to do so; another is that he had only recently encountered a number of major works by Bach and Handel, and that he was dissatisfied with his own efforts to assimilate these discoveries; still another is that the marriage to Constanze was by now a year old, and that the experience of domesticity hardly inspired a work of religious thanksgiving; and yet another is that his Catholicism was giving way to his new interest in the Masonic movement.

There was actually very little contradiction, at least not in the Vienna of Mozart's time, between Catholicism and Freemasonry. Pope Clement XII disapproved profoundly of the movement and actually prepared a papal bull against it in 1738, but the document was never published because the Holy Roman emperor, Francis of Lorraine, was already a member of the order. His wife, Maria Theresa, eventually banned Freemasonry, but nobody took the ban too seriously, for her son and heir, Joseph II, was, if not a member, at least a sympathizer.

When Mozart was applying, in 1791, for a post as second *Kappellmeister* to the court of the new Emperor Leopold, he claimed a special qualification: "Prompted by a desire of fame, by a love of work, and by a conviction of my wide knowledge, I venture to apply for the post of second Kappellmeister, particularly as Salieri, that very gifted Kappellmeister, has never devoted himself to church music, whereas from my youth up I have made myself completely familiar with this style." The Requiem is indeed a summation of Mozart's mastery of the ecclesiastical style, of vocal polyphony and Baroque counterpoint. It is not, however, among his very greatest works. There are great moments in the *Introit,* in the *Recordare* and *Lacrimosa,* but there are also a number of passages that lumber and strain. As a whole, the Requiem lacks the intensifying power of *Don Giovanni* or the triumphant elegance of the late piano concerti. Yet there is a compelling quality in the very text of the Requiem Mass, which, when we remember the circumstances of the composition, requires us to give it the special attention that courts of law give to a deathbed confession. In setting to music the words *Sanctus, sanctus, sanctus,* there can be no evasions, no lies.

But there were evasions and lies. The very commissioning of the work was an act of fraud, as was the acceptance of the commission, and when Mozart realized that he could never finish the work, he conspired further to defraud the fraudulent Count Walsegg. On his deathbed, he sketched ideas for the uncompleted sections on various scraps of paper and discussed their completion with his young pupil, Süssmayr. After his death, Constanze tried to get the work finished secretly by another court *Kappellmeister,* Joseph Eybler. And so the work was finally delivered to the man in gray, and, more than two years after Mozart's death, on December 14, 1793, Count Walsegg did conduct it at his private chapel, in honor of his dead wife.

We are left with the mystery of what Mozart actually wrote. The score was published in 1800 by Breitkopf & Härtel, and Süssmayr, when questioned about his part in the affair, wrote a letter to the publishers in which he "confessed" to having completed the *Lacrimosa* and to having composed, on his own, the *Sanctus, Benedictus,* and *Agnus Dei,* and to having had the inspired idea of concluding the mass by resetting the *Kyrie* fugue to the text of *Cum sanctus tuis in aeternum.* His "confession" seems to have remained more or less secret (he died in 1803), and the authenticity of the Requiem was not publicly challenged until 1825, when a music critic named Gottfried Weber denounced it, largely on stylistic grounds, as a forgery. Mozart's surviving friends rallied to the defense, and although they acknowledged Süssmayr's role in the fraud, they argued that he only did what, in Constanze's words, "anyone could have done." Despite all evidence, she insisted that the Requiem was "only Mozart's work." Scholars have been analyzing the archives ever since, but they have never been able to produce a satisfactory answer to the basic question: If Mozart never got beyond the first eight bars of the *Lacrimosa,* the last passage that he is known to have written, how could Franz Xaver Süssmayr, a young student who never again wrote anything of any particular distinction, have composed the five concluding sections of the mass, including such a marvel as the *Benedictus*?

Perhaps the most plausible answer comes from a scholar named A. Schnerich, who edited a 1913 edition of the Requiem, and whose researches are quoted by another scholar named Friedrich Blume (in *The Creative World of Mozart*). His thesis is that the various sections of the Requiem were written out of sequence, and that Mozart may have assigned the details to his colleagues well before his death. "Is it not conceivable," Blume suggests, "that he looked over the completing of the Requiem by Eybler-Süssmayr only once in a while but that he turned his attention again to finishing the work after the performance of *Die Zauberflöte* (September 30, 1791) freed him from the most pressing labors? This is no more than a hypothesis, but . . . is not a hypothesis, even a rather daring one, better than accusing the survivors of fraud?"

Mozart to Puchberg: May 17, 1790: "Dearest Friend and B.O. . . . I am at the moment so destitute that I must beg you, dearest friend, in the name of all that is sacred, to assist me with whatever you can spare. . . . Alas, I must still ask you to wait patiently for the sums I have already been owing to you for such a long time. If only you knew what grief and worry all this causes me. It has prevented me all this time from finishing my quartets. . . ." [Puchberg's annotation: Sent 150 gulden.]

June 12, 1790: "Dearest friend and B.O.... My wife is slightly better.... Dearest friend, if you can help me to meet my present urgent expenses, oh, do so...!" [Puchberg's annotation: Sent 25 gulden.]

August 14, 1790: "Dearest Friend and Brother.... I am absolutely wretched.... Can you not help me out with a trifle? The smallest sum would be very welcome just now...." [Puchberg's annotation: Sent 10 gulden.]

April 13, 1791: "Most Valued Friend and Brother! I shall be drawing my quarterly pay on April 20th, that is, in a week. If you can and will lend me until then about 20 gulden, you will oblige me very much, most beloved friend...." [Puchberg's annotation: Sent 30 gulden.]

June 25, 1791: "Dearest, Most Beloved Friend! Most Honorable Brother!... My wife writes to say that ... the people with whom she is living would be glad to receive some payment for her board and lodging and she begs me to send her some money.... If you, most beloved friend, can assist me with a small sum ... you will oblige me exceedingly. I require the loan only for a few days, when you will receive 2,000 gulden in my name, from which you can then refund yourself." [Puchberg's annotation: Sent 25 gulden.]

When Mozart died, less than six months later, he still owed Puchberg 1,000 gulden. Puchberg was one of the few who did not press any claim against the composer's estate, and so he was not paid. Several years later, he finally asked Constanze to repay him, and so she did. Puchberg died poor.

Antonio Salieri was one of Mozart's most important rivals—and perhaps even an enemy—but by most of the standards of the day, he was also Mozart's social superior. As *Hofkappellmeister* at the court of Joseph II, he held a position for which Mozart yearned in vain. And Salieri was well qualified, a composer of more than forty operas, and much more besides. He acted as teacher to Beethoven, Schubert, Liszt, Czerny, Cherubini, and, for that matter, Mozart's younger son, Franz. And during the season of 1787, when Viennese audiences responded coolly to *Don Giovanni,* the triumph of the year was Salieri's *Axur, Re d'Ormus.* Salieri seems to have felt some envy of Mozart, though, and he was reported to have said, on hearing of Mozart's death, "Good riddance—otherwise we would all soon have been out of work."

Salieri devoted his last twenty years to writing church music, then went mad, and confessed to a priest the crime of which he had occasionally been maliciously accused. As Johann Schickl scribbled the news in the deaf old Beethoven's conversation book: "Salieri has admitted poisoning Mozart after all, and in his guilt he has cut his throat, but he is still alive." Beethoven's response was characteristically egocentric: "Gossip! Salieri taught me more than anyone else."

Gossip, to be sure, but the scandalous rumors fascinated Alexander Pushkin. Just five years after Salieri's death in 1825, Pushkin found himself confined to his estate in Boldino because of an epidemic of cholera. Thus isolated, he felt inspired, for some reason, to write a series of short plays. In just a few days, he wrote *The Covetous Knight;* in just a few days, he wrote *The Stone Guest;* in just a few days, he wrote *Mozart and Salieri.* Pushkin's melodrama is hardly more than a sketch, yet it begins on a grand scale as Salieri declares his grievance against God: "Men say: there is no justice upon earth. / But neither is there any justice in the Heavens. . . . / For I was born with a great love for art: / When—still a child— I heard the organ peal / I listened all attention—and sweet tears, / Sweet and involuntary tears would flow. / Though young I spurned all frivolous pursuits: / All studies else than music were to me / Repugnant. . . ."

Salieri goes on to narrate his rise in the musical world, and he scorns the idea "that ever proud Salieri / Could stoop to envy, like a loathsome snake / Trampled upon by men, yet still alive / And impotently gnawing sand and dust." But now the arrival of Mozart in Vienna has reduced Salieri to that snakelike state. "Now / I do know envy! Yes, Salieri envies, / Deeply in anguish envies.—O ye Heavens! / Where, where is justice, when the sacred gift, / When deathless genius comes not to reward / Perfervid love and utter self-denial, /

And toils and strivings and beseeching prayers, / But puts her halo round a lack-wit's skull, / A frivolous idler's brow? . . . O Mozart, Mozart!"

Mozart enters and immediately displays his lack of serious pur pose by bringing along a blind fiddler whom he has heard sawing away at an aria from *Figaro*. Salieri is shocked and disapproving. "Mozart, you are unworthy of yourself!" he says. After Mozart wanders off again, Salieri decides that he must murder him. "For I am chosen to arrest his course," he says. "If he lives on, then all of us will perish— / High-priests and servants of the art of music."

This is all written in a kind of narrative shorthand, undeveloped, unexplored. In the second and last scene, Salieri and Mozart meet for dinner at an inn, and Mozart tells about the mysterious stranger. "A man, dressed all in black, / With courtly bow, commissioned me to write / A *Requiem*—and vanished. . . . / Day and night, my man in black gives ne'er / A moment's peace to me. Behind me ever / He hovers like a shadow. . . ."

Salieri is unmoved and undeterred. "You think so? / *(Pours poison into Mozart's glass.)* / Well, now drink."

Mozart drinks, then goes to the piano and announces that he's going to play his Requiem. The music makes Salieri weep. "Yes, these are the first tears I've ever shed," he says. "I feel both pain and pleasure, like a man / Who has performed a sad and painful duty. . . ." Mozart says he feels sick and goes off to bed. "You'll sleep a long sleep, Mozart," says Salieri.

This is scarcely the Pushkin of *Eugene Onegin* or *The Queen of Spades*. His little ten-page playlet was unsuccessfully produced in 1832 and then sank into that Limbo where Salieri himself probably lives. Rimsky-Korsakov resurrected it as a little opera in 1898, and that kept it alive, after a fashion. Then somehow the old legend came to the attention of Peter Shaffer, the author of such theatrical successes as *Equus* and *The Royal Hunt of the Sun,* and he was fascinated. There are still a few faint traces of Pushkin in Shaffer's *Amadeus,* notably in Salieri's account of his origins: "By twelve, I was stumbling about under the poplar trees humming my arias and anthems to the Lord. My one desire was to join all the composers who had celebrated His glory through the long Italian past! . . ." But where

Pushkin's sketch had been thin and half-formed, Shaffer really seized hold of the fundamental idea: the rage of an industrious mediocrity who wants to devote his music to God and then hears the voice of God in the music of somebody else. (Thus *Amadeus,* beloved of God.) Shaffer even had the courage to re-create that moment of recognition in the most difficult way, making Salieri describe a piece of Mozart's music. "It started simply enough," Salieri says of the Adagio from the Serenade in B-flat (K. 361), "just a pulse in the lowest registers—bassoons and basset horns—like a rusty squeezebox. It would have been comic except for the slowness, which gave it instead a sort of serenity. And then suddenly, high above it, sounded a single note on the oboe. . . . It hung there unwavering, piercing me through, till breath could hold it no longer, and a clarinet withdrew it out of me, and sweetened it into a phrase of such delight it had me trembling. . . . I was suddenly frightened. It seemed to me that I had heard a voice of God—and that it issued from a creature whose own voice I had also heard—and it was the voice of an obscene child!"

An obscene child? In Shaffer's eagerness to dramatize the fascinating idea of a devout mediocrity's rage against God, he fell victim to the temptation to exaggerate everything. See, here is Salieri playing a march to welcome Mozart to the imperial court, and Shaffer specifies only that it is "an extremely banal piece"; see, here is Mozart playing Salieri's banal march from memory, after just one hearing, and then beginning to improvise variations ("It doesn't really *work,* that fourth, does it? . . . Let's try the third above"), and then turning it into the famous *"Non più andrai"* from the yet-unwritten *Marriage of Figaro.* "He himself remains totally oblivious," Shaffer insists on telling us, "of the offense he is giving."

But an obscene child? Yes, there were a few youthful letters that Mozart once wrote to a cousin and filled with adolescent scatological buffoonery. From this titillating bit of evidence, Shaffer created a Mozart of morbid perversity—"he is possessed of an unforgettable giggle—piercing and infantile"—and a Constanze almost equally debauched. Here, for example, is Mozart gibbering at Constanze as he begs her to beat him:

MOZART: ... *(He snatches up the ruler.)* Beat me. Beat me.*
... I'm your slave. Stanzi marini. Stanzi marini bini gini. I'll just
stand here like a little lamb and bear your strokes. Here. Do it ...
Batti.

CONSTANZE: No. . . .

MOZART: Stanzerly wanzerly piggly poo!

CONSTANZE: Stop it.

MOZART: Stanzy wanzy had a fit. Shit her stays and made them
split!

(She giggles despite herself.)

CONSTANZE: Stop it.

MOZART: When they took away her skirt, Stanzy wanzy ate the
dirt!

CONSTANZE: Stop it now! *(She snatches the ruler and gives him a
whack with it. He yowls playfully.)*

MOZART: Oooo! Oooo! Oooo! Do it again! Do it again! I cast
myself at your stinking feet, Madonna!

And so on. In defending his loathsome falsification of Mozart,
Shaffer has said, "We were not making an objective 'Life of Wolfgang
Mozart.' This cannot be stressed too strongly." Other defenders argue that anyone who attempts historical fiction should have complete freedom to invent what he pleases. Does anyone complain that
Tolstoy made up the details of Napoleon's appearances in *War and
Peace,* or, for that matter, that Shakespeare invented speeches for
Julius Caesar? No, but there is a kind of implicit social contract in
the writing of historical fiction, a contract by which the author
pledges to try to imagine the truth about his characters, not just
some salable variation of the truth. If *Amadeus* were about a composer named Amadeus Schmitt, after all, nobody would ever have
paid the slightest attention to it. By invoking the name of the composer of *Don Giovanni,* Shaffer implied that he had genuine insights
or revelations to offer, and then they turned out to be on the level

---

*This is presumably intended as a reference to Zerlina's beautiful plea for forgiveness in *Don
Giovanni,* "Batti, batti."

of those fake romans à clef about the Kennedy White House, a great artist begging to be beaten as he says, "Stanzerly wanzerly piggly poo!" The only thing that could have made Shaffer's script worse was for it to be cast accordingly, and so it was. Tim Curry, whose celebrity derived mainly from his female impersonations in *The Rocky Horror Picture Show*, played Mozart on Broadway as though he were a character in *The Rocky Horror Picture Show*. Jane Seymour, all slinky and provocative, played Constanze in much the same way. Before the first act was over, my overwhelming desire was to go home, disgusted.

It seemed to me not just exploitation but desecration to claim historical sanction for such a vulgar caricature. Worst of all, the caricature was not just exaggerated but essentially untrue. That's not what Mozart was like, as anyone who has ever listened to his music knows. The seeming paradox of Mozart's sublime music emerging from "an obscene child" is a false paradox because he was not an obscene child, and an obscene child could not have written such music, and did not do so. It is possible to argue that Shaffer was only dramatizing Salieri's view of Mozart, but I doubt it; I think he was dramatizing something that could be successfully presented as a sort of historical scandal.

I say this not as an expression of the old-fashioned view of Mozart as an ingenue, all charm and innocence. Mozart's letters show him to be quite capable of deceptions, of fawning and hypocrisy. He was often bigoted, ill-mannered, irritable. And sometimes simply wild. A novelist named Karoline Pichler once described an extraordinary scene. She was playing Mozart's *"Non più andrai"* on the piano when Mozart came up behind her, began beating time on her shoulders, then pulled up a chair and made it a duet. He "told me to keep playing the bass and began to improvise variations so beautifully that everyone present held his breath, listening to the music of the German Orpheus. But all at once he had had enough; he jumped up and, as he often did in his foolish moods, he began to leap over table and chairs, miaowing like a cat, and turning somersaults like an unruly boy. . . ."

But this was just one of "his foolish moods," not particularly characteristic of the man himself. What was characteristic was his music, which he took very seriously, which he was proud of, and which he loved. "When playing [the piano]," according to one account, "he appeared completely different. His countenance changed, his eyes settled at once into a steady calm gaze, and every movement of his muscles conveyed the sentiment expressed in his playing." That is the real Mozart, who appeared only occasionally in *Amadeus*, usually ending with a giggle.

The melodrama of Mozart as an "obscene child" enjoyed a succès de scandale in London's West End, and then played for months on Broadway, and such theatrical triumphs acquire an irresistible momentum. Miloš Forman, the Czech director, acquired the film rights and persuaded Shaffer to join in the ordeal of turning his play into a quite different movie. "We spent well over four months together in a Connecticut farmhouse—five days a week, twelve hours a day—seeing virtually no other company," Shaffer wrote later. "These were four months of sustained work, punctuated by innumerable tussles, falterings, and depressions, but also by sudden gleeful breakthroughs. . . . We made an Odd Couple, yoked together in a temporary form of marriage, cooking for each other in the evenings, and each day exploring . . . countless versions of each scene, improvising them aloud. . . ."

Part of this was a matter of shortening and simplifying. The camera needs time to pan across snowy landscapes, and people who make pictures basically regard all talk as "talky." "Mr. Shaffer stripped away philosophical digressions and concentrated on the story line," as Michiko Kakutani wrote in the *New York Times*, politely ignoring the fact that the "philosophical digressions" *were* the story line. But behind all the anticipatory publicity about how Shaffer and Forman had struggled to avoid the danger of what Shaffer called "a stagy hybrid," one senses a different and more fundamental mandate. One can imagine Forman wondering whether a mass audience would really identify with a hero who kept giggling about coprophilia and wanted his wife to beat him. No, no, it won't play out there in the shopping malls. If Mozart is our hero, we've got to make him more sympathetic, more of a nice guy.

And so, just as in the see-no-evil Hollywood of a generation ago, a wondrous transformation took place. Instead of that dark drama about Salieri's rage against God, Forman created (or persuaded Shaffer to help create) a rather charming and very beautiful film about the trials and tribulations of young Mozart, a nice guy. Shaffer's original script wasn't eviscerated, just toned down, and cut, and then toned down some more. Casting helped a lot, just as it had exaggerated the malignities of the theatrical version. In contrast to the perverse Tim Curry, Tom Hulce created a rather engaging Mozart, still given to manic giggles but nonetheless capable of sincere effort and good works. In contrast to the perverse Jane Seymour, Elizabeth Berridge was not only an extremely pretty Constanze but a Constanze played as a sort of suburban soubrette. Even the murderous Salieri became, as played by F. Murray Abraham rather than Ian McKellen, quite amiable. Then there was the city of Prague, where it was all filmed, Prague playing the role of Vienna, and though the two cities do not really look alike, and though Forman had to suppress any shots that would allow Prague to look like Prague, the self-exiled Czech director made the Baroque districts of his capital look beautifully Viennese.

And finally, there was Mozart's music. On the stage, when Salieri described that oboe solo as the voice of God, we heard only a dim, tinny recording from the wings. In the film, we heard Neville Marriner's highly accomplished orchestra of St. Martin's-in-the-Fields play every gorgeous note, and play it gorgeously. The music alone—even if the script and the casting had remained unchanged—would have changed everything. The music overwhelmingly refuted all Salieri's denunciations of Mozart as an "obscene child." But the music also changed *Amadeus* from an interesting drama of ideas—Salieri's ideas—into a pleasant tale of a talented composer who dies young. *Requiescat.* And that's how the movie won all those Academy Awards, best this, best that. *Requiescat.*

One of the strangest aspects of Shaffer's tale of how Salieri poisoned Mozart is that he gradually eliminated the poisoning. At the beginning of the play, Shaffer strongly implied this murder in a series of whisperings by two characters called *"venticelli,* purveyors of information, gossip, and rumor throughout the play."* Thus:

VENTICELLO 1: There was talk once before, you know. . . . When Mozart was dying.

VENTICELLO 2: He claimed he'd been poisoned!

v 1: Some said he accused a man.

v. 2: Some said that man was Salieri!

And then, of course, Shaffer showed the demented old Salieri crying out his confession: *"Mozart! Mozart! Perdonami! . . . Il tuo assassino ti chiede perdono!"* But he never actually showed that Pushkin scene of Salieri adding poison to Mozart's glass, and in the movie version, he seems to imply that Salieri was simply trying to frighten Mozart to death. He has Salieri dress himself up as the dark-cloaked messenger, a figure vaguely reminiscent of Mozart's dead father. At the end, Mozart simply faints during a performance of *The Magic Flute,* and after one climactically absurd scene in which the dying Mozart supposedly dictates a section of the Requiem to Salieri, who supposedly will then try to claim it as his own work, the obscene child dies at dawn.

Well, Mozart did claim that he had been poisoned. "Someone has given me acqua toffana," he said to Constanze during a walk in the Prater. Acqua toffana was a celebrated poison of that era, a mixture of arsenic, antimony, and lead oxide, invented in about 1650 by a Sicilian woman named Teofania di Adamo. Its most notable quality was that it worked very slowly and was very difficult to detect, even after death, at least by the forensic medicine of the time.

It seems quite odd, though, that Mozart offered Constanze no explanation, no theory on who had poisoned him, or why. Indeed, the accusation itself only came to light nearly forty years later, when an English couple named Vincent and Mary Novello went to Vienna and interviewed the aging Constanze as part of what they wrote in *A Mozart Pilgrimage.* It is also rather odd that Mozart made this statement, if he did make it, in June of 1791, and then went on to write *La Clemenza di Tito* and the clarinet concerto and *The Magic Flute,* and all the rest, all those very unpoisoned works of his last year. It was not until December that he died.

But what did he finally die of? Perhaps the most exhaustive analysis of this question is a two-part study by Dr. Peter J. Davies in the British journal *Musical Times,* in 1984. And perhaps the most striking aspect of that study is the list of diseases and afflictions that Mozart had suffered ever since his childhood years as a wandering virtuoso. The eighteenth century may well have been an age of enlightenment, but it was also an age in which medicine had barely emerged from medieval monasticism, an age in which open sewers ran through the streets, and rotten meat was simply spiced with pepper, in which women routinely gave birth to ten children and routinely expected half of them to die. Mozart's medical history included smallpox, typhoid fever, rheumatic fever, pneumonia, dental abscesses, and jaundice. During his last days in the winter of 1791, he suffered from fainting spells, swollen hands and feet, vomiting, diarrhea, and recurrent fevers. What was the cause of it all? Dr. Davies rejects the popular legend of acqua toffana and the rival legend of mercury poisoning on the ground that the symptoms don't match. His own conclusion is that Mozart died from a combination of ailments: "Streptococcal infection—Schönlein Henoch Syndrome—renal failure—venesection(s)—cerebral hemorrhage—terminal bronchopneumonia." For those unfamiliar with Schönlein Henoch syndrome, Dr. Davies defines it as "an allergic hypersensitivity vasculitis in which immune complexes are deposited in the small blood vessels of the skin, joints, gastrointestinal tract and kidneys, resulting in purpuric lesions and edema of the skin and inflammatory changes in the other three organs."

What all that means is that Mozart died of kidney failure, aggravated by a severe throat and lung infection. And aggravated by poverty, cold, bad food, debts, and anxiety. Those were poisons enough.

"Death, when we come to consider it closely, is the true goal of our existence," Mozart once wrote to his father. "I have formed during the last few years such close relations with this best and truest friend of mankind that his image is not only no longer terrifying to me but is indeed very soothing and consoling. . . . I never lie down at night without reflecting that—young as I am—I may not live to see another day."

Mozart was thirty-one when he wrote that, and he may have intended it as a consolation for his father's anxieties. As his own death approached, it may have seemed less welcome. Precisely because death is indeed the true goal of our existence, it is, when we "consider it closely," both terrifying and repulsive—a confusion of pain and hypodermic needles and bedpans and meaninglessness. *The Magic Flute* ignored all that. The trials by fire and water are not real trials; the fire does not burn, the water does not strangle, and the lovers can overcome such dangers simply by singing at them. The text of the Requiem resounds more darkly: "While the wicked are confounded, / By devouring flame surrounded. . . . / Lo, I pray. . . ."

Mozart appeared in public for the last time on the evening of November 18, 1791, to conduct his newest and last finished work, a brief cantata on a text by Schikaneder entitled *"Laut verkünde unsere Freude"* (Loudly proclaim our joy, K. 623). The concert took place at Mozart's lodge, The Newly Crowned Hope, and the assembled Masons did loudly proclaim their joy. The cantata is a simple but charming piece, reaching an elegant sort of climax in the penultimate duet for tenor and baritone. Both of them overflow with Masonic pieties: "Let us share every burden / With the full weight of love. . . ."

Soon afterward, Mozart complained of a chill, and on November 20, two days after the concert, he stayed in his bed. A distinguished doctor named Thomas Closset was summoned and prescribed various drugs, but Mozart did not recover. The swelling of his body grew worse, the fever came and went, and it became painful even to move around in bed. He was too sick to take part in the celebration of his mother-in-law's name day, St. Cecilia's Day, November 22, but he promised to pay his respects the following week; the week passed without his gaining enough strength to keep his promise. His pet canary, which he loved to hear, had to be removed from his room because its singing was too much for his nerves. He often thought of *The Magic Flute*, which was still being played at Schikaneder's theater. He kept a watch by his bed so that he could tell when the curtain went up and imagine what was happening onstage. During one of these last days, when he foresaw his future, he said to Constanze: "I should like to have heard my *Zauberflöte* once more." Then he began to hum Papageno's first song, *"Der Vogelfänger bin ich ja. . . ."*

The night of Saturday, December 3, was very bad. Mozart's fever rose dangerously, and Constanze was afraid that he would not survive the night. The next day, when Constanze's younger sister Sophie came to visit the little apartment on the Rauhensteingasse, Mozart urged her to remain with him. "You must stay here tonight and see me die," he said. "I am already tasting death." Constanze sent Sophie off to the nearby church of St. Peter's to see if she could persuade a priest to come to the apartment "as if by chance." Sophie apparently had some difficulty at the church, for although she and Constanze had once been parishioners, and two of the Mozarts' children had been baptized there, the composer was now notorious as a Mason.

That afternoon, Sunday afternoon, they sang the Requiem around Mozart's deathbed. Benedikt Schack, the tenor who had first sung the role of Tamino in *The Magic Flute,* took the soprano part; Franz Hofer, a violinist who had married Constanze's sister Josepha, sang tenor; Franz Xaver Gerl, the original Sarastro, sang bass; Mozart himself sang the alto part. The only listeners, apparently, were Constanze and Süssmayr. They sang the opening *Introit* and *Kyrie,* then the *Dies Irae*—"Day of anger, day of mourning. . . ." Mozart had not yet finished all of the *Dies Irae.* He had only sketched the outline of the final part, *Lacrimosa*—"Ah, what weeping in that morrow . . . / Gentle Jesus, gracious Lord, / Grant Thy servants peace and rest. . . ." The singers around the deathbed sang the first few bars, and then Mozart broke into tears, and the others stopped.

Mozart's fever ran high again that night. His head was burning, and the painful swelling of his body was worse than ever. Constanze and Sophie sent a messenger to bring Dr. Closset. The messenger found him at a theater, but he said he couldn't come until the performance had ended. When he finally arrived, he inspected the dying man, and said there was nothing to do except to apply cold compresses to bring down the fever. Sophie wrapped the cold cloths around Mozart's head. The shock was too much. Mozart fell into a coma. From time to time, all unconscious, he puffed out his cheeks, and Sophie thought he was imagining or even performing some grand trumpet blast that would complete his own Requiem. At about midnight, he opened his eyes, struggled up in bed, and then turned to lie with his face to the wall, saying nothing to anyone. Less than an hour later, at 12:55 A.M., December 5, 1791, he died.

Constanze, who was destined to live another half century, to marry and survive a second and more prosperous husband, was apparently prostrated, so all the funeral arrangements fell to Baron van Swieten, a diplomat who occasionally acted as Mozart's patron. Somebody made the death mask that Constanze later broke. Somebody made an inventory of the composer's possessions, some books and music and old clothes (one mouse-colored overcoat, one nightcap, eighteen pocket handkerchiefs ...) and a few simple pieces of furniture (one iron stove with pipes, one papier-mâché screen, one rolltop writing desk, one clock in gilt case ...). The only notable items were his billiard table (60 florins) and his piano (80 florins). His total debts amounted to some 3,000 florins, about $8,000.

The funeral service for Mozart was held at the cathedral of St. Stephen—attended not only by friends like Süssmayr (where was Schikaneder?) but by the enigmatic figure of Antonio Salieri—but Baron van Swieten had apparently ordered the cheapest possible funeral (eight florins and thirty-six kreuzer, about fifteen dollars), and none of the mourners even followed the hearse from the cathedral to St. Mark's cemetery. According to the romantic tradition (echoed in *Amadeus*), the gray and wintry skies loosed torrential rains upon the hearse as it wheeled through the cobblestone streets to the graveyard. Modern scholarship alleges that the weather that day was actually rather mild, but the mourners may have been frightened away by reports of new outbreaks of the plague. Constanze's behavior remains somewhat mysterious. Is it perhaps true that she was angry about reports of an affair between Mozart and his young pupil, Magdalena Hofdemel, the one whose husband subsequently attacked her with a razor? When the hearse arrived at St. Mark's graveyard, Mozart's body was simply dumped, along with fifteen or twenty others, into a hole, a pit that was to be periodically "opened and cleared." The distracted Constanze never ventured to the cemetery to visit Mozart's grave until nearly twenty years later. By then, nobody knew where it was.

1972/1986

Pilgrims to Iona

Nolo ut pueri mei mendacium legant . . .
—The Venerable Bede

■ BOSWELL WAS, AS USUAL, THE MORE IMPRESSIONABLE OF THE
two. He observed in his journal that the houses around the famous
shrine were "poor cottages," and that the cottagers had been "without scruple" in building their homes out of stones they had taken
from the ruins of the nearby abbey. He was "disappointed" to find
that "what are called monuments of the kings of Scotland, Ireland
and Denmark" turned out to be "only some gravestones flat on the
earth." And "shocked" to see that the nuns' chapel had been turned
into a cattle barn, with its floor "covered a foot deep in cow-dung."
Despite these dispiriting sights, however, Dr. Johnson considered the
whole prospect inspiring. "That man is little to be envied," he subsequently wrote in his *Journal to the Western Isles of Scotland*, "whose
patriotism would not gain force upon the plain of Marathon, or
whose piety would not grow warmer among the ruins of Iona!"

The challenge is irresistible, and so, as pilgrims, secular pilgrims,
we have flown to Glasgow, and driven a rented car along Loch
Lomond and reached the little Argyllshire port of Oban, and as we
sit eating poached salmon among the potted palms in the waterfront
hotel dining room, the unrelenting drizzle relents for a few moments, and across the harbor we can see the setting sun gleam on
the somber hills of Mull, and beyond these hills, poking out into a
remote corner of the North Atlantic, lies the island of Iona. It is a
tiny place, only three miles long, one and a half miles wide, but large
in its meanings and implications.

"Iona of my heart, / Iona of my love . . . ," St. Columba wrote some fifteen centuries ago of the spot he had discovered. It was to become, according to the familiar legends of disaster, one of those few invulnerable sanctuaries of civilization in the gathering night of the Dark Ages, one of those places where, in Kenneth Clark's words, "Western Christianity survived by clinging on to . . . a pinnacle of rock." Even in our own time, the name of Iona still hints at the possibility of surviving the ultimate holocaust. "Seven years before the end of the world," one of Columba's followers once prophesied, "a deluge shall drown the nations; the sea at one tide shall cover Ireland and the green-headed Islay—But Columba's Isle shall swim above the flood."

The vessel that bears us across the Firth of Lorne the next morning is the *Clansman,* a sturdy craft, broad-beamed, flying the cross of St. Andrew and the red lion of Scotland. There are two or three hundred other pilgrims lined up on the pier, slowly climbing the ramp. It is raining again, but the pilgrims are prepared. Scots, most of them, they wear blue windbreakers, and thick brown tweeds, and plaid scarves over their gray heads. One fat girl with crooked teeth displays on her jacket that grinning symbol known as a "happy face" and the machine-stitched injunction SMILE! JESUS LOVES YOU! Pilgrims, it occurs to me, are quite different from tourists. Whether religious or not, they march to different drummers, dance to different pipers. The tourist is much concerned with the conditions of travel, savoring the wines and complaining of exorbitant prices, for the purpose of his voyage is the voyage itself, and the only goal is the escape from home, or the eventual return there. Since the pilgrim knows his destination, however, he remains more cheerful in dark weather, indifferent to lumpy beds or cold potatoes.

To get to Iona, the pilgrims first must disembark at the village of Craignure and climb onto buses for the thirty-mile trek across the island of Mull. It is a great lobster claw of land, a volcanic eruption of rock sparsely covered with turf and heather, and every mile of the twisting one-lane road inspires our bus driver to some new tale of violence and treachery. There is the promontory where Lachlan Maclean of Duart left his wife to be drowned by the incoming tides, and that roofless stone farmhouse over there was burned by the

English during the ruthless "clearing of the highlands" after the defeat of Bonnie Prince Charlie at Culloden, and there on that hillside is the unhallowed ground where lie nine illegitimate children, forbidden, because of their illegitimacy, in the graveyards of the church.

The silver-haired driver seems to relish all the misery he describes. But then, he relishes everything else too. He tells us the height of the tallest mountain on the island, Ben More (3,185 feet), and he stops his bus to show us the gray seals sunning themselves on some distant rocks, and he declaims to us long stanzas of Robert Burns (as well as a few verses of his own), so it is hard to tell whether his repeated charges of English injustices are a matter of national feeling or mere showmanship. The former, I think. When we tour the capitals of Europe, we see the monuments of the victors, the kings who created nations and wrote the histories of their wars to suit themselves, but whenever we travel outside those capitals, we become more aware that much of Europe consists of conquered provinces and wasted cultures. Provence, Catalonia, Wales, Bohemia, they all once had their own ruling families, their own languages and laws. In Scotland, the references to King James I as James VI (his royal title north of the Tweed) are more than a regional affectation. Bannockburn is now little more than a second-rate *son-et-lumière* show, but the slaughter of the highlanders at Culloden is still quite real. So are the years of economic exploitation and more or less forced emigration. The main certainty about the new oil fields being developed off the Scottish coast is that most of the profits will flow toward London. Still, even in defeat, the Scots cherish their long history of combativeness. It was a battle that brought St. Columba to Iona.

The bus stops in a speck of a village called Fionnphort, and the pilgrims all clamber down an embankment of red granite and into the rocking hull of a battered brown dinghy named the *Staffa* (an uninhabited nearby island containing Fingal's Cave). Across about a mile of water, we can finally see not just the low-lying outline of Iona but a few white houses huddling along the shore, and the squat gray tower of St. Mary's cathedral, built on the site of the old abbey. This narrow channel often turns rough in the winter, and Iona can be cut off for days at a time, but now the water lies soft and gentle, thumping rhythmically against the plowing hull of the *Staffa*. The sun has come out again, and the water shines blue—green—even purple. The approaching island seems to radiate, as it has to many visitors, a quality of serenity. "I never come to Iona . . . without feeling that 'some God is in this place,' " Kenneth Clark wrote. "It isn't as awe-inspiring as some other holy places—Delphi or Assisi. But Iona gives one more than anywhere else I know a sense of peace and inner freedom. What does it? The light, which floods round on every side? The lie of the land which, coming after the solemn hills of Mull, seems strangely like Greece, like Delos, even . . . ? Or is it the memory of those holy men who for two centuries kept western civilization alive?"

That last answer, perhaps. But I was thinking not just of the survival but of the disaster that threatened it, and of the disasters that threaten still. There are many prophets in these northern islands, and John McPhee has recorded the remarkably accurate predictions of Kenneth MacKenzie, the Brahan Seer of the sixteenth century, who, for using his skills undiplomatically, was condemned to being plunged into a vat of boiling tar. Like the monk who predicted a tidal wave over all of Ireland, MacKenzie foresaw physical calamity, but of a sort particularly appropriate to our age: "The whole country will be so utterly desolated and depopulated that the crow of a cock shall not be heard north of Druim-Uachdair. . . . The deer and other wild animals in the huge wilderness shall be exterminated by horrid black rains." Yes, black rains, and I wondered what it would be like to try to survive in a monastery in Iona in a time when the black rains of nuclear ash begin to fall.

Disasters seem to fill a fundamental need in our collective memory. The Garden of Eden is far less vivid than the expulsion, and in almost every culture there is a mythical flood, a devastating plague, a destruction of great cities by hellfire. In our time, there is hardly a need for mythology, for disasters of unprecedented savagery really happened, but as we look back toward the past, perhaps seeking analogies or explanations, the cataclysm that still haunts our imagination is the fall of the Roman Empire. Barbarian tribal invasions, cities sacked and plundered, women and children put to the sword, law and learning inexorably extinguished throughout the civilized world—all these images cluster around the symbolic date of 476, when young Augustulus, the ninth Roman emperor in twenty years and the last to hold that title until Charlemagne, abdicated his feeble powers to the usurping King Odoacer. The fall caused no abrupt changes—it was, someone observed recently, a process rather like those announcements that from now on, the railroad trains won't stop here any more, and the garbage will only be collected twice a week—but by 476, the victorious Franks ruled most of Gaul, the Visigoths most of Spain, and the Saxons most of Britain. Beyond that, to the north and east, lay what the cartographers called *terra incognita,* a land of monsters. The historian Procopius specifically wrote that north of Hadrian's Wall, only serpents could survive.

In British history, the symbolic date of Roman collapse is 410, not because of any disastrous assault but because that was the year in which the Emperor Honorius, when begged to send new troops for the defense of Britain, wrote back to tell the British *civitates* to defend themselves. The emperor, sequestered behind the walls of Ravenna, could do little else, for Rome itself was under siege by Alaric, king of the Goths, and when the Gothic slaves within the city opened the gates to their liberator, the capital of the world was delivered, in Gibbon's hyperbole, "to the licentious fury of the tribes of Germany and Scythia." Yet the barbarians who threatened Britain in the early fifth century were mainly the same Celts and Picts who had occupied the islands long before the Roman conquest. And the main reason for the absence of Roman troops in Britain was that their commanders kept leading them back across the channel to claim the imperial throne. Magnus Maximus managed to seize control of both Gaul and Spain before being killed in 387; Constantine III had led the British legions as far south as Provence by the time the emperor wrote to Britain, perhaps a little vindictively, that Rome had no more troops to spare.

Sometime in the middle of the fifth century, an obscure King Vortigern invited the fierce and pagan Saxons to help defend Britain, and the newcomers eventually began quarreling with their hosts. This was the period in which the shadowy King Arthur is supposed to have been victoriously defending the Roman heritage in remote

Cornwall, but the Saxons kept pressing westward and northward. They decisively defeated the British outside Salisbury in 552, and after another battle in 577, they captured Bath and Gloucester. "Both public and private houses fell to the ground, and priests far and wide were slain standing at the altar . . ." wrote the Venerable Bede, himself a Saxon, in his *Ecclesiastical History of the English Nation.* "Some of the miserable leavings being taken in the hills were there killed in heaps; others being starved with hunger were fain to come forth and submit themselves to the enemy. . . . Others in sorrow made for lands oversea [or] passed their life in want in the mountains, woods and high cliffs with minds ever in apprehension of evil."

On Whitsunday Eve, May 12, 563, a basket-shaped leather coracle bumped ashore on the southern tip of Iona, and out stepped St. Columba, followed by twelve disciples. Columba was then forty-two, a tall man, big-boned, square-faced, with curly red hair and large gray eyes. He was of royal blood—Colum was his Irish name—a great-grandson of King Erc and a descendant of King Niall of the Nine Hostages. He had been trained by St. Finnian at the monastic school of Clonard—where the monks taught not only theology but classical literature and elementary science to some 3,000 students—and even as a youth he could perform miracles. At the age of twenty-five, he founded his first monastery, in an oak grove in Derry, and during the course of fifteen years of wandering around Ireland, he founded three dozen more. This was the mission of the Irish saints—isolated from a Rome that had never conquered their land—not to govern a diocese but to explore, to teach, to establish colonies and then move on. As missionaries among the pagan tribes on the continent, they reached as far as St. Gall's outpost in Switzerland; to the west, they sailed their implausible coracles to Iceland and perhaps even to Newfoundland.

With all his sanctity, Columba was also a warrior. He quarreled with his teacher, St. Finnian, and even with the reigning King Diarmit. In both disputes, he was at least partly in the wrong, but he stubbornly refused to admit it. Instead, he gathered his clansmen to fight against King Diarmit and then turned all his miraculous powers to praying to the Archangel Michael for victory. According to legend, the archangel appeared to him, rebuked him for his request, granted the victory but warned him that he would never again have God's blessing until he had exiled himself from Ireland. Columba's army crushed King Diarmit, killing 3,000 of his men, but the Irish clergy assembled in a synod and denounced Columba for the bloodshed. It ordered him to go and convert as many men as he had killed. So Columba set sail—*"pro Christo peregrinari volens,"* as Iona's seventh-century Abbot Adamnan wrote—first to Kintyre, then to Oronsay, where some of his clansmen had formed a colony along the Scottish shores, but each time he climbed a hill, he could see the green coast of Ireland in the distance. Only at Iona could he look to the southwest and see nothing but the waves, so there the thirteen exiles dug a pit and buried their coracle.

Iona was not uninhabited. There were at least two men who welcomed Columba and mysteriously identified themselves as bishops. There was also a burial ground named after St. Oran, who had died almost twenty years earlier. Is there indeed a holy place anywhere that was not holy in some previous era, and in some era before that? Even Chartres was once the annual meeting place for the Druids of Gaul. But God "revealed" to Columba, according to the old Celtic account, that the welcoming bishops "were not true bishops, whereupon they left the island to him." So Columba and his disciples established their headquarters just north of the old burial ground, began building their huts, their cow barns, their mill. And there, today, right now, is the narrow door to the shrine at the site of Columba's own cell. A shepherd's crook hangs from the wall, and a cowbell, and a Bible lies open on the table, and next to it is a list of names of people who are sick and need your prayers.

Or rather, not quite there. Columba's cell was about a quarter of a mile away, for the shrine is part of the abbey church, which was not founded until 1203. The oldest surviving element of the abbey is the noble Cross of St. Martin, a granite Celtic cross perhaps ten feet high, ornamented with carvings of the temptation of Eve, Daniel in the lions' den, and David playing his harp for Saul. Next to it stands a similar St. John's Cross, but this was pieced together out of fragments in 1926, and blown down and smashed by gales in the winter of 1951, and restored by the Ministry of Works in 1954, and blown down by gales once again in the winter of 1957—clearly, there is a pattern in all this—and what stands on the spot now is a concrete replica scarcely four years old.

"But none of what you see now was here in the time of Columba," says the guide standing in the doorway of the church. "They didn't use stone at all in those days. They built with wood, and wattles. Everything was very crude—like Africa today. So you have to use your imagination."

The guide speaks with an odd intensity. A young man in his twenties, wearing gold-rimmed spectacles and a blue windbreaker, he seems to be not a professional guide at all. Guides are, by and large, surviving members of the servant class; they receive their tips with shows of gratitude. This guide has the nervous manner of a seminarian.

He leads us now into the Romanesque nave of the church, which, just as Columba's cell did not really fit into the thirteenth-century church, is not really of the thirteenth century itself. The original building fell into such disrepair that the abbots decided on a complete remodeling in the fifteenth century. Then came that ruthless process euphemistically known as "the dissolution," by which King Henry VIII and his followers seized and sold the treasures of the church to whomever they judged worthy. Iona ended as the possession of the dukes of Argyll, who finally decided late in the nineteenth century that the ruins that had inspired Dr. Johnson deserved total restoration.

It was characteristic of the historic sense of the Argyll restorers that the south transept now includes a colossal marble statue of Duke George and Duchess Louise, daughter of Queen Victoria, lying in funereal repose in full ducal regalia: crowns, robes, insignia, and all.* Nor does the process of modernization end there. In the garden of the renovated cloister stands a bronze statue, by Jacques Lipchitz,

---

*The feudal traditions of the house of Argyll subsequently collided with twentieth-century tax laws in 1979, when the twelfth duke decided that there was no way to pay the $1 million due in inheritance taxes except by offering the island for sale. His asking price was $3.3 million. The National Trust for Scotland began a fund-raising drive, amid dark talk of foreign real-estate developers despoiling the national heritage. The purchase price was finally pledged by Sir Hugh Fraser, the former owner of Harrods department store, who had squandered millions in gambling but apparently felt some Scottish tribal need to save Iona from the heathen.

of strange and confused symbolism. At the center is an erect figure of what seems to be the Virgin Mary. From between her legs streams what an explanatory pamphlet calls a "coiling mass of meaningless matter." Beneath her, as though newly born, is a lamb. But several coils of this "meaningless matter" curve upward like tusks and join together, just over Mary's head, in the beak of a dove. The Iona authorities hopefully offer an interpretation: "The Holy Spirit enters the material world to make the body holy. . . ."

One senses that the newest occupiers of tranquil Iona have been tormented by the search for social relevance, and indeed the guide in the blue windbreaker is now telling us earnestly about Columba's heirs, who call themselves the Iona Community. There once was a Rev. George MacLeod, who served as pastor during the worst years of the Depression in the worst slums of Glasgow, and he resigned his parish in 1938 to lead a small group of ministers and craftsmen out to Iona to work on the physical restoration of the abbey buildings (until then only the church itself had been renovated). Each summer, he re-created his commune for work and discussion and prayer; each autumn, the members returned to their various parishes to struggle with the problems of unemployment and alcoholism and crime. "That's what Columba himself taught, that we must go out into the world, and work together to help people," the guide says as his listeners begin to stray toward the souvenir stand at the far corner of the cloister. "And in Ireland, where Columba came from, we have members of the Iona Community organizing prayer groups, because we believe that we can only help stop the fighting if we can get people to pray together. From little acorns, great oaks grow."

True enough. But it sometimes seems that the church is never so irrelevant as in just these situations in which it is trying its best to be relevant. And it suddenly occurs to a pilgrim to wonder whether the heathen Picts and Saxons, fully occupied with their lands and their herds, might have held much the same opinion of the newly arrived St. Columba, hardly the savior of Christian civilization so much as a minor nuisance on a remote island, insignificant and essentially harmless.

, , ,

Columba was not by any means a hermit. He had been at Iona scarcely more than a year when he set off for Inverness to preach to King Brude, leader of the northern Picts. He impressed the pagan king by defeating the Archdruid Droichan in a number of contests of magical powers. On the road between Iona and Inverness, he even vanquished the Loch Ness monster, which rose from the deep to devour one of Columba's monks but retreated underwater again when the saint thunderously shouted at it. Nor did he hesitate to return to Ireland to take part in various political intrigues. Since he was supposed never to see his homeland again, he returned with a veil over his head, and since he was not supposed to tread on his native soil, he kept pieces of Scottish turf fastened to the bottoms of his shoes. Some of these tales of Columba's activities may be a little fanciful, but there can scarcely be any doubt that he was a very resourceful man.

For the most part, though, the once restless wanderer seems to have been quite content to remain on his little island for the next thirty-four years. He sent his monks as missionaries all over Scotland and England, but he himself spent his time farming, teaching, copying manuscripts (he is said to have transcribed 300 works in all, including "numerous" copies of the Bible). Even before his death in 597, at the age of seventy-six, Columba's island was becoming (as it may once have been before his arrival) one of the holiest places in Europe. From all over the northwest, kings' bodies were brought there for burial—forty-eight Scots (including both Duncan and his murderer, Macbeth), four Irish, and eight Norwegians—so that they would be lying in sanctified ground on Judgment Day.

Sanctity was not, however, the sole concern of the church. In 596, the year before Columba's death, Pope Gregory I sent St. Augustine to reassert the church's presence among the pagan and apostate tribes of Britain. And among those judged to be in need of Rome's authority were the wandering missionaries from Ireland. In long years of isolation from the south, the Celtic church had developed its own traditions on matters as diverse as ecclesiastical rank (the Irish abbots outranked bishops) and monks' tonsures (the Irish shaved the whole front half of the skull). Among all those differences, both sides found that the most intractable was the date of Easter.

The day is supposed to be celebrated on the first Sunday after the first full moon after the vernal equinox, but this occurs at different times in different longitudes. Moreover, the changes in the relation of sun and moon more or less repeat themselves during different cycles of years. The Jewish calendar was based on a cycle of eighty-four years, which was adopted by Rome, but while the isolated Celts continued to use that system, astronomers in Alexandria developed a more accurate system based on a cycle of nineteen years, and Rome shifted to that. The Celts refused to change, partly as a gesture of defiance toward Roman claims of supremacy. The Romans insisted, partly for the same reason. At one point, the Northumbrian court had to celebrate Easter twice, once for the king, an Ionian convert, and once for the queen, a follower of Rome. The church convened a synod in Whitby in 664, and after days of learned controversy, the Roman arguments prevailed. Some of them were not entirely astronomical. As St. Wilfrid, abbot of Ripon, said of the Celtic claims, "Is one corner of the uttermost island of the earth to be put above the universal Church of Christ?"

That was a typically Roman definition of the terms of conflict, but only in hindsight does it appear inevitable. "It may be suggested, without extravagance, that our modern Western Civilization would probably have been derived from an Irish instead of a Roman embryo . . ." Arnold Toynbee wrote in *A Study of History*, "if Colman instead of Wilfrid had won the Synod of Whitby in A.D. 664." The Celts gave in grudgingly, and Iona most grudgingly of all. For nearly fifty years, the monastery had two abbots representing the hostile factions for and against Roman orthodoxy. Not until 767 did Iona finally celebrate Easter on the same day as Rome.

And then came the Vikings. Their very first appearance was at Lindisfarne, a tiny spit of land off the Northumbrian coast, approachable only when the receding tides expose a narrow road across the mud flats. Here, the followers of Columba had built what was known as "a second Iona," famous to this day for its beautifully illuminated copies of the Gospels. Here, on June 7, 793, a fleet of Vikings sailed up out of the North Sea and plundered the monastery. "Never before," wrote Alcuin, when the news reached the Northumbrian scholar at the court of Charlemagne, "has such terror appeared in

Britain as we have now suffered from a pagan race, nor was it thought that such an inroad from the sea could be made. Behold the church of St. Cuthbert [one of Lindisfarne's first leaders, a man of such sanctity that two seals once swam ashore to warm his feet while he prayed at the water's edge] spattered with the blood of the priests of God. . . ."

That was only the beginning. The following year, 794, Viking raiders attacked another Northumbrian monastery, probably Bede's home in Jarrow; in 795, they circled Britain and descended on Iona itself, sacking the monastery. By the end of the century, they were pillaging as far south as the coast of Aquitaine. It was a time of wolves, even in the sunny wine country around St.-Émilion. That notable saint was himself a wandering Celt who came here in the eighth century, and today a gray and toothless guide will still point her flashlight down into the dismal cave where he lived, illuminating for the curious the stone bed where the saint lay, the stone desk where he wrote, and the miraculous fountain that sprang to life at his command. When the ubiquitous Benedictines came to build a church nearby, they did not dare raise even a humble spire but instead dug what is called an *"église troglodyte"* down into the molish safety of the subterranean dark.

It was partly because they were pagans that the Vikings aroused such horror among the ecclesiastical scholars who wrote what history we have. And partly because they were pagans, they concentrated their raids on the rich and largely undefended monasteries. In 801, they returned to Iona, set fire to the abbey, and destroyed it. In 806, they returned again and massacred sixty-eight defenseless monks on the sands of the beach. It is the beach where the dinghy now lands with pilgrims from Mull. The little inlet is called Martyrs' Bay.

The survivors decided to retreat. More than three centuries after Columba had set out in his coracle, his followers resolved to move their headquarters back to Ireland, to Kells. They opened Columba's grave, placed his relics in a gold and silver case, and took it to Down, to lie next to St. Patrick and St. Brigid. (It was a great time for the moving of saints to escape barbarian desecrations. From ruined Lindisfarne, the second Iona, the monks carried the crated remains of St. Cuthbert, as well as the head of his friend St. Oswald, to the greater safety of Chester-le-Street, where the crates remained for 113 years before being moved to Durham and made the hagiological foundation of the magnificent cathedral.) After twelve years of relative quiet, however, someone decided that Columba's shrine should be taken back to Iona, and five years after that, the Vikings returned yet again. They demanded to know where the shrine of Columba was hidden. The Abbot Blaithmac refused to tell them, and so he was cut down, together with all his monks. He now lies buried in the doorway of the abbey that the triumphant Benedictines built when the last Columban monks departed almost four centuries later. Nearby lies the coffin that is said to contain all that remains of St. Columba.

John Gardner demonstrated, in his marvelously witty novel *Grendel,* that even the most monstrous enemies have a self-justifying point of view that is rarely recognized in epics like that of the anonymous *Beowulf.* The Vikings, similarly, were somewhat less ogreish than their victims' chroniclers claim. They were, after all, exploring and trading from Newfoundland to the Middle East, an area far broader than anything within the experience of the Ionian monks, and the treasures recently unearthed in Scandinavia include not only Arabic coins but even a bronze Buddha from northern India. The Vikings' own art, too, their stone statues and silver brooches and runic inscriptions and even their splendidly ornamented warships, are quite the equal of anything they might have found in ninth-century England or France. To them, the remote monasteries of Iona or Lindisfarne may have seemed no more significant, no more worthy of veneration, than a temple on the Gold Coast might have seemed to Sir Francis Drake. Indeed, after the Danish king known as Sweyn Forkbeard conquered all of England in less than a year (1013), he left the important part of his kingdom, namely Denmark, to his older son, Harold, bequeathing only England to his younger son, Canute.

The English have a way of belittling everything alien, and so schoolchildren learn nothing more of Canute than that he tried to command the incoming tide to stop, but he was actually a redoubtable commander and an able monarch. When he died, he was buried alongside the Saxon Kings Cynegils, Cenwalh, Egbert, and Ethelwulf, in what is now Winchester Cathedral. "But when Cromwell's soldiers came here in the 1640s," the mustachioed guide gloatingly tells an awed troupe of tourists, pilgrims of another sort, "they dug out all those bones and played football with them. And later, when the church tried to sort them out, nobody could tell who was who. So they put all the bones into those three chests that you see up there on top of that wall. That's where he is today, King Canute and his wife, Queen Emma."

Who, then, are the barbarians? The question echoes through all of British history, perhaps through the history of all peoples. The terrifying metaphor of Roman civilization succumbing to heathen barbarians is basically a metaphor created for the age of European imperialism (scarcely half a century separates Gibbon's masterpiece from the British attack on China for its unwillingness to accept British Indian opium in payment for its silks and spices). From a postimperial (or preimperial) viewpoint, the invasion by the Roman legions, bringing their war chariots and their legal codes and their stone highways and what the French still call, applying it to themselves, a *"mission civilisatrice"*—all this may seem less self-evidently beneficent than it once did. As a Britannic chieftain protested, "You make a wasteland and call it peace."

Conversely, the decaying fifth-century empire that relied on mercenaries for its defense and on slaves for its labor had little reason to despise such kings as Alaric or even Odoacer as "barbarians." The Saxon Bede was hardly an impartial witness, but it was probably not entirely through partisanship that he described the inhabitants of late Roman Britain as "cowardly" people who indulged in "all manner of lewdness, specially cruelty [and] love of lying." A proud Danish historian in the time of King Canute might have said the same of the decadent Saxons under King Ethelred the Unready, just as both Saxons and Danes might have joined in expressing their horror of the bloodthirsty Norman invaders led by William the Conqueror. And in virtually all wars from that day to this, it has remained the custom of the winners to denounce their enemies as immoral, and of the losers to consider themselves victims of barbarism. According to the rules by which history is written, however, the Normans and their successors, being the last invaders, reestablished civilization in Britain forevermore.

Today, we know that their predecessors, whether Celtic saints or Arthurian knights, are just semilegendary figures of prehistory, mere symbols in the imagination of romantics like Tennyson or Wagner, so when we come to stand in the emerald courtyard of the abbey at Glastonbury and look down at the thin stone edging that actually marks the outlines of King Arthur's grave, it no longer overwhelms us to learn that the troops of King Henry VIII came here in 1539 and dug up the grave and scattered the bones. Like the nearby thorn tree that is not truly the same tree that did or did not suddenly sprout from the staff that St. Joseph of Arimathea stuck into the ground somewhere around here, the grave is not quite real. Nothing here is so real that it need trouble us. And when we make our way to King Arthur's castle at Tintagel, a ruin perched high on the windswept granite cliffs of North Devon, we can park the car in the King Arthur Car Park and drink a cup of tea at the King Arthur Café and buy a guidebook that steadfastly assures us that "no evidence whatever has been found to support the legendary connection of the castle with King Arthur. . . ."

So it is, in a way, at Iona. The ruins, wrecked for the last time by the soldiers of Queen Elizabeth, are all rebuilt in the approved medieval style, and electricity was brought to the island about thirty years ago, and now, at the edge of Martyrs' Bay, where the sixty-eight monks died by the Vikings' swords more than a thousand years ago, there is a restaurant called, appropriately enough, the Martyrs' Bay Restaurant. We pilgrims all sit three abreast on plastic chairs and eat from plastic tables. The waitress brings us plates of fried haddock and chips for eighty pence, then just under two dollars. As we chew on the fish, we can look out a picture window and watch the sea gulls jostling each other and cawing their sad, harsh, persistent cries. What attracts them to this spot is a pile of trash that has spilled out of some bin, potato peels, torn bits of white paper. Nearby, a waste pipe leads from one of the new buildings down toward the radiant waters of Martyrs' Bay.

1976

Scarlatti and the Princess

▪ CONFRONTING THE INFINITELY DELICATE PROBLEM OF WHERE
Crown Prince Fernando of Spain should marry Princess María Bárbara of Portugal, while Crown Prince José of Portugal simultaneously
married Princess María Vittoria of Spain, the court officials in charge
of such things decided to build a royal pavilion across the Caya River
on the border of the two countries. The Portuguese royal family
arrived from Lisbon with a retinue of courtiers and liveried servants
that required 185 horse-drawn coaches, together with an escort of
6,000 troops in splendid new uniforms; the Spanish party was of
comparable size and splendor. As the two families met on the river
in January of 1729, the Spanish prince saw for the first time his
future queen. "I could not but observe," wrote Sir Benjamin Keene,
the British ambassador to Madrid, "that the princess' figure, not-
withstanding a profusion of gold and diamonds, really shocked the
prince. He looked as if he thought he had been imposed upon. Her
large mouth, thick lips, high cheekbones and small eyes, afford him
no agreeable prospect. . . ."

Prince Fernando was then fourteen, and his bride sixteen, and
she had had smallpox too, but though her unfortunate appearance
may have shocked the Spanish prince, such judgments had little
effect on the course of royal betrothals. The young strangers took
their vows of marriage, and then, after what an official chronicle
described as "much grief at parting," Princess María Bárbara joined
the Spanish court on its voyage homeward into what was, for her,

the unknown. Since María Bárbara was a gifted musician who passionately loved her art, the royal procession from the Portuguese border back through the oak forests of Estremadura included several harpsichords tied to the backs of mules. And since King João V of Portugal indulged his daughter's fancies, he sent along with her, almost as part of her dowry, her own music teacher, Domenico Scarlatti.

He was then forty-four, a musical genius who until this time had accomplished nothing of any special significance. He would serve the homely but good-hearted María Bárbara for the rest of his long life. Unlike any other artist one can recall, he would find in this remarkable patron, whom he had trained at the harpsichord since childhood, a talented, receptive, and wealthy audience of one. He would never need any other. Within the limits of the court, his artistic freedom was total. The princess could understand and appreciate and support whatever her own composer wanted to write. So he wrote, purely for her and for himself, the 550 harpsichord sonatas that are one of the great marvels in the history of music.

This year, as we all know, marks the three hundredth birthday of Bach and Handel, and we have all admired once again the Brandenburg Concertos and the *St. Matthew Passion* and the *Messiah*. It is no denigration of these masterpieces to ask why no one has organized a comparable celebration of the three hundredth birthday this October 26 of a scarcely less gifted composer. Like Chopin, who greatly admired him, Scarlatti wrote no grand symphonic works, but his miniatures express extraordinary varieties of feeling, of tonal color and harmonic innovation, of elegance, exuberance, wit, joy, and beauty. There is a deplorable tradition of piano virtuosos playing two or three Scarlatti sonatas as tinkly exercises at the beginning of a recital, so Vladimir Horowitz is perhaps the best witness to testify that many of Scarlatti's works "are quite poetic, nostalgic, and even dreamy," and that his "freshness and unbelievable daring in the use of harmony and rhythm make him one of the most original composers of his century."

The reason that Scarlatti had accomplished so little by the age of forty-four is probably that he was the sixth of the ten children of one of the most famous musicians of his time, Alessandro Scarlatti.

It was a daunting heritage. When this sixth child was born into this overwhelmingly musical family, Alessandro, himself the son of a musician in Palermo, was just twenty-five and newly appointed *maestro di cappella* to the Spanish viceroy in Naples. One of his brothers was a professional violinist, another a comic tenor, and a sister also sang. There is no evidence that Alessandro Scarlatti ever trained any of his children, as Bach did, or Leopold Mozart. He was undoubtedly a dominating presence, but perhaps he was simply too busy for domestic tasks. He served the Vatican, he served the Medici dukes of Florence, and he rarely turned down any commissions. He wrote, in all, some 115 operas, and the record catalogues of today still include a score or more of his myriad cantatas, concerti grossi, motets, sonatas, and sinfonie. His house must have been full of music and musicians, singers, fiddlers, impresarios.

Young Domenico, known as Mimo, listened and absorbed. There is no record of his receiving any formal education in any conservatory, but when he was fifteen he won an appointment as organist and composer in the royal chapel of Naples. When he was seventeen, his first three cantatas were performed; when he was eighteen, his first two operas were staged. "This son of mine is an eagle whose wings are grown," Alessandro wrote hopefully to Ferdinando de' Medici. "He must not remain idle in the nest, and I must not hinder his flight."

Domenico's compositions were intended mostly for private performance, however, and he seems to have avoided public appearances. One of the rare accounts of his youthful virtuosity comes from an Irish harpsichordist named Thomas Roseingrave, who was touring Italy in 1710 and received an invitation to perform at the home of a Venetian nobleman. "Finding myself rather better in courage and finger than usual, I exerted myself, my dear friend," Roseingrave wrote to Charles Burney, the eminent English musicologist, "and fancied by the applause I received, that my performance had made some impression." While Roseingrave was still basking in these praises, the harpsichord was taken over by "a grave young man dressed in black and in a black wig, who had stood in one corner of the room, very quiet and attentive." When Scarlatti began to play, as Burney later wrote in his *General History of Music* (1776–1789),

"Rosy . . . thought ten hundred d——ls had been at the instrument; he never had heard such passages of execution and effect before. The performance so far surpassed his own . . . that, if he had been in sight of any instrument with which to have done the deed, he should have cut off his own fingers."

Handel and Bach, it has often been remarked, never met. Handel and Scarlatti did, at the insistence of a Roman cardinal who wanted them to compete against each other. The details are obscure, but most of the listeners apparently believed Scarlatti the victor on the harpsichord while Scarlatti himself declared Handel his superior on the organ. Handel was appropriately pleased, according to his first biographer, John Mainwaring, and "used often to speak of this person with great satisfaction . . . for besides his great talents as an artist, he had the sweetest temper, and the genteelest behavior."

Sweet and genteel, Scarlatti was the classic younger son, living and working in the shadow of an illustrious father. This father found him a handsome position at the court of Queen Maria Casimira of Poland, a vain and quarrelsome woman who had been exiled by her own son and had reestablished herself in Rome. Scarlatti's first composition for her private theater was an oratorio entitled *La Conversione di Clodoveo, Re di Francia* (1709). Then came two operas, *Orlando* and *Tolomeo*. Virtually all of these commissioned works of Scarlatti's Roman years have been lost, but history has relied on Dr. Burney's judgment that the admirers of Scarlatti's later harpsichord sonatas "would be surprised at the sobriety and almost dullness of his songs."

Queen Maria Casimira eventually ran out of money. With a little Vatican prodding, she returned to her native France in 1714 to become a lifelong dependent of King Louis XIV. Scarlatti, like many a suddenly unemployed artist in Rome, turned to the Vatican for assistance. Thus he became *maestro di cappella* of the Basilica Giulia. For a chorus of sixteen, and a monthly salary of fifteen scudi, this future rebel against churchly counterpoint began composing in churchly counterpoint, a *Stabat mater*, two *Misereres*, whatever was needed. At the same time, other offers opened other possibilities. Scarlatti received a commission from the Portuguese ambassador to compose a salute to the birth of that nation's crown prince, so he wrote *Applauso Genetliaco del Signore Infante di Portogallo.*

This was the golden age of Portugal, for large deposits of gold had been discovered in the colony of Brazil in 1680, and King João V claimed one-fifth of everything that was unearthed. "The king had a large building filled with diamonds," John Wesley wrote in piously scandalized tones, "and more gold stored up, coined and uncoined, than all the other princes of Europe together." King João indulged himself in all the usual vices, and yet he was pious too. "This monarch's gaieties were religious processions," Voltaire wrote. "When he took to building, he built monasteries, and when he wanted a mistress he chose a nun." João guiltily donated huge sums to the Vatican, perhaps as much as $500,000 a year, and the Vatican rewarded him with the title of *Fidelissimus.* What could be more natural for this king, when his homely but gifted daughter reached the age of nine, than to turn to Rome for a music teacher, someone recommended by both the Vatican and the Portuguese ambassador, a relatively obscure but capable craftsman named Domenico Scarlatti?

He sailed for Lisbon in 1719. He probably did not think of this as a permanent expatriation, but he was to return to Italy only twice more. The first return, in 1724, was to visit his aging father, who died the following year, thus finally liberating Scarlatti from the curse of filial submission and respectability. It has been said that the death of a father freed Shakespeare to write *Hamlet,* and Mozart *Don Giovanni;* Scarlatti was freed only to find his own way, which he did not yet know. He made his second voyage back to Naples in 1728 to acquire a Neapolitan wife, Maria Catalina Gentili. She was sixteen, nearly thirty years younger than her husband. It was presumably an arranged marriage, but well arranged. Scarlatti not only took his bride off to Portugal but later brought her mother and brother to Spain, where they all lived on, in apparent good harmony, for the rest of his life.

King João of Portugal was to die insane in 1750, but the Spanish court to which he sent his daughter and her music teacher was already dominated by the even more overwhelming madness of King Felipe V. At this distance in time, it is impossible to tell what ailed these Iberian monarchs, and there is little scientific evidence in such contemporary judgments as the comte de Saint-Simon's statement on Felipe that "the least act of will caused him total exhaustion." A grandson of Louis XIV of France, Felipe arose from his bed at five in the afternoon, dined at three in the morning, and expected all his exhausted courtiers to behave accordingly.

To the extent that the court functioned at all, it kept on the move, reappearing at the Buen Retiro palace in Madrid mainly on such holidays as Christmas and Easter. Most of the year, it circled Madrid, trekking from the grim Hapsburg palace of the Escorial in the autumn to the rustic amiability of Aranjuez in the spring to the newly begun mountain retreat at La Granja in the summer, and then back to the Escorial in the fall. But there were periods in which the king refused to get out of bed at all. Melancholia was the puzzled doctors' name for his affliction. The king would not change his linen for months on end, or allow his hair to be cut for years. The only person who could exert any influence over him was his domineering young Italian wife, Isabella Farnese, whose authority was absolute.

The melancholy king tried at one point to abdicate in favor of his oldest son, who was also of a somewhat unstable intellect. When this son shortly died, Felipe had to resume his unwanted throne. From then on, to avoid any further abdications, Queen Isabella never allowed Felipe to have or use a pen except under her supervision. And in contrast to King João of Portugal, Felipe was allowed no nuns, only a ruthless wife, who was always ruthlessly available. Saint-Simon wrote loftily of the troubled king that he indulged in *"trop de nourriture et d'exercice conjugal."*

Queen Isabella did not welcome her Portuguese daughter-in-law to the lunatic court with any particular affection. Since Isabella and Felipe had both been married before, Prince Fernando, officially known as Prince of the Asturias, was only her stepson. The queen was determined to find principalities for her own two sons to rule. She had little time for art, and, as the British ambassador reported, "The king . . . has a natural aversion to music." But then there appeared at court a touring Italian castrato named Carlo Broschi, who called himself Farinelli. The king had been lying in bed "for a considerable time," according to a contemporary chronicle, and the queen asked Farinelli to try to rouse him by singing some songs. "Philip [Felipe] was struck by the first air sung by Farinelli," this account continues, "and at the conclusion of the second, sent for him, loaded him with praises, and promised to grant whatever he should demand. The musician, who had been tutored by the queen, entreated him to rise from his bed, suffer himself to be shaven, and dressed, and attend the council. Philip complied. . . ."

The king thereupon hired Farinelli as his music master at an immense salary of 50,000 francs a year. To fulfill Farinelli's expensive ideas of what a music master should accomplish, the king had a magnificent new theater built in Madrid. It opened in Carnival Week of 1738 with a performance of Metastasio's *Demetrio*. Farinelli was by now too exalted to sing in public. He was the impresario, recruiting other singers, designers, and directors from all over Europe. He inevitably became an unofficial minister to the bewildered king, almost a prime minister. But Farinelli was apparently a man of great probity as well as charm. He never abused his position of trust.

Together with his power as the king's musical favorite, Farinelli had to suffer two stern restrictions. One was that he had to abandon all the applause of the world outside the Spanish royal court, for he was forbidden by Madrid protocol to sing anywhere else at all. The other was that he had to sing for the king, every night for the next ten years, the same four songs that he had sung the first night the king had heard him. There was one last unpleasantness: the king yearned to imitate him, and since the king was totally unable to sing, the nocturnal court had to endure bursts of royal screeching and wailing that lasted until three or four in the morning.

Scarlatti lived under similar restrictions. He could give no concerts, win no popular applause, achieve no artistic reputation. Conversely, he was cut off from musical influences from the rest of Europe; there is no evidence that he knew anything of such contemporaries as Rameau or Bach. Scarlatti was even more confined than Farinelli, for the singer served the king, while Scarlatti served only the Princess María Bárbara, and relations between the two royal households were inevitably strained. A Spanish queen had extraordinary authority while a Spanish princess had virtually no power at all beyond the anticipation of someday becoming queen, at which point the widowed dowager would be driven from her throne on whatever terms the new queen chose to inflict. Isabella once carried her domestic tyranny to the point of sending a servant to order

Farinelli never again to sing or play in Princess María Bárbara's apartments. Farinelli displayed his characteristic combination of honor and discretion when he answered: "Go and tell the queen that I owe the greatest obligations to the prince and princess of Asturias, and unless I receive such an order from Her Majesty's own mouth, or the king's, I will never obey it."

It was probably María Bárbara who asked her father in 1738 to honor her Scarlatti with a knighthood in the Portuguese order of Santiago. This required an elaborate ritual, in the course of which a Capuchin priest made Scarlatti swear that he was free of the taint of Moorish ancestry, and that he was "prepared to defend the gates against the Moors." The priest also asked Scarlatti whether he was sufficiently humble and obedient, so "that even if we sent you to keep the pigs you would do it." Scarlatti gave the required pledge: "Thus I promise."

In response to this knighthood, which Scarlatti seems to have regarded as a great benefaction, the composer honored the king that same year by dedicating to him his first published collection of harpsichord sonatas. With knightly humility, Scarlatti called these thirty splendid pieces merely *Essercizi,* or Exercises, a humility that was not again matched until Chopin published the masterpieces of his opus 10 under the bleak title *Études.* Scarlatti was vain enough, however, to identify himself on the title page as "Knight of St. James and Master of the most Serene Prince and Princess of the Asturias &c." His dedication to King João seems fawning even for an age in which great artists customarily fawned on secondary potentates. "Do not disdain, O Most Clement King, such Tribute as this may be from an obsequious Servant. . . ." And so on. Scarlatti also included a few honeyed words about María Bárbara: ". . . the immortal Honour vouchsafed me by your Royal Command to follow this incomparable Princess. The Glory of her Perfections, of Royal Lineage and Sovereign Education, redounds to that of the Great Monarch Her Father. . . ."

Only at the end of these extravagances did Scarlatti offer a few rare and ironic words to anyone who would strive to play his music in the future. "Do not expect any profound learning," Scarlatti wrote, "but rather an ingenious jesting with art, to accommodate you to the mastery of the harpsichord. . . . Perhaps they will be agreeable to you. . . . Show yourself then more human than critical, and thereby increase your own Delight. . . . Fare well."

With that mocking *envoi*, at the age of fifty-three, Scarlatti left us thirty marvels. The D Minor Pastorale was perhaps the most beautiful and the most enduringly famous piece he ever wrote. The G Minor Fugue that later generations of Romantics insisted on calling the Cat Fugue, because its odd theme was supposedly created by Scarlatti's cat creeping across his keyboard, was the strangest. But everything about this unprecedented collection of pieces was strange. "In some sonatas," as Ralph Kirkpatrick wrote in his authoritative biography of Scarlatti, "the brittle tensions and intoxicating rhythms of the Spanish dance are heightened by the wail of a harsh flamenco voice accompanied by guitars and castanets and punctuated by shouts of *olé* and the cross accents of stamping feet." And more: "Many of them extend . . . into an impressionistic transcription of the sounds of daily life, of street cries, church bells . . . fireworks, artillery, in such varied and fluid form that any attempt to describe them precisely in words results in colorful and embarrassing nonsense." Yes, better simply to say, as Kirkpatrick finally does, that "Scarlatti's real musical career began with the *Essercizi,* as if some complete break and miraculous process of regeneration had taken place in his life."

But we really know only the bare outlines of that life. Just three months after the *Essercizi* went on sale in London in the late winter of 1739, Scarlatti's twenty-seven-year-old wife, Catalina, died in the king's summer capital of Aranjuez, leaving behind, under the tutelage of her mother, five children under the age of ten. Within a year or two (the date is uncertain), Scarlatti married a Spanish woman named Anastasia Ximenes, and in 1743 she gave birth to a girl named María Bárbara, the sixth of Scarlatti's nine children. His original mother-in-law, Margarita Gentili, apparently took charge of the whole brood. And Scarlatti provided for them all. His only known vice was gambling.

In 1746, the pitiful King Felipe finally suffered an attack of apoplexy and died in the arms of his infuriated wife. So María Bárbara, after seventeen years of quasi-servitude, finally became the queen, and Isabella Farnese was dispatched to a quasi-exile among the elaborate fountains of the palace that her late husband had built at La Granja. There she perpetuated the all-night hours to which she had become accustomed, but her former court never again came to visit her.

The new Queen María Bárbara had by now become extremely fat, but one contemporary account described her as "a woman of agreeable address, sprightly wit, and uncommon gentleness of manners. She was cheerful in public and extravagantly fond of dancing and music. . . ." The new king, now Fernando VI, was already showing signs of his father's chronic melancholy, but he remained devoted to María Bárbara and shared in her love of music. Spain, it must be admitted, was not well governed by these two, but the arts flourished. Farinelli became an even more grand producer of operas, and an even greater power at court, but he remained honorable, declining offers of bribes from even such distinguished corrupters as King Louis XV of France. "It seems," Dr. Burney observed, in one of the kindest judgments ever made on a castrato, "as if the involuntary loss of the most gross and common of all animal faculties had been the only degrading circumstance of his existence."

Scarlatti, in the shadow of such powers, kept writing. His later sonatas became ever richer and subtler and more complex. He abandoned such virtuoso tricks as the crossing of hands, but his increasing virtuosity as a composer became correspondingly remarkable. By remaining within the miniature formula that he had made his own, he compressed all his daring ideas until they burst forth with extraordinary vitality. Radical modulations that Haydn would avoid, Scarlatti seized upon; transitions to which Brahms would devote pages occupied Scarlatti for only a measure or two. Perhaps the one indisputable judgment to be made on Scarlatti's miniatures is that they are not miniature.

But we know almost none of the details of how they were written. We know only that between 1752 and 1757, some trusted scribe copied out thirteen volumes of Scarlatti's sonatas for Queen María Bárbara to play on one of her seven harpsichords. These copies were made in various colored inks and then bound in red morocco, and they finally ended in the Biblioteca Marciana in Venice.

No manuscript copy of any of Scarlatti's 550 sonatas has ever been found anywhere. The idea that they may all survive in some chaotic Spanish royal archive remains a dim but intoxicating possibility.

In 1752, when this copying started, Scarlatti suffered a major illness. In one of his very few surviving letters, he wrote to the duke of Alba: "I cannot go out of my house. Your Excellency is great, strong, and magnanimous, and full of health; why not come therefore to console me with your presence?" Scarlatti had already made his will three years earlier, filled with pieties, "recommending my soul to God our Lord who created it and redeemed it with the infinitely precious blood of his Son. . . ." But the copying went on.

In the midst of it, Lisbon was struck by the devastating earthquake of 1755, which killed about 50,000 people, stunned Europe, filled Madrid with Portuguese refugees, including many musicians, and destroyed whatever records there may have been of Scarlatti's years in the Portuguese capital. But still the copying of Scarlatti's sonatas went on, and while it did, so did Scarlatti's creation of new sonatas. Hearing time's winged chariot hurrying near, he seems to have been more productive in his sixties and seventies than he had ever been before. Scarlatti was one of those artists who never declined in old age, who kept finding new depths to explore and new ways to explore them. His last known work, strangely, was not for the harpsichord but for the instruments of his youth, a *Salve Regina* for soprano and strings. *In hac lacrimarum valle. . . .*

Scarlatti died in his seventy-second year, on July 23, 1757, and was buried in a convent near the University of Madrid. (As often happens, the convent was abolished in the nineteenth century, and Scarlatti's grave destroyed.) Queen María Bárbara had made a will in which she left 2,000 doubloons and a ring to "my music master who has followed me with great diligence and devotion." Now that he had died before her, she paid off his gambling debts and provided a pension to the widow and each of the children to honor *"la buena memoria de Dn. Domingo Scarlatti."*

María Bárbara herself had little time left. By now forty-three, grossly fat and wheezing with asthma, she died just a year after Scarlatti, in the summer of 1758. King Fernando soon followed. "From the moment of her death, his folly knew no more limit . . ."

according to one contemporary account. "The monarch continued walking alone, refusing all food for more than a week, then eating the impossible for eight days, forcing himself to yield nothing by sitting on the pointed knobs of the antique chairs in his room. . . ." The king died childless the following year, in the summer of 1759, and so the Spanish throne passed to his younger brother, Carlos, king of Naples, who cared nothing for music, loved only hunting, but began to rule Spain according to the rational principles of the Enlightenment. Of Farinelli, the new king remarked that capons were good only for eating.

Farinelli quietly retired to Bologna, built himself a fine house, and filled it with fine furniture that he brought back from Spain, including three harpsichords that had been bequeathed to him by María Bárbara. About ten years later, he received a visit from the indefatigable Dr. Burney, who "prevailed on him to play a good deal," and persuaded him to "furnish me with all the particulars concerning Domenico Scarlatti. . . . [He] dictated them to me very obligingly, while I entered them in my pocketbook." That is how we know most of what little we know about Scarlatti's long sojourn in the secluded court of María Bárbara—that and the wonderful scores of the 550 sonatas that somebody copied out for her, and for us to enjoy forever.

1985

The Lion on the Mountain

■ "LIKE A LION IT CROUCHED," THE YOUNG AMERICAN LIEU-
tenant thought as he looked up toward the great abbey on top of
the mountain, "dominating all approaches, watching every move
made by the armies down below." This was Monte Cassino, the
mother of all Christian monasteries, created by St. Benedict himself
more than fourteen centuries ago, and now it stood blocking the
U.S. Fifth Army's march on Nazi-occupied Rome, just eighty miles
to the northwest. It would have to be destroyed.

The lieutenant, Harold L. Bond, was surprised by both the grandeur and the serenity of the doomed monastery. "Its stone walls
were yellow and unexpectedly warm on that cold January day," he
wrote later. "The sun reflected from some of the glass in the windows, and the great towers and dome were notably outlined against
the sky. . . . Some soldiers in the yard told me that the Germans were
using it for an observation post, and that was the reason they had
been able to fire with such deadly accuracy on all of our positions."

Bond and his men spent a week clawing their way up that mountain, clawing through snow and rain and frozen mud, short of food
and even ammunition. The American attackers finally captured a
ridge within 1,000 yards of the monastery's wall, but then they could
go no farther. Though they took 80 percent casualties during that
dreadful week, every attack was beaten back by the equally brave
and determined German defenders. When the shattered American

force had to be replaced by New Zealanders for the final assault, the monastery still stood there, still watchful as a lion.

"Oh, it was malignant," said an English sergeant who served with the New Zealanders. "It was evil somehow. I don't know how a monastery can be evil, but it was looking at you. It was all-devouring, if you like—a sun-bleached color, grim. It had a terrible hold on us soldiers. . . . It just had to be bombed."

"Can you imagine what it is like to see a person's head explode in a great splash of gray brains and red hair, and have the blood and muck all over you, in your mouth, eyes, ears?" asked another British officer. "And can you imagine what it is like when that head belonged to your sister's fiancé? I *knew* fucking Jerry was up there in that fucking bloody monastery directing the fire that killed Dickie, and I know that still. . . ."

It wasn't true—there were no Germans inside the monastery— but the invaders all thought it was true. And so, at 9:28 on the sunny and nearly cloudless morning of February 15, 1944, a flight of 147 B-17 Flying Fortresses unloaded 287 tons of explosive bombs on the undefended monastery, along with 66 tons of incendiary bombs. Great clouds of smoke rose to cover the top of the mountain. Later that day, 86 medium bombers returned with a second round of devastation. The total: 453 tons of bombs, the heaviest attack ever launched against a single building.

Through a reasonably typical series of military miscalculations, the raids were staged both on the wrong day and at the wrong time of day. The New Zealanders were not ready to begin their assault, and when they belatedly did begin it, they failed. The bombing that was supposed to shorten the Allied march to Rome probably lengthened it. All that the bombing accomplished was to reduce St. Benedict's monastery, which once had preserved the relics of civilization through the long centuries of the Dark Ages, to smoking rubble.

I was driving through that region not long ago, on the superhighway from Rome to Naples, and I had made a mental note to watch for some sign of the ruins of Monte Cassino, perhaps some roadside plaque marking the spot where the monastery had once stood. But the bone white gleam of the stone wall caught my eye from miles away, that jagged wall outlined against the brownish green of the surrounding mountains and the serene blue of the Italian sky. As I drove closer, I saw that the wall was still there, the whole monastery was still there, still watching from its mountaintop. The Americans had not been the first to destroy Monte Cassino— Lombards and Saracens had destroyed it too—and the monastery had taken as its motto the words *Succisa virescit,* meaning, "Struck down, it will live again."

So it has all been rebuilt, stone by stone, just exactly as it once was. And over the one entrance through the ten-foot-thick walls into the domain of St. Benedict, there is a message painted in large and bloodred letters. It is the monastery's message to all who come as conquerors. It says, in its scarlet letters, just one word: PAX.

St. Benedict would approve, one likes to think, but perhaps not. He was a combative man, after all, and much convinced of the rightness of his cause. When he first came here, in the year 529, he found many of the inhabitants still loyal to the long-outlawed worship of the gods of Olympus. On top of the mountain, as Pope Gregory I wrote about Benedict in his *Dialogues,* "stood a very old temple, in which the ignorant country people still worshipped Apollo as their pagan ancestors had done, and went on offering superstitious and idolatrous sacrifices in groves dedicated to various demons." Benedict's reaction was forceful. He destroyed the revered statue of Apollo, overturned the altar, and cut down the sacred groves. He might therefore be described as the first man to desecrate the shrine of Monte Cassino, except that some earlier priest of Apollo quite possibly destroyed an Etruscan temple on this same site, and some Etruscan priest may well have destroyed a still older sanctuary.

The Ancient Enemy of Mankind, as St. Gregory cautiously identifies the Devil, was angered by Benedict's missionary labors and came to berate him. Satan was invisible to Benedict's followers, but the saint later told them that he "had an appearance utterly revolting to human eyes. He was enveloped in fire and . . . flames darted from his eyes and mouth." Though the monks could not see this apparition, they were said to have heard it roaring at their leader, "You cursed Benedict . . . ! Why are you tormenting me like this?" Benedict apparently gave no answer, and the Ancient Enemy departed. So St. Gregory tells us.

Gregory's *Dialogues,* written in about A.D. 594, some fifty years after Benedict's death, is our only real source of biographical information about the saint, and Gregory was interested more in recounting miracles than in recording what a modern biographer would call facts. So we have no idea, for example, when St. Benedict was born. Most historians guess at around A.D. 480. That would be four years after the quasi-legendary event now referred to as the Fall of the Roman Empire.

Benedict's parents, whom Gregory describes only as "distinguished," were probably unaware that the Roman Empire had fallen, since the only thing that had happened in 476 was that the barbarian usurper Odoacer had declined the supine Senate's offer of the traditional imperial title of Caesar. Benedict's parents behaved quite conventionally in sending their young son from his native district of Norcia to study in Rome. The ways of the metropolis apparently shocked him. "When he saw many of his fellow students falling headlong into vice . . . " Gregory tells us, "he turned his back on further studies, gave up home and inheritance, and resolved to embrace the religious life."

The exemplars of the religious life in these early years of Christianity were the hermits like St. Anthony, who withdrew into the Egyptian desert, fasting and scourging themselves and generally pursuing an ideal of ascetic self-denial. Benedict went to live by himself in a cave near the ruins of Nero's villa at Subiaco. His self-sacrifice inspired a monk named Romanus, who lived in a nearby monastery, to bring bread to Benedict every day. Because a steep cliff jutted out between the monastery and the saint's cave, Romanus devised a system of lowering the daily bread on a long rope. He even attached a little bell to the rope to signal to Benedict that his food was there. The Ancient Enemy was irritated by such good works, so he threw a stone at the bell and broke it, but Romanus continued to feed the saint, and the saint to eat. So St. Gregory tells us.

"One day, when the saint was alone," Gregory's chronicle continues, "the Tempter came in the form of a little blackbird, which began to flutter in front of his face." This fluttering seems to have been some form of preliminary temptation, but Benedict made the sign of the cross, which caused the blackbird to fly away. The moment it left, Benedict was "seized with an unusually violent temptation." The Devil had recalled to his mind a woman he had once seen, and this seems to have brought on a kind of crisis of loneliness, for Benedict nearly decided to give up his life as a hermit. Then he saw a chance for salvation in a nearby patch of briars and nettles. "Throwing his garment aside, he flung himself into the sharp thorns and stinging nettles," Gregory reports. "Then he rolled and tossed until his whole body was in pain and covered with blood. Yet once he had conquered pleasure through suffering, his torn and bleeding skin served to drain the poison of temptation from his body. . . . From then on, as he later told his disciples, he never experienced another temptation of this kind." So St. Gregory tells us.

Only now that he was free from such temptations, according to Gregory's account, was Benedict ready to instruct others in leading the religious life. He appears to have been by now nearly fifty, a sturdy man with a thick white beard, if the devotional paintings in Monte Cassino are to be believed. He attracted converts and disciples not only by his "zealous preaching" but by his ability to perform miracles. These were of the traditional sort, retrieving lost objects or mending broken ones, healing the sick with a touch of his hand, and in one case discovering a hidden stream of water. Heeding the numerology of the Bible, he soon founded twelve monasteries and assigned twelve monks to each.

Such success naturally aroused envy. A priest named Florentius grew so jealous that he sent Benedict as a gift a loaf of poisoned bread. Benedict knew immediately that the gift was deadly, so he gave it to a raven and told it to hide it where no one would ever find it. Florentius then decided to attack the saint by corrupting his disciples. "For this purpose," says Gregory, "he sent seven depraved women into the garden of Benedict's monastery. There they joined hands and danced together for some time within sight of his followers, in an attempt to lead them into sin." Benedict saw all this, feared that some of his younger monks might be tempted, and, in a most uncharacteristic retreat from combat, decided to depart and "let envy have its way." As soon as he left, God punished the gloating Florentius. The balcony on which he stood surveying his new domain suddenly fell to earth and killed him. So St. Gregory tells us.

Cassino, where Benedict arrived with only a few of his most loyal followers, had been a fortified city since time immemorial. Casinum was its Roman name, and it sat astride the via Casilina, now known as Route 6, which was and still is one of the main roads southward to Naples. Hannibal had occupied Casinum during his ill-fated attempt to overthrow Rome. Mark Anthony later owned a splendid villa here and used it for scandalous orgies. Entirely within the walls of the ancient fort, some 1,500 feet above the Liri Valley, Benedict built his new monastery (it was originally called the Citadel of Campania). And here he wrote his *Regula,* or *Rule,* his guide and manual for the monastic life, which would eventually become the standard book of rules for all monasteries in the empire for the next seven centuries.

"Listen, my son," Benedict begins the *Rule,* "and with your heart hear the principles of your master. . . . My words are meant for you, whoever you are, who, laying aside your own will, take up the all-powerful and righteous arms of obedience to fight under the true King, the Lord Jesus Christ." One hears again that Benedictine note of combat, but Benedict was an eminently practical man, and one reason for the triumph of his *Rule* was its eminently practical advice on how to organize a communal life amid the confusions of the sixth century, how to arrange a compromise between the ascetic ideals of the Eastern hermits and the demands of peasant life. The monks were to rise and pray at regular intervals between midnight and dawn, but then they were to go out and work in the fields, raise the crops and harvest them. *Laborare est orare.* The monks were to avoid eating meat, but Benedict was not averse to their drinking a modest amount of wine along with their bread and fresh vegetables. "Though we read that wine is not at all suitable for monks," he wrote with characteristic pragmatism, "in our day it is not possible to persuade the monks of this truth." In what time remained after their work, Benedict's followers were to read the Bible and the works of the church fathers. They went to bed early and probably slept soundly.

Benedict went on performing miracles, which were now of a somewhat more spiritual sort. He "began to manifest the spirit of prophecy," as Gregory puts it, "by foretelling future events and by describing to those who were with him what they had done in his absence." King Totila of the Ostrogoths, who was fighting General Belisarius's attempt to reconquer Italy for the Eastern Empire, came to visit Monte Cassino and tried to test Benedict by that classic ruse of sending a servant disguised as himself. "Son, lay aside the robes you are wearing . . ." Benedict said to Totila's dressed-up sword-bearer, Riggo. "They do not belong to you." King Totila, suitably impressed, came and prostrated himself before the saint. Benedict foretold the Ostrogothic ruler's future and urged him to behave more virtuously. "Put an end to your wickedness," he said. "You will enter Rome and cross the sea. You have nine more years to rule, and in the tenth year you will die." And so it happened.

Unlike many prophets, St. Benedict could foresee his own future, and that of his followers, and the prospects grieved him. A monk named Theoprobus once discovered him weeping and asked him what the matter was. "Almighty God has decreed that this entire monastery and everything I have provided for the community shall fall into the hands of the barbarians," Benedict answered. "It was only with the greatest difficulty that I could prevail upon him to spare the lives of its members."

Benedict had a sister named Scholastica, who had been "consecrated to God in early childhood," and who came from her convent to visit Benedict once every year. Since she was not allowed into the monastery at Monte Cassino, Gregory reports of the last such visit, the two of them sat at a nearby farm and "spent the whole day singing God's praises and conversing about the spiritual life." At dusk, Scholastica wanted Benedict to stay and talk further, but the saint said he had to return to his brethren. So Scholastica put her head down and prayed, and immediately there came a thunderstorm so fierce that Benedict could not leave his shelter. This was, Gregory wrote, "a miracle almighty God performed in answer to a woman's prayer."

Three days after Scholastica returned to her convent, Benedict was standing in his room and looking out at the sky. "He beheld," as Gregory puts it, "his sister's soul leaving her body and entering the court of heaven in the form of a dove." After giving thanks to God for having granted Scholastica "eternal glory," Benedict sent for her body and had it brought to Monte Cassino to be placed in the tomb that he had already prepared for himself. At about this same time, according to Gregory, he saw another remarkable vision in which "the whole world was gathered up before his eyes in what appeared to be a single ray of light."

Benedict foretold to his disciples the exact day of his death, and six days before that day, he gave orders that his tomb be opened for him. "Almost immediately," Gregory records, "he was seized with a violent fever that rapidly wasted his remaining strength. Each day his condition grew worse until finally, on the sixth day, he had his disciples carry him into the chapel, where he received the body and blood of Our Lord to gain strength for his approaching end. Then, supporting his weakened body on the arms of his brethren, he stood with his hands raised to heaven, and as he prayed, breathed his last."

At that very moment, two of Benedict's followers, who were in two different places at the instant of the saint's death, saw an identical vision. They saw a magnificent road, covered by rich carpeting and illuminated by thousands of glittering lights. It extended straight eastward from Monte Cassino, according to Gregory's account, "until it reached up into heaven." Standing by the side of this road, the two disciples both saw "a man of majestic appearance," who said to them, "This is the road taken by blessed Benedict, the Lord's beloved, when he went to heaven."

But what of Benedict's predictions of disaster at Monte Cassino? Did the saint ever imagine that on some distant January morning, waves of American bombers would destroy his monastery? If so, the vision was not included in the *Dialogues* of St. Gregory, who recorded only that occasion on which Benedict told Theoprobus that God had decreed that the monastery would fall into the hands of barbarians, and that only Benedict's strenuous arguments had persuaded God to spare the lives of the monks. Of this prediction, Gregory observed, "We have seen its fulfillment in the recent destruction of his abbey by the Lombards. They came at night while the community was asleep and plundered the entire monastery without capturing a single monk."

This was the sacking of Monte Cassino in A.D. 591 by Zotto, the Lombard duke of Benevento, and though the monks all survived, the ruin of the monastery was total. The monks fled to Rome and took refuge in the Lateran monastery, bringing with them only the manuscript of Benedict's *Regula,* their official measuring cups for bread and wine, and their motto that what had been struck down would live again. The motto was actually an understatement. If Monte Cassino had not been sacked by the Lombards, it is quite possible that the Benedictines would have remained in quiet provincial obscurity, harvesting their crops and saying their prayers. As refugees in Rome, however, they brought to Pope Gregory not only a skillfully organized system of communal life but a vocation to serve that pope who had given them shelter.

And of all popes who might have given the Benedictines shelter in Rome, few could have been more adept at seeing the possibilities in this newly acquired flock of followers. A stocky, forceful man with a bald head and bearded chin, Gregory was not only an experienced administrator (a former prefect of Rome) and diplomat (ambassador to Constantinople) but also the founder of seven monasteries and indeed the first pope to be drawn from the ranks of the monks. When Gregory decided to send an envoy to the apostate shores of Britain to undertake the conversion of the pagan King Ethelbert of Kent, it was natural for him to turn to the Benedictine Augustine, who went and established the first new Christian church at Canterbury. And from the Benedictines' conversion of the British, much else followed.

While the Benedictine missionaries were spreading the *Regula* throughout Britain, France, and Germany, however, the plundered shrine at Monte Cassino remained in ruins. Not until the year 718, more than a century after the Lombard attack, did Pope Gregory II send a monk named Petronax of Brescia to visit the mountaintop. Petronax found there a few local followers—"solitaries," they are called in the official church account—who still honored Benedict's grave. Petronax remained in Monte Cassino and began organizing the rebuilding of the monastery, and in 742 Pope Zachary honored the effort by returning to the revived abbey the original manuscript of Benedict's *Regula.* He also decreed that the abbey should be subordinate to no authority except that of the Holy See itself.

The fate of Benedict's actual bones was more ambiguous. By the time St. Petronax arrived at Benedict's grave in Monte Cassino, the tomb had apparently been opened, and the saint's bones had somehow been conveyed to the monastery of St.-Benoît-sur-Loire at Fleury, near Orléans. There a new shrine had been built in their honor, and pilgrims came from all over Europe to worship them. Pope Zachary issued orders that these bones be returned from Fleury to Monte Cassino, but there is some doubt whether his orders were carried out. The monks at Fleury may have returned only some of the bones, for the relics of Benedict were worshiped for years in both places.

The cult kept growing. Charlemagne came to visit Monte Cassino in A.D. 786 and inspected the original manuscript of the *Regula,* and when he returned to his court at Aachen, he asked the Benedictines to send him a copy, which they did. This imperial copy made for Charlemagne was eventually lost, as was Benedict's original, but when Charlemagne's son and successor, Louis the Pious, ordered in A.D. 817 that Benedict's *Regula* be made the basic law for all monasteries in the empire, he ordered a new copy made from Charlemagne's copy, and it is this new copy, listed as Sangallensis 914, at the famous monastic library in St. Gall, in Switzerland, that survives to this day.

The abbey kept growing too. Abbot Gisulf (797–817) rebuilt the modest church erected by Petronax into a three-nave basilica. He also built a new church and monastery at the foot of the mountain. This was what attracted Saracen marauders in A.D. 883. They broke into the new monastery and butchered Abbot Bertharius. The monks fled once again, this time carrying the precious manuscript of the *Regula* to the nearby monastery of Teano. Fire destroyed the monastery at Teano in 896, and that was how Benedict's manuscript disappeared. Another century passed before Abbot Aligernus once again led the monks back to Monte Cassino and once again rebuilt the ruins, grander than ever.

It was now, in the eleventh century, that Monte Cassino reached the height of its grandeur. Its control of the surrounding fields and vineyards extended for miles. The copyists in its scriptorium produced more new copies of both classical and Christian texts than any other institution in southern Italy. Monks from Monte Cassino occupied many of the highest positions in the church, and three of them became popes (Stephen IX, Victor III, and Gelasius II; there have been twenty-four Benedictine popes in all). One of these, Pope Victor III, settled the old problem of Benedict's missing bones by announcing that he had discovered in Monte Cassino a secret hiding place where the bones had originally been stored, and that the fragments removed to Fleury were therefore inauthentic, that the true relics of the saint remained and had always remained at Monte Cassino. The only event needed to complete this new cycle of rebirth and revival was a new moment of destruction. In 1349, an earthquake cracked open the walls of the monastery and brought the great towers tumbling to the ground.

Each rebuilding seemed to take more time and more elaboration, and the Baroque palace that now arose on top of the mountain seemed far removed indeed from the humble establishment that St. Benedict had once created. A rough rectangle of carved stone, it stood about 200 yards long and 150 wide, its basilica walls covered by murals by Luca Giordano, its library filled with more than 80,000 volumes. A painting by Paolo de Matteis still portrays the dedication ceremonies that were finally held in 1727, amiable festivities that featured bewigged dancers and musicians. By then, of course, the church of St. Benedict had slipped into its long centuries of slumber.

Henry Wadsworth Longfellow climbed the mountain on a visit in 1874 and then wrote some characteristic musings:

> The silence of the place was like a sleep,
>   So full of rest it seemed; each passing tread
> Was a reverberation from the deep
>   Recesses of the ages that are dead. . . .

When General Mark Clark first saw Monte Cassino, from a jeep parked in the snowy hills on the far side of the Liri Valley, he saw only the prospect of misery and suffering for his men. "When I think back on the weeks and finally months of searing struggle," he later wrote, "the biting cold, the torrents of rain and snow, the lakes of mud that sucked down machines, and, most of all, the deeply dug fortifications in which the Germans waited for us in the hills, it seems to me that no soldiers in history were ever given a more difficult assignment than the Fifth Army in that winter of 1944."

The man who gave them that assignment was Mark Clark himself, an ambitious man all too new to the hardships of combat. Son of a career officer, Clark had graduated from West Point in 1917 just in time to see a few days of actual fighting in World War I. His chief role in the second war had been as a planner of military training, an assignment in which he impressed Chief of Staff George Marshall and made a friend of Marshall's protégé, Dwight Eisenhower. Eisenhower had asked for him to help plan the North African invasion of 1942, and now, at forty-seven, Clark was the youngest lieutenant general in U.S. army history. This was not necessarily the best recommendation for the officer assigned to command the U.S. Fifth Army on its march to the capture of Rome. The Fifth Army included not only veteran British and Canadian troops but Gurkhas from the Himalayas, Moroccan cutthroats under French command, some remnants of the Polish army, and even a few Brazilians.

Facing these polyglot invaders stood about 70,000 of the best troops in the German army, organized in the five divisions of the Fourteenth Panzer Korps under the command of General Frido von Senger und Etterlin. A professional soldier of fifty-three, Senger had served with distinction in both the conquest of France and the defeat at Stalingrad. He was also a Rhodes scholar and a devout Catholic. He was one of those who misguidedly believed that it was a soldier's duty to fight as well as possible in even a doomed and disgraced cause. "According to the creed of Thomas Aquinas," Senger wrote, "no man can be blamed for the crimes of others insofar as he has no influence over them. However, the power is not in the hands of the generals but of Hitler and the German people who have voted him into power. . . ."

One of the major powers in Hitler's hands was the authority to decide whether and where to make a defense against the Allied invasion. The Italians had signed an armistice on September 3, 1943, shortly after the Allied conquest of Sicily, and that enabled the British Eighth Army to cross the Strait of Messina unopposed. Clark's Fifth Army landed at Salerno on September 9 and entered Naples by the end of the month. Hitler drew a line—the so-called Gustav Line—that would enable the *Wehrmacht* to organize a defense south of Rome (he could decide later whether to abandon Rome and fall back to the Gothic Line, just north of Florence). The Gustav Line—to be reinforced by mines, pillboxes, machine-gun nests, barbed wire—extended all across the mountainous peninsula from Gaeta on the Tyrrhenian coast to Ortona on the Adriatic. It ran right through the middle of Cassino. Though General Senger could take a measure of pride in his refusal to make any military use of the monastery, he could hardly have deluded himself about what would happen when he fortified the surrounding hills. One of the orders issued from Senger's headquarters specifically said: "Evacuate civilians as soon as possible, and make no use of abbey buildings, but make defenses right up to the abbey wall if necessary."

Not only was the monastery itself one of the great art treasures of the world but its library was filled with priceless medieval manuscripts. Indeed, the Italian authorities in Rome, who still lived under the illusion that the monastery would remain safe from attack, had shipped other art there for safekeeping. From the Naples Museum, there were eleven Titians, including the gorgeous *Danaë,* and Brueghel's *Parable of the Blind,* and the only two Goyas in Italy. And more: thirty crates of things unearthed at Pompeii, and seven crates of ancient coins from Syracuse, two boxes of Keats and Shelley manuscripts from the Keats house in Rome, and more crates unopened and uncatalogued, all lined up in the underground vaults.

The obvious vulnerability of this hoard was at first realized only by a Dr. Maximilian J. Becker, who had been an archaeology student before the war and who now served as a medic in the Hermann Goering Division. When Becker heard from some Franciscan monks about what had been stored at Monte Cassino, he made a private visit there to persuade the abbot, Gregorio Diamare, to let the Germans remove his treasures for safekeeping in the north. The abbot, a stooped and paunchy little man of seventy-nine, declined. He lacked authority, he said; besides, God's will would be done. Becker joined forces with a Lt. Col. Julius Schlegel, the transportation officer for the Goering Division, and the two of them finally persuaded the abbot that only they could save the treasures of Monte Cassino from almost certain destruction. When the advancing Americans were only about fifty miles away, and the town of Cassino had already been hit by the first Allied air raids, the Germans loaded up more than one hundred truckloads of art and carted them away to their supply depot at Spoleto. Only then did Becker, having pledged his personal honor to the abbot for the safety of the treasures, learn that the ambitious Schlegel was now currying favor with Marshal Goering by offering him the pick of the Monte Cassino pictures for his personal collection. (And only after the war did the Allies retrieve Goering's loot from Nazi hiding places in Austria.)

What the Germans called "clearing" the abbey also meant clearing out its inhabitants. Abbot Diamare, who had ruled over Monte Cassino for thirty-four years, refused to leave his post in the face of the coming attack, but the Germans forcibly removed all but ten of the monks, as well as several hundred refugees who had taken shelter in the monastery. More hungry refugees soon began to gather outside the walls, though, swarms of them. Ten women finally pounded on the monastery gate and demanded to be let in. The monks refused. The women threatened to set fire to the gate. The abbot gave way, ordered the gate opened, and about 800 terrified peasants came streaming into the abbey.

One of the monks kept a diary:

"Jan. 20: Around seven o'clock hellish firing started on the plain, which looked as if it were erupting all over; an awful noise shook the whole monastery. . . . This was the first great battle for Cassino. . . .

"Jan. 21: . . . During the night, an Anglo-American shell penetrated the basilica. . . . A cloud of dust covered everything. The confessionals were smashed and so were some marbles. The most important damage was done to the great painting by Luca Giordano; it was torn and disfigured, on its left side as you face it. . . . The stained-glass window was also ruined. . . .

"Jan. 24: Hellish firing started at around 9:30 P.M. and continued until about 11:30. Several shells fell on the monastery. One on the *collegio* where it smashed the roof; two on the novitiate, one at exactly 11:30, where it blew into pieces a column standing near the observatory. Fragments flew all over the place. . . ."

Mark Clark had launched the great offensive by ordering the Thirty-sixth Division, a Texas National Guard division, to cross the Rapido River just east of Cassino on the night of January 20. He could hardly have chosen a worse place for his attack. The fast-flowing Rapido was fifty feet wide and too deep to wade. Senger's defenders were fully prepared. They had mined the eastern banks of the river, they had flooded the surrounding fields to halt American armor, and they had cut down all nearby trees to give themselves a free field of fire. The Americans, on unfamiliar terrain at night, were supposed to pick their way through the minefields, cross the river on rubber boats, establish a bridgehead on the opposite shore, and then build pontoon bridges for the units that would follow. "We might succeed, but I do not see how we can," Maj. Gen. Fred L. Walker wrote in his diary before leading his Texans to the river. He was right. He lost nearly 2,000 men in that night's debacle.

The French and Moroccans finally led the way across the Rapido, much farther upstream, and then Clark sent his Thirty-fourth Division to climb the heights 1,500 feet above Cassino and to seize the monastery. The attackers succeeded in scaling the heights, but then came a deadlock. The Germans were too well entrenched to be dislodged, and each assault met with a counterassault. By the time the New Zealanders crept up to replace the Americans at the end of a week's hard fighting, they found the hillside strewn with frozen corpses. Fifty Americans still guarding the uppermost ridge were so exhausted that they could not even stand and had to be carried down the mountainside on stretchers. And the snow kept falling.

On February 12, the New Zealand commander, Lt. Gen. Bernard Freyberg, called up Clark's headquarters to request more air support for the new offensive that had been assigned to his Fourth Indian Division. "We will make every effort to give you what you want," said Clark's chief of staff, Maj. Gen. Albert Gruenther.

"I want the convent attacked," said Freyberg.

"You mean the monastery?" Gruenther said. "The monastery is not on the list of targets."

"It is on my list of targets . . ." Freyberg retorted. "I want it bombed."

So the Allied commanders finally had to come to grips with the question of whether to destroy Monte Cassino. It was a question that they had barely begun to analyze in any depth, and it threatened to confront them again and again. What would happen, for example, if the Germans decided to make a major military stand in front of Rome? Or Paris? If they could assign artillery spotters to Monte Cassino, why couldn't they make the same use of the Vatican or the Cathedral of Notre Dame? Eisenhower had tried to set out the basic guidelines just a month earlier, but those guidelines remained ambiguous. "Today we are fighting in a country which has contributed a great deal to our cultural inheritance . . ." Eisenhower declared in a December 29 message to "all commanders." "We are bound to respect [its] monuments so far as war allows. If we have to choose between destroying a famous building and sacrificing our own men, then our men's lives count infinitely more and the buildings must go. But the choice is not always so clear-cut as that. In many cases the monuments can be spared without any detriment to operational needs. Nothing can stand against the argument of military necessity. That is an accepted principle. But the phrase 'military necessity' is sometimes used where it would be more truthful to speak of military convenience or even of personal convenience. . . ."

What, then, is "military necessity," except what some general says it is? When the Americans were leading the advance toward Cassino, none of their generals had demanded the destruction of the monastery. Major General Geoffrey Keyes, commander of II Corps, and his divisional commanders, both General Walker of the Thirty-sixth Division and Maj. Gen. Charles Ryder of the Thirty-fourth, none of these had seen any "military necessity" for an air raid. Now here was General Freyberg of New Zealand arguing precisely that. And Freyberg was not just another general. When Clark's own superior, Sir Harold Alexander, the British commander of the entire Italian campaign, assigned the New Zealanders to the Fifth Army, he had told Clark, "Freyberg is a big man in New Zealand, a big man in the Commonwealth. We treat him with kid gloves and you must do the same."

Freyberg was indeed a big man, a rugged figure more than six feet tall, his nation's leading war hero. At the beginning of World War I, Freyberg had barged into Winston Churchill's office at the Admiralty and won himself a position on the expedition to the Dardanelles. Freyberg was subsequently wounded four times on the Western Front—he once showed Churchill more then twenty scars on his body—and won Britain's highest military honor, the Victoria Cross. He was already fifty when the new war began, but he led the New Zealand Corps through arduous combat in Egypt, Crete, North Africa, and Italy (it had lost 18,000 of 43,500 men). Most important, the New Zealanders could go home any time their leaders decided that these troops were needed for defense against the Japanese (as the Australians had done). And when the New Zealand Parliament had debated that very question in the spring of 1943, one major reason why the New Zealanders remained in Italy was that Freyberg urged his countrymen to stand behind their commitment.

Another problem was that Clark's attention was much distracted by the dangers threatening the new Allied beachhead at Anzio, about fifty miles up the coast, behind the Germans' Gustav Line. Originally, Clark had pressed the disastrous crossing of the Rapido on January 20 to divert German attention from the prospective landing at Anzio on January 22; now, when the Allies found themselves pinned down on the Anzio beachhead, they needed new pressure exerted against Cassino or they risked defeat in both places. Thus, when Gruenther had to respond to Freyberg's demand for a bombing raid against the monastery, he had to deal with commanders much concerned about other things. He could reach Clark only by radio, during an inspection of the Anzio front, and Clark only grumbled that "Freyberg's strong viewpoint . . . was putting me in a very difficult position."

Alexander's chief of staff, Lt. Gen. Sir John Harding, called Gruenther later that day with a secondhand version of the commander's verdict: "General Alexander has decided that the monastery should be bombed if General Freyberg considers it a military necessity. He regrets that the building should be destroyed, but he has faith in Freyberg's judgment. If there is any reasonable probability that the building is being used for military purposes General Alexander believes that its destruction is warranted."

Considering the explicitness of that decision, Gruenther sounded almost insubordinate in his defense of his own commander's view. "General Clark does not think that the building should be bombed," he said, according to his own recollection of the argument. "If the commander of the New Zealand Corps were an American commander, he would give specific orders that it should not be bombed. However, in view of the situation, which is a delicate one, General Clark hesitated to give him such an order without referring the matter to General Alexander. General Clark is still of the opinion that no military necessity exists for the destruction of the monastery. He believes it will endanger the lives of many civilian refugees in the building, and that a bombing will not destroy its value as a fortification for the enemy. In fact, General Clark feels that the bombing will probably enhance its value."

General Harding was icy. "General Alexander has made his position quite clear on this point," he said to Gruenther. "If General Clark desires to talk personally to General Alexander about the subject, I'm sure that General Alexander will be pleased to discuss it with him."

Gruenther had no choice then but to report this exchange to Clark. Clark equivocated a bit longer by telling Gruenther to call Freyberg once more and "to let Freyberg know that I still did not consider it a military necessity and was reluctant to authorize the bombing unless Freyberg was certain that it could not be avoided." Freyberg was quite willing to accept the responsibility that Clark sought to avoid. He declared that he was "convinced of the necessity" and added a warning "that any higher commander who refused to authorize the bombing would have to be prepared to take the responsibility for failure of the attack."

It was apparent then, and it has become even more apparent since then, that there was a clear difference between the American and British judgments on the bombing of the monastery. And if it is not too cynical to suggest that Supreme Court justices pay attention to election returns, the same can reasonably be said of generals (as

Mark Clark was to learn all too well when the Texas representatives in Congress began inquiring about the heavy casualties in the crossing of the Rapido). President Roosevelt was facing a reelection campaign later in 1944. Americans of Italian origin and other Catholic voters both represented large and sensitive constituencies. (General Clark, be it noted, was also a Catholic.) In Britain, by contrast, Churchill faced no immediate election, and whenever he did, the Catholic vote would be a small one, and the Italian vote even smaller.

Yet even in these ill-defined currents of opinion, there were strong crosscurrents. The British, who had recently seen much of London go up in flames, were more emotionally aware than the Americans of what mass bombings might do to Italy. The archbishop of Canterbury certainly knew of the wreckage surrounding his own cathedral when he asked the House of Lords to consider the dangers threatening Ravenna, Padua, Venice. "Think of Rome itself," he said. "Rome doesn't belong to Italy; it belongs to the world." Harold Nicolson, the eminent diplomat and memoirist, spoke even more passionately. "Works of art are irreplaceable," he said. "Human lives are replaceable." And lest anyone think that he was speaking in abstractions, Nicolson said that if he had to sacrifice his own son in the service to preserve Monte Cassino, then he would accept that sacrifice. (He did not know at the time that his son Nigel actually was serving at Cassino; the son, equally unaware of the price that his father had put on his head, survived.) Some of the listeners in the House of Lords were quick to rebut such statements. "I do not wish," said Lord Latham, "to see Europe stocked with cultural monuments to be venerated by mankind in chains and on its knees. . . . The people of this country will not submit to their boys being sacrificed—even one of them being sacrificed—unnecessarily to save whatever building it may be."

Though American leaders may have been keenly aware of Italian and Catholic sensibilities in an election year, they were also aware of the American press's noisy commitment to the welfare of the ordinary GI. Any signs of favoritism brought trouble. CLARK ORDER PROHIBITS 5TH ARMY FROM ATTACKING CHURCH PROPERTY, one critical headline in the *New York Times* announced over a dispatch from C. L. Sulzberger on the fighting at Monte Cassino. "There seems little doubt that [the Germans] are employing it as an artillery observation post. . . . The Fifth Army's abstention from shelling Monte Cassino Abbey . . . hampered our advance greatly. . . . Many lives may be lost." Though Sulzberger suggested that there was "little doubt" about the Germans' military use of the monastery, other American reporters indicated that there was no doubt at all. "Allied artillerymen were still carefully avoiding the Abbey with artillery fire though officers say the old monastery was definitely being used as an observation post," according to a dispatch from Associated Press correspondent Lynn Heinzerling. "Many soldiers are bitter that it is left unmolested while their comrades die below it." Unmolested was hardly the word, since Allied shells were landing inside the monastery every day, but the debate over an all-out assault continued.

Strangely enough, the most powerful voice demanding such an assault came not from the highest ranking officer involved but from the lowest ranking one, and not from a man who wanted to destroy the monastery but from a man who didn't want to attack it at all. His voice was so powerful, according to the excellent account by David Hapgood and David Richardson, because he was the commander who had been assigned to lead the actual attack. Tuker was his name, Maj. Gen. Francis Tuker, commander of the Fourth Indian Division, a unit within the New Zealand Corps that was one-third British, two-thirds Indian and Gurkha. A waspish professional soldier (also an artist and a poet), Tuker was one of the few generals on the scene who actually had experience in mountain warfare, having fought on the North-West Frontier in India. He had a low opinion of most of the officers who now outranked him in the battle for Monte Cassino. He regarded Freyberg as "an obstinate dunce," a man who was "personally brave" but "without any tactical talent . . . no brains and no imagination." Still higher, General Alexander impressed him as "an indolent fifth wheel" and General Clark as "a flashy ignoramus."

It was typical of Tuker, when he heard nothing from any intelligence officials on how the monastery was actually built, that he sent an aide hunting through the used-book stores of liberated Naples to find some prewar tourist guidebooks. "After considerable trouble . . ." he tartly reported to Freyberg, "I have at last found a book, dated 1879, which gives certain details of the construction of the Monte Cassino Monastery." Specifically, the old guidebook disclosed that the monastery's stone walls were ten to fifteen feet thick, and that there was only one gate, built out of "large stone blocks 9 to 10 metres long." How in God's name was an infantry unit supposed to break into such a fortress? In his experience, Tuker said, the only answer was first to reduce the place to rubble. "If we were to be forced to attack," he said in a memo to Freyberg, "then it would have to be a matter of obliterating the *whole* Monte Cassino feature with bombs day after day and following up the bombs with artillery, and then shoving the infantry up at dusk on the heels of the shelling, leaving them the whole night to do the job."

As Tuker made clear with that preliminary *if*, he thought such an onslaught both unnecessary and undesirable; the monastery could easily be bypassed and isolated. "I went through hell on earth during the early days urging desperately that no attack on Monte Cassino should be contemplated," Tuker said later. "I could never understand why the Fifth Army decided to batter its head again and again against this most powerful position, held by some of the finest troops in the German Army in heavily wired and mined and fixed entrenchments." The reason why was that General Clark wanted it, and he wanted it because his Fifth Army was supposed to conquer Rome as soon as possible, before the D day landings that were now planned for only four months in the future. The Americans were getting irritated, moreover, by repeated British suggestions for delaying and diversionary actions on every front. They were beginning to think, to put it bluntly, that the British were afraid to risk heavy casualties. It was true, of course, that the British had been at war for four years, twice as long as the Americans, and while fighting alone against Germany, the British had suffered heavier losses than anything yet inflicted on the Americans. So why must more British soldiers now be sacrificed to the American appetite for combat, Tuker might well have asked, or if they must be sacrificed, why should anyone hesitate about bombing a monastery?

What a cat's cradle of contradictory arguments! Clark didn't want to bomb the monastery, but he did want it captured. The only available troops were the New Zealanders, who said they had to bomb the monastery before they could capture it. The British supported whatever the New Zealanders said for political reasons, but the New Zealanders thought it was a mistake to attack the monastery at all. But Clark insisted on the attack, and the only available troops were the New Zealanders, and so on. Such complexities were actually somewhat beyond Freyberg, who thought it an officer's duty to do as he was told. He supported both his superiors' demands for an attack and his subordinate's judgment on how the attack should be carried out. Tuker's delusion was that he could somehow persuade Freyberg to persuade Clark to change his mind. "I always told Freyberg quite clearly," Tuker said later, "that nothing would induce me to attack this feature directly unless the garrison was reduced to helpless lunacy by sheer unending pounding for days and nights by air and artillery. . . ."

Tuker tried to reduce Freyberg and Clark to helpless lunacy by the pounding of his snappish memoranda, but he was suddenly silenced by a crippling attack of rheumatoid arthritis. That put the Fourth Indian Division under the command of the more pliable Brig. Harry Dimoline and enabled Freyberg to get on with the job. On February 11, Dimoline formally requested the U.S. Army to bomb the monastery; Freyberg approved and forwarded the request. Gruenther arranged the details. When the weather cleared, the bombers would strike on February 13. Even then, however, Clark sought an escape in another meeting with Alexander, and even then Alexander based his definition of military necessity on political expediency. "Remember, [Freyberg] is a very important cog in the Commonwealth effort," Alexander said, according to Clark's recollections. "I would be most reluctant to take responsibility for his failing and for his telling his people, 'I lost five thousand New Zealanders because they wouldn't let me use air as I wanted.' " Clark squirmed to the end. "I said, 'You give me a direct order and we'll do it,' and he did."

As soon as the raid was finally ordered, it had to be canceled. Freyberg telephoned Gruenther at midnight to report that his troops had not had time to move back from their exposed positions near the monastery. Then the next day, it snowed heavily, so the raid was postponed again. The Fourth Indian Division finally sent back word from the mountaintop that it would be ready to attack on the night of February 16–17, so the air raid was scheduled late on February 16. Then Freyberg got a call from the Americans saying that the air raid would be staged not late on February 16 but the very next morning, February 15. There were reports of more rainstorms coming, and all available bombers would soon be needed at Anzio. The troops on the mountain said they could not evacuate their positions by the following morning. Freyberg said that they would have to do the best they could, that "this delay from day to day is making us look ridiculous." When the first bombers arrived over Monte Cassino the next morning, a British officer on the mountain shouted into a field telephone that the men weren't ready. "Even as I spoke," he recalled, "the roar drowned my voice as the first shower of eggs came down."

President Roosevelt called a press conference later that day to explain the raid. "The reason it was shelled was because it was being used by the Germans to shell us," Roosevelt said. "It was a German strongpoint—had artillery and everything up there in the abbey." Since there were actually no Germans in the abbey, no "garrison" of the kind that Tuker wanted to pound into "helpless lunacy," the only people killed were about 150 of the Italian peasants hiding in the cellar. Stray bombs also wounded twenty-four of the unready Indians. When it was all over, Abbot Diamare, carrying a large wooden crucifix, led a procession of monks down the mountainside the following morning. Along with them came about thirty of the surviving refugees, some badly wounded. One woman who had lost both feet was carried on a ladder.

When the Indians finally attacked the battered monastery on the night of February 17, they were beaten back like all their predecessors, and the same thing happened on the next night and the night after that. The third attack, by the light of a waning moon, was supposed to be the last and fiercest, irresistible. Two companies of Gurkhas crawled up to a ridge only 400 yards from the ruins of the monastery, then made for the cover of some shrubbery at the edge of a ravine. The shrubs turned out to be thorns, all festooned with German mines and trip wires. Two-thirds of the Gurkhas were shot down within fifteen minutes, and some of the corpses seen dangling among the thorns the next morning had as many as four wires coiled around their legs.

The "obstinate" Freyberg wanted to resume the attack next day, but after the Fourth Indian lost 530 men in that third night alone, Dimoline persuaded him to give up. Two days later, the Germans finally took advantage of the lull to move up inside the monastery walls and establish stronger defensive positions among the heaps of rubble. And the snow kept falling.

The next month, the scarred and numbed Indians were replaced, like the Americans before them, this time by Gen. Wladyslaw Anders's Polish Corps. These were some 50,000 men who had been captured by the Soviets during the monthlong nightmare in which both Hitler and Stalin attacked Poland from opposite sides. Only after Hitler invaded Russia in 1943 did Stalin agree to release his Polish captives from their Siberian prison camps to go and join the British forces in Iran. From there, they had worked their way to Italy, to the snow-covered ridges of Monte Cassino. Here they too attacked, and they too were beaten back, until finally, on the morning of May 18, an assault by the Twelfth Podolski Lancers met no resistance. The Germans had quietly pulled out during the night. The Poles raised their red-and-white banner over the ruins.

What should be done when a great and noble place is destroyed? Should it be rebuilt as it was, or as something else, or should it be abandoned? History provides no clear answer, for much depends on what the building represents, and how it was destroyed, and by whom. If we want to preserve it, what are we preserving? It is hard now to imagine the disappearance of the great pyramids of Egypt, yet they were once only one among the so-called Seven Wonders of the World. Who of us now feels a sense of loss at the passing of the Temple of Artemis at Ephesus or the Mausoleum at Halicarnassus?

Most ancient ruins, in fact, we insist not on restoring but on preserving as ruins, for that is the form in which we have always known them. Stonehenge and the Acropolis must now be protected from roving tourists, but no one would ever advocate rebuilding them to the state they were in when they were new. If anyone tried to restore the Roman Colosseum, it would look about as inspiring as a soccer stadium. It needs repairs, of course, to keep it from falling down, but just enough repairs to keep it looking like a classical ruin. Anything more would only imbue this noble relic with the revivalist rhetoric of the Mussolini era, a rhetoric partly brutal and partly burlesque.

Sometimes, then, people decide to preserve ruins as ruins precisely because they do remind viewers that the process of ruin is often a consequence of the lust for glory. The Kaiser Wilhelm Church in Berlin, for example, with its clock perpetually stopped at the moment of an Allied air raid, implies that the bustle of surrounding commerce was not always so peaceful. Still, one does wonder occasionally who is delivering this message to whom, and at what price. Would the Berliners have decided to preserve such a monument to the destruction of their city if the decision had been freely theirs to make? And are they perhaps preserving not a confession of Nazi wrongs but rather an accusation of wrong inflicted on Berlin by Allied bombers? One can also hardly help observing that the institution preserved in its ruin is a rather ugly church and not, for example, the Brandenburg Gate.

The Romans preserved ruins as a form of exemplary punishment, but it was they who did both the preserving and the punishing. The wreckage of Carthage, its stones seeded with salt, provided a striking message to anyone who might think of challenging Rome, but the Carthaginians probably would have interpreted the message in their own way. The Romans felt equally assertive when they ordered a similar devastation of Jerusalem. Messages can change, however. The once-buried stones of Jerusalem now express a whole chorus of differing concepts of preservation, and they are more fiercely contested than any monument in Rome.

Unless it be the function of a ruin to be a ruin, then, we want it repaired to fulfill some other function. When the Campanile in Venice collapsed in 1912, for example, nobody suggested that it would look picturesque as a ruined stump. Its function was to overawe tourists in the piazza San Marco, and so it was rebuilt from the ground up, rebuilt so skillfully that few now realize that this Renaissance masterpiece is younger than the Eiffel Tower. Function serves even better to explain the restoration of churches. When the Cathedral of Rheims was gutted by shellfire during World War I, for example, nobody suggested that it be venerated as a shrine to peace. The Rockefellers paid handsomely to have it rebuilt just as it had been. In London, similarly, the complex of political and religious buildings around Westminster Abbey strikes a newcomer as dauntingly medieval, but the Gothic towers are about as Gothic as those of Yale or the University of Chicago, and for much the same reasons.

There are times, unfortunately, when the need to restore ruins conflicts with a passion for modernism, for "a contemporary statement." The Roman architects who were commissioned to rebuild St. John of the Lateran in the seventeenth century, for example, could not bear the idea of re-creating a Romanesque masterpiece when they had before them all the possibilities of the Baroque. All over southern Italy, indeed, Romanesque churches were encrusted with Baroque "improvements," and though a modern restorer might happily strip away nineteenth-century neo-Gothicism, he feels qualms about destroying a seventeenth-century restoration that hides a fourteenth-century original. How much more sensible in every way were the authorities in Assisi, who frugally preserved a beautifully pillared temple to Minerva by simply reconsecrating it as a Christian church.

Political fashions also change unpredictably. The enthusiasm for commemorating military bloodshed in marble and bronze seems to have crested after World War I. Even the most peaceful village in Bavaria or Provence insisted, with a certain complacency, on asking every bypasser to admire some heroic rendition of Mars or Mariana and to contemplate the carved lists of the local martyrs. The killing in World War II was so much greater that the desire to memorialize it seems to have wearied. Or perhaps there was something too painful about commissioning another statue on the same public square so soon after the unveiling of the last one. Many a village, whether out of exhaustion or economy, simply added the new names to its roster of the dead.

And just as the greater physical destruction required more rebuilding, the traditional enthusiasm for brand-new plazas and memorial buildings now tended to give way to a preference for restoring things just as they had been before the great destruction. The first rebuilding in London and Berlin was either bleakly functional or pretentiously neo-Bauhaus, a "statement," but once there was more money available, and more time for reflection, it was largely devoted to the re-creation of a lost past. Let every stone in Wren's bombed churches be put back just the way it used to be (how deplorable, though, if Wren himself had felt the same way after the Great Fire!), and every timbered roof in the back alleys of Nuremberg. Before Hitler, before Wagner, there was always Hans Sachs.

Only in America, where there is relatively little to be restored, and where most of the destruction is something that we have inflicted on ourselves, only here are questions of historic restoration usually mixed up with real-estate deals. Thus, although Madison Square Garden is a historic name associated with the talents of Saint-Gaudens and Stanford White, only New York operators would create a new version of this establishment by tearing down the handsome facade of Pennsylvania Station to make room for it.

And only years afterward do we realize that profound self-judgments are involved in such public decisions, and that the lack of self-judgment is part of the judgment. Suppose, then, that the Empire State Building or St. Patrick's Cathedral were suddenly destroyed. What would we build in their place—if anything?

For the U.S. government to play any role in the reconstruction of Monte Cassino might have implied that the U.S. government acknowledged having done something wrong, and the U.S. government acknowledged no such thing. And so, among its many postwar activities, activities both benevolent and destructive, not one penny out of all the billions of dollars disbursed around the world went for the rebuilding of the monastery of Monte Cassino.

But something had to be done. First, of course, there were the people to be cared for, the 25,000 or so survivors of what had once been the industrious town of Cassino at the foot of the mountain. The actual fighting, week after week, had been fiercest not around the walls of the monastery but down here in the town. Tanks and artillery had pushed forward, block by block, firing at anything that moved, then retreating again, block by block, still firing.

Now that the war was over, the survivors had to live on in the rat-infested rubble, without food, without fresh water, without money or jobs. A whole generation of children was growing up without even knowing what a school was.

Three months after the Polish capture of the monastery, Mayor Gaetano di Biassio had written a letter to President Roosevelt, appealing for help for what he called his "martyred city." This had received only a cool reply from the U.S. embassy in Rome ("The American government endeavors to assist Italy as best it can . . ."), but the mayor seemed to think that this constituted a White House promise of aid. When an American reporter stopped by for a visit in 1947, he found that only six new houses had been built in the devastated town, and the mayor sounded aggrieved. "If only the United States would help," he said. "President Roosevelt promised. I have the letter. But he died. Now I get no answer."

Even then, though, about thirty-five monks and about one hundred workmen were slowly clearing away the debris in the shell of the monastery. Though the main bell had been destroyed, like almost everything else, the monks had strung up a shell casing to sound the hours for prayer. As they sifted the wreckage, they followed a basic rule that the new Abbot Ildefonso Rea had laid down, that everything should be reestablished *"dov'era, com'era,"* or "where it was, as it was." But all this would take ages. "It goes very slowly," said Dom Francesco Vignanelli, as he sat in a shack and catalogued fragments of stone. "Still, we've rebuilt six statues." Another monk, Dom Oderisco Graziosi, offered a comparison with the thousands of olive trees that once bloomed on the mountainside. "It takes an olive tree thirty years to bear fruit . . ." he said. "For us it will be decades, perhaps centuries. But that day will come. . . ."

The late 1940s brought the realization that Washington would have to finance Europe's recovery, brought the Marshall Plan and a quickening of Italian economic life, and eventually new concrete apartment blocks arising in Cassino. Another reporter came to visit in 1950, and the villagers proudly took him on tours of their new homes and showed him the new marvel in each apartment, a porcelain bowl of water that flushed itself empty with a softly rolling gurgle whenever you pushed that little steel lever over there on the side, there, like that. Then, inevitably, the reporter climbed the mountain to see what progress had been made on the monastery.

"The basilica, which was begun only four months ago, is half finished," Alan Moorehead reported in *The New Yorker*. "One sees besides St. Benedict's tomb there the crater made by an unexploded bomb. In the courtyards of the monastery, some two hundred men are working, under the direction of the monks, among a network of dump-car tracks, fallen pillars and decapitated statues. By groping about in the rubble, they have rescued and reconstructed statues and slabs of inlaid marble that had been broken into as many as fifty pieces. A kind of jigsaw-puzzle game goes on. . . ."

It still seemed beyond possibility that the rebuilding could be finished in this century. But the Italian government, which had officially owned Monte Cassino ever since all monasteries were nationalized as part of the risorgimento a century ago, managed to provide nearly $4 million over the years, and $4 million can be stretched a long way in the rebuilding of an Italian monastery. The Benedictines, who number about 12,000 around the world, one-quarter of them in the United States, also managed without a great deal of noise to raise a substantial sum, and such sums, too, can be stretched a long way in the rebuilding of an Italian monastery. In 1964, then, Monte Cassino was all ready to be reconsecrated by Pope Paul VI. There is still work going on today—is any church ever really finished?—but Monte Cassino is once again there, alive.

The most impressive part of the building is the central cloister, which is not closed in and sheltered like most cloisters but open to the Italian sky. Here you can stand under a simple stone arcade and look out over the Liri Valley, which, after all the centuries of conquest, lies once again as fertile and peaceful as when Benedict first saw it. A statue of St. Benedict with his shepherd's rod stands there now, looking out over that same view; beside him, robed and haloed, stands St. Scholastica. *"Est nam certa quies fessis venientibus illuc,"* Charlemagne wrote after his visit more than a thousand years ago. "For there is certain rest for the weary who come here."

If you turn your back on the view over the valley, a long stone stairway leads you to an upper level, and there, on the far side, stands the new basilica, all richly ornamented with gold and inlaid marble, exactly like the old one. And from out of nowhere, the voices of the monks sing their evening prayers, exactly as they always have. There are just a few changes. The bronze doors that depict the ravages of the Lombards and the Saracens now depict the ravages of the Americans too. A Latin plaque records the deed without rancor, one more act of destruction among many.

Pax.

The view out over the Liri Valley includes one sight that was not here in the time of Benedict, or even that of Longfellow. It is a large cross formed out of cypresses, and it stands watch over the graves of more than 1,000 Poles who died here. Down at the entrance to the monastery, a sign points to the Cimitero Polacco, and more cypresses lead the way.

The graves are identical, row on row of them, and from each cross dangles a string of plastic rosary beads. Nearby stands a large and defiant Polish eagle. These men died in exile, hoping that they would earn some honored place in Poland after the war. The Polish government pays their graves little attention or respect. Accordingly, they are still heroes to the Solidarity resistance movement. The busloads of Poles who come here now bring the emblems of Solidarity along with their red and white carnations. They stand together in the cool mountain breeze and sing Polish songs. Their voices are thin but determined, determined even in their thinness, not hopeful but enduring.

"We Polish soldiers, for our freedom and yours," says the plaque that overlooks the place where the visitors sing, "have given our souls to God, our bodies to the soil of Italy, and our hearts to Poland."

The British are buried in a separate cemetery down at the foot of the mountain, the British and the Canadians and the New Zealanders and Cypriots and Gurkhas. In contrast to almost any other spot in Italy, the grass grows thick and green here, as thick and green as an English lawn, and on every third or fourth grave a red rose blooms.

The Italians have provided a plaque in honor of these *"valorosi*

Britanni" who fell *"per la causa della giustizia e della libertà. . . ."* The graves themselves each bear a name and two dates, of birth and death, two dates usually separated by only twenty years or so, and then one of those historic regimental names that labeled and identified each dead youth at the moment of his death: The Leicestershire Regiment, The Saskatoon Light Infantry, The Royal Wilshire Yeomen. On some graves, the parents or wives added a few lines of their own. Of Royal Artillery Gunner G. T. Smith, who died in 1944 at the age of twenty-eight, somebody wrote

> *Deep in our hearts*
> *Your memory is kept*
> *We who loved you*
> *Will never forget*

The Americans were all gathered up and taken to the cemetery at Anzio, but the Germans, too, lie not far from here, on the outer edge of Cassino, not only the Germans killed here but those who died all over southern Italy. There are 20,000 of them in all, lying under the pines and the ivy.

There is a quiet statue of two grieving parents here, and a mosaic of a dove, and a plaque which states only that these soldiers lie *"zum letzten Ruhe."* There is not a word saying why they fought here or why they died their futile deaths. They are packed closely together in these graves, three names on each stone cross, and they too were very young, born in 1922 or '23, dead in 1944.

Pax.

1986

The Last Empress of Rome

■ SHADOWED BY A ROW OF ELEVEN MOURNFUL PINE TREES, IN-side a reddish brown brick building shaped like a Greek cross, there stands a huge stone sarcophagus. It is empty, apparently unfinished. Above it, around it, on all sides, some of the most beautiful mosaics ever created gleam in the twilight. Here two fawns stretch forth their necks to feed, here white doves sip from a bowl, here six lambs flock around the Good Shepherd, and over all this arches a vault of the richest blue, some universal continuum that encompasses both the stars of the sky and the white-capped waves of the sea.

This noble tomb in the Adriatic city of Ravenna was designed, according to tradition, to guard the remains of a most remarkable woman, the Empress Galla Placidia. Scholars insist that she is not here, that she died in Rome in November of the year A.D. 450, and so she must have been buried there in the Theodosian family mausoleum, probably underneath what is now the basilica of St. Peter's. But proof is hard to find. No pilgrim to Ravenna can enter the little tomb of Galla Placidia and not feel that the empress, dead for more than fifteen centuries, is still very much here.

We must rely considerably on imagination, for documents of the fifth century are rare and unreliable, and portraits are rarer still. The only surviving image of Galla Placidia—which may not be her at all—is a painting on glass that dates from about A.D. 430, when the empress was already past forty. The portrait shows a woman of no extraordinary beauty but of great strength, intelligence, character, and determination. She has huge dark eyes, dark hair parted in the middle, a narrow, intense, and slightly twisted mouth.

In her later years, when the mosaics in the mausoleum were designed, Galla Placidia was a devout Christian. Her earlier years were more ambiguous. She was hardly more than a girl when she was abducted by the fierce Visigoths and then became their queen, then was widowed, then more or less forcibly married to a Roman general. Roman law forbade any woman to command troops, much less to rule the empire, but by a combination of intrigue and force, Galla Placidia acquired and exercised the imperial authority for nearly thirty years. She was its emblem and embodiment, the last real ruler of the Western Empire, which crumbled to its inglorious end just twenty-six years after her death.

The empire that Galla Placidia was born to rule had long been moribund. Divided between the inept and intrigue-ridden courts of Milan and Constantinople, the onetime republic now suffered repeated attacks by the so-called barbarians from the north and east, the Goths and Vandals, the Alemanni, Franks, and Burgundians, and yet Rome's own armies consisted largely of soldiers recruited or captured from these same tribes. The last true emperor who proved able to reunite and rule the legacy of the Caesars was Theodosius the Great, a hot-tempered Spaniard who was summoned to the eastern throne in Constantinople after his predecessor was killed in battle by the Visigoths in A.D. 378. The Western Empire, including Rome itself, was supposedly ruled at this time by a seven-year-old princeling named Valentinian II, who had been propped up on the throne at Milan after the murder of his father. When the boy was threatened by yet another military revolt, his mother, Justina, fled to Constantinople with all her children to seek the support of the Emperor Theodosius. As part of her plea, she exhibited her three fetching daughters to the newly widowed Theodosius and indicated that one of them might serve him as his new empress. Theodosius promptly married the youngest of the three, Galla, and then marched off to crush the revolt in the West. Within a year, in 388, Galla gave birth to a girl and named her Galla Placidia.

Her childhood was precarious. The young Empress Galla died in childbirth when her daughter was six. The Emperor Theodosius sent the child to Rome to be raised and educated by his favorite niece, Serena, who was married to an eminent general of Vandal descent named Stilicho. The very next year, Theodosius himself suddenly swelled with dropsy and expired, leaving not only Galla Placidia but the whole Roman world in the tremulous hands of the two worthless sons of his first marriage. Arcadius, then seventeen, inherited the throne of Constantinople, and Honorius, aged ten, was installed by General Stilicho on the throne at Milan. Arcadius resented and disliked his half sister Galla Placidia; Honorius felt for her a fawning but faltering affection.

"Honorius was without passions, and consequently without talents," Edward Gibbon concluded in his *Decline and Fall of the Roman Empire.* "His feeble and languid disposition was alike incapable of discharging the duties of his rank or enjoying the pleasures of his age. . . . The amusement of feeding poultry became the serious and daily care of the monarch of the West." Perhaps the most significant single act of Honorius's growth into manhood was his withdrawal of the imperial capital in 404 from the crossroads of Milan to the secluded Adriatic port of Ravenna. There, protected on the inland side by trackless swamps and marshes, the frightened young emperor thought he would be safe. "The son of Theodosius," wrote Gibbon, "passed the slumber of his life, a captive in his palace, a stranger in his country, and the patient, almost the indifferent, spectator of the ruin of the Western empire."

In such a situation, General Stilicho naturally acquired imperial ambitions. Twice, he had saved Honorius by beating back the invasions of King Alaric and the Visigoths, and now he dreamed of uniting the imperial family and his own. First, he arranged a marriage between the Emperor Honorius and his elder daughter, Maria. When the hapless emperor produced no heir—Stilicho's daughter was later said to have died a virgin—the general began regarding Galla Placidia as the natural heiress and laid plans to have her marry his son Eucherius. According to some accounts, Eucherius himself tried courting Galla Placidia, and she rejected all his advances. Before Stilicho's plan could reach fruition, still another mutiny in the army threatened the imperial court. The trembling Honorius heard charges of treason against both Stilicho and his son and then acquiesed in their being murdered. So Galla Placidia was living in Rome and still un-married at the relatively advanced age of twenty-one when King Alaric of the Visigoths once again invaded Italy, besieged the imperial court at Ravenna, and then swept virtually unopposed to the gates of the city that still imagined itself the capital of the world.

We know all too little about this famous Gothic assault on Rome in the summer of 410, and we can only guess why Galla Placidia was trapped there. Perhaps she thought a royal princess was invul-nerable or inviolable; perhaps she thought the same of the city itself; perhaps she didn't care. We do know that the Roman authorities showed very little of their ancient fortitude toward the invaders. They tried to bribe the Goths into sparing them, then tried to avoid paying their own ransom. Looking for a scapegoat, the Senate fixed its murderous attention on the widow of Stilicho, Serena, once Galla Placidia's guardian, and ordered her strangled on suspicion of trea-son. On the night of August 24, A.D. 410, some Gothic slaves ap-parently opened the Salerian Gate to the besiegers, and there followed three days of tumult and plunder. The Visigoths then marched south-ward, taking with them all the loot they could carry. They also took along one very valuable captive, young Galla Placidia.

King Alaric seems to have thought that he could sail to North Africa, which was then the abundant granary of Rome, but no sooner had he assembled an armada of crude sailing vessels off the coast of Sicily than a sudden storm overwhelmed it. Alaric himself soon fell ill with a mysterious fever and died. The mourning Goths diverted a river near Cosenza and buried him among the plundered treasures of Rome, in a riverbed grave that has never since been found. Then they elected as their new king Alaric's brother-in-law, a sturdy war-rior named Ataulf, and Ataulf began leading his people on their slow march back toward the north.

In all the Goths' wanderings—they had originally come from Swe-den and across Poland about three centuries earlier—they had been trying to find themselves a secure and prosperous homeland, and even now they continued negotiating with the imperial court at Ravenna about where they might go and on what terms, what ransom in corn and cattle. The new element in these negotiations was Galla Placidia. Ravenna demanded her return; the Goths appeared willing to bargain. They had not simply kidnapped her; they treated her with the courtesies due to a royal hostage. They were also Christians. The Goths did not travel in royal luxury, however. Their oxcarts lumbered through the countryside like caravans of Gypsies; they ate by the fireside; they slept in the rain.

It took three long years after the sack of Rome for the Goths to trek as far south as Sicily and then all the way back again, and then across the Alps into southern France. During these years of intermittent negotiations, their price for the return of Galla Placidia kept increasing. Ataulf's real price was extravagant: He wanted to marry Galla Placidia and to make her the queen of the Visigoths. What was even more astonishing was that Galla Placidia seemed to share this desire. The Emperor Honorius was appalled by the barbarian's proposal. His chief general, Constantius, sent a message demanding once again that the emperor's sister be returned to Ravenna. The Goths ignored it. So did Galla Placidia.

It is possible that Galla Placidia's betrothal was coerced. That was common enough in Roman times, and even women of the highest rank were often made to marry against their will. Galla Placidia had by now been for more than three years a captive of an invading army on the march, so she had very little opportunity for free choice. Still, it is not mere sentimentality to imagine that the king of the Visigoths and the emperor's sister fell in love. Not a great deal is known about Ataulf, but the one surviving description portrays him as "a man outstanding both in mind and body, not very tall but beautifully molded in figure and most attractive in face." Of Galla Placidia, even the supercilious Gibbon suggested the impression created by "the splendour of her birth, the bloom of youth, the elegance of manners, and the dexterous insinuation which she condescended to employ." One can easily imagine the barbarian king bewitched.

Ataulf's march across southern Gaul did not go unopposed. When he laid siege to Marseilles, he was not only beaten back but severely wounded in the foot by a Roman officer named Boniface. Ataulf marched on, seized Toulouse and Bordeaux. Early in 414, when Galla Placidia was twenty-six, she and Ataulf defied all the imperial injunctions and celebrated their marriage at Ataulf's new headquarters in Narbonne. It was a grand ceremony. In honor of the Roman princess, Ataulf put aside the tribal furs of the Goths and assumed a Roman toga. He gave Galla Placidia as a present fifty young slaves in silken costume, and each bore two platters heaped with gold and precious stones.

Perhaps at the urging of his Roman bride, the king of the Visigoths began to imagine great political possibilities. A Roman aristocrat who knew him in Narbonne later reported to St. Jerome that Ataulf had told him of these imaginings: "At first he had ardently desired to eradicate the Roman name and to make all the Roman territory an empire of the Goths ... that *Gothia* should be what *Romania* had been, and that Ataulf should now become what Caesar Augustus had once been. But when he discovered from long experience that the Goths were not at all capable of obeying laws ... he chose to seek for himself the glory of restoring and increasing the Roman name by the power of the Goths, and to be regarded by posterity as the author of Roman restoration."

For all these grand visions, however, Ataulf remained no more than the commander of a wandering tribal army. He tried to establish a permanent state in Aquitaine, but the imperial General Constantius blockaded the main harbor at Narbonne. Ataulf decided to march south across the Pyrenees and reestablish his people in Spain. In the Goths' new capital of Barcelona, Galla Placidia bore her first child. Following Ataulf's vision of a Gothic-Roman restoration, she gave her son the name of her father, who had ruled from Persia to the Atlantic: Theodosius. The future ruler of Gothia and Romania lived only a few days, however. Somewhere near Barcelona, Galla Placidia buried her infant son in a silver coffin (years later, when she had achieved imperial power, she would somehow retrieve that tiny coffin and have it brought back to her).

There was to be no second chance. Within a few months of the baby's death, in 415, Ataulf himself was attacked while inspecting his stable of horses. An attendant named Dubius, once the servant of a rival Gothic chieftain who had been defeated and slain by Ataulf, caught the king by surprise and stabbed him in the groin. Ataulf had time only to gasp a dying wish that Galla Placidia be sent home to Ravenna, and that the Goths live in peace with the Romans. Galla Placidia, at twenty-seven, suddenly found herself not only widowed but isolated among an alien people who no longer regarded her as their queen.

The Goths elected their kings. Ataulf's immediate successor, however, was a rival named Sigeric, who may have conspired in his murder and then simply proclaimed himself king. This Sigeric celebrated his triumph by forcing Galla Placidia and a cluster of Roman prisoners to walk on foot for twelve miles in front of the horses that bore him in royal splendor. The prayers that may have run through Galla Placidia's mind during that dismal procession were soon answered. After just a week in power, Sigeric was murdered at the behest of another Gothic chieftain named Wallia, who restored Galla Placidia to a position of honorable captivity. Wallia was quite ready to sign a new peace treaty with the Romans, and to sell Galla Placidia back to Ravenna as part of the agreement. General Constantius, who had been harrying the Goths ever since Ataulf moved out of Italy into Gaul, now agreed to a settlement. The Goths received not only their lands but a large supply of Roman grain; in return they vowed to defend the Romans against all other barbarians. And they agreed to send home Galla Placidia.

She must have regarded this treaty as a godsend, but there was one difficulty. General Constantius, her rescuer, had wanted for years to marry her himself. It was he, in fact, who had constantly insisted that the feckless Honorius make his sister's return an essential element in any peace treaty with the Goths. A worthy suitor, in short, but not one whom Galla Placidia could regard with much enthusiasm. He was an Illyrian of heavy middle age, who liked to carouse with his fellow officers, and according to a contemporary chronicler named Olympiodorus he "tried hard to rival the mimes and actors in their jest and sport." More commonly, though, he "peered out upon the world from his large eyes in somewhat gloomy and sullen mood. His head was flat. His neck was thick and broad. When he rode his horse, he leaned forward, crouching on its neck; swiftly he glanced now to one side, now to the other, obviously wanting to look like a man worthy of the throne."

There is no evidence that Constantius had ever seen Galla Placidia before beginning his courtship, but after some years in the service of her weakling brother, he must have decided that a marriage to the emperor's sister would provide a gateway to the emperor's throne, if not for himself then for the sons she would bear him. And when he did finally see the attractive young widow he had recovered from the Goths, how could he have failed to savor the prospects? Galla Placidia did her best to fend off his advances. She rejected any thought of remarriage, or anything else, and more than once. Constantius was patient but persistent. The Emperor Honorius had apparently promised his sister to the general if the general could rescue her, as he had just done. And no matter how unattractive Galla Placidia may have thought this thick-necked and aging general to be, she was quite able to calculate her various prospects. For the third time, now, someone was pursuing her as a means of winning the imperial throne, as a dynastic instrument, a vehicle. Yet that was what she seemed to be. On the one hand, she faced all the difficulties of life as a widow at the imperial court of Ravenna, isolated and helpless among the scheming eunuchs and courtiers; on the other, she faced the obvious advantages of marriage to the most powerful general in the Western Empire. The choice, if she actually saw any choice at all, could hardly have been pleasant.

On January 1, 417, Honorius and Constantius together celebrated their accession to that antique annual honor, the consulship. In front of an adulatory crowd, the emperor pointedly took his sister's hand and pressed it into that of his chief general. Her decision had been made for her. If Galla Placidia grimaced, history does not record it. Her subsequent marriage to Constantius was fulfilled the next year by the birth of a daughter, Justa Grata Honoria, and the year after that, a son, Flavius Placidus Valentinianus. Then came a sequence of imperial honors: the designation of General Constantius as the co-emperor, and of Galla Placidia as augusta, or empress, and of the young Valentinian as Nobilissimus, or "most noble," a princely title that made him heir presumptive.

In all these honors, one can infer the increasing influence and dynastic determination of Galla Placidia, but though the honors presumably satisfied Constantius's ambitions, they seem to have brought him little pleasure. Isolated from his military comrades at the elaborately ceremonious court of Ravenna, he drank heavily, quarreled, raked in bribes, and suffered from ominously prophetic nightmares.

It is reasonable to suspect that Galla Placidia was less than an ideal wife to the general she had been forced to marry. In one of Constantius's nightmares, he heard a sepulchral voice intoning, "The sixth month has gone, the seventh is beginning." During that seventh month of his co-emperorship, in the year 421, Constantius suddenly fell ill with pleurisy and died.

Galla Placidia probably did not mourn very deeply, but she must have been afflicted with anxiety. A widow again at the age of thirty-three, she now had two small children to raise. One of them, the two-year-old Valentinian, she regarded as the only rightful heir to the western throne and thus the key to her own future fortunes. A line of royal succession from an uncle to an infant nephew could hardly be considered secure, however, particularly in an age when ambitious generals repeatedly challenged any sovereignty other than their own. For the time being, all legitimate power remained in the hands of Honorius, and as Galla Placidia tried to impress him with her son's claims to the imperial inheritance, he now began responding with an affection that appeared to be more than fraternal. "Indecent familiarity" is Gibbon's tart phrase for the emperor's behavior. He kissed his sister on the lips, publicly and often. The courtiers gossiped maliciously. Galla Placidia's personal servants inevitably heard the gossip and told her about it. The next time Honorius seemed too familiar, Galla Placidia rebuked him. The emperor angrily denied everything, with the anger of guilt, and ended by banishing his seductive sister from his court.

Where could she go? Honorius told her to move back to Rome, but Galla Placidia apparently feared for her safety there, within reach of Honorius's henchmen. Or perhaps she saw a different way of pursuing her dynastic ambitions. With her two children, she abruptly departed from Italy and set sail for her distant birthplace, Constantinople. She had not seen the eastern capital since the death of her mother when she was six, and the rulers of the east regarded her entire family with mistrust. The Emperor Theodosius II, who had succeeded Honorius's brother Arcadius on the eastern throne, never acknowledged Galla Placidia's rank of empress, much less any imperial claim on behalf of her son. Theodosius, too, was Honorius's nephew, and he liked to imagine himself reuniting the two empires that had once been ruled by the grandfather for whom he himself had been named.

Just a few months after Galla Placidia's troubled flight to the east, a messenger arrived from Ravenna with the news that Honorius had died of dropsy, on August 15, 423. Theodosius seems to have thought that he could reacquire the Western Empire by a kind of osmosis. Instead of either claiming the western throne or supporting another new emperor, he designated the commanding general in Ravenna, a man named Castinus, who had long been hostile to Galla Placidia, as his co-consul for the coming year. The implication was that the western throne should remain vacant while Castinus acted as the unofficial surrogate for Theodosius. This scheme soon disintegrated. The Roman commander in North Africa, Boniface, that same officer who had wounded Ataulf at the siege of Marseilles, now proclaimed himself loyal to Galla Placidia and her son. Faced with the threat of having their food supplies from Africa cut off, the courtiers at Ravenna conspired to create an emperor of their own, a leading civil servant generally known only as Johannes, or John.

In Constantinople, Theodosius had to decide whether to support his aunt Galla Placidia, whom he disliked and distrusted, or to let the western throne pass to a usurper to whom he bore no relationship at all. Theodosius chose his family. He belatedly granted Galla Placidia and her son, Valentinian, the imperial rank they had enjoyed in the west. There was, as always, a price. Galla Placidia had to renounce all western claims to eastern Illyricum (Greece and all lands north of it), and she had to agree to the betrothal of her young son to Theodosius's only daughter, Licinia Eudoxia, who was then three years of age. With all that settled, Theodosius began the laborious process of organizing an invasion fleet. Galla Placidia refused to be left behind. She took her two children in hand and sailed westward with the invaders. This was no easy voyage, for the ship carrying her across the Adriatic was engulfed in a sudden tempest that began tearing it apart. Galla Placidia fell to her knees, according to pious legend, and began praying to John the Evangelist, promising that she would build a church in his honor if she and her children survived this storm. Miraculously, the sea became calm.

Galla Placidia proceeded on to Aquileia, which was then the

main fortress north of what is now Venice, and there she learned that a worse fate had befallen the commander of the invasion force. The commander, Ardaburius by name, had become separated from the rest of his fleet during another Adriatic storm, and his isolated ship had been captured by pirates. The pirates had put him in irons and then sold him as a prisoner to the usurper John.

This John seems to have been a ruler all too mild for his own survival. Instead of treating the captured Ardaburius as he himself would soon be treated by his enemies, he allowed him to roam freely within the fortified capital of Ravenna. John apparently felt secure within the city walls, but he also was relying on a gifted officer named Aetius, whom he had sent into the wilderness beyond the Danube to persuade the ferocious Huns to strike Theodosius's invasion force from the rear. The captured Ardaburius skillfully used his freedom inside Ravenna to subvert John's forces, and after no more than a skirmish, he managed to overthrow the usurper and take him prisoner. The wretched John was taken to the hippodrome in Aquileia, where Galla Placidia presumably sat and watched his degradation. His right hand was cut off. Then he was seated on a donkey and paraded before the cheering crowds of his former subjects. Then he was beheaded.

So Galla Placidia had won. Just barely. Scarcely three days after John was beheaded, his envoy Aetius arrived at the gates of Aquileia with 60,000 Huns ready to fight for the fallen usurper. Galla Placidia managed to have them all paid off and sent home. She not only pardoned Aetius but prudently gave him a promotion and assigned him to distant Gaul. So she had won. She took her six-year-old son to the imperial forum in Rome and proudly watched as he was hailed, on October 23, 425, as the Emperor Valentinian III. Officially, according to Roman law, an emperor must rule his own empire, and so there could be no such thing as a regent, but the real occupant of the western throne, supreme ruler of the western world, was now Galla Placidia. She was still only thirty-six, and she was to reign for yet another decade.

She also kept the promise that she had made to John the Evangelist when she thought that she and her children were drowning. She began building, perhaps in that same year of 425, the stately brick church now known as San Giovanni Evangelista, and she covered the walls with elaborate mosaic portraits of herself and her family and the scene of the Evangelist saving her from the storm at sea. "Blessed are the merciful," says one of the Latin inscriptions, "for God will have mercy on them." When this church was to be consecrated, though, no relic of St. John could be found, so Galla Placidia went there to spend a night in prayer. Suddenly, she and her attendants saw St. John himself, dressed in the vestments of a bishop, spreading incense around the church. As he approached the altar, the empress fell to her knees and clutched at his feet. The vision promptly vanished, but not without leaving one shoe in Galla Placidia's hands. The passing years brought all kinds of changes to this church—a vast rebuilding in the thirteenth century, with a new campanile 140 feet high, and frescoes by Giotto, who had come to Ravenna to visit Dante, and then another vast rebuilding in the Baroque style in 1747, and then the pulverizing Allied air raids of 1944. One of those raids ravaged the whole front section of the church and destroyed the mosaics of Galla Placidia being saved from drowning. All that remains of that section, in the carefully rebuilt church, is a courtyard where the grass grows richly green within three walls standing open to the sky.

The empire that Galla Placidia had finally acquired for her young son was already disintegrating. It had been overrun several times by the Germanic tribes from the north; some had settled within the empire as allied *foederati,* some simply wandered where they chose, plundering as they went, and yet still more implacable tribal armies kept emerging from that endless wilderness beyond the frontiers on the Rhône and the Danube. The Visigoths had been more or less assimilated in the provinces along the Pyrenees, and the marauding Vandals seemed to be confined in southern Spain, but both Romans and barbarians dreaded the approach of the savage Huns, who now controlled much of the territory from the Black Sea to the Rhine. The Eastern Empire's only defense against these Huns was a lavish and degrading payment of annual tribute, first 350 pounds of gold, then 700, then, by a treaty of 443, no less than 2,100. Attila, the king of the Huns, understandably considered himself the master of the crumbling empire. Against such enemies, Galla Placidia could rely on neither aides nor allies. As an unofficial regent, she lacked full sovereignty over the administration of the state; as a woman, she could never enforce her will by taking command of what remained of the legions. Instead, she had to depend on her ability to manipulate the various rival generals, to play them off against the court officials, the great landowners, and against one another. It was a game that she played instinctively, shrewdly, desperately—and ultimately lost.

There were two principal generals competing for power on the day that Galla Placidia took over from the usurper John. One was Boniface, the brave and loyal commander in Africa, who seems to have been an ox among men, an Ajax, profoundly attached to Galla Placidia throughout the crisis, but moody, temperamental, and probably rather stupid. Quite the opposite was Aetius, the commander in Gaul, wily, clever, treacherous. He had spent part of his boyhood as a hostage among the Huns, had made friendships among them, and had used those friendships as a means of blackmailing his imperial superiors. "Each of these men, if the other had not been his contemporary, might have been called the last of the Romans," wrote the sixth-century historian Procopius. But since they were contemporaries, they were destined to fight each other to the death.

Then there was Felix, the official commander in Ravenna, who should have helped Galla Placidia to control the other two. He never had a chance. Aetius apparently became convinced that Felix was plotting against him, as he probably was, so he began spreading money among the troops in Ravenna, and in May of 430 there was a sudden uprising. Felix was trapped and cut down on the steps of the Ravenna cathedral. Who was responsible? Nothing was ever proved. That left only the stolid Boniface in Africa and the crafty Aetius in Gaul.

Aetius had already begun an almost classic intrigue against Boniface. He suggested to the anxious Galla Placidia that Boniface, newly married to a wife suspected of the Arian heresy, might be plotting to separate Africa from the imperial control of Ravenna. This suspicion might easily be tested, Aetius said, if Galla Placidia ordered Boniface back to Ravenna for questioning. "If you summoned him to your presence," Aetius predicted, "he would not obey the order."

Aetius then wrote to Boniface to warn him of conspiracies against him in Ravenna. Galla Placidia "is plotting to rid herself of you," he confided. "The proof . . . will be your receipt of a letter from her, ordering you, for no earthly reason, to wait upon her in Italy."

The consequences of Aetius's scheme were disastrous. Galla Placidia summoned Boniface to Ravenna for consultations; Boniface refused to come; Galla Placidia bitterly declared him a traitor and began organizing an invasion fleet to regain control of North Africa. What Galla Placidia did not anticipate was that Boniface would decide to defend himself against her invasion by inviting the Vandals in Spain to cross the Strait of Gibraltar and reinforce the troops under his command. Some historians have questioned whether even the most oxlike of commanders could really have made such a suicidal offer, but Boniface certainly acquiesced as the Vandals came streaming across the strait, in the year 429, some 80,000 strong.

Boniface seems to have thought that he could somehow control these invaders. Within a few months, their lamed but ruthless King Gaiseric had swept about a thousand miles to the east and besieged Boniface within the walls of Hippo Regius (now the Algerian city of Bône). The celebrated bishop of Hippo, St. Augustine, aged seventy-five, had written eloquently that all good Christians owe their allegiance to the City of God. Now, he reached the end of his days with the Vandals at the city gates, "gently released," as Gibbon put it, "from the actual and impending calamities of his country."

The Vandals were not skilled at sieges, and Boniface eventually fought his way out of Hippo, arranged a truce with King Gaiseric, and returned to Ravenna to confront his destiny. He told Galla Placidia everything. And Galla Placidia forgave him everything, promoted him to a higher rank than Aetius, and even dismissed Aetius from his command in Gaul. Aetius, however, refused to accept Galla Placidia's orders. He gathered his most loyal troops and marched on Italy. The two generals clashed near Rimini, just south of Ravenna. The loyalist forces of Boniface defeated Aetius's rebels, but Boniface himself was mortally wounded. Once again, Galla Placidia decided that she had no choice but to forgive the treacherous Aetius. He more or less forcibly married the supposedly heretical widow of the fallen Boniface and became for the next two decades the supreme commander of Galla Placidia's crumbling armies—and the most dangerous threat to the reign of her son.

Though Galla Placidia had ultimately failed in her effort to prevent any one general from challenging her authority, she had gained time, which is more than can be said for many of the later emperors, time for her infant son to grow into manhood and to take from her the burdens of state. In the summer of 437, when Valentinian was eighteen, he set sail for Constantinople to marry his fifteen-year-old cousin, Licinia Eudoxia. After a betrothal of more than a decade, the wedding was a great occasion, uniting once again the eastern and western thrones, and the medallions struck for the occasion provide evidence of the official euphoria about the future. *Salus orientis felicitas occidentis,* says one in honor of Licinia Eudoxia, "the well-being of the east, the happiness of the west." When Valentinian returned to Ravenna in 438, he was ready to take command of the imperial heritage that Galla Placidia had preserved for him, and she, at the age of nearly fifty, could contemplate a dignified retirement.

The character of her children ruined this fair prospect. Her son, Valentinian, seems to have been completely unworthy of the throne that his mother had won him. A voluptuary, hot-tempered, sulky, lacking either constancy or judgment, he was described by one contemporary writer, Apollinaris Sidonius, as a "half man out of his head." Procopius was even more harsh, condemning him as "weak and womanish . . . lascivious . . . utterly worthless." Perhaps this was an inevitable result of Valentinian's perilous upbringing, and there are those who blame the strong-willed Galla Placidia for dominating and even emasculating her son, but there was a strange parallel between the relationship of Galla Placidia to her feeble half brother Honorius and that of Valentinian to his older sister, Justa Grata Honoria.

In Honoria, Galla Placidia could hardly help seeing a younger and wilder copy of herself. Not only was Honoria willful and disobedient, even perverse, but as long as Valentinian had no male heirs, Honoria could claim the imperial succession for any son of hers. Her hand in marriage was therefore a goal for any aspiring nobleman or general, and for the same reasons she was forbidden to marry anyone at all. Still unmarried at what was then considered the advanced age of thirty-one, she gave herself to an official named Eugenius, who had been appointed to administer her household and property. Honoria apparently hoped to inspire Eugenius to overthrow the Emperor Valentinian. In due course, she became pregnant.

Sexual intercourse with a member of the royal family was legally considered to be *maiestas laesa (lèse-majesté,* or high treason), so Eugenius was duly executed. The fate of Honoria presented a more difficult problem. The conciliators at the court of Ravenna, presumably including Galla Placidia, urged that the errant princess be married off to an aged senator named Herculanus Bassus. Honoria refused. The conciliators insisted. Honoria still refused. The court's guardians of morality then urged that Honoria be sent off to Constantinople until she could accept the wisdom of her superiors. And so she was exiled to the east, just as Galla Placidia had once been, but Honoria had no sense of returning to any childhood home in Constantinople, no sense of anything but condemnation, banishment, and a yearning for revenge.

Who, then, could rescue Princess Honoria from the royal command that she marry an aged senator? Honoria was nothing if not imaginative. She summoned a favorite eunuch named Hyacinthus, gave him her ring as a proof of good faith, and sent him northward into the wilderness to find her a rescuer—none other than the empire's most dangerous enemy, Attila, king of the Huns. Attila's appearance was as fearful as his reputation. He had, by one account, "a large head, a swarthy complexion, small, deep-seated eyes, a flat nose, a few hairs in the place of a beard, broad shoulders, and a short, square body of nervous strength." It is not certain whether Honoria actually offered herself in marriage to the Hun or simply asked him to help her. Attila, who already had several wives, chose to believe that marriage had been proposed. He sent the eunuch Hyacinthus back to Constantinople with the message that he accepted Honoria's offer, and that he expected to receive half the Roman Empire as her dowry.

This message caused consternation in Constantinople. The eunuch Hyacinthus was seized, tortured to tell his story, and then beheaded. Honoria was unceremoniously shipped back to Ravenna.

Attila, having been ignored by Constantinople, redirected his message to Ravenna: he was willing to marry the emperor's sister in exchange for half the empire. Valentinian was outraged. He decided that the only punishment appropriate to Honoria's conspiracy was execution. Despite the obvious evidence of high treason, Galla Placidia could hardly permit her son to kill her daughter. Her arguments—and what must they have been, how passionate, how cold and commanding, how tearful, even hysterical?—prevailed. Honoria was pardoned. And though Attila threateningly repeated several times his demand for Honoria's hand and dowry, she was quietly married off to old Herculanus Bassus and thereupon disappeared from the pages of history.

Galla Placidia was determined, in these last years, to put her life in order. That meant, among many other things, a large program of building churches in homage to God and filling them with mosaic murals to illustrate her own troubles and trials. Pious historians have claimed that Galla Placidia had always been pious, from the days of her stern upbringing in the household of General Stilicho, but it seems more probable that she had once been wild and headstrong and fiercely independent. Certainly if piety implies docility, there was little sign of that in her forbidden marriage to Ataulf, her conflicts with Honorius, or her march into war against the usurper John. One contemporary chronicler speaks of her "blameless life after her conversion," which apparently meant a conversion not to Christian belief but to a religious way of life, a transformation that seems to have taken place after she had established her son on the throne. Yet even the piety of her old age, inspired by years of struggle and intrigue, was that of a builder, an empress. A surviving sermon of Peter Chrysologus, bishop of Ravenna, speaks of her as the "mother of the Christian, enduring and faithful empire."

In Rome itself, Galla Placidia financed the rebuilding of the basilica of St. Paul's-Outside-the-Walls after it had been badly damaged by a thunderbolt. In Rimini, she erected a church to St. Stephen. Most of her efforts, however, were centered in Ravenna. She contributed substantially to the cathedral known as the Basilica Ursiana (torn down and replaced in the eighteenth century by the inexorable ravages of the Enlightenment); she commissioned as an adjunct to the royal palace the Church of the Holy Cross (also destroyed by subsequent rebuilders). She constructed, as has been described, the church honoring St. John the Evangelist, and among the mosaics that once ornamented this much-battered building, she listed all the members of her royal family, including "the Most Noble Theodosius," that baby she had borne to Ataulf so many years ago, and buried in a silver coffin in Barcelona, and retrieved at last for reburial here in Ravenna.

Very little of Galla Placidia's building has survived fifteen centuries of warfare, wind, and cultural revolution, but her masterpiece remains: the little brick cross known as her mausoleum. Perhaps her spirit protected it; perhaps no one thought enough of it to tear it down; it asks nothing, troubles no one. Its exquisite mosaics illustrate a message, but that message remains muted and elusive. The central figure over the great sarcophagus is a white-robed saint marching forward with great determination toward a flaming grill. With his right hand, he bears a large cross on his shoulder; in his left, he carries an open book. The flames before him leap up with an orange brilliance that defies all the limitations of conventional mosaics. But who is he, and what is he doing?

Some scholars used to argue that he was an angry paragon of orthodoxy, bringing some heretical text to be burned. But perhaps he is St. Apollinaris, the semimythical first bishop of Ravenna, who overthrew the idols of paganism and was reputed to have been made to stand on burning coals. Modern analysts more commonly declare that this is St. Laurence, one of the seven deacons of Rome in the middle of the third century. Commanded to surrender the riches of the church to the city authorities, according to pious legend, Laurence assembled the poor and sick and told the Roman prefect: "Here is the church's treasure." He was probably beheaded in 258, though the tradition insists that he was burned to death on a grill. But why should the martyred St. Laurence, if it is indeed St. Laurence, be so honored directly above the sarcophagus of Galla Placidia? The riddle remains a riddle.

Galla Placidia died—apparently peacefully, though none of the details are known—in Rome, on November 27, 450, at the venerable age of sixty-one. So she could only have guessed at the disasters that threatened her ill-fated family and her ill-fated realm. The most prominent of her descendants, in a strange way, was to be her granddaughter, Eudocia, the elder of Valentinian's two daughters, whose potential claims to the throne attracted the attention of King Gaiseric of the Vandals. Having seized control of most of North Africa, Gaiseric sought a treaty that would confirm his conquests. The Emperor Valentinian agreed in 442 to cede land in exchange for an annual tribute, but the king of the Vandals also wanted Eudocia as a bride for his son, Hunneric. The Romans agreed in principle but objected that Hunneric was already married to the daughter of King Theodoric of the Visigoths. Gaiseric was not to be deterred. He abruptly accused the Gothic princess of trying to poison him, ordered her ears and nose cut off, and sent her home in mutilated disgrace to her father. King Theodoric vowed terrible vengeance on Gaiseric, but his plans were interrupted when Attila the Hun, urged on by Gaiseric, suddenly invaded Gaul. Theodoric's Visigoths and Aetius's Roman legions joined forces to beat back the Huns at the great Battle of Troyes in 451, and Theodoric died on that battlefield.

The victorious Aetius, whom Galla Placidia had checked and counterchecked for two decades, now determined to pursue his imperial ambitions by demanding that his son be betrothed to Valentinian's younger daughter, Placidia. He pressed his demand so arrogantly, and Valentinian resented his pretensions so angrily, that the emperor finally summoned Aetius to a private meeting in September of 454 and stabbed him to death. Now, he must have thought, free of both his mother and his general, he could be emperor at last. That dream lasted scarcely six months. Then two of Aetius's devoted followers accosted Valentinian while he was practicing archery in the Campus Martius. One of them slashed him across the temple with a sword, and as he turned toward his attacker, he received another blow across the face and fell dead. And so, on March 15, 455, the line of succession from Theodosius the Great was extinguished.

Chaos bred chaos. A hugely wealthy landowner named Petronius

Maximus, who may well have hired the two assassins to kill Valentinian, now claimed the imperial throne, and, when nobody objected, further claimed Valentinian's widow, Eudoxia, as his wife. Eudoxia appealed for help, like several other harassed females in this royal family, to the barbarians—in this case, to King Gaiseric of the Vandals. Gaiseric responded by sailing to Italy in June of 455 and seizing Rome. The hapless Emperor Petronius Maximus tried to flee but was stoned and then torn to pieces by his own subjects. Gaiseric spent two weeks methodically plundering the city, stripping even the gilt bronze roof from the Capitol, and when he sailed back to Carthage, he took with him both the Empress Eudoxia, who had imprudently invoked his aid, and her two daughters, Galla Placidia's granddaughters. The elder, Eudocia, now aged seventeen, was then married to Gaiseric's son, Hunneric, as Gaiseric had intended from the start. In due course, she gave birth to a son, Hilderic, Galla Placidia's great-grandson, who became in time the king of the Vandals. As for poor Eudocia, who had fulfilled her dynastic function, she finally pleaded for her release after twelve years as a captive queen. The Vandals allowed her to go to Jerusalem (they had already released her mother and sister after seven years) and to spend the rest of her life in a convent.

The throne of the Western Empire, meanwhile, passed on to a series of warlords, usurpers, and puppets. Nine inconsequential emperors were crowned in the twenty years that followed Gaiseric's invasion, but their momentary authority scarcely extended beyond the borders of Italy. One of them was a nobleman named Olybrius, who had married Galla Placidia's younger granddaughter, Placidia, the girl Aetius had wanted for his son; Olybrius ruled all of three months. The last of these phantom emperors was a handsome boy of fourteen, portentously named Romulus Augustulus but actually no more than the creature of his father, a rebel General Orestes. After the boy had reigned less than a year, another rebellious general named Odoacer, probably a Hun, overthrew Orestes in September of 476 and had him beheaded. The new conqueror disdainfully sent Romulus Augustulus into exile at a villa near Naples. And when the obsequious Roman Senate offered to make Odoacer the new emperor, he rejected the worthless honor and ruled as king of Italy. So ended, until the arrival of Charlemagne more than three centuries later, the Roman Empire.

But there remains one story to tell about the tomb of Galla Placidia. It contains not one but three sarcophagi, and until relatively recently, the two on either side were thought to have contained the ashes of Galla Placidia's feckless brother, Honorius, and her feckless son, Valentinian. The central sarcophagus, according to tradition, had long contained not the ashes but the embalmed corpse of Galla Placidia, dressed in imperial robes and seated upright on a throne of cedarwood. She had refused to be buried. She had refused to die. She sat there in her tomb, proudly erect, waiting for Judgment Day, and there she continued to sit for more than a thousand years. This ghostly figure could just barely be seen if one held up a burning taper at the entrance to the tomb, and so there came a day, in 1577, when some curious children thrust their taper too close to the mummy. An edge of Galla Placidia's desiccated robe caught fire. Then in one great roar of flame, the withered empress and her robe and her cedar throne all burst upward into oblivion.

Modern scholarship assures us, however, that none of this is true. The giant sarcophagi were probably not placed in Galla Placidia's mausoleum before the fourteenth century—there is no documentary reference to their existence earlier than that—and in fact the mausoleum itself was probably not a mausoleum at all but simply an oratory. So whatever it was that burned in 1577 was not the embalmed cadaver of Galla Placidia, for according to all the scholarly evidence, she was never buried here at all. She is not here, they say, not here at all.

1982

The Trial of Sergeant Walker

▪ THIS IS IN HONOR OF SGT. WILLIAM WALKER, OF THE 3RD
South Carolina Infantry Regiment, a young black soldier who believed in the United States government's promises of equal rights.
This is in honor of Sgt. William Walker, who was brave enough to
act on his belief in his rights. This is in honor of Sgt. William Walker,
who died in disgrace, executed by the United States government for
having acted on his belief in its promise of equal rights.

The main charge against him was mutiny. The specifications of
the court-martial at Hilton Head, South Carolina, dated January 11,
1864, provide the basic details: "That he, Sergt. William Walker, Co.
'A,' 3rd S.C. Infy, did unlawfully take command of his Company 'A,'
and march the same with others of the Regiment in front of his
Commanding Officer's tent (Lt. Col. A. G. Bennett), and there ordered them to stack arms; and when his Comdg Officer Lt. Col.
A. G. Bennett inquired of the Regiment what all this meant, he, the
said Sergt. William Walker, replied, 'We will not do duty any longer
for seven dollars per month'—and when remonstrated with, and ordered by their Comdg Officer (Lt. Col. A. G. Bennett) to take their
arms and return to duty, he, the said Sergeant Walker, did order his
Co. ('A') to let their arms alone and go to their quarters, which they
did—thereby exciting and joining in a general mutiny."

But now we must go back a little way, for although it is customary at present to think that dark-skinned people have a constitutional
right to equal treatment, this was not true in January of 1864, not

true during most of the Constitution's first century. In the Dred Scott decision of 1857, the Supreme Court specifically ruled that a black who claimed to be a freedman could not argue his claim in federal court because he was by definition not a citizen. And though the Civil War was implicitly fought over the issue of slavery, neither the new President Lincoln nor the Congress made any great effort to free any slaves. On the contrary, the original version of the Thirteenth Amendment, passed by Congress (with Lincoln's approval) in March of 1861, promised that the federal government would make no attempt to interfere with the institution of slavery. It was only the Southerners' attack on Fort Sumter in the following month that nullified this remarkable amendment, and not until four years later, when the war was over and Lincoln dead, did Congress finally pass a new Thirteenth Amendment, proclaiming that "neither slavery nor involuntary servitude . . . shall exist within the United States."

A few radicals had argued that view from the beginning. "Our cry now must be emancipation and arming the slaves," wrote the young Henry Adams. But even the most idealistic of presidents has to make compromises with political reality, and Lincoln was probably correct in believing that any attempt to abolish slavery would inspire slaveholding states like Kentucky and Maryland to join the Southern rebellion. Only in 1862, in fact, fully a year after Fort Sumter and the Battle of Bull Run, was slavery finally outlawed in the national capital, in the District of Columbia, and there was considerable doubt whether Lincoln would actually sign the bill into law.

Some of the men directly in charge of fighting the war were less sensitive to politicians' anxieties. Major General John Charles Frémont, who had been the Republican candidate for the presidency in 1856 and who now commanded what was known as the Department of the West at Saint Louis, decided to act on his own. In a proclamation of August 30, 1861, he declared martial law throughout Missouri and the liberation of all rebels' slaves. "The property, real and personal, of all persons in the state of Missouri who shall take up arms against the United States . . . is declared to be confiscated to the public use, and their slaves, if they have any, are hereby declared free men." Lincoln responded by giving the adventurous general a direct order, "in a spirit of caution, and not of censure," to go no further than Congress had authorized, and Congress had authorized nothing resembling Frémont's proclamation.

These official hesitations about freeing the slaves applied all the more to the idea of arming them. There was actually a law against blacks serving in the United States armed forces, though they had done so with distinction in both the Revolution and the War of 1812. Throughout the South—and not only in the South—the image of black slaves acquiring weapons conjured up hideous scenes of revenge, massacres and atrocities. Again, the men charged with waging war had to confront reality, and the main reality was that the Union army needed a great many soldiers. "If it shall be found that the men who have been held by the rebels as slaves are capable of bearing arms and performing efficient military service," Secretary of War Simon Cameron said in a report issued in December of 1861, the end of the first year of war, "it is the right, and may become the duty, of this government to arm and equip them. . . ." Lincoln was angered not only by Cameron's views but by his audacity in making such a statement public without the president's approval. "He was especially displeased with that part which assumed to state or enunciate the policy to be pursued by the Administration in regard to slaves . . ." wrote Gideon Welles, the secretary of the navy. "The President ordered that part of the report which he deemed intrusive and objectionable to be expunged. . . ."

Though many Union generals regarded blacks as worthless, a few kept pressing Lincoln to make use of them. The first serious attempt to recruit and arm former slaves took place on the Sea Islands off the coast of South Carolina. Here in the lovely old mansions of Beaufort, on Port Royal Island, among the magnolias and the orange trees and the live oaks dripping Spanish moss, the cotton barons of South Carolina had plotted the Southern insurrection, so it was eminently fitting that the Union navy should invade their headquarters by sending southward an armada of seventy-four steam frigates, steam sloops, gunboats, and transports loaded with 12,000 seasick troops. At 9:25 on the morning of November 7, the Northern fleet arrived in Port Royal Sound and was fired on by the two strongholds guarding the entrance, Fort Walker and Fort Beauregard. Led by the Frigate *Wabash,* with its guns roaring, the Union fleet proceeded in stately measure from Bay Point to Hilton Head and then back again, three times, cannonading the two forts until they lowered their rebellious flags.

The victorious Union fleet did not hurry its invasion, however. By the time its leisurely landing parties ventured into the two forts, they found no occupants except for a flock of turkeys. The commander of the invaders, Brig. Gen. Thomas W. Sherman, issued a conciliatory proclamation announcing to the slaveholders that his soldiers came "with no feelings of personal animosity; no desire to harm your citizens, destroy your property, or interfere with any of your lawful rights, or your social and local institutions. ..." He waited five days for some answer before a military vanguard entered Beaufort, but there could be no answer because every white inhabitant had fled. Only the slaves were left.

There were about 10,000 of them, more than 80 percent of the islands' prewar population, and their appearance rather dismayed some of their liberators. "Nearly all the Negroes left on the islands were in densest ignorance," wrote one arriving Northern officer, Capt. Hazard Stevens, "some of the blackest human beings ever seen, and others the most bestial in appearance. These ignorant and benighted creatures flooded into Beaufort ... and held high carnival in the deserted mansions, smashing doors, mirrors, and furniture and appropriating all that took their fancy." A correspondent for the *New York Tribune* was equally dismayed by the spectacle of "costly furniture despoiled; books and papers smashed; pianos on the sidewalk, feather beds ripped open, and even the filth of the Negroes left lying in parlors and bedchambers."

The Northerners had no idea what to do with these blacks. They were hardly slaves now, since their masters had fled, but they had not been officially freed, so they were not really people either, much less citizens. Out in the Southwest, in New Orleans, Gen. Benjamin Butler had devised a solution to this problem by decreeing that escaped slaves were "contraband." The word ordinarily referred to smuggled property—property, in any case—and the application of this term to slaves seemed to satisfy everyone's sense of legality and propriety. So the 10,000 contraband objects on the Sea Islands, who needed, after all, to be fed and clothed and sheltered, were assigned to the United States Treasury Department. The Treasury Department appointed a bright young Boston lawyer named Edward Pierce to go to Port Royal and take charge of the contraband. He sent his charges back to the work they had always done, planting, hoeing, and picking cotton. He rewarded them, however, with something they had never seen before: cash wages.

Then came Maj. Gen. David Hunter, West Point '22, who had spent nearly forty years reaching the rank of major, then found himself suddenly promoted to general, then wounded at Bull Run, now commander of the grandly named Department of the South, which actually included little more than these beautiful but swampy islands off the Carolina coast. Scarcely a month after his arrival in Port Royal in March of 1862, Hunter issued a decree proclaiming that all people "heretofore held as slaves" in the three nearest coastal states, South Carolina, Georgia, and Florida, "are . . . declared forever free." On the same day on which he freed the slaves, however, Hunter ordered his subordinate officers "to send immediately to these headquarters, under a guard, all the able-bodied negroes capable of bearing arms."

Pierce of the Treasury was outraged at this autocratic conscription of his contraband cotton workers. They "were taken from the fields without being allowed to go to their houses even to get a jacket . . ." Pierce wrote to Washington. "Wives and children embraced the husband and father thus taken away, they knew not where, and whom, they said, they should never see again." Once again, Lincoln himself struck down an overzealous general. "The government of the United States," he declared, "had no knowledge, information, or belief of intention on the part of General Hunter to issue such a proclamation."

But though Lincoln thus disavowed Hunter, disavowed both the emancipation of slaves and the arming of slaves, he remained under pressure to do both. Edwin Stanton, who had replaced the corrupt Cameron as secretary of war, gradually came to favor the recruitment of blacks, and Congress drifted nervously toward the same view. The Second Confiscation Act, passed in July of 1862, authorized the president "to employ as many persons of African descent as he may deem necessary and proper for the suppression of this rebellion." Congress suggested but did not insist that blacks should be used as auxiliary forces, for hard labor and garrison duty. In the Militia Act, passed that same month, it authorized the president "to receive into the service of the United States, for the purpose of constructing intrenchments, or performing camp service, or any other labor, or any military or naval service for which they may be found competent, persons of African descent." It also specified that persons of African descent would be paid $3.00 a month less than white soldiers, $10.00 a month instead of $13.00, and $3.00 of that pay would be deducted for clothes, whereas whites could spend or keep their $3.50 clothing allotments.

So although General Hunter was forbidden in May to emancipate or draft blacks into his forces, Gen. Rufus Saxton, the new military governor in Port Royal, was authorized on August 25 to recruit 5,000 of them. And these recruits, Stanton told Saxton, were "to be entitled to receive the same pay and rations as are allowed by law to volunteers in the service." That declaration by the secretary of war amounted to a pledge of equal pay and equal rights. It was understood as such not only in Port Royal but wherever Union officials undertook the recruitment of black soldiers. But Congress had never authorized any such pledge, nor, when challenged, would Congress honor it.

Captain Thomas Wentworth Higginson, who knew nothing of these complications, was having dinner with two other officers in the barracks of the Fifty-first Massachusetts Regiment when he received a letter from General Saxton announcing that he was "organizing the First Regiment of South Carolina Volunteers" and offering him the colonelcy and command of what was to become the first Union regiment of freed slaves. Higginson was astonished. "Had an invitation reached me to take command of a regiment of Kalmuck Tartars," he recalled, "it could hardly have been more unexpected." But Saxton had heard good reports about Higginson, and they were all true. Higginson embodied many of the characteristics that Bostonians like to consider elements in the classic Bostonian persona: courage, independence, eloquence, idealism. He was an ordained Unitarian minister, but also an ardent swimmer and football player, also an ardent abolitionist, a friend and comrade-in-arms to John Brown, also an ardent feminist, one of the signers of the call to the first National Women's Rights Convention, and author of a celebrated polemic entitled *Ought Women to Learn the Alphabet?* After his antislavery activities forced him to resign from his wealthy parish in Newburyport, he declared, "An empty pulpit has often preached louder than a living minister." And after he discovered the reclusive Emily Dickinson, whose poems he was the first to publish, she wrote to him: "Of our greatest acts we are ignorant— You were not aware that you saved my Life. . . ."

Higginson was reluctant to abandon his comrades in the Fifty-first Massachusetts Regiment, but on making a quick trip to Port Royal, he found that he could not resist the challenge of leading "eight hundred men suddenly transformed from slaves into soldiers, and representing a race affectionate, enthusiastic, grotesque, and dramatic beyond all others." Though that may sound a little patronizing, Higginson soon came to love his black troops, and they loved him. One of their most extraordinary confrontations occurred on New Year's Day of 1863, when ten cattle were slaughtered and barbecued for an open-air feast to accompany the reading of Lincoln's new Emancipation Proclamation. Then there was the presentation of a new regimental flag. "Then followed an incident so simple, so touching, so utterly unexpected and startling, that I can scarcely believe it," Higginson wrote in *Army Life in a Black Regiment.* "Just as I took and waved the flag, which now for the first time meant anything to these poor people, there suddenly arose, close beside the platform, a strong male voice . . . into which two women's voices instantly blended, singing, as if by an impulse that could no more be repressed than the morning-note of the song-sparrow—'My country, 'tis of thee, / Sweet land of liberty, / Of thee I sing.' People looked at each other, and then at us on the platform, to see whence came this interruption. . . . Firmly and irrepressibly the quavering voices sang on, verse after verse; others of the colored people joined in; some whites on the platform began, but I motioned them to silence. I never saw anything so electric; it made all other words cheap; it seemed the choked voice of a race at last unloosed. . . ."

The Emancipation Proclamation was a grand gesture, but it was not really designed to emancipate any great number of slaves. It specified that those who were to be "thenceforward and forever free" were only those who were "held as slaves within any State or designated part of a State, the people whereof shall then be in rebellion against the United States." These designated parts, all listed by name, were precisely those Confederate territories over which Lincoln had no control. In every area where the president did have control, like Tennessee or Missouri or Maryland, the proclamation went on to declare that the institution of slavery was to be "for the present left precisely as if this proclamation were not issued."

Lincoln's posthumous reputation as the Great Emancipator has always been something of a legend. "I am not, nor ever have been, in favor of bringing about in any way the social and political equality of the white and black races . . ." he had said in his fourth debate with Stephen A. Douglas in 1858. "I am not, nor ever have been, in favor of making voters or jurors of Negroes, nor of qualifying them to hold office nor to intimacy with white people; and I will say in addition to this that there is a physical difference between the white and black races which I believe forbids the two living together on terms of social and political equality. . . . There must be the position of the superior and inferior, and I as much as any other man am in favor of having the superior position assigned to the white race."

If any slaves actually became emancipated, or somehow escaped to the North, Lincoln planned not to accept them into white society but to ship them overseas, to Africa or the Caribbean. In his first annual message to Congress in 1861, he requested funds for this purpose, and Congress responded with an initial appropriation of $600,000. The House Committee on Emancipation and Colonization recommended spending $20 million to find for every freed slave "a congenial home and country." A few hundred blacks actually did emigrate in 1862, but far more shared the views of a freedman named Robert Purvis, who declared to a government emigration agent, "Sir, we were born here, and here we choose to remain."

Once Congress had authorized the recruiting of black soldiers, Secretary of War Stanton established a Bureau for Colored Troops in May of 1863 and asked the War Department's solicitor, William Whiting of Boston, to look into the vexing question of what the black recruits should be paid. Despite Stanton's promise of equal treatment, Whiting replied that the only applicable law was the Militia Act of 1862, in which Congress had specifically stated that "persons of African descent" were to be paid ten dollars per month (minus three dollars for clothing), or three dollars less than white soldiers received. "There seems to be inequality and injustice in this distinction," Stanton said in his annual report for 1863, "and an amendment authorizing the same pay and bounty as white troops receive, is recommended." Lincoln was not convinced. Since blacks "had larger motives for being soldiers than white men . . . they ought to be willing to enter the service upon any condition," the president said to Frederick Douglass, the black leader. The decision to grant them lower pay, Lincoln added, "seemed a necessary condition to smooth the way to their employment at all as soldiers." For the time being, Stanton wrote to the governor of Ohio, all blacks who had relied on his promises of equal pay "must trust to State contributions and the justice of Congress at the next session."

Colonel Higginson was furious. The refusal to grant equal pay, he declared, "has impaired discipline, has relaxed loyalty, and has begun to implant a feeling of sullen distrust in the very regiments whose early career solved the problem of the nation, created a new army, and made a peaceful emancipation possible." Colonel Robert Gould Shaw, who commanded the Fifty-fourth Massachusetts Regiment, the first black unit recruited in the North, was even more furious. Though the Massachusetts legislature appropriated funds to provide equal pay for Shaw's regiment, which was already stationed on the Sea Islands and ready to go into action, the regiment refused to accept the bargain, refused to accept any pay at all unless it was given equal pay. These soldiers should either be "mustered out of the service or receive the full pay which was promised them," Shaw wrote to Massachusetts Governor John Andrew. "Are we *soldiers* or are we *laborers*?" wrote one of Shaw's black soldiers, James Henry Gooding, in a letter to President Lincoln. Then, in the flowery rhetoric of his time, Gooding answered his own question: "Mr. President . . . the patient, trusting descendents of Afric's clime have dyed the ground with blood in defense of the Union and democracy."

Unpaid, the Fifty-fourth Massachusetts marched into combat,

leading a hopeless charge against Fort Wagner, in Charleston harbor. The hopelessness of it was hardly accidental. According to Nathaniel Page, a special correspondent for the *New York Tribune,* Brig. Gen. Thomas Seymour decided on the fate of Colonel Shaw and his black troops by saying to another general, "Well, I guess we will . . . put those damned niggers from Massachusetts in the advance. We may as well get rid of them one time as another."

And so it was done, the murderous orders given. After a long but ineffective cannonading, Shaw's outnumbered troops had to charge uphill and across a deep ditch into a storm of Confederate gunfire. Colonel Shaw, who was twenty-five, led them all the way, reached the fort's parapet and climbed it. "He stood there for a moment with uplifted sword, shouting, 'Forward, Fifty-fourth!' " as William James said many years later in dedicating Saint-Gaudens's great monument on Beacon Hill, "and then fell headlong with a bullet through his heart." More than half of Shaw's unpaid black troops died in that heroic charge before the remnants were finally beaten back. And after the dead were all dumped into a common trench, the Confederate commander was said to have remarked of Shaw, "We have buried him with his niggers."

It was a fact that black casualties in the Union army were far higher than white casualties. Of the nearly 200,000 black troops eventually recruited, almost 40,000 died. That death rate amounted to slightly more than 20 percent, as compared with a death rate of 15.2 percent among white troops and only 8.6 percent in the regular army. The disparity occurred not because blacks were regularly used as cannon fodder, as they were at Fort Wagner, but because most Civil War casualties, white and black alike, resulted from sickness. Among blacks, the remarkable statistics are that 2,870 died in combat, 29,756 of illness. In fact, the regiment with the second-highest number of deaths in the entire Union army was the Sixty-fifth U.S. Colored Infantry, which lost 755 men without ever going into combat at all.

There were a number of reasons for this. High among them were inferior food, inferior clothing, inferior medical care, inferior everything. All wars breed corruption, after all, and the Civil War, fought in the golden age of freewheeling capitalism, probably bred more than most. The young J. P. Morgan, for example, financed a friend named Simon Stevens in buying 5,000 obsolete army carbines for $11.50 each from one of Stevens's friends, who had bought them on credit at a New York armory for $3.50. The carbines were then peddled to General Frémont, who was recruiting troops in the West, and who persuaded the government to pay $22 each for the $3.50 weapons. Morgan himself took in $26,345.54 on the deal, a profit of about 50 percent on a three-month loan. "An expedition was dispatched to the Mississippi in rotten hulls for which the government often paid nine hundred dollars a day," as Thomas Beer wrote in *Hanna.* "Bayonets of polished pewter, tents of porous shoddy, coffee made of pulse and sorghum, carbines that exploded on the drill ground . . . and many other versions of the wooden nutmeg were offered to the Army between 1861 and 1864. Often nothing could be done. The actual vendor vanished in a cloud of agents and guileless middlemen. . . ." And who could be more vulnerable to this sort of operation than the fledgling black regiments? One of their commanders, Brig. Gen. Daniel Ullman, complained to a correspondent from the *New York Post* about "arms almost entirely unserviceable, and . . . their equipment have been of the poorest kind."

And woe to anyone who fell ill. Since black troops were supposed to be led by white officers, only eight black doctors were taken into the army, and six of these served in Washington hospitals. White doctors generally refused to serve in black regiments, and so, according to one general's report, "in very many cases hospital stewards of low order of qualification were appointed to the office of assistant surgeon and surgeon." There were "well grounded objections," the general went on, "against the inhumanity of subjecting the colored soldiers to medical treatment and surgical operations from such men."

The basic reason for the high black casualties, though, was that the black troops were used mainly to dig trenches and fortifications, to cut trees and haul supplies, to provide, for seven dollars per month, what they had once provided for nothing, slave labor. "My men were . . . put into trenches and batteries, or detailed to mount guns, haul cannon and mortars, and were kept constantly and exclusively on fatigue duty of the severest kind . . ." said Col. James

Montgomery of the Second South Carolina Volunteers. "I frequently had to take men who had been on duty from 4 o'clock in the morning until sundown to make up the detail called for, for the night, and men who had been in the trenches in the night were compelled to go on duty again at least part of the day." Or as another officer wrote, "where white and black troops come together in the same command, the latter have to do all the work."

The maw of war kept demanding more men. In the maw of Gettysburg, both sides together suffered more than 50,000 casualties before the Union forces finally beat back Robert E. Lee's invasion of Pennsylvania. The following week in July of 1863, Lincoln's draft law went into effect, the first names were chosen by lottery, and mobs of antidraft rioters began tearing New York City to pieces. It is not known to this day who organized the four-day Draft Riots, or whether they were organized at all. There was considerable opposition to the war in New York, though, and there is a certain amount of evidence that the mob of predominantly Irish rioters had some kind of covert leadership. It started marching early in the morning, not ordinarily a time for spontaneous rioting, and it proceeded quite directly toward the armories where weapons were stored. It also started by cutting the telegraph wires and the railroad lines to the outside world. But though the rioters started out with banners against the draft, and though they spent much of their energy in battling the police, their favorite sport was chasing and catching blacks.

One of their first targets was the Colored Orphan Asylum, a handsome brick building on Fifth Avenue at Forty-third Street. The superintendent was smart enough to barricade the front door and then lead his 200 orphans, none older than twelve, out a back door. By the time the rioters broke down the barriers, they found only one terrified black girl hiding under a bed, and killed her.

On the Lower East Side, just off the Bowery, the rioters wrecked a well-known restaurant named Crook's because it employed black waiters. They chased several blacks to the roof of a building, set the building on fire and then waited, roaring in excited expectation. One by one, the trapped blacks fell to the ground and were beaten to death. On the second day came the first lynching. A black named

William Jones, who lived on Clarkson Street, near the Hudson River docks, ventured out to buy a loaf of bread. The mob caught him. Somebody threw a rope over a branch of a tree. Somebody else lit a fire under the hanging man. Women in the mob threw stones at the dying victim. When the police arrived to cut down the corpse, they found that he still held a charred loaf of bread under his arm.

By the time army troops arrived in New York, they found three blacks hanging from lampposts at the corner of Eighth Avenue and Thirty-second Street. Confronting a wild mob of thousands of rioters, the army reacted in the only way it knew, with cannonades of grape and canister. "Give them grape and plenty of it," urged the *New York Times*. Such urgings sound horrifying—the rioters were largely unarmed civilians, after all, and many of them were women—but the mob itself was hardly less horrifying. When the soldiers cut down the lynched blacks on Eighth Avenue and then marched on, the rioters recaptured the corpses and strung them up on the lampposts all over again, and there they hung, all day long.

Nobody knows the final death toll. Police Commissioner Thomas Acton estimated it at around 1,200. Nobody knows the damages either, though reasonably reliable investigators estimated 200 buildings burned and financial losses at about $5 million, a handsome sum in an age when a slave could be bought for a couple of hundred dollars or recruited into the army for seven dollars per month.

Nobody knows, finally, how much of this kind of news reached the Sea Islands off South Carolina, or what impression it made on black recruits like William Walker in the Third South Carolina Infantry Regiment. One can imagine that they heard quite a lot, and that the effects of what they heard were considerable.

And when his Comdg Officer Lt. Col. A. G. Bennett inquired of the Regiment what all this meant, he, the said Sergt. William Walker, replied, "We will not do duty any longer for seven dollars per month."

We do not know a great deal about William Walker. For most of his young life, he belonged to that large class of people on whom history keeps no records. There are only some military documents—notably a fifty-five-page handwritten transcript of his court-martial—

and not many of those. One says that he was born in Hilton Head, another that he was born in Savannah. One says, "Occupation: Servant." It adds: "Name of former owner not of record." From this we can deduce that William Walker had been born and reared a slave, and that if anyone asked him who his master was, he probably refused to say.

He was five feet seven inches tall, according to these army documents. Eyes black, hair black, complexion black. He was illiterate, which should hardly be surprising, since it was against the law in South Carolina to teach a slave to read, and any black found in possession of writing materials, a pencil or paper, was liable to flogging. He was twenty-three when he died.

On Walker's death certificate, his occupation was given not as "servant" but as "pilot." In his last appeal for mercy, just three weeks before his execution, he said that he had served six months as pilot on a *Monitor*-type armored gunboat, the USS *Montauk*. (Before that, he had apparently served as pilot on another warship blockading the Carolina coast, the USS *Wissahickon*.) This implies, surely, that he knew the region well; it also implies a certain intelligence, energy, eagerness to serve the Union cause.

Walker may indeed be the anonymous ex-slave who turned up in a report by Comdr. John L. Worden, captain of the *Montauk*, about the blockading fleet's venture up the Big Ogeechee River to attack Fort McAllister early in 1863. "I learned through the medium of a contraband, who had been employed upon these waters as a pilot, the position of the obstructions below the fort . . ." Worden wrote on January 28. "This information, with the aid of the contraband, whom I took on board, enabled me to take up a position nearer the fort in the next attack upon it. . . ." The *Montauk* accomplished little in its exchange of gunfire with Fort McAllister, but it discovered the Confederate raider *Nashville*, a paddle-wheeled merchant steamer that had been newly outfitted with cannon, lying aground near the fort. "A few well directed shells determined the range," Worden reported on February 20, "and soon we succeeded in striking her with XI-inch and XV-inch shells . . ." The *Nashville* caught fire, then exploded. But a Confederate torpedo blew a hole in the *Montauk* and nearly sank it before its engineer could patch the leak. We know no details of Walker's role in all this, only that he proudly stated in his appeal: "I also destroyed the rebel steamer Nashville in the Big Ogeechee River. . . ."

One day in April of 1863, Walker got a pass to return home and visit his family—he had a wife named Rebecca—and there he heard that a third regiment of South Carolina blacks was being organized to join Colonel Higginson's First and Colonel Montgomery's Second. He knew that his job as a pilot exempted him from conscription, but the cause called out to him. To join the Union infantry in combat must have seemed better than being just a river pilot. "On the promise solemnly made by some who are now officers in my regiment," he later said, "that I should receive the same pay and allowances as were given to all soldiers in the U.S. Army, [I] voluntarily entered the ranks."

Not quite. He enrolled as a sergeant from the start, on April 24, 1863, and that also implies that he had a certain quality of self-possession, authority, leadership, some quality unusual for an illiterate ex-slave of twenty-three. It did not earn him any extra pay, however. Black recruits were all paid the same seven dollars per month, regardless of rank. And they soon found that their white officers could be as harsh as any slavemasters. "For an account of the treatment that has been given to the men of the 3rd Regt of S.C. Vols by a large majority of their officers," Walker declared at his court-martial, "nine-tenths of those now in service there will be my witness that it has been tyrannical in the extreme. . . ." Walker's judgment was corroborated, after his death, in a statement by a Col. P. P. Browne of the provost marshal's office, about some other blacks accused of taking part in Walker's "mutiny." All his interrogations, said Colonel Browne, led him to the conclusion "that during the summer and fall of 1863 . . . the regiment . . . was under bad management and in a greatly demoralized condition; that several of the officers who had most to do with these men have either been dismissed [from] the service or are under charges which will cause their dismissal . . . ; that being made up of South Carolina slaves their great ignorance of their duties and responsibilities as *soldiers* led them to commit errors which more intelligent men would have avoided; that the officers of the Regiment were [more] to blame than the men. . . ."

Sergeant Walker, eager and enthusiastic, signed up for three years' service in April of 1863. By that August, just four months later, he was embittered, quarrelsome, insubordinate. The indictment listed several instances of "mutinous conduct" that occurred long before the protest demonstration about equal pay. The first specification charged that on August 23, he did "join in a mutiny, at Seabrook Wharf [in Hilton Head], when on detail, and go away to camp when ordered not to do so by 1st Lieut. Geo. W. Wood." The second specification charged that Walker "did use threatening language, such as 'I will shoot him,' meaning 1st Lieut. Geo. W. Wood. This he said in a loud voice, so as to be heard all over camp, having, at the same time, a gun in his hand."

Lieutenant Wood was absent from the court-martial, but a Lt. Adolph Bessie testified for the prosecution in support of this charge. In doing so, however, he made it sound as though the quarrel had been started by Wood rather than Walker. "I was sick at that time," Bessie said. "The accused came to my tent, and several others of the company. He complained of Lt. Geo. W. Wood as having maltreated him, of having threatened to shoot him, or something of that kind. I told the accused I would see about it. He left my tent, and shortly after I heard considerable noise in the company street. I went out and saw the accused with a gun in his hand, and heard him say he would 'shoot Lt. Geo. W. Wood.' He repeated it several times, in front of the tent of the orderly. . . ."

QUESTION, BY JUDGE ADVOCATE (Lt. S. Alford of the Eighth Maine Volunteers): What was his tone of voice when threatening to shoot Lt. Wood?

ANSWER: It was loud, and could be heard quite a distance. He seemed to be talking in a rage.

Captain Edgar Abeel attempted to arrest Walker, according to the third specification, but Walker "did refuse to obey." Abeel testified that he had ordered Walker to go to his tent under arrest. "He refused to go in arrest," Abeel said, "and said he would not for any man."

Q: Where did he go after the order?

A: He walked up and down the street of his company, but did not go in his tent.

Q: What was the conduct of the men present at the time?

A: They seemed to uphold the sergeant. A number of them said they "would go to the Provost with him."

Abeel seems to have given up his attempt to arrest Walker, and the whole quarrel died down. That was in August. In October Walker got into another angry argument, this time with a Sgt. Sussex Brown, at Drayton's Plantation. The troops were supposed to be inspected, Brown testified, but Walker didn't appear. "I went in Sergt. Walker's tent and two men was there playing cards," he said. "I asked them, 'What are you doing?' They told me they was 'coming out now.' Sergt. Walker said, 'Let's play on,' and I told Sergt. Walker he must fall in. He cussed and said I was a 'damned son of a bitch.' I said, if you don't fall in the ranks, I will have you arrested. . . . He told me he 'didn't care a damn' about any man. He said if I didn't mind he'd put a ball in his gun and shoot me. . . ."

Q: About how many times, if more than once, did he say he would shoot you?

A: Three times.

Walker subsequently denied most of this. He claimed that he and his comrades had each had only one more card to play, and that he had said, "Play your card and get out." He further claimed "that my threat of 'putting a cartridge in my gun and blowing his brains out' was only in answer to his threat that he would 'smash my head in with the butt of his gun.' " By now, though, Walker's insubordination was almost habitual, and he resisted discipline not only for himself but for other men. Drum Maj. William Smith testified that when he tried to arrest a man named Ranty Pope for refusing to go on fatigue duty, Walker intervened. "I told him [Pope] I would tie him up," Smith said. "Sergt. Walker told me if I tied Ranty Pope up I would also have to tie him, Sergt. Walker, up."

Q: What did you then do with the said Pope?

A: I did not do anything with him.

Q: Why not?

A: The camp was in a state of excitement, and I did not like the looks of Sergt. Walker at the time.

Q: You say you did not like the looks of the accused. How did he look or act at the time?

A: He eyed me sharply. I was actually afraid of him.

Q: Did the words or looks of the accused prevent the arrest of Ranty Pope . . . ?

A: His words and looks both.

This all happened on the morning of November 19, the day of the "mutiny." The prosecution made no effort to establish any chronology, so it is not clear whether Walker's rescue of Ranty Pope came before or after the equal-pay demonstration outside Colonel Bennett's tent. The prosecution also made no effort to establish any reason for the "mutiny," any background of grievances and arguments about pay or living conditions or anything else. Walker later stated that he had not received any pay at all since August, but we don't know whether his regiment was another unit rejecting unequal pay or what the reason was. Clearly Walker was in a state of rage, and clearly he was not alone in that rage. The whole camp was described as "mutinous," but nobody at the court-martial paid much attention to the reasons. On the main charge of stacking arms and refusing to serve without equal pay, the judge advocate simply asked Colonel Bennett whether he had seen Walker that day and then asked him to "state his conduct as it came under your observation."

"On the morning of November 19, 1863, when a portion of the command was in a state of mutiny," the colonel began, "I noticed the accused, with others of his company and regiment, stack his arms, take off his accoutrements, and hang them on the stack. I inquired what all this meant, and received no reply, and again repeated the question, when the accused answered by saying, that they 'would not do duty any longer for seven dollars per month.' I then told the men the consequences of a mutiny. . . . I told them that if they did not take their arms and return to duty, I should report the case to the Post commander and they would be shot down. While saying this, I heard the accused tell the men not to take their arms, but leave them and go to their street, which command of his they obeyed. . . ."

Q: Where was the accused at the time you told the men to take their arms, and told them the consequences if they did not?

A: He stood on the right of the line when I first saw him. He afterwards moved to the rear, moving back and forth. . . .

Q: Do you know the object of the accused passing to and fro . . . ?

A: He was advising the men "to go back to their quarters without their arms."

But then it became apparent that there was a gap in what the colonel had seen.

Q: Did you hear the accused order the company to stack their arms?

A: I did not. The arms were stacked when I came out of my tent. . . .

Q: Did you hear the accused give the command to march the company back to their street?

A: He did not give the command, "March." He merely told them to go.

Walker attempted to dodge responsibility, or perhaps it was the defense lawyer assigned to him, Lt. J. A. Smith of the Forty-seventh New York Volunteers, who made that attempt. The court-martial record says only:

QUESTION BY ACCUSED: Have you had any conversation with the accused since his confinement . . . ?

ANSWER: I have once. . . .

Q: Did you, in that conversation, say that you were satisfied, from the information you had received, that he was not the person who used the language relative to not serving any longer for seven dollars per month . . . ?

A: No, sir, I did not.

Though there was some hearsay in Colonel Bennett's testimony, the prosecution also produced an eyewitness account from 2d Lt. John E. Jacobs, who said he had seen Walker lead the demonstration from the start. "The first I saw of him after roll call, he was at the head of the Company, apparently in command of it, marching up to the Colonel's quarters," Jacobs testified. "At the front of the Colonel's quarters, he gave the command, 'Stack arms.' They stacked arms. . . . The Colonel asked, 'What does all this mean?' The accused replied, they were 'not willing to be soldiers for seven dollars per month.' The Colonel first advised them to take arms, and then commanded them to take arms. Sergt. Walker then left his place at the head of the company, and walked up and down in the rear of the company, telling the men not to take their arms. He came to the left of the line, and the company left, without taking their arms."

Lieutenant Jacobs also had difficulties, it then turned out, with one of the privates in Walker's company, Jacob Smith. He said he had ordered Smith to stand guard but Smith "absented himself from camp till evening." When Smith returned, Lieutenant Jacobs attempted to arrest him and handcuff him.

"He resisted, and the guard would not help me," Jacobs testified. "He called on his company to come and release him. Sergt. Walker, the accused, called to Company 'A' to fall in. They fell in, quite a portion of them, and marched to the Guard House. Sergt. Walker, the accused, said, 'Snatch hold of him, pull him away,' or 'Take him away, my Bully Boys.' They obeyed his order and released him, or took him from me."

Once again, going back to the main episode of mutiny, the stacking of arms, Walker tried to deny responsibility.

QUESTION BY ACCUSED: Was there more than one person made a remark to the effect that they would not serve any more for the $7 per month . . . ?

ANSWER [by Jacobs]: There was.

Q: Was that remark made previous, or subsequent to the accused's speaking?

A: I heard it before and after, both.

Q: Was there more than one person gave the order to "stack arms" when the men were in front of the Lt. Col's quarters . . . ?

A: I did not hear any other man give the order.

Walker never testified in his own defense. Nor did he make any attempt to argue that the demonstration for equal pay expressed a justifiable grievance. Perhaps he (or the presumably white lieutenant acting as his assigned attorney) realized that a court-martial would not allow such a line of argument. All of the defense's intermittent attempts to cross-examine the prosecution witnesses were attempts to deny involvement, to spread blame or to spread confusion. The handful of defense witnesses served much the same purposes. Private James Williams, from Walker's own Company A, was asked, "Did you hear anyone say that the 'men wouldn't serve any longer for $7 a month,' and if so, who was it?" Williams testified that the only man he had heard make such a statement was a Sergeant Bullock. And so on.

Instead of testifying, Walker and his lawyer submitted to the court a long statement in which he denied everything. About the alleged dispute with Lieutenant Wood, for example, he said: "I positively declare that I had not a gun in my hands that day, neither did I threaten to shoot Lieut. Wood." On the rescue of Jacob Smith, "I was not there at the time and had no part or lot in the occurrence." More generally, Walker declared that he and his fellow blacks were "entirely ignorant" about the rules of military law and behavior. "We have been allowed to stumble along," he said, "taking verbal instructions as to the different parts of our duty, and gaining a knowledge of the services required of us as best we might. In this way many things have occurred that might have been made entirely different had we known the responsibility of our position."

As for the equal-pay demonstration outside Colonel Bennett's tent, Walker could not deny his participation but he did once again deny his responsibility. "I believe that I have proved conclusively by the testimony of the non-commissioned officers and men of my company that I did not then exercise any command over them," he said, "that I gave no word of counsel or advice to them in opposition to the request made by our commanding officer, and that, for one, I carried my arms and equipment back with me to my company street." In other words, he denied being a rebellious hero and claimed to be a docile subordinate. Perhaps that was the lesson all slaves had to learn in order to survive, or perhaps it was just the basic teaching of the army. But though Walker denied all responsibility for the demonstration that the army regarded as a mutiny, he did remind the court that the demonstrators had been "an assemblage who only contemplated a peaceful demand for the rights and benefits that had been guaranteed them."

In the middle of the signature at the end of that statement, between the names William and Walker, there is an *X*. Remember that any slave in South Carolina who learned to read or write could be punished by flogging. Over and under the *X* are the words "his mark."

The court-martial, a lieutenant colonel from Connecticut, a major from Pennsylvania, two captains and two lieutenants, considered the accusations and the defense and then returned their verdict. Of the first charge, guilty. Of the second charge, guilty. Of the third charge, guilty. Of the fourth charge, guilty. Of everything, guilty. "And the Court do therefore sentence him, Sergeant William Walker, Co. 'A' 3d S.C. Vol Infantry (two thirds of the members concurring) to be shot to death with musketry at such time and place as the Commanding General may direct."

The commanding general directed that the execution take place the following month, February, at the Union outpost in Jacksonville, Florida. Walker was still imprisoned at the provost guardhouse in Hilton Head early in February, when he addressed his last appeal to the provost marshal general. By now, he was reduced, as many prisoners eventually are, to pleading and whining. "I am a poor Colored soldier . . ." he began. He was "entirely guiltless" and had "always done my duty as a soldier and a man." He had not been paid anything at all for the past six months, and he was "suffering very much in consequence of my close confinement and absence from my family who are suffering from want and destitution." If the provost marshal general would "use your influence in the proper quarter," he went on, the evidence would lead to his release and return to duty. "I assure you, Sir," he said, "I shall never give you cause to regret your kindness."

The next document is a discharge form filled out by the lieutenant who commanded the firing squad in Jacksonville. He did not even bother to cross out the inapplicable parts. With preprinted courtesy, the discharge form said that Walker, by now reduced to the rank of private, had "served HONESTLY and FAITHFULLY with his company to the present date," but then the lieutenant wrote in a flowery script that he "was shot to death for mutiny at Jacksonville, Fla., Febry. 29th 1864. . . ."

The form then proceeded to summarize the financial relationship between the late Private Walker and his government. "The said William Walker was last paid . . . to include the 31st day of August, 1863, and has pay due him from that time to the present date," the document said. "He is entitled to pay and subsistence for travelling to place of enrollment and whatever other allowances are authorized to volunteer soldiers, or militia, so discharged." In other words, equal pay. On the other hand, the document continued, "he has received fifty-nine ⁶/₁₀₀ dollars, advanced by the United States on account of clothing." It further said that he had "lost" one Prussian musket, one bayonet, one bayonet scabbard, one cartridge belt, and forty rounds of ammunition. Perhaps those were the weapons he had stacked in front of the colonel's tent and denied having stacked in front of the colonel's tent. Trying to estimate their value, to be repaid by the late Private Walker to the government that had just executed him, the lieutenant could only write, "Price list has never been furnished." As for the rest of the printed form, which said, "He is indebted to ——, sutler, —— dollars," and "He is indebted to ——, laundress, —— dollars," the lieutenant just crossed all that out. And so the United States government declared that its account with the late William Walker, who had believed its promises, was settled in full.

Three months later, Congress took up once again the question of equal pay for black soldiers and once again defaulted on the government's obligations. It voted to grant equal pay to black soldiers, but not to ex-slaves like Walker, only to those who had been freedmen on the day the Civil War started. There then began a series of deceptions in which officers like Col. Edward Hallowell, Robert Gould Shaw's successor as commander of the Fifty-fourth Massachusetts, told his men, "You do solemnly swear that you owed no man unrequited labor on or before the 19th day of April, 1861. So help you God." And all the ex-slaves who felt that they owed no man unrequited labor then or at any other time chorused their agreement.

But even then, Congress's laggard bill only offered equal pay retroactive to January 1, 1864, fully a year after the so-called Emancipation Proclamation had inspired the serious recruitment of black soldiers. Colonel Higginson was eloquent in his indignation. His black troops were not mercenary, he wrote to the New York Tribune. If they felt that Lincoln's government could not afford to pay them, he said, they "would serve it barefooted and on half-rations, and without a dollar—for a time." But when they saw white troops earning more than they earned (Higginson did not mention the earnings of people like J. P. Morgan), they felt understandably resentful. And their white officers would have to continue "to act as executioners for those soldiers who, like Sergeant Walker, refuse to fill their share of a contract where the Government has openly repudiated the other share." Finally, on March 3, 1865, finally, just a month before Lee surrendered at Appomattox, finally, Congress passed the Enrollment Act and granted retroactively equal pay to all black soldiers.

Including the late William Walker's old regiment, the Third South Carolina Volunteers, which, because of a new regulation banning state names for army units, was now known as the Twenty-first U.S. Colored Troops. They had not seen a great deal of combat, but in these last days of the crumbling Confederacy, they were the ones assigned to march triumphantly into the slaveholders' citadel of Charleston, to recapture Fort Sumter, where the first shots had been fired, and Fort Wagner, where Colonel Shaw and his brave black troops had been slaughtered. Before fleeing Charleston, the Confederate Gen. W. J. Hardee ordered the burning of all shipyards, cotton warehouses, and anything else that might be of value to the Union forces.

Colonel Bennett, the survivor of that confrontation with the late William Walker, arrived in Charleston by rowboat from Morris Island, out in the harbor, and sent a message to the mayor to demand a surrender and to promise "every possible assistance to your well-disposed citizens in extinguishing the flames." Then into the city marched the Twenty-first U.S. Colored and two companies of Hallowell's Fifty-fourth Massachusetts. A reporter for the *Boston Journal* tried to describe the extraordinary scene. Here were ex-slaves, he wrote, "with the old flag above them, keeping step to freedom's drum beat, up the grass-grown streets, past the slave shambles, laying aside their arms, working the fire-engines to extinguish the flames, and, in the spirit of the Redeemer of men, saving that which was lost."

There is just one postscript to add. In 1894, thirty years after the execution of William Walker, his wife, Rebecca, now remarried to somebody named Morrison, filed a claim for a pension due to a widow of a veteran of the Civil War. If she was about twenty at the time of her husband's execution, she was about fifty now, in the age of President Grover Cleveland, and perhaps she thought that everybody had forgotten the case of Sergeant Walker. Perhaps she thought everybody had forgotten that her husband had told his men to stack their arms in front of Colonel Bennett's tent, forgotten that he had said, "We will not do duty any longer for seven dollars per month."

The military bureaucracy never forgets anything, never remembers either but also never forgets. On the application by Mrs. Walker/Morrison for a pension deriving from the execution of her husband, because he had asked for equal pay for black soldiers, a War Department examiner named J. M. Paxtero recommended "rejection on the ground that soldier's death from gun shot while resisting authority in a state of mutiny was not in line of duty."

Quite true. Sergeant William Walker did not die in the line of duty. Let us honor him for that.

1988

There Are OO Trees in Russia

"OF COURSE I'M SURE—I READ IT IN *NEWSWEEK.*" FOR SEV-
eral years, this slogan appeared in large advertisements all over the
country. The advertisements usually showed no people, simply some
scene of affluence and presumed influence, a new skyscraper, or a
boardroom, or a golf club. From some unseen figure of authority,
whose statements on current affairs had apparently been questioned,
came a huge, white cartoon-style balloon filled with the crushing
rejoinder, "Of course I'm sure—I read it in *Newsweek.*"

The theory behind the advertisements was probably sound. Since
Newsweek has less reporters, writers, and editors than its omniscient
rival, *Time,* since it has less circulation, less influence, less importance than *Time,* its only real claim to attention is that it makes a
reasonable effort at fairness in summarizing the week's events. *Newsweek*'s advertisements often return to this theme. They claim that
you get all the news "and you get it straight." By boasting of its
congeries of columnists, *Newsweek* manages to imply that everything
else it publishes is the simple factual truth. Its recent ads promise a
magazine "where you can always distinguish fact from opinion."
One of them, portraying Walter Lippmann next to Washington bureau chief Benjamin Bradlee, emphasizes the special qualities of the
latter: "The facts he gets are often 'first'—are always *facts.*"

Time, of course, has never admitted the validity of these accusing
insinuations from its smaller doppelgänger. *Time* has always opposed
the idea of mere objectivity, and it acknowledges a certain bias in
favor of democracy, free enterprise, and the enlightened human

spirit, but it insists that its experienced staff simply distills the facts of the news into the truth. In one recent issue, the weekly "Publisher's Letter," which normally serves as a medium of self-congratulation, sadly criticized the Soviet Union for expelling *Time*'s Moscow correspondent. With a certain amount of unconscious humor, *Time* observed: "Soviet officials have never been able to understand or accept or even get accustomed to our kind of reporting." What the Soviets couldn't understand, *Time* went on, was that "our stories on the Soviet Union come from a wide array of sources available to our writers and editors in New York and to our correspondents elsewhere around the world." Thus *Time*'s kind of reporting doesn't depend primarily on having a reporter at the scene of the event; indeed it doesn't even need one there at all. "From these many sources . . ." *Time* concluded, "we will continue to report frankly and deeply on the Soviets despite last week's reading-out of our correspondent." (There is still one other smaller and less interesting newsmagazine, but both *Time* and *Newsweek* understandably ignore the Brobdingnagian claims of *U.S. News & World Report,* which purports to be "America's class newsmagazine . . . number one in importance of content, number one in quality of readers.")

Despite the competing claims of *Time* and *Newsweek,* there is a certain identity of both purpose and technique. Not only is the basic function of the two magazines almost the same, but the editor, national editor, and foreign editor of *Newsweek* are all alumni of *Time,* and there is a kind of all-purpose newsweekly office jargon that involves phrases like "the cosmic stuff" and "give it some global scope." To anyone who has ever been introduced to these concepts and techniques, the easy equation of facts, news, and truth can be rather disturbing. Any philosopher knows that the facts do not represent the truth; any journalist knows that neither one of them represents the news. That men should live at peace with one another might be described as truth, but it is not a fact, nor is it news. That a certain number of children were born yesterday in Chicago is a fact, and the truth, but not news. Even the *New York Times* does not claim to publish "All the Facts That Are Fit to Print." While news is at least as undefinable as truth, journalism does involve an effort to discover, select, and assemble certain facts in a way that will be not only reasonably true but reasonably interesting—and therefore reasonably salable. These truisms are easily forgotten because of the eagerness with which an anxious and uninformed public buys anything which promises "the real story," and the most forgetful people of all are those who boast of producing the facts and the truth in the name of freedom of the press and "an informed electorate."

Behind this forgetfulness lies an enduring and endearing myth of American journalism, the myth of the police reporter and the city editor. Like all myths, it once had a certain reality. When I first went to work on the *Des Moines Register,* I was the police reporter, and I turned in my copy to a lean and dour assistant city editor, who spoke with a cutting Missouri accent and didn't believe in anything. No three-paragraph story about a minor burglary was immune to his questions about the number of floors in the burgled house, the denomination of the stolen bills, or the location of the shards of glass from the broken window. Of all possible answers, the least acceptable was "I guess so." "Let's not guess, let's know," the assistant city editor would retort. Sometimes I had to telephone him a half dozen times from my bare, yellow-walled cubicle in the Des Moines police station to verify trivial details in trivial stories. I have never been sure whether the assistant city editor wanted to browbeat or simply to educate a very inexperienced and inept police reporter, but the copy that he finally sent to the composing room was, as nearly as possible, the facts.

Almost twenty years have passed since then, and I no longer expect reporters to know the answers to questions about their stories. I have grown accustomed to their complaints that the facts in question can't be discovered, and to their complaints about being questioned at all. They have a certain justification, for what happens in the Senate or the French cabinet simply can't be covered like a mugging on Sixth Street in Des Moines. The "facts" are more elusive, and, in a way, less important, for the physical details of who spoke to whom are relatively meaningless until they are molded and put into perspective by an act of judgment and a point of view. The average news story is a mixture of facts, background knowledge, and speculation, all carpentered into some kind of shape by the craftsmanship of a writer who knows how to create Potemkin villages. In other words, the legendary police reporter and the legendary city editor no longer exist as criteria; their talents and techniques are irrelevant to most of the major news stories.

The newspapers and news agencies acknowledge this, just as they acknowledge human fallibility. Later editions of newspapers correct the factual mistakes and the misjudgments caused by the need for speed in getting out the first edition; a wire service revises a story with the euphemistic confession of error: "First lead and correct." It is among magazine editors, many of whom have never worked for newspapers or wire services, much less seen the inside of a police station, that the myth of "reporting the facts" remains strongest. Since a magazine must go to press several days, or even weeks, before it appears on the newsstands, and since it remains on display for at least a week, errors and all, magazine editors have developed a fetish about absolute accuracy on the most inconsequential facts, a fetish that even makes "the facts" a substitute for reality. To be sure that you can be sure because you read it in *Newsweek* (or *Time*, or, for that matter, *The New Yorker* and a number of other magazines), there has come into existence an institution unknown to newspapers: the checker.

The checker, or researcher, is usually a girl, usually in her twenties, usually from some middle-level eastern college like Smith or Wellesley, usually pleasant looking but not a femme fatale. She came from college, unqualified for anything, but looking for an "interesting" job. After a few years, she usually gets married or embittered, or both, since she feels, rightly, that nobody appreciates her work. Her work consists of assembling newspaper clippings and other research material early in the week and then checking the writer's story at the end of the week. The beginning of the week is lazy and lackadaisical, and so is the research, but the pressure increases day by day. Toward the end of the week, when typewriters clack behind closed doors and editors snap at intruders, there are midnight hamburgers and tears in the ladies' room. For the checker gets no credit if the story is right, but she gets the blame if the story is wrong— blame administered at periodic scoldings by the "chief of researchers," a lady of authoritative age and temperament. It doesn't matter if the story is slanted or meretricious, if it misinterprets or misses the point of the week's news. That is the responsibility of the editors. What matters, and what seems to attract most of the hostile letters to the editors, is whether a championship poodle stands thirty-six or forty inches high, whether the eyes of Prince Juan Carlos of Spain are blue or brown, whether the population of some city in Kansas is 15,000 or 20,000.

The first question about this fetish of facts, which no newsmagazine ever questions, is whether these facts, researched and verified at such enormous trouble and expense, really matter. Obviously, there is an important difference between saying that Charles de Gaulle accepts Britain's entering the Common Market, which a number of prominent reporters used to report, and saying that de Gaulle opposes Britain's entering the Common Market, which mysteriously turned out to be the case. But how much does it really matter whether a newsmagazine reports that de Gaulle is sixty-seven or sixty-eight, six feet one or six feet two, that he smokes Gauloises or Chesterfields, that he eats a brioche or a melon for breakfast, that he has a telephone next to his bed or not, that he responded to some crisis at 2:00 A.M. or 3:00 A.M., that Madame de Gaulle puts fresh roses or does not put fresh roses on his desk every day? Judging by the legend of the police reporter and the city editor, and judging by the amount of space the newsmagazines devote to such minutiae, it matters very much to provide "the facts" and "provide them straight." Despite the public statements of principle, however, the men who usually care the least about such details are the men who actually write and edit the newsmagazines.

There is an essential difference between a news story, as understood by a newspaperman or a wire-service writer, and the newsmagazine story. The essential purpose of the conventional news story is to tell what happened. It starts with the most important information and continues into increasingly inconsequential details, not only because the reader may not read beyond the first paragraph but because an editor working on galley proofs a few minutes before press time likes to be able to cut freely from the end of the story. A newspaper is written and edited so that a reader can begin almost anywhere and stop almost anywhere, or skip to almost anywhere. A newsmagazine is very different. It is written and edited to be read consecutively from beginning to end, and each of its stories is designed, following the critical theories of Edgar Allan Poe, to create one emotional effect. The news, what happened that week, may be told in the beginning, the middle, or the end, for the purpose is not to throw information at the reader but to seduce him into reading the whole story, and into accepting the dramatic (and usually political) point being made. In beginning a story, without actually telling what the story is about, the newsmagazine writer often relies on certain traditional procedures, as demonstrated by the first three May issues of *Time* and *Newsweek*.

"Flowers were in bloom on the crumbling towers of St. Hilarion, and hawks turned soundlessly above Kyrenia." This is *Time*'s beginning for a story on civil strife in Cyprus. The weather lead is always a favorite because it creates a dramatic tone, because it so obviously avoids reporting the news that it implicitly promises the reader more important things to come. The following week, *Newsweek* applied the same approach to a story on Finland: "The Finnish spring comes with glacial restraint. Farm houses stand silent, ice-locked lakes mirror the stillness."

Then there is the moving-vehicle lead, most often a description of a plane landing, occasionally a report of tanks crunching through darkened streets. In one of these May issues, *Time* began a story this way: "One foggy morning in Berlin, a yellow Mercedes from the Soviet zone drew up at the tollgate at the Heerstrasse crossing point." *Newsweek*'s beginning was almost identical, though it chose to create the effect of reality by means of time rather than place: "Shortly after 5 o'clock in the morning a heavily shrouded black Mercedes bearing license tags issued by the Allied Control Commission in Germany rolled quietly into the no man's land between the Western and Russian sectors of Berlin." There is no real contradiction between the black Mercedes and the yellow Mercedes, for each magazine was focusing on a different vehicle involved in an exchange of spies, and either vehicle would provide a satisfactory, if conventional, beginning.

Weather and moving vehicles are only two of the possibilities. There is the narrative opening, involving an unidentified person: "The hooded gambler eyes tracked the jurors as they filed into the courtroom." (*Newsweek* on the trial of Roy Cohn.) There is the provocative quote involving an unidentified object: " 'She's in there,' pointed one proud Pinkerton. 'She's the most magnificent thing I've ever seen.' " (*Time* on the appearance of Michelangelo's *Pietà* at the New York World's Fair.) There is the personality lead, still involving an unidentified person: "He roared up to his classes on his gadget-laden German motorcycle, dressed in sweat shirt, corduroy trousers, and boots." (*Newsweek* on the posthumous influence of C. Wright Mills.) There are other approaches too—the complicated pun, the ostentatious epigraph, the fathomless philosophical profundity. And occasionally, the newsmagazine writer just gets bored with it all: "There was a sense of déjà vu about the whole affair—an uncanny paramnesic feeling that all of this had happened before." (*Time* on the May Day parade in Moscow.)

The writer had some reason to be bored. Presumably assigned to write a full-page lead story on the week's events in Eastern Europe, he had only two things to say—that nothing much had happened at the May Day parade, and that the Romanians were playing off the Russians against the Chinese for their own benefit. In elaborating on this, he engaged in some characteristic newsmagazine equivocation: "Dej is playing a double game in the Sino-Soviet conflict, one that could lead to plenty of trouble—or perhaps to a certain amount of freedom." But though the story has nothing much to say, it absolutely bristles with the facts that newsmagazines use as a substitute for reality. It tells us what Khrushchev was wearing (a homburg) and what he has been eating lately (cabbage rather than meat). Though Communist China has no Politburo, and though the age of most of its leaders is subject to doubt, we are told that "Communist China's Politburo is even more decrepit: its average age is 65." The story tells us how to pronounce the name of Romania's Galati steel combine (Galatz) and what its rolling mill cost ($42 million). It gives us a figure for Romanian industrial growth (15 percent) and a translation for the name of the Romanian Communist newspaper *Scinteia* (*Spark*). And to persuade us that the activity in Romania is important to people of every alphabetical persuasion, the story reports as a fact that "every Communist from Auckland to Zanzibar took note of it." At about the time this story was going to press, a rather interesting event became known—students had rioted against the government in Czechoslovakia. But there was apparently no way to work this into the fabric of Khrushchev's eating habits and Romanian economics, so it was simply wedged into the bottom of the page as a footnote. The Prague riot, which appeared on the front page of that Sunday's *Times,* may not have been worth more than a footnote—but a footnote to what?*

As a general rule, facts are not scattered around so indiscriminately, like sequins ornamenting some drab material, for the main function of facts in a newsmagazine story is to illustrate a dramatic thesis. When *Newsweek* runs a story on an African "summit conference," for example, it is apt to begin by saying (in a variation of the moving-vehicle lead, which might be called the crowd-gathering lead): "Some came in sleek Italian suits from the Via Condotti. . . ." Did any African premier really wear clothing from the via Condotti? The problem would never arise on an ordinary newspaper because it doesn't particularly matter where the African statesmen buy their clothes. But since the newsmagazine writer starts with a dramatic concept—the African leaders are a self-indulgent lot—he needs a dramatic conceit to illustrate it. Therefore he reports where the Africans bought their clothes. Yet the writer himself may not know or care where the Africans bought their clothes. The via Condotti is all right, but so is the rue du Faubourg St.-Honoré, or any other fashionable European shopping center. The vaunted fact, in other words, has in itself no inherent importance at all.

An even more characteristic opening dramatized *Time*'s recent cover story on Henry Cabot Lodge: "In the early-morning gloom of Saigon's muggy pre-monsoon season, an alarm clock shrills in the stillness of a second-floor bedroom at 38 Phung Khac Khoan Street. The Brahmin from Boston arises, breakfasts on mango or papaya, sticks a snub-nosed .38-cal. Smith & Wesson revolver into a shoulder holster, and leaves for the office." This is a fine example of the well-trained virtuoso at work, not only disguising the subject of the story but combining a series of insignificant facts into a cadenza of exotic

*A week later, *Time* decided the Czech situation was worth a story after all, a story beginning "It was in Prague in the 20s that Franz Kafka wrote his chilling allegories. . . ."

weather, breakfast food, strange street names, and gunplay. The author was so pleased with the results that he went on repeating himself for three paragraphs, which disclosed that the temperature that day was ninety degrees, with 90 percent humidity, that Lodge's moving vehicle was a Checker Marathon sedan, that the U.S. embassy building is located at 39 Ham Nghi Boulevard, and that Lodge's office desk contains yet another gun, a .357 Smith & Wesson Magnum. There are two reasons for this inundation of minutiae. The first—based on the theory that knowledge of lesser facts implies knowledge of major facts—is to prove that *Time* knows everything there is to know about Lodge. The second—based on the theory that a man who carries a gun is tough and aggressive—is to dramatize the basic thesis of the story, that Lodge would be a good Republican candidate for president.

But does the specific fact itself matter? Does it matter whether Lodge carries a .38-caliber Smith & Wesson or a Luger or a pearl-handled derringer? Does it make any difference whether he lives on the second floor of 38 Phung Khac Khoan Street or the third floor of some other building? The newsmagazines have provided their own answer by evolving a unique system which makes it theoretically possible to write an entire news story without any facts at all. This is the technique of the "zip." It takes various forms: *Kuming* (a deliberate misspelling of *coming* to warn the printer not to use the word itself), or *TK,* meaning "to kum," or, in the case of statistics, 00 (the number of zeros is optional). This technique enables the writer to ignore all facts and concentrate on the drama. If he is describing some backward country, for example, he can safely write that 00 percent of its people are ravaged by TK diseases. It obviously doesn't matter too much whether the rate of illiteracy is 80 percent or 90 percent. Any statistic will sound equally authoritative. It is the checker who is responsible for facts, and she will fill in any gaps the writer leaves.

This system has led to some extraordinary results. In times of opulence, the newsmagazines have spent enormous sums of money to fill in these "zips." One former *Time* writer, for example, recalls some problems that arose when he was writing a cover story on General Naguib, then the president of Egypt. At one point, he wrote that Naguib was such a modest man that his name did not appear among the 000 people listed in *Who's Who in the Middle East.* At another point, he wrote that Naguib disliked luxury and had refused to live in the royal palace, surrounded by an 00-foot-high wall. A cable, as the writer tells the story, duly went to the Cairo stringer. There was no answer. The editors were indignant at the stringer's irresponsibility. They changed the copy so that neither of the missing facts was needed. Then, a week later, came a cable saying something like this: AM IN JAIL AND ALLOWED SEND ONLY ONE CABLE SINCE WAS ARRESTED WHILE MEASURING FIFTEEN FOOT WALL OUTSIDE FAROUKS PALACE AND HAVE JUST FINISHED COUNTING THIRTYEIGHT THOUSAND FIVE HUNDRED TWENTYTWO NAMES WHOS WHO IN MIDEAST.

Such dedication to factual accuracy is rare, however, and it is expensive. It is much simpler to give a researcher a problem and a telephone directory and challenge her to find the answer. When both the writer and the researcher accept this as a game, the search for the key fact can become pure fantasy. On one occasion, for example, a newsmagazine editor wrote into a piece of copy: "There are 00 trees in Russia." The researcher took a creative delight in such an impossible problem. From the Soviet government, she ascertained the number of acres officially listed as forests; from some Washington agency she ascertained the average number of trees per acre of forests. The result was a wholly improbable but wholly unchallengeable statistic for the number of trees in Russia. On another occasion, when Princess Margaret married Antony Armstrong-Jones, the same editor insisted on declaring that "Jones is not the most common name. There are only 00 of them in Britain, compared to 00 Smiths and 00 Browns." The same researcher found family associations which provided the answers.

In the normal case of the 00, however, someone calls a government agency to get the official answer. The results are sometimes equally strange. One *Newsweek* researcher recalls the story of the Sudanese army, which a writer had described as the 00-man Sudanese army. No newspaper clippings could fill in the figure, and telephone calls to the Sudanese embassy in Washington indicated that nobody there had any idea of the number of men enrolled in the Sudanese army. The problem had never arisen, and the Sudanese may well have been surprised that anybody should want to know such a figure. As the weekly deadline approached, an editor finally instructed the checker to make "an educated guess," and the story appeared with a reference to something like "the 17,000-man Sudanese army." There were no complaints. The *Newsweek* story duly reached Khartoum as part of a summary of American press coverage of the Sudan. The Khartoum press complaisantly reprinted it and commented on it. Digests of the Khartoum press duly returned to Washington, and one day a Sudanese embassy official happily telephoned the *Newsweek* researcher to report that he finally was able to tell her the exact number of men in the Sudanese army: seventeen thousand.

Once you go beyond the Des Moines police station, you find yourself dealing more and more with the Sudanese embassy. The "facts," which are supposed to form the basis of the news, are often simply unknown. On one occasion, I had to write a major story about Iraq and I declared that, as I remember it, "90 percent of the people live in mud huts without electricity or running water." When the researcher challenged me on this dubious statistic, I proudly pointed to a paragraph in a previous *Time* cover story, from which I had cribbed it. The researcher accepted this as adequate documentation—not because it was true but simply because it was documentation, and at deadline time any old clipping from any old newspaper or magazine becomes acceptable evidence. "After all," said the researcher, who had to face the periodic meetings with the chief of researchers, "we have to protect ourselves." A year or so later, I was again writing a story about Iraq, and, since I didn't feel very energetic, I once again wrote that 90 percent of the people lived in mud huts without electricity or running water. The forgetful researcher challenged me once again; once again I cited the *Time* cover story. This time, fortified by a year of increasing cynicism, she rebelled: "How the hell do *they* know?" To placate her, I abolished the statistical computation of the number of Iraqi hut-dwellers, and yet in any week's issue of any magazine of journalism, you can find very similar statistics—00 percent of the people of Brazil are illiterate, or the per capita income of the Burmese is $00.

In actual fact, newsmagazine writers play a number of statistical games with totally unverifiable statistics. With the cooperation of partisan groups, they make comparative projections of the American and Russian gross national product in 1970 when nobody has more than a vague estimate of what these figures will be a year from now. The birth-control lobby issues horrendous statistics about the number of human beings who will be living on every cubic yard of earth in the year 2000, and yet all such projections are based heavily on the estimated future populations of China and India, estimates that vary even today by hundreds of millions. All over the world, in fact, estimates of population, illiteracy, illness, industrial growth, or per capita income are no more than the wildest of guesses. "Let's not guess, let's know," the assistant city editor in Des Moines used to say, expressing a characteristically American desire for certainty. At one point during one of the periodic crises in Laos, however, an American correspondent bitterly complained to a Laotian government spokesman that he had spoken to sixteen government officials and got sixteen different versions of the facts. The Laotian was bewildered. It seemed perfectly natural to him, he said, that if you spoke to sixteen different officials you would get sixteen different answers.

The Laotian was wise in acknowledging and answering the first fundamental question about the fetish of facts—does it really matter which "fact" is to be officially certified as "true"? He was equally wise in acknowledging and answering a second question—does anyone really know which "fact" is "true"? He was equally wise in raising a third question, and implying an answer, that every man sees the "facts" according to his own interests. Governments and business corporations have long acknowledged this by employing public-relations men and "information officers" to make sure that any facts make them look virtuous. *Time* once quoted a French spokesman's poetic definition of his job: *"Mentir et démentir."* And in the world of newsmagazines, seeking the certainty of the unascertainable facts, the official government statistics carry a surprising weight. On one occasion, for instance, I was writing a story about the economic problems of Sicily, and I wrote that approximately 30 percent of the inhabitants were unemployed, which I believed to be roughly true. When I saw the story in print, I read that something like 8 percent of the Sicilians were unemployed. In other words, one of Europe's poorest areas was scarcely worse off than the United States—but this was the official statistic that the Italian government had given to the researcher. "After all," as one of them had said, "we have to protect ourselves."

The basic purpose of the newsmagazines' facts, however, is not to report the unemployment statistics in Sicily, or the shopping habits of African statesmen, but to provide an *appearance* of documentation for what are essentially essays. The fact-choked opening of the *Time* cover story on Lodge, for example, eventually leads to the question of whether the Republicans might nominate Goldwater because no Republican can defeat President Johnson anyway. "This defeatist attitude is pretty silly," reports *Time, The Weekly Newsmagazine*. "Sure as his political moves have been, Johnson could still stumble politically. And healthy as the President may seem, there is always that dread possibility of disablement or worse. The Republican nomination is therefore nothing to give away for the mere asking." After that Olympian declaration, the *Time* story goes on to outline the Lodge supporters' hopes for their candidate's triumphant return to the United States. "A foolish fantasy?" *Time* wonders. "Perhaps. But that is one of the most enchanting things about U.S. politics: dreams can and do come true."

Unfortunately, the perils of prophecy are high. The week after the Lodge story, which assumed that the ambassador would sweep onward from a victory in the Oregon primary, *Time* had to rush out with a cover story that began, a little hysterically: "Battling Nelson did it! Battered, bloodied, beaten, taunted, hooted, and laughed at during bitter, frustrating months, Republican Nelson Rockefeller never gave up, never stopped swinging." This story, too, concluded with a warning to Republicans not to accept defeat: "Nelson Rockefeller doesn't think like that—and in Oregon he demonstrated that perhaps it is a pretty poor way of thinking." No man waits for *Time*, however, and when Barry Goldwater finally won the Republican nomination, the editors declared that it had been inevitable: "Goldwater won the presidential nomination by arduously cultivating support at the precinct and county levels. . . . What helped clinch it for Goldwater was the fact that a strong conservative tide was running in the U.S., fed by a deep disquiet at the grass roots over the role of an ever-expanding Government. Goldwater and the tide came together, and the one could not have succeeded without the other."

On a less exalted plane, the typical newsmagazine story almost invariably reaches a point where the writer drops the factual ballast and summarizes his views on the importance of the week's events. And there is nothing wrong about this. In view of the general ignorance of the American public—if everyone read the *New York Times* there would be no newsmagazines—an informed evaluation of the week's news is something to be commended. Yet if the reality were candidly admitted, it would antagonize the newsmagazine readers. The English, who read newspapers on a scale that should shame most Americans, have no major newsmagazines, but they appreciate magazines that frankly comment on a body of presumed knowledge, *The Economist, The New Statesman, The Spectator.* Most Americans, however, taught to believe that they should assimilate "the facts" for themselves, reject such American counterparts as *The New Republic* and *The Nation.* They accept the newsmagazines not as magazines of commentary or interpretation but as magazines which will tell them yet more facts, "the real story."

Here is the Achilles' heel of the newsmagazines. For if you assume that nobody really knows or cares how many men there are in the Sudanese army, as newsmagazine editors do every time they use the term "00," you acknowledge the hypocrisy of your claim to be reporting the facts (it is worth noting that newsmagazine reporters chronically complain that their files are ignored), and you assume the sacerdotal role of providing not the facts but "the truth." Apart from the size of the Sudanese army, what is really going on in the Sudan? Apart from the number of trees growing on the steppes, what is really going on in Russia? Or in London and Paris and Washington? It is in the major political capitals, where the major news is made, that the police reporter in pursuit of the facts has become particularly irrelevant. A skillful police reporter turned loose in the Pentagon not only wouldn't be able to get the right answer, he wouldn't even be able to find the person who knew the answer. A reporter may ring doorbells in the Bronx and ask anybody anything he chooses, but the officials of the State Department or the Quai d'Orsay only speak to people they know. And the reporter who persuades himself that he represents the so-called Fourth Estate soon does become an unofficial representative of the government, as any correspondent visiting foreign countries realizes about the press in every capital but his own. At the very least, the capital correspondent thinks he is the intermediary divinely chosen to interpret the activities of the politicians to the electorate; quite often, he acquires a vocation to educate and inspire the politicians themselves; rarely does he realize that in representing a "Fourth Estate" he serves the government as an instrument for leaks, propaganda, and outright lies. After all, if you're having a candlelit dinner with the secretary of state, isn't it the better part of valor to assume that anything he tells you is "the truth"?

The situation remains much the same from one administration to another, for the "facts" come from the power establishment, and any reporter who wants to get any facts must remain on good terms with that establishment, and with the establishment's view of what the facts are. One incident that still seems most illustrative occurred during the Kennedy years. At a time when no Berlin crisis was visible in the daily press, the Washington bureau manager of a newsmagazine telephoned his superiors to say that a major Berlin crisis was imminent. Having access to the president, he reported that "the only thing on the president's desk" was a melodramatic plan to evacuate dependents, to mobilize reserves, and to behave as though war were imminent. This was a little puzzling since the Russians apparently hadn't done anything about Berlin recently, but the newsmagazine was so impressed by the president's supposed anxiety that it printed a major story about the supposed "emergency plan." When that issue of the newsmagazine appeared, the president affected to be distraught. He telephoned the head of the magazine and asked how he could jeopardize the national interest with such an article. He even announced publicly that he was calling in the FBI to investigate the Pentagon to see who had leaked such a dangerous story to the magazine.

The editors of the magazine, who had innocently thought they were acting for rather than against the national interest, were very embarrassed. But the FBI somehow never succeeded in finding or punishing the culprit who had leaked the story. And while the Pentagon was upset at the idea of the FBI undertaking an intelligence job that the Pentagon normally performs on itself, it remained for the *New York Times,* one of the last redoubts of independent journalism in Washington, to suggest that the president had called in the FBI to investigate the leaking of a phony "emergency plan" so that the Russians would think it was a real emergency plan.

By that time, the president was on the air, urging Americans to build bomb shelters because of the impending Berlin crisis. And the newsmagazine, which spends tens of thousands of dollars every year to verify the per capita income of nonexistent peasants in Thailand, was left wiping the pie off its face. It could only wipe in dignified silence. For unlike the daily newspaper, which can publish a political "leak" one day and the official denial the next, the newsmagazine purports to tell not just the facts but the inside, authoritative, "real" story, and thus it remains peculiarly vulnerable to inside, authoritative, real propaganda. It cannot deny what it was authoritatively told as the truth without denying itself.

And yet the myth survives—we must report the facts. Every statement must be checked and double-checked. One day in March of 1958, when it seemed that France was drifting toward chaos, a newsmagazine editor assigned me to write a generally sympathetic story about Charles de Gaulle and his views on France's future. Our Paris bureau chief was an ardent Gaullist and sent a long file to explain de Gaulle's policies. And since I had long been an admirer of de Gaulle, I felt no misgivings about writing an article outlining the hopeful prospects for a Gaullist France. But there was nothing in the Paris file and nothing in de Gaulle's own writing that seemed to provide an adequate summary of the Gaullist contempt for the Fourth Republic. And so I concluded, on a note of typical newsmagazine rhetoric, that France's main problem was to remake itself. This, I added, involves a change in outlook and atmosphere, an end to the meanness, corruption, squabbling that have darkened the past decade. When I saw the published version, I saw to my surprise that my own rhetoric had somehow become de Gaulle's rhetoric. "This, he adds," it said, referring to de Gaulle, " 'involves a change in outlook and atmosphere ...' " And so on. When I asked the researcher how my words had become de Gaulle's words, she said that the quotation marks had been added by a man who was then one of the chief editors. She said she had gone to remonstrate with him, and to tell him that de Gaulle had never said any such thing, and she reported that he had answered: "Well, that's his idea, isn't it? He *could* have said it."

So the matter rested, for a few weeks, and then I went on vacation. During my vacation, the army and the mob seized control of Algiers, and France shook, and de Gaulle announced his readiness to return to power, and the researcher sent me a full page torn from that morning's edition of the *New York Herald Tribune,* quoting de Gaulle's views on every known issue. And what was his view on the basic condition of France? France must remake itself, he said, and "this involves a change in outlook and atmosphere, an end to the meanness, corruption, squabbling that have darkened the past decade. . . ."

By now, I can only assume that this statement is a documented "fact," like the "fact" that 00 percent of the Iraqis live in mud huts without electricity or running water. Until some researcher angrily asks, "How the hell do they know?" Or some Laotian, who never met a Des Moines police reporter, suggests that neither facts nor news is necessarily the truth.

1964

Reunion in Concord

■ "COME AND GET REACQUAINTED," THE MIMEOGRAPHED SHEET
said. "Concord Rod and Gun Club. Strawberry Hill Road. . . . Smorgasbord Dinner, Dancing and Chatting. . . . SEE YOU THERE!"

The Concord Rod and Gun Club is a long, low building, set in
some rather nondescript woods. Its founders apparently designed it
as an isolated citadel of masculinity—a large stone fireplace, exposed
ceiling beams, antlers on the walls—but there are signs that the
women have been at work. Ears of corn hang by the doorways, and
streamers of crepe paper, in harvest colors of brown and orange,
flow from the ceiling. . . .

I was there to attend the twenty-fifth reunion of the Concord
High School class of 1945. I have always remembered, with embarrassing clarity, a rather unpleasant adolescence in Concord, and
now, trying to rediscover my own past, I wanted to see what the
surviving evidence of youth could reveal to the observation of middle
age.

Everyone seemed to remember me quite well. They laughed
cheerfully and clapped me on the shoulder. They remarked that I
had grown a good deal since those days. But I myself, the returning
ghost, remembered almost none of them—not even after we had
bowed toward one another for a quick inspection of lapel badges,
with names and photographs from the class yearbook of 1945—not
even then could I remember who they were, or how we had once
been children together.

* * *

"You could never guess what I have most missed in my life," Henry Luce once announced to a group of dutifully attentive executives. There is no evidence that any of his listeners hazarded a guess—there was so much that was missing, after all—and the celebrated publisher went on to give his own answer. "It is the fact that I have never had—and cannot have—a hometown, an American hometown. 'Where do you come from? Where were you born and raised?' These are basic questions. . . . I would give anything if I could say simply and casually, 'Oskaloosa, Iowa.' "

I have actually been in Oskaloosa, Iowa (whose leading citizens responded to Luce's yearnings by awarding him an honorary citizenship in the last year of his life), but I can testify that its attractions are limited. The average Oskaloosan would probably find it vastly gratifying to be able to say, like Luce, "I was raised in Tengchow, China." But Luce believed, as so many Americans do, in the legendary "hometown," that mythical village somewhere between Hannibal, Missouri; Oxford, Mississippi; and Peyton Place, a scene of elm-shaded streets and frolicking dogs and kindly widows knitting on whitewashed front porches—a place of security and stability and sanctuary. Luce seemed to think that he alone had been deprived of an experience that all native-born Americans had shared, but I suspect that the large majority of native-born Americans share his sense of deprivation. For most of us, raised in apartments or farmhouses or suburban split-levels, and forced to move every few years because of the vagaries of the family finances, there never was a hometown. And so we must create one.

My own childhood was more stable than many, I think, since my father held the same job throughout the Depression. Year after year, he lectured on government at Harvard, and so we never moved very far from Harvard Square. I had been born in Boston, but I spent my childhood years in Cambridge, and from those years I still retain the meaningless recollections of neighborhood oddities—old Miss Carruthers going out every day for a drive in her mysteriously silent, bottle-green electric automobile, and Mrs. Sperry, the wife of the dean of the Divinity School, appearing on her side porch at ten o'clock every night to cry out for her roving Scotch terrier: "Peter! Peter! Peter!"

Martin Luther once said that even if he knew the world was coming to an end, he would go on planting apple trees. At the beginning of 1933, when my father's world was beginning to come to an end, he planted an elm tree at the corner of our front lawn to celebrate the birth of my sister Liesel. But this was just a gesture. Cambridge was (and is) too large and too heterogeneous to be any-one's hometown, and besides, we didn't live there much longer. Now that Hitler had come to power and we couldn't go back to Germany in the summers any more, my father bought a farm in the hills outside Brattleboro, Vermont.

As the Depression tightened, he sold the house in Cambridge and tried for a time to commute to Brattleboro, which, in the middle of winter, was a rather rough hundred-mile trip. My mother learned to live with ten-foot snowdrifts, and we—my brother Paul, Liesel, and I—staggered out onto the road every morning to catch the an-cient Ford station wagon that carried the farm children five miles to school in Brattleboro. There, in the Green Street School, every-thing was very old-fashioned. The bright children learned to conju-gate verbs and parse sentences, and the dumb children flunked, year after year, until, at the age of sixteen, they finally dropped out of the fourth or fifth grade and stayed home on the farm. We also learned to fight for dear life. The only fights in Cambridge had been wrestling classes, in gym suits, but here every challenge had to be settled in the mud of the playground. My sister Liesel, newly enrolled in the first grade, soon announced proudly, "I can beat every boy in the first three grades."

But Brattleboro was not really a hometown either. Every day, the school bus took us back out to the farm, where the nearest house was half a mile down the road, and only once or twice in those years did we ever lure some other boys out from town to play base-ball among the thistles in the cow pasture (using mounds of half-hardened dung as the bases). At about this time, my mother decided to take up the violin, practicing Beethoven every night in one remote corner of the house, but that did not put off the inevitable break-down for long. Suddenly, not long after I had started the eighth grade, and the nights were getting cold again, we all moved back to the suburbs of Boston, to a rented house in Belmont. But Belmont is not a town; it is a series of boxlike houses on rows of neat streets, without any sense of cohesion or community. I spent much of our year there in flight from roving gangs of toughs, and when I later planned for a time to write a pseudo-Dostoyevskian novel about a mindless, motiveless sex murderer, I inevitably set the scene in Belmont. No, Belmont was not a hometown at all.

My father had always had an inquisitive feeling about real estate. Houses and plots of land affected him the way jewelry affects women—treasures to be savored, inspected, priced, considered, reflected upon. So as he drove between Cambridge and Vermont, during these hard years, he kept track of a number of places that were marked for sale, places that kept sinking in price during every year of the Depression. There was a large and beautiful house in the very center of Concord, a former colonial inn, of white clapboard, with four living rooms and ten bedrooms and a long garden out in the back. In the middle of 1941, my father noted that the price of this grand old house at 54 Main Street had dropped to $8,000, and then he bought it.

I lived there only three years, plus one year of commuting to college, so Concord is really no more of a hometown than Cambridge, or Brattleboro, or even Belmont. But Concord is where I went to high school and got my first job and went on my first date, and such a town becomes, in memory, one's hometown. That's really all it is, Mr. Luce, nothing more than that.

"The town of Concord is unique in all America," says the guidebook, "because it has three famous periods in its history, any one of which would be a sufficient claim to distinction. First, its history reaches back more than three hundred years to the days when the early Puritans made here in the wilderness the first Massachusetts settlement away from the tidewater. Second, it was the scene of the first battle in the war of the Revolution. Third, it was the home of

Emerson, Alcott, Thoreau, and Hawthorne, great authors of the period aptly called the 'Flowering of New England.' Moreover, it is not just a museum but a beautiful, elm-shaded town of homes, schools, farms, and businesses, growing from year to year...."

Yes, Concord is a town unlike any other, and there are a great many bronze plaques to celebrate that fact. Here, at the end of Main Street, is the site of Jethro's Tree, where, in 1635, Maj. Simon Willard first bought from the Indians "6 myles of land square." And over there, that stately white Unitarian church with the blue dome and the massive Doric pillars, that church was founded in 1636, rebuilt in 1673 and rebuilt again in 1712, and John Hancock presided here over the First Provincial Congress, and then the church was turned sideways, and then it burned down, and then it was rebuilt once more. And out on Monument Street, the famous Minuteman stands perpetually on guard over what Emerson called "the rude bridge that arched the flood," preparing to fire "the shot heard round the world." For well over a century, these plaques and pillars have established Concord's identity, its view of itself as a national treasure. The citizens of Concord consider it natural and proper that outsiders should come from far away to admire their monuments, and when the citizens of Concord refer to the local aristocracy of "families who were here before the fight," they mean, literally, those farmers who were here in 1775, the Buttricks and the Barretts and the Bulkeleys.

But let us begin less heroically. Let us begin at the railroad station. The Boston & Maine used to provide regular and dependable service from Boston and Cambridge out to Concord, Fitchburg, and points west. The Concord station was of a type found all over New England, a small, square building with an almost pagodalike roof that swooped steeply down in a four-sided pyramid. Every few years, the painters would come and apply a new coat of paint, usually gray, sometimes a muddy brown.

The station was known as the depot, and it formed the social center for many of the tough boys who lived nearby. They were a mixture of Irish, Italian, and French Canadian, known as "the depot kids." Some of them were among the best linemen on our football team, but most of them remained rather small—wizened and toughened by years of bad food and the knowledge that they had no future. They were not vicious, in a sadistic sense, but they did not tolerate competition, arguments, or uppityness from any newcomers to their territory. In recent years, it has become popular to argue that no white man can ever know how Negroes feel, but I suspect that anybody who ever grew up in a standard "hometown" got a very good idea of how Negroes feel every time he encountered that town's "depot kids." What I felt, in any case, were all the emotions that one might attribute to Stepin Fetchit—terror, helplessness, and a doomed desire to please. One could not please the depot kids; one could only hope that they did not notice one's existence. (Outside their territory, the roles were reversed, of course, and the depot kids become our Negroes, the slum children of a rich town. Concord had only one real Negro, though, the fat, elderly cook at Freddy Childs's restaurant, who was known as Pappy. It also had one Jew, a tailor named Arkin.)

The reason that I had to pass among the depot kids was that Massachusetts law forbade anyone under the age of fourteen to acquire the working papers required in such prestigious institutions as the A & P on Main Street or Tirrell's garage on Walden Street. Since I was twelve, the only job open was to deliver newspapers for Harry Bullard, who tended the newsstand at one end of the railroad station. Harry Bullard was a bald, stout old man, about sixty, with red veins in his cheeks. He always wore a flat, checked cap on his head and a dirty brown cardigan to keep him warm in the winter. My brother, Paul, a year older than I, was the first one to get a paper route from Harry Bullard, and then he arranged to get one for me. It seemed a great honor, one's first job, and a real income—half a cent per paper, about three dollars a week in all.

The depot kids, who didn't mind tending Harry Bullard's newsstand from time to time, refused to deliver the papers, and as fall turned into winter, I learned why. I had to get up at six-thirty every morning and bicycle to the station in the darkness. Harry Bullard was already there, standing behind the counter in his little stall, waiting for some early commuter to buy a paper. His breath made faint clouds in the air, and since the railroad office didn't open until seven, the only light came from the bare bulb that hung over his head. By this time, Harry Bullard had already dragged into his lair the bundles of *Heralds* and *Globes* that had been thrown off the train. He had cut the wires that bound them, and he had stacked the papers on his battered wooden counter. And now we, the paperboys, arrived on our bicycles to load our share of papers into our white canvas bags and wheel off across town.

My brother Paul and I each started with a route of about fifty papers, but as the winter descended, and the temperatures sank to twenty below zero, and the snowbanks remained four feet high, week after week, and I set out at a little after seven o'clock every morning in a kind of blue woolen sailor cap that folded down over my mouth and formed icicles as my breath froze—as all this happened, the other paperboys dropped out, and by the end of the year there were only two of us left. One was a small boy named Bruno, who stayed within his own neighborhood on the south side of the railroad tracks. Throughout the rest of Concord, I was the one who delivered the newspapers—about 200 every morning, about 100 every afternoon.

Sometimes, though, when the weather got warmer, my sister, Liesel, drove along after me on her bicycle, helping me to spin the folded papers onto the front porches. At the age of nine, she was still too young to have a route of her own, but she was content to tag along behind me, because she wanted company, or because she had nothing else to do. I would send her up the long driveways, particularly those which contained troublesome dogs, and she would always ride off with a sense of pride that I had assigned her to the mission of delivering that day's *Globe* or *Traveller*. Occasionally, she would ask if she could take over the whole route for a day or two, deliver all the papers, assume all the responsibility. I always refused her, declaring that she didn't know the complete details, and I couldn't be sure that she would do the job right. So she just went on following me around my route, one bicycle wobbling after another, delivering the *Globe* to old Mr. Lee, the chairman of the Esperanto Society, and two copies of the *Traveller* to the Dees' Funeral Home, and the *Monitor* to Mr. James, who was reputed, even during the war, to be a Fascist.

When I try to remember Liesel now, I really remember rather little. There are pictures that tell me what she looked like, a square, sturdy girl who liked to play football, not pretty but handsome, in a sisterly sort of way. She wore her dark blonde hair in pigtails. The thing I remember most clearly about her was a quality of eagerness and hope. She wanted very much to please people, and, as the only girl after two brothers, she felt that nobody cared about her very much. To a certain extent, she was probably right. Old Harry Bullard liked her a lot, though, and he fussed over her whenever she came to the depot to help me with the papers. He sold her Life Savers at cost, three cents a pack.

During the summer of 1943, I stayed in Concord by myself, delivering the papers and sweeping the floor at the bookstore and packing the china for Mary Curtis's gift shop and washing dishes at Freddy Childs's restaurant, which he called The Mill Dam, and one day my mother telephoned from Brattleboro to say that Liesel had drowned. Nobody knew how it had happened. Liesel had had the measles that spring, and the measles have strange aftereffects, but the doctor had pronounced her cured. So she went to the swimming pool of some neighbors called Holbrook, who lived in a bizarre old Victorian mansion called Naulahka, which had been built by Rudyard Kipling, during his Vermont phase, and was still something of a local museum. My father was hoeing a vegetable patch along the road that led to the pool, and he shouted after Liesel to ask whether she really felt well enough to go swimming in such cold water. Liesel said she did, so my father waved to her as she climbed the steep hill to the pool. And she waved back.

There were two other children at the pool, younger ones, children of a farm family that lived on the other side of Naulahka. After a time—nobody knows how long—they wandered home and told their mother that Liesel was lying at the bottom of the pool. I was not there, but I can see the rest, even now—the woman telephoning our house, yes, they say that Liesel is lying at the bottom of the pool, and my mother throwing down the telephone and slamming through the screen door and shouting wildly across the vegetable garden, and my father shouting back, What? What? and then dropping his hoe and starting to run, panting, unbelieving, up the hill to the pool. He jumped into the freezing water and dragged Liesel's body up onto the mossy brick walk that ran along the edge of the pool. And pressed his thick, strong hands against her back and tried to force the water out of the lungs. And did force some water out, trickling out onto the stone pathway by the side of the pool, but too late.

The telephone call made very little impression on me. I was fourteen years old, and fourteen-year-olds live in the world of their own selves. Liesel was dead. Well, so Liesel was dead. This was a Saturday, and Saturday was the day we had to go down to Harry Bullard's newsstand and put together the Sunday newspapers. The Sunday papers arrived in great bundles—hundreds of sports sections, hundreds of comic sections, hundreds of rotogravures and society sections—and we arranged the bundles on the floor and slipped a copy from one pile to the next pile until we had a complete Sunday paper.

"Liesel drowned," I said to Harry Bullard as I started my work. The old man looked at me in amazement and then simply rejected what I had said.

"Don't make jokes like that," he said, angrily.

"I'm not making a joke," I said. "My mother just called me about it from the farm."

Harry Bullard turned away, saying nothing, fussing with a new bale of papers. I set to work then on my own job of folding sports sections into comic sections—feeling nothing more, really, than a sense of self-importance. I had delivered big news, I had impressed and startled my boss, Harry Bullard. And as I look back on it, I think they were right, in ancient times, to whip the bearers of bad news. Despite their pretense of neutrality, those bearers enjoyed their bad news, and the effect it had on their victims.

Harry Bullard had no way to say what he felt, perhaps because he was a poor and uneducated man, or perhaps because I was a callow boy who could not have understood anything he said. So Harry Bullard said nothing. What he did, in silence, was to get down on his knees next to me on the floor of the depot and help me fold the rest of my Sunday papers.

⟡　⟡　⟡

Where is Harry Bullard now? Dead, I suppose. I drive my rented Hertz Ford to the depot to see whether the place is still there.

Yes, it is still there, and with a new coat of gray paint, too, but it is not a railroad station any more. The railroad still runs through here, but now you buy your ticket on the train—not a bad idea, it seems to me—what was the point of all those little stations at every stop along the line? The building itself is occupied mainly by a store called Stop, Look, and Listen, Inc. It sells rock 'n' roll records. Out in front, there are two wooden barrels full of petunias. In the wing that used to be Harry Bullard's newsstand, there is a real-estate office. In back of the station, alongside the tracks, there stand three blue metal boxes, which contain the *Herald Traveller,* the *Globe,* and the *Record-American* (these papers used to be separate entities, when I delivered them, and there was also a *Post,* now dead), and you deposit coins in the slot and get your paper. The job that got Harry Bullard up at six o'clock every morning no longer needs a Harry Bullard. The machine works by itself.

"All stories like this are always the same," my wife says. "You go back to see the places where you grew up, and you find that everything has changed, and everything looks smaller than it used to, and that's that."

This is certainly true for Cambridge, which has become the Greenwich Village of New England, and it is certainly true for Brattleboro, where a superhighway now cuts through the woods just below our farm, and it is probably true for Belmont, though it's a little hard to tell, since change has relatively little effect on places that scarcely exist. But I am here to report that Concord, Massachusetts, has not changed at all. Or rather, it has not given way to the supermarket and the superhighway. On the contrary, to the extent that Concord has changed, it has become more colonial (which means pseudocolonial) than ever. It is full—almost too full—of little boutiques that sell leatherwork and pottery and framed etchings and old coins.

There are still just two banks, both of red brick, with large lawns in front. Most of the sidewalks are of earth, not concrete. The two drugstores, Snow and Richardson's, still confront each other at the corner of Main Street and Walden Street. And there is still no traffic light at this main intersection. A policeman stands in a box and directs traffic by hand.

Behind the policeman, there is Anderson's grocery store. Thirty years ago, any logical forecast of Concord's future would have predicted Anderson's inevitable death. There was already an A & P on the other side of Main Street, and a Grand Union on Walden. They were both cheaper than Anderson's, and, since food was rationed during the war, relations between grocers and their customers became rather peculiar. Butter, for example, was generously rationed, but hard to find. The A & P, which had no friends, sold butter at random, one pound to a customer, whenever a new supply became available. Mr. Anderson, on the other hand, kept his butter for regular customers, which was his right, though my mother considered his system undemocratic.

Mr. Anderson was fighting for his life, and in many towns he might have lost, but in Concord, he won. Today, his descendants still operate an old-fashioned grocery store, where fowl roast on spits before your eyes, and staples like coffee still lie in barrels, to be sampled and bought by the scoop. Across the street, the A & P has disappeared. In fact, along the whole Main Street of Concord, there are no longer any supermarkets at all. And there are no gas stations either.

So let us start over again, approaching the town not by its railroad line but by the main highway that stretches about fifteen miles out from Boston. It used to be a narrow blacktop road called the Cambridge Turnpike, which wound past a few small farms and then across some marshland into the center of town. This was where I expected to find the standard kind of destruction—the rows of split-levels, the felled trees, the filled-in marshes, the dead uniformity of suburbia. It was not so. The superhighway swerves off to the left before it reaches Concord, and the maple trees along the road into

town still stand, as they have always stood, fat and round and complacent, turning yellow now and shedding their leaves onto a road
that is still narrow, and a marsh that is still a marsh.

The Cambridge Turnpike leads to a forked junction with Lexington Road, and here, at this junction, you can observe, on the left,
the splendid white mansion where Ralph Waldo Emerson used to
live, but as I approached the junction, I looked to the right, because
that was where the McKennas used to live.

Late at night, at the Concord Rod and Gun Club, four of us
alumni are sitting around a table, drinking beer, and one man says,
"I saw Leo McKenna the other day."

"Yeah?" says someone else. "How was he?"

"Okay," the first man says. "Okay."

I missed the full, almost mythological impact of the McKennas,
since the only one in school with me was Tommy McKenna, who
was a year or two ahead of me, a rather gawky boy with a large
Adam's apple. He ran like the wind, though—a quarter-miler, half-
miler, miler, cross-country runner. Indeed, he was the state champion in several of these categories, and in Concord, to be a state
champion was a very big thing to be. But Tommy McKenna was
only a cousin of the McKennas who lived in the house across from
Ralph Waldo Emerson. It was a plain wooden house, plainly furnished, for the McKennas were not rich, but nobody ever went
inside, where Mrs. McKenna ruled over a large kitchen, for the
social center of the McKenna place was the large square lawn where
a football game was always in progress.

Concord, being a rich and progressive town, had an enormous
playground, complete with a baseball diamond, a quarter-mile track,
tennis courts, and a football field, but, as sometimes happens, the
enormous playing fields were empty most of the time, and everybody
who wanted to play football would migrate over to the McKennas'
house on Lexington Road. To me, the great virtue of the McKennas'
permanent football game was that I was one of the older players,
and so I got to play in the backfield, along with my brother, Paul;

and Doc Flavin, the son of the dentist who lived farther out on Lexington Road, and occasionally Jimmy Walker, the class radical. The oldest of the McKennas themselves was Joey, who was a year or two younger than we. Since it was his football, he generally played end, which enabled him to run and shout and occasionally catch a pass. As for the little ones, the eight-year-olds, Leo McKenna and various small neighbors, they had to play in the line. "Get in there and block out," Doc Flavin would shout at the start of every play. Day after day, we assigned these little ones to their fate, never to run or pass or even catch a pass, only to block and suffer on behalf of their elders and betters.

Several years later—how many years? five? ten?—I was living in Paris and trying to write a novel, and my brother Paul wrote me that the Concord High School football team had become a kind of legend. Did I remember Bernie Meigin? The Concord football coach, once of Notre Dame? A heavy man with a rapidly receding hairline, a professional coach interested in nothing but his profession, he was not exactly a Knute Rockne but rather an imitation of Pat O'Brien playing Knute Rockne in that movie. Anyway, my brother, who had also gone his own way, to Yale, to Russia, to Mexico, was now back in America, watching on television the high-school football national championship. The game was taking place somewhere in North Carolina, and there, in the maroon jerseys, was Concord High School, which, under Bernie Meigin, had won something like eighty-five games without a defeat, and there, at quarterback, throwing long passes and leading a flawless T-formation offensive, was none other than little Leo McKenna.

"Hey, what ever happened to Leo McKenna?" I asked, in the Concord Rod and Gun Club, of the man who had seen him on the street.

"He got a scholarship to Dartmouth," the man said, "and he played there, of course, and now he's in business, and says he's doing pretty well."

He spoke as though he had seen St. Paul or St. Francis, one of us, but one of us who had really made it.

*   *   *

As an old town, Concord has many generations of the dead, and many monuments to those many generations. The first settlers lie in the Old Hill Burying Ground, or in the cemetery near our house on Main Street. Sleepy Hollow, out on Bedford Street, has an "Authors' Ridge," which contains the graves of Emerson, Thoreau, and Hawthorne, but this is really the town's new, modern graveyard, established after the old places were full.

At the center of town, where Main Street, Lexington Road, and Monument Street all converge, the town commemorates its war victims. There is a boulder listing twenty-five dead in "The World War," then, across the street, a large tombstone with a plaque naming forty dead in "World War II." Beneath that, on the same stone, they have economized by simply adding another plaque for the two dead in Korea. And Vietnam? Is there another plaque being cast in some foundry, or are they waiting for the war to end?

At the center of the square is the Civil War Monument. Two college students, boy and girl, stand in front of the ugly monolith that commemorates the forty-eight who died in "The War of the Rebellion." They both wear blue jeans, and they hold hands, and the girl touches her long blonde hair as she says to the boy that she had always heard it called the American Revolution, so why does this plaque call it the War of the Rebellion? The boy does not know the answer. He mumbles an evasion. And the dead who are commemorated by this squat, square pillar do not know that we have forgotten which war it was that killed them.

We, the good Germans, were in favor of America going to war—my father lectured for all kinds of lobbying groups with names like Committee to Defend America by Aiding the Allies—and the Concord establishment was naturally Anglophile—the big charity was "Bundles for Britain"—but when the war actually came, it was shocking.

On the afternoon of December 7, I was lying on my bed, as usual, and listening to the regular rut of moronic radio shows—*Joe and Mabel* and *The Great Gildersleeve*. Nobody who knows only the depths of television comedy, which at least provides a picture for the glassy-eyed viewer to contemplate, can imagine the noncamp, nonfunny mindlessness of radio, which required the glassy-eyed listener to stare into space. This was the way I spent two or three hours during every day of my youth. And while I lay vegetating, my father, who thought it unseemly to have a radio, sent my brother upstairs to ask that I switch to the news. Some guests for afternoon tea had heard a report of a Japanese attack on Pearl Harbor. About ten minutes later, I went running downstairs with the confirmation that Japanese bombers had sunk our battleship the *Arizona*. My father's guests, a gray-haired couple of some distinction, insisted that the report couldn't be true, the attack couldn't be happening. Then they all moved into the dining room to have tea.

The next day, when the *Herald* told us that war was certain, I was surprised to find the world much the same as before. I felt that the trees should have turned red, the sun should shine green. We were going to war. In a state of great emotion, we trooped into the high-school auditorium to hear Mr. Roosevelt tell us that this was a date that would live—pause—in infamy. We all looked at one another with a sense of awe, and wondered how long it would be before we could get into action. It would be quite a while, of course, since my brother was then fourteen and I was twelve, but from that very first day we became the creatures of a vast propaganda machine, which began teaching us to hate and to kill, and which has never been turned off since then. That week, *Life* magazine showed us pictures not only of the sunken *Arizona* but of California barbershops where various patriotic barbers hung out signs offering free shaves to any Japanese who would dare to step inside. And we began singing those jingo songs—"We've Done It Before and We Can Do It Again," and "Johnny Got a Zero," and "Don't Sit Under the Apple Tree with Anyone Else but Me." And how long was it before Earl Warren began herding the nisei into concentration camps? And was there no connection between the patriotic barbers, the jingo songs, and the concentration camps?

As I look back on "the home front," in which we all now enrolled, I think that its most extraordinary element was the idea that we were all in danger of imminent enemy attack. On the third floor of our house, for example, we kept a number of pails filled with sand, because we had been warned that the Nazis' new phosphorous bombs could not be extinguished with water, only with sand. And we went to nighttime classes at the high school to hear uniformed Red Cross instructors explain how to apply tourniquets to air-raid victims. And to alert the town to such dangers, we signed up as air-raid spotters. On a hill not far from Main Street, where everybody went skiing in the winters, there now appeared a square wooden tower, perhaps thirty feet high, and we, the volunteer air spotters, reported here in regular shifts and scanned the horizon for signs of Hitler's Heinkel 111 bombers. And not just Heinkels. In the training manuals that showed the silhouettes of enemy planes, we also learned to recognize the shape of Mitsubishi bombers from Japan. God only knows how a Mitsubishi could ever have flown from Tokyo to Concord, Massachusetts, but as I stood on those wooden ramparts, hour after hour, tightening inside every time I saw a mosquito in the middle distance, it never occurred to me to doubt that I was serving in the defense of my threatened country.

Not everyone was so patriotic as I, of course, because not everyone was an adolescent trying to live with the curse of a very German name. In fact, the home front was in many ways a rather unattractive spectacle. As soon as essential goods were rationed, people began cheating on the rationing system. Are you old enough to remember the A and B and C gasoline cards that everyone had to stick on the car windows? Or the food stamps, blue for canned goods and red for meat? Then you remember how easy it was to buy extra supplies for a little extra cash. And you remember the black market in unrationed goods, in rubber tires and silk stockings and whiskey. Yes, in response to wartime shortages and rationing, American free enterprise responded in the traditional manner of free enterprise everywhere, with a black market.

But adolescents yearn to believe. It has become commonplace to shudder at the fanaticism of the Hitler Youth, or, more recently, the Red Guards in China, but every time a society really needs patriotic energy, it appeals to its adolescents. And during those first years of the war, there was no appeal from Washington that I did not answer. I not only learned first aid and searched for enemy bombers, I invested every penny I earned in war bonds, and then sold more bonds to anyone who would hear me. I prowled through all the woods around Concord, collecting scrap rubber for the war effort, and then again to collect scrap metal. I saved tin cans, cut out at both ends and neatly stamped flat. I went to the Red Cross and rolled bandages for wounded soldiers. I even knitted woolen scarves and hats for sailors on patrol in the North Atlantic.

What kept me in this fever of patriotic activity, I think, was the Veterans' Hall, where, every Friday and Saturday night, we went to the movies. It was an ugly white clapboard building on Walden Street, a dingy hall with folding wooden chairs, and the town laws forbade any marquee, or, in fact, any advertisement more dramatic than a small cardboard poster. The movies were months old, too—for anything current, one had to board an irregular bus and ride about five miles to the neighboring town of Maynard—but in this little temple of patriotism, where every show ended with a flapping-flag film of "The Star-Spangled Banner," we learned not only about the war but about the whole world outside of Concord.

It was here that I fell in love with Rita Hayworth, dancing through the streets with Gene Kelly and Phil Silvers in *Cover Girl,* and with my other great idol, Ingrid Bergman in *Casablanca,* and, to a lesser extent, with all those other beautiful creatures who suffered so nobly—Greer Garson in *Mrs. Miniver,* and June Allyson in *Two Girls and a Sailor,* and even Betty Hutton in *And the Angels Sing.* The war dominated all those movies, in one way or another, and we all felt that we would not be worthy of June Allyson, much less Rita Hayworth, until we enlisted in the Marines. But the most extraordinary propaganda of all came in the war movies themselves. Leni Riefenstahl would have blushed, perhaps even Joseph Goebbels would have blushed, at those scenes in which American nurses, when rescued from Japanese captivity, stared hollow-eyed into the distance as they reflected on their implicitly sexual disgrace, or those scenes in which Japanese admirals squeaked and gibbered on the bridges of their doomed battleships as they pointed in terror toward the diving American bombers. Of all these absurdities, the one that still remains with me the most clearly is the final scene of a movie called *Bataan,* in which Robert Taylor, surrounded by Japanese who will attack through the misty rice paddies at dawn, resolves never to surrender—

it was an article of faith at MGM and Warner Bros. during those years that the Japanese not only raped American nurses but tortured captive American soldiers—and so the picture simply ends with Taylor showing his teeth as he fires his machine gun into the dawn mist.

"Why is it that so little has changed in Concord?" I asked one of my classmates at the Concord Rod and Gun Club. Ed Damon is his name, and he always got better marks than I did in every test of math and science—not much better, only a point or two, but he was always number one in this field, and I was always number two. It used to infuriate me, but now I don't much care. He has a gray crew cut, and he teaches courses on laser rays at Ohio State University.

"It's all a matter of that thing called zoning," says Ed Damon. "Two acres is the minimum, I think, and all new buildings are supposed to be made of red brick, and with pointed roofs. That's the way Mrs. Hosmer and the board of selectmen always wanted it. You remember Mrs. Hosmer, don't you? Out on Main Street?"

"She didn't mind telling people what she thought either," says Kathleen, another one of the classmates. "When Woolworth's put up an ugly neon sign outside their store, she made them take it right down again. And when she died last year, she left instructions that the hearse be drawn by horses, and so it was."

"Mrs. Hosmer wanted everything to stay the way it had always been," says Ed Damon. "So they still don't even have a movie theater, in a town of fifteen thousand people, unless they're still showing movies in the Veterans' Hall, and I don't think they are. The selectmen think it would keep people out on the streets after nine o'clock, and they might throw chewing-gum wrappers on the sidewalks."

I guess I have led a very sheltered life, because the only dead body I have ever seen was that of my sister Liesel, who was brought down to Concord in a hearse and installed on the dining-room table in a silvery coffin with a velvet lining. Friends and neighbors passed through intermittently to pay their respects.

I hated having to do what we all had to do, to go and look at her lying in the coffin, but we did all have to do it. The undertakers had done quite a good job, with rouge on the cheeks, so she looked, serious and earnest as ever, as though she might open her eyes at any moment. But there was also an extraordinary quality of stillness, motionlessness, which made one feel that this is what death really is: the end of everything. Her rouged face looked like that of a very large doll, made of marzipan.

Outside, in the living room, my father played a record of the Allegretto from Beethoven's Seventh Symphony, which is, I think, as mournful and despairing a piece as anyone ever wrote—but theatrical, too. I have disliked it ever since then. My father sat on our ugly purple sofa and stared into space while that morose theme sounded over and over again. My mother just wept, for no specific reason. In the middle of a meal, or while washing the dishes, or just sitting in a chair, the tears would suddenly start welling up, and she would blow her nose loudly, and no one could help her.

"Onward, Christian Soldiers" was Liesel's favorite hymn, so that was what the organist played as we gathered in the Episcopal Church at the far end of Main Street. The minister—I don't remember him or his name—we were not very regular churchgoers—said the usual things over the coffin, and then we paraded out, my brother and I pushing the coffin along on its dolly wheels. Our own friends—Doc Flavin, Jimmy Walker, and Joe Wheeler—served as embarrassed pallbearers. They had not known Liesel very well. She was just a kid sister who tried to play football and tagged along on my newspaper route.

The procession drove up Main Street to Sleepy Hollow, where, on a gentle hill under some pine trees, a deep, rectangular hole had already been dug. The closed coffin was placed on two thick, gray canvas straps, and then lowered into the hole. The minister said the familiar words about dust unto dust and threw the first handful of earth onto the silver coffin. Then a workman with a shovel began shoveling more earth onto the coffin until it slowly vanished from sight, as though sinking into the ocean, and I remember thinking: How can she ever get out of there?

At the long dinner tables of the Concord Rod and Gun Club, where we eat slices of roast beef and piles of creamed potatoes, I am sitting next to an amiable lady named Nancy Halpin, who served on the organizing committee and therefore knows where people are.

"But what about the teachers?" I ask. "What has become of Miss Camilla Moses, for example?"

"She's with the flowers of the field, as they say," says Mrs. Halpin. "Died some years ago."

"And Mrs. Freeman? And Miss Weir?"

"Mrs. Freeman remarried, I think. And I don't know what happened to Miss Weir."

High-school teachers are among the most important influences on one's life, not just intellectually but psychologically as well. The pity is that so many of them are so rotten—so incompetent and so indifferent. But in any average school there are usually a few teachers who can somehow make any subject fascinating. In Concord High School, I had two.

Miss Weir, who taught French by means of pure terror, was a small, stocky woman in her fifties, as I remember, with her gray hair in a bun, and I have no idea why she terrified us so. She never raised her voice, never inflicted any punishment, but she managed to radiate a quality of sarcasm and contempt that made us ready to do anything to win her good will. Not praise. Miss Weir did not give praise. A grunt of satisfaction was the most we could hope for.

On the first day of class, she began by picking up a book and saying, with the appropriate gestures, *"Je prends le livre. J'ouvre le livre. Je tourne la page. Je ferme le livre. Je mets le livre sur la table."* We all sat there in utter bewilderment. Then Miss Weir called on a large, bovine girl in the front row, who had flunked the previous year, to repeat the mysterious words she had just said. (Miss Weir issued no textbooks until two weeks later.) The fact that I can still remember this sequence of sentences almost thirty years later gives some indication of the mysterious power that Miss Weir exercised over her little group of ignorant adolescents. Miss Weir's class for beginners, the sophomores, took place during the sixth period, after lunch, and when I was a freshman, I could not understand why all of her pupils spent their lunch hour studying French. When I was a sophomore, I understood, for we, too, gobbled our food and then devoted the remaining time to a hopeless effort to avoid Miss Weir's scorn. And all through class, it was the same—every eye on the clock, praying that Miss Weir would call on someone else, until the minute hand finally reached twenty to three, when a bell would ring, and we would be free. But two facts remain: Miss Weir treated everyone exactly alike, teaching the dumb children as ruthlessly and relentlessly as the bright ones, and when she was through with us, we had learned more than we ever learned from any other teacher. In short, we had learned French.

Mrs. Freeman was the exact opposite. She was probably about forty, and scarcely a great beauty, but whereas Miss Weir radiated cold, hard authority, Mrs. Freeman radiated glamour. She dyed her hair a reddish brown, cut in bangs, and she wore harlequin glasses, and Mexican bracelets that jangled on her wrists. And unlike Miss Weir, she more or less ignored the dumb children, whom she seated at the back of the class, so that she could concentrate on the bright children in the front. I had an enormous crush on her, and just as I would work like a slave to avoid Miss Weir's gravelly sarcasm, so I would work equally hard to win from Mrs. Freeman a smile of approval and affection.

She taught ancient history, but ancient history was only her point of departure. Indeed anyone who knows Muriel Spark's *Prime of Miss Jean Brodie* knows Mrs. Freeman. She loved to make preposterous assertions, and the more preposterous they were, the more vividly we remembered them. I still recall being baffled by her announcement that Katherine Dunham, whom I had never heard of, was "the greatest dancer in the world." I recall even more strongly her declaration that "anyone who doesn't think P. G. Wodehouse is the funniest man alive should be taken to a hospital to have his head examined." She was not completely absurd, however. She taught us, in her ancient history class, about such hitherto unknown phenomena as the paintings of El Greco and Renoir. We sat and gaped and absorbed, and when, several years later, my brother Paul had to send me money via Western Union and had to compose some question that only I could answer, and thus, as by a code, prove my identity, a bewildered Western Union clerk recited to me this riddle: "What are the three centers of ancient Persian civilization?" Any of Mrs. Freeman's prize pupils could have answered without the slightest hesitation: "Persepolis, Pasargadae, and Susa."

About that same time, when I was hitchhiking between home and college, a rather battered car stopped to pick me up one day, and there at the wheel sat Miss Weir. I was almost afraid to get into her car. And when I did get in, I was astonished to hear her ask cordially about my studies and my general welfare. Her voice was husky but quite gentle, and she seemed genuinely interested in me. In fact, she even seemed to like me. And all of a sudden, after those years of terror, I liked her. But then we came to a fork in the road, and she let me out, and I never saw her again.

Nor Mrs. Freeman either.

On the afternoon of the reunion, I went to look at the Concord High School, but it was locked, and so I could only note that everything looked much the same. A plain stone building, designed and built in the year of my own birth, 1929, in the post-office style of the period. Over the door there is a bas-relief showing some ambiguous figures who may be studying or conferring or taking part in a legal judgment, and the motto says: PROGRESS, EDUCATION, HISTORY.

And now, at about one in the morning at the Concord Rod and Gun Club, Leo Duggan and I are drinking beer, and Leo Duggan says, "High school? That wasn't the high school you saw. The high school nowadays is a huge place out where the town dump used to be. That building where all of us went to high school, you know what that is? That's just the *sixth grade* in the Concord school system. That whole place is just nothing but the sixth grade!"

I delivered the papers in the morning, and then went to school, and then took part in the debating club, and the theatrical society, and edited the school newspaper, and ran the electric scoreboard at the basketball games, so I still had enough time to go looking for more work. I found a job sweeping the floors in the Concord Book Shop, and packing the china for Mary Curtis, who ran a gift shop in one corner of the bookstore. I got fifty cents an hour, which seemed very good pay at the time, much more than Harry Bullard paid me.

Aside from money, though, the bookstore served as a kind of sanctuary. All adolescents seem to yearn for any home and parents other than their own, and in the bookstore, down on Walden Street, next to the Veterans' Hall, I found not only a place that was filled with books and crystal candlesticks and sets of china teacups but also a place ruled by a half-dozen tweedy, chain-smoking, middle-aged ladies: Mrs. Baldwin, Mrs. Taft, Mrs. Warren, and Miss Curtis. In my Oedipal way, I loved them all. I would have been happy to work for them for nothing.

The only one who reciprocated my feeling was Mrs. Warren, a vague, windy, bright-eyed lady known to everyone as "Fidee," and I suspect that her affection had less to do with me than with the fact that I had been born in 1929, the same year as her daughter, Susan, who had died at the age of seven, and now, through some mysterious circumstance in the selling of graveyard plots, lay next to my sister Liesel on the hill in Sleepy Hollow. Mrs. Warren once said to me, in fact, that she knew, she *knew,* that when she died, she would meet Susan in heaven. And in the meantime, I think, she looked on me as a symbol, a classmate in the birth year of 1929, of what her daughter might have been. And so she would pursue me, while I was sweeping up the cigarette butts that the other ladies had snubbed out next to the Crime & Mysteries section of the lending library, with questions about the books I was reading nowadays. I was not really worthy of such attention. While my brother was working his way through *The Brothers Karamazov,* I had become obsessed with the effort to "keep up with" everything that appeared on the *New York Times* best-seller lists, and so I proudly said to Mrs. Warren that the two most interesting books I had read that year were *The Robe,* by Lloyd Douglas, and *Hungry Hill,* by Daphne Du Maurier, and Mrs. Warren said, "Well, that certainly is very interesting."

Miss Curtis, who had a husky, sexy voice, caused mainly by

smoking too much, was more interested in why the wedding gifts of china plates kept arriving in ruins.

"Are you *sure* you packed that shipment carefully, with lots of excelsior?" she would inquire after each disaster report.

"Yes, honestly," I would protest, quite truthfully, for I did indeed pack the china carefully, and if the postal and shipping systems consisted of other adolescents who threw my boxes around like footballs, who was to blame for that?

"And it was Spode, too," Miss Curtis would say bitterly.

Now, twenty-five years later, I had no passionate desire to see Miss Curtis again, but I couldn't help being impressed by the fact that there was a large, prospering store in the middle of Main Street with an awning and a sign saying THE MARY CURTIS SHOP. Vast displays of glassware, china, linen, silver. One could gather that every wedding for miles around brings the local matrons to the Mary Curtis Shop, and that all sales are recorded on opulent charge accounts.

A pleasant and elegant gray-haired lady asked me what I wanted. I said I wanted to know if Mary Curtis was still around.

"You mean Mrs———?" asked the gray-haired lady, offering a name I hadn't heard before.

"I mean the original Mary Curtis," I said, "the one whose name you have on the sign over the door. I used to work here, many years ago, and I'd like to know what became of her."

"Oh, then you don't know," the gray-haired lady said. "Then I'm sorry that I have to tell you the news—she passed away, about a year ago. She'd just come back from a trip around the world, and she suddenly fell unconscious. . . ."

So I asked about the bookstore, and about its former proprietors. Mrs. Warren was dead too, and Mrs. Baldwin "hasn't been around for years." The bookstore itself had split away from the gift shop and moved into a vacant space farther up Main Street—a space which, if my memory is accurate, once housed the defeated A & P. "You should go and look at it," the gray-haired lady said, "and perhaps they can tell you about what has become of everyone."

I did go and look at it—a surprisingly large and well-stocked store for such a small town—but I did not introduce myself or ask for anyone, since I didn't know whom to ask for. I only asked the lady at the desk—younger and less tweedy but also less maternally attractive than the ladies of my day—whether she had a comprehensive history of Concord.

"There isn't any," she said. "I just wish there were."

One of the things one learns in going back to Concord is that the people change and move and die, but the buildings remain, and the buildings are what express the spirit of the town. Many people don't appreciate the importance of buildings, viewing them as mere objects, things of brick and wood and plaster. Real-estate developers do not appreciate buildings either. That is why, in midtown Manhattan, there are so few places that date back even to World War II, and why so many occupants of the new places feel a sense of uncertainty, restlessness, and vague danger.

Concord is more like London, or Paris. Its rows of white-painted clapboard houses, with lilacs growing tall behind the picket fences, its ivy-covered red-brick public buildings, wearing and weathering through the years—all these convey a sense of time passed, time endured, and therefore of tranquillity. A building needs perhaps fifty years to acquire a personality, but then, once it has a personality, it not only outlasts generations of inhabitants but inspires each such generation of inhabitants with a sense of their own proportion, their relation to the surrounding world, and thus their value.

Finally, I went back to our old house at 54 Main Street, but slowly, circuitously, as though I were going to a rendezvous with an ex-wife whom I still wanted. I wandered first through the center of town, and then, instead of staying on Main Street, drifted off along Walden to the red-brick post office and the red-brick gymnasium, then back past the former high school to the red-brick library— savoring, not quite consciously, the delay in the moment of recognition. Walking over the lawn of the library, I couldn't avoid eventually looking across the street and seeing that the house was still there, and that it was, like the beloved ex-wife, marvelously familiar and yet hideously altered. It had a new master now, and the new master had imposed his will.

Once it had been a long, elegantly simple building, perhaps forty feet across the front and seventy-five feet in depth, three stories high, but with a third story that was empty and haunted. I used one of these attic rooms for the workshop where I built model airplanes, and my father used one as a sort of garden storeroom, where he kept ripening pumpkins and gourds, but otherwise there were only the ghosts of past occupants, now long forgotten. When my father finally sold the house, he sold it to the Concord Academy, a girls' boarding school that was expanding cancerously through a whole row of old houses along Main Street, and now that this is a dormitory packed with adolescent girls, the authorities apparently live in terror of a holocaust. They have built a vast rectangular stairway up and down one whole outer side of the house, so that if fire breaks out among the girls who are packed onto that once-haunted third floor, they can all come tripping down to the ground in safety.

I had some compunctions about marching into a girls' dormitory and asking to inspect the place, and so I stood for a minute on the sidewalk across the street, looking up at the windows of my room on the second floor. When we first moved in, back in 1941, my brother and I both lived in this corner room, not because there weren't plenty of other rooms for each of us to have to himself but because we had always shared a room, and it seemed the natural way to live. My brother, however, soon developed a passionate desire for apartness. He moved out into the hall, where he erected a screen and devised a sort of living area for himself. During all those lolling, lounging hours of adolescence, while I was listening to my radio, my brother was lying on his stomach on his bed in the hall, occasionally reaching down to turn a page in the Dostoyevsky or Tolstoy that lay on the floor beside the bed.

For a time, I felt hurt and rejected, but I soon came to realize that I now had a splendid room all to myself, my own fireplace, four windows looking out over Main Street, my own desk and bookcase. In due time, I went off to college, where the dormitories were built in lavish pseudo-Georgian style, with courtyards and bell towers, but also with cockroaches crawling out of the fireplaces and occasionally appearing in the soup, and so, when it came time to write my thesis for graduation, I came home to entrench myself in this room. Freed of virtually all responsibility, except to get this one thing written, I reverted to my natural hours, sleeping well into the afternoon and working all night, and here, to everyone's surprise, I finally did produce a "scholarly" treatise on the development of centralized government in France under the rule of Cardinal Richelieu. And then, without waiting for graduation day, I sailed on a freighter to Le Havre, determined never to return.

Still, there is no law barring one from one's own house—and this house is mine, just as any house I have lived in is mine, and I haunt it now, just as other people haunted it when I first came there. (Or, as someone said in a third-rate movie I saw on TV the other night, "No room in an old house is ever really empty.") And, in fact, the house door now stands wide open. Inside, in what used to be the front living room, with the French provincial sofas, and that Rembrandt, the man in the golden helmet, there are now half a dozen girls lounging around on double-decker bunks. On the walls, there are college pennants—Harvard, Brown, Yale—and signs saying things like BEWARE OF THE DOG.

I ask who is in charge of this place, and one of the girls goes off to fetch a housemaster, an amiable blond man of no more than thirty, in Bermuda shorts. He seems surprised that anyone ever lived here—in the sense that one lives in a house, as contrasted to a dormitory—but he says that the building is virtually empty because of vacations, and he has no objection to my wandering around. It is a novel and unpleasant experience, for although I have often read in various glossy magazines about the rehabilitation of ruined buildings, old barns in Pennsylvania magically converted into streamlined studios for some investment banker with a wife who does pottery, I have never read a single article about how a worthy institution, on buying a handsome building, proceeds to wreck it.

This was once a splendid house, large, well proportioned, and aristocratic, if aristocracy implies the ability to waste space for the sake of aesthetic pleasure. Within a few years, then, it was turned into an upper-class slum, a place where rich people spend thousands of dollars to confine their children within a living space about the same as that of a welfare family in Harlem. Here, where there was once a single family of a half dozen people, there is now a herd of perhaps fifty adolescent girls, perhaps more, and so, as I might have suspected from the outside stairway, and as I might suspect in any slum, the fear of fire is constant. In the stately front hall, where we once had a mahogany table that bore a silver salver for calling cards—yes, there really was a time, once, when people left calling cards on silver salvers—there are now thick pipes running along the ceilings, with a series of valves and faucets and spouts that will start sprinkling if the young ladies of the Concord Academy are ever threatened by fire.

The pipes along the celing make the whole front hall look rather like the entrance to a factory, not a modern factory but one of those dingy textile plants that Melville described as the Tartarus of Maids. But the front hall itself no longer really exists, for it has been cut in half, then blocked. The first rule in converting a house into a slum, in Concord just as in Harlem, is to break up halls and rooms into cells and cubbyholes, into the least possible amount of cubic space. This process of destruction might be laudable if each cell provided privacy to an individual occupant, but no, once a slum has been built, the owner invariably puts two or three people into each of his cells. That was the basic purpose in creating the slum in the first place. And the two or three people in each den fight back in the only way they can, by creating the mess and clutter that they hope will enable them to retain their own identity and their own sanity.

As I climbed the stairway, once lean and flowing, now dominated by a hideous wallpaper of nesting cranes, I felt a sense of acute claustrophobia. Every niche or corner had become a separate room; every original room had been chopped up into two rooms; and every one of the new rooms, occupied by a trio of girls, overflowed with teddy bears, record albums, cashmere sweaters, and tennis rackets. The space around the bay window where my mother used to sit on a chaise longue and read Thomas Mann, veiled by a perpetual haze of blue cigarette smoke, was now, all by itself, a warren. The end of the hall, where my brother used to sulk over his Dostoyevsky, was yet another. My own room, in the corner, had become two rooms, each with three girls in it. And even on the third floor, once so empty and so frightening, there were now rows of stuffed ducks, and Beatles posters, and all the paraphernalia of adolescent girls. I speak not a word against the girls—the few I saw were bright and pretty and charming—but only against a system that turns such a house into such a tenement. For although I may be a prejudiced witness, I sensed that the whole building had become a dungeon, terribly overcrowded and terribly oppressive.

The blond young man, whom I met once again on the ground floor, was no more than a warden. He seemed to occupy an apartment that had been hacked out of what were once the laundry and the butler's pantries. He escorted me to the back door, where I used to set out on my paper route, and he asked me whether that old garage had always been there.

"Yes, that was our garage," I said. "But what has been happening next door?"

Between our place and the cemetery, there had been a white Victorian house, all turrets and verandas, occupied by Mr. Pratt, a businessman of some sort, who used to annoy my parents by fertilizing his front lawn with wagonloads of fresh horse manure. And beyond that, in the graveyard corner of the Pratts' property, there had been the cottage of Mrs. Merwin, the piano teacher, who, together with Miss Darling, a nervous violinist who lived farther out on Main Street, used to join my father for evenings of Haydn trios. Now I could see only a large, square brick building, looking like a cross between a hospital and the back of a supermarket.

"That's a parochial school," the housemaster said, "but it's going out of business."

"How come?"

"I really don't know," the housemaster said. "It's not a matter of money. More complicated than that."

"And how about the back garden? Is that still there?"

"What back garden?" the young housemaster said.

Someone had once conceived a rather formal design behind our house—an entry, shielded by shrubs, opening onto a long, oval lawn, all surrounded by a wide bed of perennials, tulips in the spring, iris

and various lilies in the summer. At the far end stood Miss Bowditch's garden house, actually a sort of toolshed, its broken windows
providing proof that my brother and I had repeatedly violated my
father's ban on baseball games. When my father repeated the ban
very loudly, we moved our fantasy diamond out into Miss Bowditch's
hayfields, which stretched from our lawn down to the river. My
brother's idol was Bob Feller, whose father had taught him to pitch
by throwing baseballs at a barn door. My heroes were the champion
Dodgers of 1941—Dixie Walker and Ducky Medwick and Dolph
Camilli, and above all, Pete Reiser—who had presumably learned to
bat, just as Feller had learned to pitch, in rural isolation. And so we
confronted each other in Miss Bowditch's hayfields: my brother, who
couldn't pitch, and I, who couldn't hit, flinging a baseball to and
fro, constantly losing it in the two-foot-high grass, and cursing one
another's incompetence.

It was at about this time that my brother developed his sense of
apartness, and began reading Thoreau, and lost all interest in baseball, and began building, without guidebook or instructor, a kayak.
Any professional carpenter would have ridiculed this vessel—weak
in its framework, heavy to carry, and lopsided—but when my brother
finally finished building it, a bony, ungainly canvas boat, water-
proofed only by three coats of dark green paint, he carted it down
to the river, and it really did float.

Some people used to say that you could live all your life next to
the Concord River and not know which way it flowed, which was
just a sarcastic way of saying that it was a marvelously peaceful river,
silent and still, sometimes covered for a considerable distance with
a rippling light green blanket of duckweed. In this soporific stream,
one could paddle along for hours in a state of almost narcotic isolation, until one reached Fairhaven Bay, where the river widened a
bit, and the water got somewhat rough for the lubberly kayak. At
this point, whenever I borrowed the kayak, I invariably turned back,
mistrustful of my brother's carpentry, but my brother just as invariably paddled on, determined to prove that his creation could not
sink. And here, now that I think of it, we always looked up in awe
at the bluff that contained the pillared mansion of Charles Francis
Adams, for Mrs. Freeman, in explaining the social structure of the

ancient world, had once informed us that Mr. Adams would have been a member of the Roman Senate, and all of us would have been his slaves.

The metaphor has lasted, but the reminiscence takes too long. It took me only a few minutes to walk through the clumps of shrubbery behind our house—forsythia, I think they were—and to see that the back lawn is gone, and Miss Bowditch's garden house is gone, and all the hayfields are gone. There is only a parking lot here, and an asphalt roadway that circles past various administration buildings. Beyond that, the fields have become a "campus"—odd that two such different words should be theoretically synonymous—and the girls are playing field hockey.

All theory aside, all history and sociology and literary pretenses aside, what I have remembered most vividly about Concord is, of course, the girls. For almost thirty years, I have remembered them just as they were, beautiful and immaculate, their long hair bouncing on their shoulders as they walked, and their bodies swiveling to and fro under their thin dresses. They seemed only half aware of their own sensuality, and scarcely aware of the fact that we, the boys, thought of little else. In retrospect, it is difficult to judge the quantity or variety of sexual behavior in any given situation, but my guess is that in the Concord High School of the 1940s, sex remained largely a matter of daydream and potentiality, and that there was very little actual fornication. If this is true, then we all have the same memory, all the classmates of 1945, of possibilities unfulfilled, and this is part of what draws us together.

When I first heard of these class reunions, at the time of the twentieth, I decided not to go, partly because it was inconvenient, but also partly because I knew that the beautiful girls of 1944 could no longer be so beautiful, and I preferred to have them remain in my memory as they had once been. But then, when I got another chance, the twenty-fifth reunion, I decided that no matter how fat and wrinkled and complacent they might have become, I wanted another look at Phyllis and Sue and Marcia and Ruth and, above all—

("I don't think you should use her real name," my wife re-marked. "Why not?" I protested. "It was just a date. Nothing happened." "Well, you make yourself look like a fool," my wife said. "So it makes her look like a fool for having gone out with you.")

I must first explain, though, that I was and have always been a victim (or beneficiary) of the theory that bright children should skip grades for the sake of their intellectual development. I started school at five, and I taught myself to read, the following summer, by memorizing Stephen Vincent Benét's *Book of Americans* ("Oh Daniel Drew, Oh Daniel Drew, it makes me sick to think of you . . ."), and so, slipping ahead of my contemporaries, and developing a fierce sense of intellectual competitiveness, I eventually enrolled in college at the age of fifteen without ever achieving the two things that mattered much more to me than my splendid grades in Latin and algebra. I hadn't made the varsity baseball team, and I hadn't kissed a girl.

In athletic competition, the difference between a boy of fifteen and a classmate of seventeen or eighteen is clear. In the matter of courtship, the difference between a boy of fifteen and a girl of seventeen is almost overwhelming. Year in, year out, I did nothing but moon over the girls of Concord High School, staring fixedly at the underwear faintly visible through the backs of their dresses, dreaming fantastic dreams about kissing them in the back garden, but I hardly dared even to speak to them, much less take them to the war movies at the Veterans' Hall. One result of these inhibitions was that I scarcely even knew these beautiful creatures, and the second result was that when I finally got up enough nerve to ask one of them to go out with me, I felt I had to offer her the most extravagant rewards.

The girl whom I then adored, with more silent misery than I had ever devoted to her predecessors, was named—well, let me call her Marianna. I knew her only slightly, but she was large and soft and round, with freckles, and long, brown hair, and I went to bed every night thinking about that long, brown hair, and—well, yes—that bosom, and so I finally told my mother that I wanted to buy my first sports jacket. I gave no reason or explanation. She took me to Pete's Clothing Store and reluctantly bought the jacket that I picked out, an ugly brown model with leather buttons, rather like one that my brother had. The price was $17.50. Then I sent a letter to the Colonial Theater in Boston to order two tickets for Ethel Barrymore in *The Corn Is Green*. As soon as the tickets arrived, I called up Marianna, and, after some terrified clearing of the throat, blurted out my invitation: "Would you like to go to the theater in Boston next Saturday to see Ethel Barrymore in *The Corn Is Green*?" The poor girl must have been too startled to decline. "Why—uh—yes, all right," she said, agreeing to our first (and last) date.

I had no idea what the rules for dates were (only two years later, when I went back to Europe, did I discover that there are no rules), and so the whole evening became a marathon of boredom and self-consciousness and embarrassment. The first problem was the transportation problem. Nowadays, everything has changed to such an extent that I have sent my oldest daughter off on dates with boys who are driven to and from the movies by their mothers, but in the Concord of the 1940s, I had to walk, in my new brown sports jacket, to Marianna's house on Lexington Road, and then escort her on a twenty-minute hike to the railroad station. Marianna, too, had a brown jacket, with a matching, flaring skirt, and a frilly white blouse. She was also taller than I was, already a woman, really, whereas I, the scrawny and stumbling suitor, kept blushing furiously and hoping that nobody would recognize us as we marched, mostly in silence, the length of Main Street.

At the station, Harry Bullard's newsstand was shut down for the day, so I was spared the observations of the depot kids, but then we had to face each other, Marianna and I, for the long evening ahead. First we must clamber onto the train to Boston—Great God, look at Marianna's bottom as she climbs the steep iron stairway!—and then we sit for the better part of an hour on the red plush seats that rattle and sway as we creak into Lincoln and Waltham and all stops to North Station. Then we descend into the subway and look brightly at one another as we screech along to Park Street, where we have a choice of changing to the Boylston train or walking down Tremont Street for another quarter of an hour. We walked. On the way, we stopped in Schrafft's for an ice-cream sundae with chocolate sauce.

By this time, Marianna seemed quite numb. She didn't really want an ice-cream sundae, but she was ready to go along with whatever was proposed.

Finally, we climbed up into the balcony of the Colonial Theater, the oldest and mustiest in Boston, and watched Ethel Barrymore stride about the stage and strike out at her partners with all the weapons in that reverberating voice. Or half-watched. For all through Miss Barrymore's struggles with the problems of the Welsh coal miners, I was preoccupied with the fact that Marianna was sitting next to me, plump and luscious, with nothing between us but a hard wooden armrest. But I did not dare to put my arm around her, or even to take her hand, much less to, God help us, pinch her pretty leg. The most I could bring myself to do was to press my arm against hers, as though accidentally, on the armrest that separated us. Marianna's arm naturally offered a certain amount of resistance, but I never found out whether this was part of the courtship or simply part of a girl's defense against what must have seemed a bizarre pushing and shoving from the adjoining seat.

And so we endured, for two hours or so, while Ethel Barrymore coughed and cackled down there on the stage, and then we had to start the extravagant hour-plus-long trek home again—long walk to Park Street, subway to North Station, train back out to Concord. . . . Poor Marianna must have suffered as much as I during those long silences while the subway clattered around a curve, and the loud-speaker in North Station said that the train would soon be leaving, and then we bounced along on the red plush seats that always smelled of old cigars. What on earth did we talk about, we who scarcely knew each other, during almost three hours of traveling from Concord to Boston and back? The question occurred to me the other day, while shaving, and just as suddenly the answer, stored away in my mind through all these years, came back to me. We talked about Frankenstein. I had just read Mary Shelley's novel, and so I told Marianna the entire plot, down to the last details of the hunt across the ice. And since she had seen the movie version, which I had not, she told me the whole plot of that, how the kite soared up into the thunderclouds, how the lightning made the electrodes sizzle in the monster's neck, and then we remarked, many times, on how different one plot was from the other.

Back in Concord, at last, we walked the length of Main Street in silence once again while I reflected on all those agonized newspaper debates about the kiss in the doorway at the end of the first date ("Will he ever respect her again?" Dorothy Dix used to ask in the *Herald*). But Marianna just said good night on her doorstep, and that was that. From then on, just as before, we hardly spoke to one another again.

I wanted very much to see Marianna at the twenty-fifth reunion, and I wouldn't have minded if she had become fat, or dyed her hair bright red—or perhaps I would have minded—but, of course, she wasn't there. And neither were the rest of those girls I had remembered so clearly for so long.

"And where is Sue?" I asked my friend at dinner, Nancy, the member of the organizing committee. I tried to sound very off-handed, with a tone of only the mildest interest.

"She's in New York, working for an advertising agency."

"And Marcia?"

"Out west, in Colorado, I think, working with some program for teaching poor children."

"And Ruth?"

"She's out west, too. I don't know exactly where."

"And Marianna?"

"She's married to an engineer or something, living just north of Boston. She said she wanted to come to the reunion, but then she decided she couldn't make it."

Quite a number of them—particularly the ones I had known best—couldn't make it. My brother Paul, for one, was off on another anthropological expedition among the Indians of central Mexico, and Doc Flavin, son of the town dentist, was now a stockbroker in New York, and Chuck Harwood, once a halfback, sent us an account of his career at the Corning Glass Company: "I have worked mostly in sales jobs in television, electronics, laboratory glassware products. From '67–'70 I was area manager for Corning's operation in Latin America. I . . . was responsible for companies in Mexico, Argentina and Brazil. . . ." As for Joe Wheeler, a farmer's son who had been a sturdy long-distance runner but also an enthusiast for student peace movements, he couldn't come because he was in Rawalpindi as head of the U.S. foreign-aid mission to Pakistan. "In the long run," he wrote to the class committee, in the foreign-aid-bureaucracy rhetoric that he had made his own, "what happens here in Pakistan, the fifth largest country in the world, will make a difference to the people living in Concord. We Americans have a new appreciation of this. . . ." And so on.

There was another group that didn't come either. The depot kids. Rene, who regularly filched my bicycle and hid it behind a warehouse; Bill, the track star who was known to smoke cigarettes, and thus doomed to sin and degradation; and—what shall I call her? Josie?—the girl who, on dates, sometimes made sexual advances to her terrified escorts. Had they all left Concord? I suspect not, but they were the kind of people who moved from one job and one rented cottage to another, and perhaps the mail didn't get forwarded, or, if there were questionnaires soliciting information on what had become of our young hopes, then perhaps the depot kids, now in their forties, would be inclined not to answer.

Who, then, came to the reunion? Or in other words, who were we, the reunited?

It was rarely acknowledged in Concord High School—it is rarely acknowledged anywhere in America—that we live within a jungle gym of class relationships, and that the sense of class governs every aspect of our lives—what jobs we get, whom we marry, what we tell our children. This is not strictly a matter of race or religion, nor is it even a matter of wealth, since any one hundred rich people, like any one hundred Negroes or one hundred Catholics, will soon form some sort of hierarchy within their own group. It comes simply from the fact that we need to judge people, and even more to judge ourselves in relationship to other people.

Much of the upper level of the class of 1945—selected by any standard or index you prefer—left Concord and went out into the world, to college, to jobs in New York or Chicago, or, for that matter, Rawalpindi. And most of them never came back. Many people on the bottom level apparently also drifted away—I say "apparently" because nobody ever keeps track of the bottom level—and they have not been heard from since. So we, the reunited, represented that celebrated Middle America that President Nixon keeps addressing, and the *New York Times* keeps analyzing. And despite all the rhetoric of election-year politics, this Middle America shows very little sign—to me, at least—of the fears and hatreds that various experts generally attribute to it. Middle America, if I am any judge, has no passionate desire to assault Negroes or student radicals, because Negroes and student radicals are utterly irrelevant to the basic realities of Middle America's life, to its jobs and families, houses and schools. Middle America appears indifferent, yes, but it also appears quite industrious, prosperous, and cheerful. Any Washington pundit can argue, I suppose, that there is no political or sociological value in statements submitted to class yearbooks, that the classmates' testimonials not only do not represent a national mood but do not even represent the true situation of the classmates themselves. They are too complacent, too sketchy and superficial, too full of mild boasts. Still, I find in them a certain interesting pattern. These people have built their own small empires—staying in the same place, and the same job, and with the same wife or husband—and they are quite pleased with what they have built.

Mildred Burk Edwardsen reports: "Married to Ted Edwardsen for 24 years and we have two daughters aged 23 and 21, plus two grand-daughters. . . . My husband and Howie Soberg own and operate a service station in West Concord. . . . I do the bookkeeping for the business and that keeps me busy most of the day. . . ."

Mary Elizabeth Shepard Dahl reports: "Married 23 years and we have two daughters 20 and 17. . . . Have lived in Concord, Pittsfield, Littleton, Greenfield and Centerfield, all in Massachusetts. Have vacationed in Florida. . . . Husband Henry's position as Supervisor of Prison Camps . . . keeps him busy. . . . I couldn't have a more pleasant life. I enjoy our home, love my family, and talk to my flowers. . . ."

Mary Harrington Valliere reports: "Married 23 years, with 3 children—22, 19 and 15 and 1 grandchild. Am accounts payable supervisor. Being the wife of a career service man I have traveled throughout most of the U.S. . . . A very happy day a year ago when I watched my husband retire from the Air Force after 25 years!"

Bud and Marge (Harmon) Larrabee report: "Married 22 years and have four children. . . . Bud is a product manager for S. D. Warren Paper Mill. . . . We decided to make our home in Maine, and after 21 years we consider ourselves practically natives! Where does one find a beautiful old 8-room Colonial house built in 1792. . . ."

Rose Brothen Chisholm reports: "Married 22 years and Jack and I have seven children. . . . Married to a fireman whose weird hours keep us crazy! I work in a nursery school which is lots of fun!"

Roy Barnhart reports: "Married fifteen years and have seven children. . . . Electrician. . . . We are all conservative Christians (born again). We are all conservative Americans. . . . I enjoy hunting deer and elk and have been lucky. . . . My greatest joy is introducing people to my Lord and Savior Jesus Christ. . . ."

Do you see the pattern? Not much of the wealth and celebrity that seem to preoccupy everyone in New York, but a good deal of stability and security, and perhaps even serenity. But it is not quite that simple either. One of my reunion comrades, whom I once knew fairly well and admired as a good football player, tells me as we stand together at the bar, getting a new round of sixty-cent Scotches, that both he and his brother have been working at the same jobs, for the same companies, for more than twenty years. And I remark, without meaning any criticism, "You guys sure do like to stay in one place." And just for a second, there is a strange look in the man's narrow blue eyes—is it anger, or resentment, or possibly even fear, of the future and the past?—before he remembers that we are all buddies drinking together at the bar, and he says, "Well—yeah—I guess so."

And then there is the problem of educating Kathleen's children. She has five, between the ages of eighteen and nine. She is a nurse, her husband an insurance man. She is very nice, very warm, and her problem is that the Catholic schools are closing down, and she doesn't know what will become of her children's education. We ourselves all went to Concord's public schools, of course, but Kathleen appears to have given up on them. It is not just the Negroes—though Kathleen is opposed (mildly) to the present program of busing a few dozen city children out to Concord for their schooling. There is also an experimental curriculum (or lack of curriculum) in the public schools nowadays, and, as the classmates of 1945 say to one another, "the kids just play games on the floor, and nobody learns anything."

Kathleen put her children in the parochial schools. "They aren't very good either," she says with a sorrowful smile, "but at least they do teach the children to read and write." But now revolution has come to the parochial schools too. The Rose Hawthorne School, that ugly brick castle next to our house on Main Street, was diplomatically named for the novelist's pious sister, but it was nonetheless considered a symbol of the advancing power of the Boston Catholics, and now it is closing down. The ugly brick building has been offered both to the Concord Academy and to the town, and neither of them wants it. But why is it closing down? "The nuns don't want to stay there any more," says Kathleen. "They want to go out into the world. They want to teach in the ghettos." Fine, but what will the middle class do with its children? Kathleen has found a new parochial school, St. Bridget's, in the nearby town of Maynard, and she drives her children there every day on her way to work. "But I don't know how long that will last either," Kathleen says, worried but stoical. "A lot will depend on the new archbishop."

They know, in other words, that there is a different world outside Concord, and they know that it is threatening to change the way Concord has always lived, and they wish, in a mild, non-Agnew way, that it wouldn't. And I am inclined to agree with them, in that I think an average citizen in Concord today lives a better life, a more peaceful and pleasant and harmonious life, than does an above-average citizen of New York, or most of our big cities and their immediate suburbs.

And I like Kathleen, in her black party dress with the transparent net sleeves and the feathers at the wrists. In the suburbs of New York, it seems to me, everyone fights with everyone else, but Kathleen is friendly and nice, and I hope very much that she somehow finds a school that will provide whatever it is that she wants for her children.

The reunion lasted until after 2:00 A.M., and then, slightly drunk, I took a wrong turn in my rented Ford and got hopelessly lost on a narrow road that wound through the dark woods. It was three o'clock before I got back to the Colonial Inn (founded in 1716, once occupied by the Thoreau family, and so on), so I slept late the next morning, but I felt it my duty, before leaving Concord, to inspect the famous battlefield. In all the time I had lived there, I had not been to the battlefield more than two or three times—and then only because the patriotic parades on April 19 and July 4 ended there, and once, my father made a little speech to the little crowd that stood by the Old North Bridge.

There is much more to it now, and all very stately. All of Monument Street, where I once delivered the papers, is now a national park, supervised by the National Park Service, and as I approach the entrance to the Old North Bridge, so do two bearded youths on motorcycles, apparently planning to go vrooming down the path to what the July 4 orators used to call "hallowed ground." This is, however, not permitted. A National Park Service patrolman orders the black-jacketed rebels to park their motorcycles in the National Park Service parking lot, and they grudgingly agree. Everyone must show proper respect. On the path to hallowed ground, mothers lead bored children by the hand. An old lady in black blows her nose and stuffs the Kleenex back into her handbag.

The Old North Bridge is not a very impressive structure, a simple arch of wooden beams, obviously quite new. The monuments have a certain elegance, though—not only Daniel Chester French's Minuteman, standing guard with his rifle and plow, but also the plaque that honors the British victims—"They came three thousand miles and died / To keep the past upon its throne. . . ."

The National Park Service has everything well organized. Signs guide the visitor from the battlefield across the stagnant river and up a sandy pathway to the Buttrick House, where, in the middle of a very formal garden of clipped hedges and cypress trees, we come to "The Lookout." Here, observing the battlefield from a hillside terrace, we can push a button and hear a recorded voice describe the skirmish in the excited tones of a sports broadcaster. But what a small and unheroic business it was. How small and unheroic most of our early history was. In my youth, I had always thought of the Battle of Concord as a mighty confrontation between massed regiments of red-coated British troopers and a relative handful of American frontiersmen, who won their great victory by a combination of courage, daring, and marksmanship. The recorded voice makes no such claims. It tells us that the British force numbered about 100 men (mostly frightened boys, probably, wandering forlorn through a strange woodland, the Vietnam of their time). There was no resistance until the gathering mob of Yankee farmers reached 400, and then the exchange of gunfire from opposite banks of the little river killed a total of two Americans and three British. Thereupon, the outnumbered British retreated back to Boston. Next to me, as the disembodied voice excitedly describes this small encounter, four Chinese—father, mother, and two children—stand and listen impassively to the strange beginnings of American history.

There is one other thing, of course, that I still have to do. The pilgrimage to Sleepy Hollow. It is an unexceptional cemetery, on the hill just north of town, but it is quiet and serene, with many pines that sigh overhead. Near the entrance on Bedford Street, one reads those grand names of the nineteenth century—Gen. Joshua Buttrick, Ephraim Farrar, Jonathan Curtis ("Soldier of the Revolution"), Capt. Artemus Wheeler, and "Sister Sarah, wife of Isaac Bridlow." As I walk up the hill, a youth with long blond hair whizzes past me on an English racing bicycle, the seat high, the handlebars low. He is apparently using the cemetery for exercise. At the curve next to a giant locust tree, he swings to the left and disappears from sight.

The newer graves are farther from the road, so, as you turn inward, you enter the twentieth century, and the headstones bear simpler names, and the families in the family plots are smaller. I

wonder whether I can find, among all these graves, the grave I have
not seen for more than twenty-five years. But perhaps I have forgotten how much I remember. I find the grave as easily as a sleepwalker
finds the garden door. It is on that gentle hillside, under that grove
of pines. Next to it is the grave of Susan H. Warren, beloved daughter of Edward and Frances Warren, 1929–36, and next to that is
the grave of Hugh Fraser Leith III, 1941–44. The gravestone for the
three-year-old has some toy trains carved across it, and on top, his
real name: SKIPPY. And beyond that—how did this quiet hillside come
to be the graveyard of dead children?—lies James Baldwin Bourquin—
1944–54.

My father commissioned some distinguished artist to create Liesel's tombstone. They agreed on a handsome stone of greenish gray,
and the artist worked for months to produce a charming design, a
flower in the center and a small duck on each side. The only trouble
was—as we saw when the artist finally arrived with the finished tombstone and stood proudly to one side to receive our praises and con-
gratulations—that he had spelled the name wrong. Well, what can
you do when your daughter's misspelled name has been chiseled in
stone? You accept the strange misfortune and you erect the monument: LIESEL FRIEDERICH.

As I sit by the grave, on a white, wrought-iron Victorian bench
that my father has installed there, I also observe that he has planted
a number of mournful plants. There is a little rhododendron, about
a foot high, and a yew, and some scraggly myrtle that creeps across
the grave. There is also a dead rosebush, quite small, still bearing its
promise on a white tag: "Nearly wild, subzero rose."

But do I remember anything new? Feel anything more deeply, or
more intensely, than before? Re-create, in some way, that small,
brave girl who died so long ago? No, there is nothing at all, here in
the silence among the dead children. Only the mysterious bicyclist,
who keeps sweeping past every few minutes along the circling paths
of the graveyard, like a vulture.

My father was surprised when I told him that I had gone back
to Concord. He wondered why I had done it. I couldn't explain. He

asked whether I had gone to Liesel's grave. I said I had. I asked him how often he himself went there. He said he went about twice a year.

"That rosebush you planted there is dead," I said.

"What?" my father said. At seventy, he can't hear very well any more, so a great many things have to be said twice.

"That rosebush you planted there is dead," I said, louder.

"Oh," my father said. "Well, then, I'll just have to plant another one."

1971

Jimmy

The age demanded an image
Of its accelerated grimace,
Something for the modern stage. . . .
                                    —Ezra Pound

◾ LATE ONE NIGHT IN PARIS—AND IT WAS ALMOST ALWAYS LATE at night in Jimmy Baldwin's Paris—he took out a ballpoint pen and began drawing a large rectangle on what was left of a tattered, crumb-strewn paper tablecloth. We were sitting in a place called Chez Inez, as I remember, and I had paid for my share of Inez's overpriced fried chicken, and Jimmy had added his share to the tab that neither he nor Inez ever expected to see paid. Inez was a matronly black woman who sang from time to time; her husband was a weary-looking Dane who tended bar. I didn't much like either her or her restaurant, but Jimmy, who was so broke that he lived almost entirely by cadging, appreciated the fact that his credit at Chez Inez was good indefinitely.

Inside the rectangle on the tablecloth, he slowly began inscribing, with a faint smile on his lips, a series of incantatory words:

Crying Holy
A Novel
By James Baldwin

Jimmy raised his head to survey the imaginary book jacket, then began redrawing the letters, widening and darkening them. This was a scene that I had witnessed before, always late at night, in the cheaper cafés of St.-Germain-des-Prés, at the Royal, the Reine Blanche, the Pergola. Jimmy's first novel did not actually exist, or rather it existed as a heap of drafts and inserts and new beginnings, new beginnings that remained unfinished. By this time, after five or six years of work on *Crying Holy*, he was trying to get started on a new novel that he called *So Long at the Fair*, but that wasn't going very well either. Blocked, frightened, penniless, he could survive only by clinging to the dream of a novel, actually printed and bound, with its title on the cover.

With a few drinks more, he might have started writing imaginary blurbs on that imaginary jacket:

"This beautiful, furious first novel."

—THE NEW YORK TIMES

"A novel of extraordinary sensitivity."

—THE CHICAGO TRIBUNE

"His writing is skilled, perceptive, beautiful, brutal, objective, compassionate . . ."

—SAN FRANCISCO CHRONICLE

Jimmy didn't actually write those praises on the wine-stained tablecloth at Chez Inez. Some years later, when *Crying Holy* finally came out as *Go Tell It on the Mountain*, they all appeared in print, all came true.

She did not ask me what I wanted, but repeated, as though she had learned it somewhere, "We don't serve Negroes here.". . . There was nothing on the table but an ordinary water-mug half full of water, and I picked this up and hurled it with all my strength at her. She ducked and it missed her and shattered against the mirror behind the bar. . . . I had been ready to commit murder. I saw nothing very clearly but I did see this: that my life, my real life, was in danger, and not from anything other people might do but from the hatred I carried in my own heart.

—NOTES OF A NATIVE SON

I was nineteen when I got out of college in 1948, having no idea what I wanted except to go to Europe and write novels. I bought a hundred-dollar ticket and boarded a converted Liberty ship named the *SS Marine Tiger*—or was it the *SS Marine Marlin?*—with a typewriter, a duffel bag borrowed from my brother, and sixty-five dollars in cash. I spent the summer with relatives in Munich, earning about five hundred dollars from German magazines, then went to Paris and found a room near the Luxembourg Gardens. The room was about four feet wide and ten feet long, with a window that wouldn't stay shut, and the September winds blew cold. This grimy little room cost eight dollars a month, so, limiting myself to one cheap meal per day, I could survive on about fifty dollars a month, which meant that I had enough money for about ten months. I began working on a novel.

It is difficult for even the most gawky and inarticulate nineteen-year-old to live for long in Paris without meeting a girl. Since I went for coffee every morning to the Café de la Mairie du VIème, an amiable little establishment next to the grandiloquent church of St.-Sulpice (where, incidentally, Djuna Barnes set several scenes in *Nightwood),* I duly met two American girls on the grand tour. As often happens with American girls seeing the sights together, one was very beautiful and the other was very friendly. I became a friend of the friendly one and a pursuer of the beautiful one, an art student from New York. The problem with beautiful girls is that they have many pursuers, who inevitably begin bumping into each other in the course of the pursuit, and so I kept bumping into an equally persistent young man, a faunish poet named Mason Hoffenberg. As it turned out, neither of us got the girl. She decided to escape from the complications of Paris by returning to New York, where, for all I know, she is now happy in grandmotherhood.

Mason Hoffenberg eventually acquired a certain celebrity for having collaborated with Terry Southern on a mildly pornographic novel called *Candy,* but after the art student returned to New York, he and I were just two more rejected suitors, and it occasionally happens that rejected suitors become friends. So I was drinking a midnight beer at the Royal with Mason and some other people when Mason suddenly leaned across the table and said to a quarrelsome leftist painter who affected the single name of Mottke: "Jimmy must be here by now, let's go get him." The painter agreed, and so three or four of us began wandering down the boulevard St.-Germain to the Boul' Mich and then up that avenue to a dismal place called the Hôtel de Rome.

It was about one o'clock by now, and the hotel was totally dark, but Mason cheerfully pressed the doorbell until a sleepy concierge let us in and waved us up, with some irritation, to the second floor. There, while Mottke held up a cigarette lighter to illuminate the numbered doors, Mason finally found the right one and began banging. From inside, there were groans and shufflings, and then the clanking of the door bolt being unbolted. A short, slightly pudgy black opened the door and stood blinking in the glow of the cigarette lighter. He wore baggy pants and a T-shirt, his eyes bulging in his dark brown face, his lips spreading into a gap-toothed smile as he recognized his persecutors.

"Mason! God, it's good to see somebody."

"Hey, come on," Mason said, Mason the poet who hated any signs of emotion. "Let's all go down to Les Halles and get some food."

"Eat? Now?" Jimmy was still half asleep.

"Sure, Les Halles," Mason said. "That's where you get the onion soup."

In some deep, black, stony, and liberating way, my life, in my own eyes, began during that first year in Paris. . . .
—NOTES OF A NATIVE SON

There is almost nothing that can be said about Paris that has not been said before, and said by masters. Like any great metropolis, it is both beautiful and stony, both inviting and hostile. It has been part of the American landscape for generations—"All good Americans go to Paris when they die" was once a fresh and amusing summation of our feelings about the magical city—and generations of Americans have gone there in search of something. They have generally found what they were looking for, though it was not always what they expected. They expect, to begin with, the good life, in a purely physical sense, the sunshine of a Renoir garden and the taste of a Burgundy that eludes description. Paris meets its visitors on any terms they choose. One of them may savor a newly discovered garlic soup while another lies prostrate in his hotel room with an intestinal attack. The visitors expect "culture" too, in a physical sense, and Paris gives each newcomer the welcome he deserves. One is exalted by the stained glass in the Sainte Chapelle while another sits on a bench in the Louvre because his feet hurt.

There are other attractions more complicated than the physical ones. Many Americans come in search of some intangible element that they couldn't find in the United States, but they don't know exactly what it is. Some search for it on the banks of the Seine, some in the striptease clubs off the Champs-Élysées, and some just sit in their hotel rooms and do the crossword puzzle in the *Herald Tribune*. Paris mirrors and exaggerates the visitors' emotions and capacities. For the rich, the headwaiter at Lapérouse exerts himself, and the opera house opens its gates at the end of a long avenue of lights. For the needy, the smell of roasting chestnuts provides its own warmth, and the spectacle of the fountains in the Tuileries its own coolness. Money can buy more things here than almost anywhere else, but the lack of money makes less difference than anywhere else. Love seekers can find love, but loneliness seekers can also find loneliness. Nowhere is there more promise than in the April daffodils that sprout in the Luxembourg Gardens; nowhere is there more finality than in the rhythmic strokes with which the blue-uniformed old witches wield their brooms of branches to sweep the fallen leaves into the gutters of the place St.-Sulpice.

You see? In writing about Paris, one soon begins to indulge in rhetoric, the easy citation of romantic sites and the easy images of passing seasons. But the writers who come to Paris—and Paris has always been a city of writers—do not come to watch falling leaves. I really do not know exactly why Henry James came here, or Gertrude Stein or Ezra Pound. Now it is 1948, and I do not really know why Jimmy Baldwin and I came here either. I argued about it once with a black friend of Jimmy's, whose name I have forgotten, and he would not accept any of the obvious reasons. To begin with, I said, one has to live somewhere—not the farm or the hometown or the family attic but *somewhere*. No, he said, that couldn't be the reason for coming to Paris. Well, it was then cheap in Paris, cheaper than any city in America, so you could eat better, live better than back there. No, he said again, that couldn't be the reason. Well, they leave you alone in Paris, so you can sit and write all day, if you want, or not write all day, if you want, and so you can get your work done, or not done. No, he said again, that's no reason for leaving home and coming here. So I finally asked him, sitting on the warm terrace of the Deux Magots, what he would consider a good reason, and he said, "I don't know, but there's got to be one."

Let us try to concentrate on specific facts. On the corner of the rue de Verneuil and the rue de Beaune, just three or four blocks from the left bank of the Seine, in the Seventh Arrondissement, there stood and still stands a grimy, tottering seven-story building called the Hôtel de Verneuil. It was then run by a cadaverous Corsican called Monsieur Dumont, who occupied a steamy ground-floor apartment with his swarthy wife, several children, and a mother-in-law. The rooms above were dark and dingy, and the whole hotel had only two toilets, of the kind in which you have to stand or squat over two footrests next to a hole in the floor, but the Dumonts were paternalistic, and they understood about the rent money being late, and they didn't mind people cooking in their rooms. So the word spread that the Hôtel de Verneuil was a convenient place to stay.

Here lived a warmhearted English girl called Mary, who worked for the Communist-run World Federation of Trade Unions by day and then cooked supper for many of the indigent writers in the neighborhood. So she inevitably found herself cooking for Jimmy Baldwin, who had just as inevitably found his way here, and for me. Mary welcomed all newcomers and tried to make them friends—if there was a lonely Danish painter on the fourth floor and a Vassar girl trying to write a novel on the fifth floor, Mary would soon be feeding them both. Actually, it was another friend of Mary's, a young writer called Priscilla Boughton, who also lived here, who had known Jimmy in New York, and who found him his room at the Hôtel de Verneuil.

And now she was giving a party in honor of a new magazine, *Zero.* Everybody in Paris in those days was involved with some kind of little magazine—*Points, Merlin, Janus,* who can remember all the names? This was long before the rich came with enough money to establish something as permanent as *The Paris Review*. *Zero* was the creation of two implausible youths, a bearded, pock-marked poet named Albert Benveniste and a pale Greek from Detroit who was experimenting with a mustache and had given himself the name of Themistocles Hoetis. The purpose of a little magazine, of course, is to publish one's own unpublishable works, and the works of one's friends, and so the first issue of *Zero* naturally contained the writings of Benveniste, Hoetis, Mason Hoffenberg, and Jimmy Baldwin's *Everybody's Protest Novel*. But that all lay in the future. This party was simply in honor of there being a new magazine called *Zero*, and so Priscilla's room on the top floor of the Hôtel de Verneuil shook with swarms of people arguing and drinking and playing jazz until Madame Dumont turned out all the lights as a signal of her displeasure, whereupon the party went on in the dark.

Almost anything was an excuse for a party—somebody finishing a novel or somebody leaving for the south of France or somebody getting a check from home—and so there were many parties, and, in time, they all merge together. I found myself one evening with Mary at Terry Southern's apartment, and the people were crowded onto the double bed like sardines, all passing hashish from one to another, and the record player was playing something by Thelonious Monk, whom I had never heard of back then, and the problem was that the hall was flooding because Mr. Soong, a bearded sage of about sixty who hung around the neighborhood cafés and cadged money for cups of tea, had passed out in the bathroom and was lying facedown in the clogged bidet, his gnarled hand gripping the running faucet. And then some girl who worked for the U.S. aid program went to Italy and left her apartment on the boulevard St.-Germain in the hands of friends, who promptly invited in the whole neighborhood, and there stood Brendan Behan, wildly drunk, singing one ferocious revolutionary song after another, and then somebody found a copy of the departed hostess's diary and began laughing and then read aloud to the whole crowd the passage that said: "There I was, naked in the prow of an old canoe, drifting down the river and wondering, 'Is this the meaning of life?'"

Jimmy Baldwin came and went. He was twenty-five then, and known to have published an article in *Commentary* and to have won a Saxton Fellowship from Harper's for an unfinished novel—fairly impressive credentials in the very uncredentialed world of St.-Germain-des-Prés. I saw him here and there, at parties and cafés, without taking any particular note of him. "Right after Thanksgiving," according to Fern Marja Eckman, who wrote a book called *The Furious Passage of James Baldwin*, "he 'went to pieces,' a process begun at home but hastened by his exposure to the chill of Paris. . . . 'I'd gone to pieces a bit *before* I left New York, y'know,' Baldwin says. 'But I really did go to pieces when I got to Paris. Thank God I went to pieces there! It was very lucky—because I fell ill in a hotel that was run by a Corsican woman who *liked* me. And so she nursed me. And I ran up a *ferocious* bill. I caught—you know, Paris was, for Americans, extremely badly heated. And I was always on the *streets*. And I—I really didn't have any *clothes*. So I—something went wrong with my bronchial tubes or something. Anyway, I was very sick.' "

The "going to pieces" sounds like some sinister kind of breakdown, but Mrs. Eckman was quite aware that she had to rely on Jimmy's highly melodramatic account of his past life. "His memory of the past," she says warily, "is inclined to be impressionistic." Actually, there was no time during the several years I knew him that Jimmy did not describe himself as "going to pieces." It was one of his favorite phrases, something that explained everything and excused everything—his other favorite being the repeated plea "God! God! God! God!" But during those first months in Paris, when I barely knew him at all, I had only a general impression of his being around, arguing, drinking, or staring into space, just like everybody else. I knew he had no money, but I knew he was picking it up here and there, also like everybody else. There were still rackets in those days—the gas-stamp racket, for instance, in which you could go to the prefecture and swear that you needed a gasoline ration for your car, and then sell the ration coupons to somebody who actually had a car. The most complicated of these rackets involved importing cars into England. Since an American was allowed to bring his car with him, bands of roving Englishmen were always looking for a willing American who would sign up as the owner of a car, accompany it to London, turn it over to its real owners, and take his chances on getting out of the country without trouble. The job paid fifty dollars and expenses, as I recall, but it wasn't really very risky, and when Jimmy left for a mysterious two-day trip to London, it wasn't any great mystery.

As that winter deepened and then faded, I saw Jimmy more and more, in a random way, and the pop-eyed black face and the drawling voice became more and more familiar. Jimmy could laugh and joke and make wisecracks, but everybody does that. What was remarkable about his café talk was an absolutely passionate concern with such fundamental questions as identity, love, fear, art, greatness—things that less elemental people feel some embarrassment about even mentioning. Jimmy talked about them endlessly, as though he had just discovered each one, offering each familiar observation as though it were a major philosophical principle. There was nothing exceptional about his views—he was convinced that nobody knew himself, that nobody was capable of real love, that innocence was a disguise for ignorance, and so on—but he managed to surround them with such rhetoric that they sounded both inscrutable and important. The one thing that he did not talk about much was being black. That was always there, and it came up occasionally, but there were never any impassioned discussions of the subject. Perhaps that was because he took the situation for granted; perhaps it was because I wasn't much interested.

It seemed to me more interesting that Jimmy had once been a full-fledged minister, preaching the Word. He used to talk about this with a slightly embarrassed but very real pride. It was an important element in *Crying Holy,* but Jimmy best portrayed his own conversion at the age of fourteen in *The Fire Next Time:* "I fell to the ground before the altar. It was the strangest sensation I have ever had in my life—up to that time, or since. I had not known that it was going to happen, or that it could happen. One moment I was on my feet, singing and clapping . . . ; the next moment, with no transition, no sensation of falling, I was on my back, with the lights beating down into my face. . . . And the anguish that filled me cannot be described. It moved in me like one of those floods that devastate countries, tearing everything down. . . ." In that condition of exaltation, Jimmy began preaching the coming end of the world, on a predetermined month and day.

"And what did you tell your parishioners," said I, the eternal skeptic, "when doomsday came and went without anything happening?"

"I told them it was our prayers that had saved the world," Jimmy said.

Jimmy's father had also been a preacher, but a man so filled with hatred that he regularly beat his children. Jimmy believed strongly that his father had been deeply wounded and eventually destroyed by white society, and when Jimmy himself looked at white society, he looked at it with his father's eyes. But if there was hatred in Jimmy too, it seemed to be focused less on white society than on that violent father. "His father's arm, rising and falling, might make him cry," Jimmy wrote of one beating in his autobiographical first novel, "yet his father could never be entirely the victor, for John cherished something that his father could not reach. It was his hatred and his intelligence that Johnny cherished, the one feeding the other."

I cannot reliably quote Jimmy's monologues after a lapse of so many years, but I was impressed, in reading Mrs. Eckman's carefully recorded interviews, by how little Jimmy's ideas and language had changed. And so I shall steal some of his words from her. I can imagine myself back on the terrace of the Royal on a spring night, drinking beer and watching the girls flow past, and here is Jimmy talking, not necessarily to me but to anyone who would listen: "Y'know, you simply cannot—I can be all kinds of *people* in public. Or to myself in front of my mirror. But in relation to someone who loves me or someone I *love*, you know, all these masks have to go. And everyone's *afraid* of that. Afraid of being seen as he or she is. But that's the *price*, you know. That's why love is so frightening, I'm *sure*. Because you really *have* to come down *front* and be who*ever* you are. And you don't *know* who you are, y'know. You discover that partly—you discover that *really* through somebody *else*. And everybody's *afraid* of this *revelation*. You know, it isn't done in a *day*. Once you've done it, it isn't so terrifying—though the hangover remains. Once you meet the barrier, I think—once you've made some crucial *turning* point, then, hopefully, you can handle it from then on out, y'know. Because *you* know you *can*."

It is unfair, I suppose, to judge anyone by what he actually says. It is particularly unfair to writers, since, while they tend to babble in interviews, they work hard on what they want to say in print. Still, if Jimmy had been forced to live according to his talk, he would have had to be a saint, and he was never a saint. For those who are not saints, the first law is survival. I had come to Europe with a duffel bag, a typewriter, sixty-five dollars, and the knowledge that I could get bailed out if I absolutely had to be; Jimmy had come with a suitcase, a typewriter, forty dollars, and the knowledge that nobody would bail him out. And since then, he had pawned his typewriter. When Mary went to Corsica for a vacation, Jimmy moved into her room and started using her typewriter. He was back at work on *Crying Holy,* the novel he had been struggling with since he was about seventeen. When Mary came back and routed him out of her room, he wanted to keep the typewriter, "just for a week."

"But it's my typewriter," Mary protested.

"But you don't need it," Jimmy said. "I have to finish this chapter. That's what I need it for."

"Well, I want to write some letters," Mary said.

"Letters, for God's sake!" Jimmy cried. "You can write them later, or send postcards, or something. Don't you see, I *have* to finish this chapter?"

"But it's mine!" Mary insisted. "Do you think you have some kind of a *right* to take people's things just because you want to write something?"

"Yes," he said. "I've got to have it."

The novel did not get done, however. He had written it and rewritten it, and it still wasn't right. Did he work on it constantly? No, he did not work on it constantly. He worked on it very little. Just as job hunting can become a full-time job, with regular hours, regular commuting, and all the aspects of a job except an income, so survival can become a full-time occupation, and instead of job hunting, the survivor spends his time negotiating loans, postponing debts, avoiding creditors, and then relaxing in the evening after a hard day's surviving. And when spring comes to Paris, it brings friends and tourists and travelers who like to roam around, so after a winter of survival, Jimmy decided to go to the Riviera. He joined forces with several people he had known in New York, who had money, and they all headed south. There were about a dozen of them, most of whom knew one another only slightly, and none of whom knew much about where they were going. All but one were young men in various stages of self-discovery, the other being a fat and noisy girl who seemed to have a considerable amount of money.

In case I have made this chronicle sound too earnest, it's worth recalling that most Americans did come to France not to write great literature but to have fun, and Jimmy was great fun to have along on the trip. He was witty and lively, and he enjoyed gossip, preferably malicious. He knew lots of funny stories, and lots of obscene limericks, and he particularly relished those ecclesiastical ones that reverberated so strangely out of his days as a storefront preacher. Like the one about the young girl from Chichester, who made all the saints in their niches stir. Each morning at matins, her bosom in satins made the bishop of Chichester's britches stir. Or the young girl named Sue, who said as the bishop withdrew, "The vicar was quicker, and thicker and slicker, and longer and stronger than you."

It had pained Jimmy that his father had often told him he was ugly, though the father had a point. Jimmy was small and pudgy, and his eyes bulged froglike, and there was a wide gap between his front teeth, but he also had a lot of charm, of a rather theatrical sort, and he could be very funny doing his melodious imitations of Bette Davis as the princess of the plantation in *Jezebel*. It amused him to flirt with the middle-aged white Americans who kept asking if they could buy him a drink, though he despised them while he flirted with them. The people he got more involved with tended to be young and French, and it was probably no accident that he and they spoke no common language. (The spectacle of Jimmy heating Madame Dumont's flatirons on the electric hot plate so that he could iron out his lover's white shirts was a scene of domestic devotion worthy of the *Ladies' Home Journal* of about 1910.) He also liked to sing torch songs, particularly "See, See, Rider"—"See what you have done. Caused me to love you, now your man has come. . . ."

The people who had taken Jimmy south left with high hopes of a summer of communal hedonism, but soon there were arguments and quarrels. Some wanted to live in tents, and others wanted to go sailing, and then they began trickling back to Paris, broke and bedraggled. Jimmy had written nothing, and money was beginning to be a serious problem again. I encountered a rather sepulchral lawyer named Tommy, who had an office and apartment on the Right Bank, where he represented some kind of chemical company. I told him about Jimmy's difficulties, and so it was that after almost a year of scrounging, Jimmy became a filing clerk. The work was not demanding, and he got the handsome salary of eighty dollars a month, plus free lunch with Tommy and his Moroccan houseboy. Now, finally, he would have a chance to get some work done on his novel.

At about this time, I began to keep a sort of journal of day-to-day events in St.-Germain-des-Prés, and after all these years, it probably documents the expatriate life in the quarter more accurately than I could describe it from memory. Most of it, of course, deals purely with me, with what I was writing and reading and thinking—I had by now finished two novels, which an agent was trying to sell in New York, and I made a relatively comfortable living translating movie scripts from French into English—but Jimmy and other people keep wandering in and out of my journal, so it is a journal of their lives as well. From any serious point of view, this chronicle is completely trivial, superficial, worthless, and I suppose I should be embarrassed by the record of my own arrogance and ambition. But that is what life in Bohemia is like most of the time. Everyone is young and hopeful and unemployed, and there is a great deal of idle imagining, and just wandering around. Wasted time.

In America, the color of my skin had stood between myself and me; in Europe, that barrier was down. Nothing is more desirable than to be released from an affliction, but nothing is more frightening than to be divested of a crutch. It turned out that the question of who I was was not solved because I had removed myself from the social forces which menaced me. . . .

—NOBODY KNOWS MY NAME

From a journal:

August 17, 1949. . . . Met Jimmy at the Royal at 7:30, and along came Lionel [Abel], and Jimmy said, "Here comes my favorite intellectual." Abel was pleased, and we all went to supper at the Basque place on the Rue Mabillon. It was fairly expensive but very good—Jimmy and I had a faux filet, which was served with Madeira sauce and champignons, and Abel bought a bottle of rosé. . . . One trouble was that Abel and Jimmy had to talk about Richard Wright, a conversation I have heard about a million times. They are still rehashing Jimmy's article in *Zero*, with Abel defending the older generation. . . . Abel was very charming, and in one of his explaining moods, so he explained Henry James, Flaubert, Faulkner, Cyril Connolly, Leslie Fiedler, Picasso's inability to sleep nights, and the absence of an influence of older French writers on younger French writers.

After dinner, Jimmy and I were going to a movie—*Back Street* with Boyer and Sullavan—but it was way out at the far end of the Rue de Babylone, and by the time we got there, with Abel explaining things all the way, it turned out that the movie had started at nine and not ten, and now it was ten-thirty, so we came all the way back to the Royal, with Abel still explaining (Graham Greene, Sartre, Bernanos, etc., etc.).

We were talking about Milton Klonsky, would-be poet, for whom Abel appropriated Lenin's term "a gangster of the pen," and then there he suddenly appeared, trying to be important, so we all ignored him. And then appeared a girl called Nina something, who had just heard Mahler's *Song of the Earth* and had just seen a bullfight and had to tell us all about them. And then somebody called Ted rode up on a tandem bicycle, the other half of which was occupied by someone called Siegfried, who had just got back his short stories that very afternoon from Mr. Baldwin, who had told him to tear them up because they were terrible, especially the one about the world-famous pianist who had no little fingers because his manager, Mr. Elbow, had made him cut them off for publicity (and he wasn't kidding). . . .

August 18. . . . Stephen, the one who wrote that awful novel, was complaining because he couldn't get his next book written, and he said, "Why don't you sell me a manuscript?" And I said, "I won't sell you one, but I'll write you one," and Jimmy said, "*I'll* write you a manuscript." Then we said we'd collaborate and write a quick best-seller for Stephen to sell to the movies. Stephen said he was very serious, and we said we were very serious. Stephen said he had already been paid an advance of $1,000, and he hadn't written a line, and what was he going to do? We said he should give us $400 apiece and we would write 100 pages to justify the advance, and then we would get half the royalties on the finished book. Stephen said, "Dumas did it, so why shouldn't I?" Why not indeed, we said. So he said we should write a beginning and meet him at the Royal the next night, and we said we would.

After he left, Jimmy and I plotted out the great novel, which was to be called *The First Time I Saw Paris,* the real and true story of Young Love. . . . We parted, the master and I, solemnly swearing that we would really do it. . . . I wrote six pages this afternoon. Jimmy read them and laughed, and Abel read them and laughed. Jimmy never wrote anything, and Stephen himself never showed up, the bastard. . . .

August 23. . . . *Life* has an absurd article called "The New Expatriates," featuring four men with beards sitting in front of the Flore, which is too expensive for anybody under thirty. Wonder who they might be. The article says: "The kids are worried about their work too. Three years, they say, and still no Hemingway." Wonder where they got nonsense like that. Imagine, not a day complete without somebody saying, "Three years and still no Hemingway."

August 24. . . . Herb Gold, another one of Mary's discoveries, introduced me to a withered man called Newman, a professional "promising young writer," now almost 40, somehow connected with the New School for Social Research. He was denouncing Jimmy, said Jimmy had "never fulfilled himself." He had a copy of the first *Zero,* and he said Jimmy's article was badly written, and I said it wasn't badly written. He said it's pretentious, and I said it's not pretentious. He said it's immature, and I said it's not immature, and he said, "You're being dogmatic." Somehow this turned into an argument with Gold and his wife about Saul Bellow, now living on the Rue de l'Université, and Edith Gold said Saul Bellow is the most talented writer in America, and they all shook hands. I said Jimmy had more talent than Saul Bellow would ever have, and they all glared at me. Edith said it was "presumptuous" of me to compare someone who had already published two novels with someone who hadn't published a single one. Newman said to Gold that "some young people" felt they had to denounce people they were afraid of (!!!).

August 27. . . . These arguments can go on and on. Jimmy was very mad at Newman and raged at him about all kinds of past history from Greenwich Village. Newman got very defensive. "Well, I may not know much about literature," he began one round, and Jimmy said, "Why, you know nothing whatever about literature." Jimmy bet Newman a dinner that within three years, he, Jimmy, would have a novel published and well reviewed, and that I would too. . . .

September 2. . . . Jimmy got a very sad letter from Themistocles because he has spent months down in Tangiers with the Paul Bowleses, trying to put together the second issue of *Zero,* and now he says the Moroccan printers have made a mess of it. They have no decent paper, so it's all done on newsprint, and the printers can't understand English, and they ignored all the corrections on the page proofs, so it's all full of mistakes. I still have no idea what's in it except for the two articles by Jimmy and me (mine on Thomas Mann), but Themistocles is bringing it back with him next week. . . .

Jimmy has found a poem that he likes, and he tacked it to his wall because he says it applies to all these people around here. It's by Louise Bogan, and the last lines say: "Parochial punks, trimmers, nice people, joiners true-blue. / Get the hell out of the way of the laurel. It is deathless. / And it isn't for you."

September 4. . . . Jimmy is still supposed to open as a singer in a nightclub in the Arab Quarter on the 15th. A little hard to imagine. . . .

September 6. . . . Everything is sultry and sticky because it rained very hard last night. . . . Wandering down the Rue des Saints Pères, I ran into Jimmy and Herb Gold having a fierce argument right out in the street next to the post office. Gold had said, "I have a bone to pick with you." He wanted to know whether Jimmy had really said various things he had been quoted as saying. Jimmy wanted to know what he had been quoted as saying. Had Jimmy really called him "a Sunday school teacher"? Well, yes. Gold said he wanted to know what Jimmy really thought of him. Jimmy said he thought Gold had a lot of pretensions. Then Gold started firing back and said Jimmy was prejudiced and cynical and "maladjusted."

Jimmy later appeared at the Royal, fuming, but claiming he had won the argument. And then who should appear but old Schaefer, the would-be *philosophe,* devotee of Gurdjieff and Ouspensky, just back from America and 25 pounds heavier, with a great fat belly under his T-shirt, stuffed with German-American home cooking. He said he had a bottle of Seagram's, so we all went to the Hôtel de Verneuil to drink it, but first we had to wake people up even though it was only midnight. We went to see Gidske, everybody's favorite Norwegian journalist, and Jimmy pounded on her door, and she said, "What is it?" and he said, "Open the door," and she said, "Are you drunk?" and he said, "No, and it's important." There were angry mutters from behind the door, and then she opened it, and she and Schaefer fell into each other's arms. Then we banged on Mary's door, and she appeared blinking in a bathrobe, and then we spent two hours chattering and drinking up all of Schaefer's whiskey. . . .

September 8. . . . I was sitting at the Royal with Jimmy and Schaef and Gidske and being monumentally bored because they all talked about nothing but *Bicycle Thief,* which I had never seen, and then Themistocles appeared in front of us, carrying the new issue of *Zero,* which we all started reading. . . . It is very nice to see one's own name in print. . . . Themistocles then started talking for hours about how wonderful North Africa is, and all his fancy new friends, Capote, Vidal, Cecil Beaton—it all sounds like a circus. . . . The plan now is that Jimmy and Gidske and I will all go down there for two weeks at Christmastime. . . .

September 12. . . . I had drinks with Tommy and the talk got around to Jimmy, and he said, "Is this on the record or off?" and I said, "Either," and he said he was going to "have to let him go," i.e., Jimmy is sacked, fired, and all his daydreams of security are finished. And he hasn't gotten much good out of them either. Since he began that job a couple of months ago, he scrapped the second version of the novel and began writing a short story, and he worked on that for a few weeks, and then scrapped it, and then he went back to being a novelist, and this time he said he was concentrating on a completely new novel, the one about Greenwich Village, *So Long at the Fair,* but what has become of it? He has to stay here until he has made the grade. Each time in his life that he made a great leap, he made it impossible to go back. Once he escaped from Harlem, he couldn't go back there, and now he can't go back to Greenwich Village. He came here without a penny, and he's been living by borrowing ever since. I asked Tommy to try to find him another job before firing him, and he said he would try, but he has been paying Jimmy out of his own pocket because there is no official budget for him to have any filing clerk at all, and he thought the company would agree to it, but he has been turned down. Now what jobs are there in Paris for somebody like Jimmy?

September 13. . . . Tommy asked whether I had told Jimmy, and I said I hadn't, and he said to say nothing because he "might not have to let him go after all." He refused to explain. . . .

September 16. . . . Went with Jimmy, Gidske, and others to see *La Tour Eiffel Qui Tue,* a kind of musical extravaganza about the Eiffel Tower going on a rampage of crime and vice. My favorite song was the one where a girl comes on stage with a baby and starts singing her complaint: *"C'est un enfant naturel. Son père est la Tour Eiffel."* Later we met Mary at the Royal and began improvising an American version. The first scene takes place on the ruined plantation where young Marybelle plans to run away to Hollywood while wise old Pappy Baldwin tries to dissuade her: "Don't go, gal, don't go. . . ."

September 17. . . . Themistocles and Jimmy went to have lunch with Sartre except that they didn't get any lunch. Themistocles says Sartre is going to write a piece for *Zero,* and Jimmy suggested that Sartre republish his piece on the Harlem ghetto in *Les Temps Modernes.* Sartre was reported to be interested.

September 18. . . . *Commentary* keeps asking Jimmy to write an article for them, and he was wondering aloud about what he should write, and I told him to write the full-scale article about Richard Wright that he keeps meaning to do, so he said he would do that. Then I began thinking of more ideas and told him to write an article about the character of Joe Christmas in *Light in August,* which he has been talking about for ages, and he liked that too. . . .

I had thought we were rid of Jacques the actor, Jimmy's latest love, but he keeps tagging around after Jimmy, even though nobody will talk to him, and he speaks no English. Last night, he got quite drunk and kept saying he wanted to buy a dog. *"Je veux un chien, un tout petit chien."* Gidske got very mad at him because he always insists on drinking Pernod while everybody else has beer, and then he never has any money, so somebody else has to loan Jimmy the money to pay for Jacques's Pernod. It came Gidske's turn again, and she said she wouldn't pay unless Jacques drank beer, and he refused. . . . Jacques asked Themistocles whether he had seen Cocteau's *Les Parents Terribles,* and Themistocles said he thought it was very bad, and Jacques said that was because Jean Marais was very bad, and that it would have been much better if he, Jacques, had been given the part. Themistocles was speechless. Jimmy has been keeping a journal on the subject, which I read today. It's about 25 pages and mostly rhetoric.

September 19. . . . Elliott was going to *L'Avare* at the Comédie-Française, but now his friend has acquired a car and wants to go to Normandy, so I have inherited two good tickets, one of which is supposed to be for Jimmy, which seems sort of silly since he can't understand what's happening on the stage. I told Mary I would try to talk Jimmy out of going, but he was adamant about how much he wanted to go. . . .

September 20. . . . My clock was slow, and so I didn't get to tell Mary that Jimmy insisted on going to *L'Avare* until 7 or so, and then I went to meet Jimmy at the Royal, but he wasn't there, so I had a quick supper and then went back to the Hôtel de Verneuil to get Mary. I left a taxi waiting outside, only to find out that she was in bed and didn't want to go—or did, but didn't want to get dressed. I told her to put on a pair of pants over her pajamas and come on, and she said, could she really? And I said, sure. So she put on a sweater over the pajamas, and then a skirt, and rolled up the pajama legs, and off we went. The play was marvelous, but Mary kept fretting because her pajama legs kept getting unrolled.

September 22. . . . Much confusion last night. I saw Jimmy and Themistocles briefly at the Reine Blanche, and Themistocles said, "This is the night Jimmy is going to blow his stack about everything." But Schaefer and I were going to play chess, so we went on to the café across from the Métro. Jimmy came by at about midnight to say good night, and then Schaef and I went on playing chess until about one, and then went to the Auberge to have a *croque monsieur*. Then Gidske appeared at about two, and Schaef went over to the Reine Blanche to see if anybody was still around. He came back saying Jimmy was there with two Cubans, so we went over there. Jimmy tried to pick a fight with me about the book translation that Tommy has been negotiating for us to collaborate on, but I didn't feel like fighting. Then Jimmy took Schaef down to the far end of the bar, and there was much earnest conversation, and then the place was closing, and we all continued to the Bar du Bac, which never closes. Jimmy took Jacques off to a separate table, and I asked Schaef what the hell was going on, and he said Jimmy was telling Jacques to "get lost and stay lost." They came back, and Jacques was weeping, with great snuffles, and with great hot tears rolling down his cheeks, and Jimmy was tearful too. . . .

September 24. . . . Jimmy is now working on the two articles I suggested he write for *Commentary,* and with those and the novel, he is now very determined to get some work done. So I had an inspiration and told him to quit the job at Tommy's place, and to tell Tommy the very next day that he had to concentrate on his writing. He said he'd like to, but he wanted to get his first check from *Commentary* before quitting. But he was supposed to be fired last Thursday, except that he didn't show up for work, and then he was going to be told yesterday, but nothing happened, so I guess it will be Monday, but if I could just get him to quit now, he would never know he was going to be fired. . . .

September 27. . . . Poor Jimmy—Tommy told him yesterday that he was through, and he is trying not to be worried, to keep working on his articles. He is also collecting various materials about himself because Tommy said he might be able to help him get an advance on a novel, which I told him not to count on, for God's sake, but I'm afraid he does. . . .

October 7. . . . Themistocles as the social lion is getting more and more fantastic. Last night at the Deux Magots, he and Jimmy were ensconced in the company of Max Ernst, Truman Capote, Stephen Spender, Simone de Beauvoir, and God knows who else. Too much for me, so I retreated to the Reine Blanche, where Jimmy and Themistocles later appeared, bringing with them a tall, gaunt fellow called Frank, who kept babbling about having to take Daphne to Chartres the next day. Frank paid for everybody's drinks, while Themistocles pushed Jimmy's writing, and Jimmy pushed Jimmy. After Frank left, Themistocles said, "Well, that's one way to get a book published," and Jimmy said, "It's the *only* way to get a book published."

But how the hell can he get it written when he spends so much time lobbying for its publication? The Richard Wright article, which was going to be in the mail to *Commentary* on Monday or Tuesday (it being now Friday) has only gotten as far as a first draft, which he doesn't like. And the new novel is only on page 19, which doesn't look very promising, although he still talks about getting it finished by Christmas. I was in his room this afternoon, and read what was in the typewriter, and it sounds just like *Crying Holy* all over again—has a character called Gabriel who discovers the Lord, and whose mother was a slave. I said, "Is this new novel just a new version of *Crying Holy?*" He said, "Well, yes and no."

October 9. . . . At the Reine Blanche again with Jimmy and Frank, who seems to have not only a large expense account but the authority to buy manuscripts for Doubleday. (The Daphne whom he had to take to Chartres turned out to be Daphne Du Maurier, a very pleasant lady.) All night long, he kept getting hiccups, because we were all drinking beer, and he says he gets hiccups when he drinks beer. Jimmy's technique for curing hiccups is that he holds the victim's ears shut while the victim holds his own nose and downs a full glass of beer. It always works, for a while. . . .

October 14. . . . I asked Tommy about this business of getting Jimmy an advance on a novel (that was the way Jimmy had put it), and Tommy said that wasn't the plan at all. What he had planned was to approach several people who knew Jimmy's work and get them to subscribe to a fund to keep him going—in other words, pure charity. I told him I thought it was a bad idea. But he hadn't done anything about it anyway. . . . Later I saw Themistocles outside the Deux Magots and asked him where Jimmy was, and he said Jimmy was inside with Frank and Capote and him, Themistocles himself.

"And don't interrupt," Themistocles said, "because they're finally talking turkey about Jimmy's novel."

October 16. . . . A long, tangled evening at the Reine Blanche ending up at the Pergola at about 5:00 A.M.—full of Africans sleeping on benches and women singing in Spanish while somebody strummed a guitar. At one point, one of the Africans got up and led a French girl to a telephone booth, and they both crammed themselves together inside it for five minutes. And nobody paid any attention. . . . I was grumbling to Jimmy about Themistocles' continual intriguing, and Jimmy said, "I know what Themistocles is doing," and I said, "I know, he's trying to sell your novel," and Jimmy said, "He's sold it." He was vague on details, but Frank is going to pay him money every month to get him through the winter while he writes it. But now he says he can't write it in Paris, so he wants to go to Tangiers in about a week, leaving all his debts behind him. Paris may be distracting, but I can't imagine him getting much done in Tangiers. . . .

October 19. . . . All of a sudden, two fat characters in raincoats appeared at the door of the Reine Blanche and said this was a raid. For what? For suspicious characters without identity papers. I had all my papers in order, so I had no trouble. Frank had all his papers in order, so he had no trouble. But Jimmy had no papers with him, no French papers, so they said, "Ah-hah, and what do you do?" He said, "I'm a writer." They said, "Ah-hah, and what do you write?" He said, "Novels, stories, articles." They said, "Ah-hah, and who do you write for?" He said, *"Partisan Review* and *Commentary* and *The Nation."* They said, *"Qu'est-ce que c'est que ça?"* They looked as though they were about to drag him away, but then he had an inspiration and said, "And also for *Temps Modernes*—for Jean-Paul Sartre." And then they said, "Ah," and there was no further trouble.

And whom should they grab but innocent, law-abiding old Schaefer, whose *carte d'identité* had expired, and who was led off smiling the smile of the unjustly accused. Jimmy was quite frantic and started asking questions like "Do they beat them?" So Frank and I went off to the local police station to see whether anything could be done. The police said they were going to hold Schaefer until they could *"vérifier son identité."* How long would that take? Overnight. Frank got very indignant and began blustering about all his friends in the embassy, but this had no effect on the gendarmes. There were about twenty-five of them all sitting around and itching for something to do, and one of them got up and came swaggering over to us, bristling, and said, *"Vous manquez de correction,"* which is about as ominous a phrase as I've ever heard from a French policeman, so I got Frank to calm down and leave. . . . It was noon the next day before Schaefer returned to the Quarter, unshaven and cheerfully smoking his pipe. They had said, "Do you go to the Reine Blanche often?" He said, "Fairly often." They said, "Do you know its reputation?" He said, "Yes, but I don't mind." They said, "Why do you go there?" He said, "To visit with old friends." So they photographed him and took his fingerprints and turned him loose. . . .

Jimmy is supposed to get his first payment from Frank on Friday. Then he and Gidske and Themistocles leave Paris on Sunday for Tangiers, where Jimmy and Gidske stay until Christmas. . . .

October 23. . . . I had quite a row with Jimmy in the Bar du Bac. I said he never got his writing done, just kept talking about it. I said a writer has to set himself a quota and get that done every day, no matter whether he feels like it or not. Jimmy said I was talking like a hack. I said better a hack writer than a nonwriting talker. . . .

October 26. . . . About midnight at the Gare de Lyon, where they were all leaving. Themistocles, with a homely but very expensive-looking American girl, and Jimmy and Schaef all at the *dégustation*, having cognac, so I had one too. I asked where Gidske was. They said she was guarding the baggage, because this was really a train to Toulon, not the Riviera, and all full of sailors, and there were two tough characters in the compartment, so they didn't want to leave the baggage alone. I went out to look for her and found the compartment with the two tough characters eyeing Gidske, who sat peacefully reading an article by Lionel Trilling about *The Princess Casamassima* in an old copy of *Horizon*. So finally it came train time, and everybody piled aboard, and there were fond farewells, and the engine began puffing forward, leaving Schaefer and me and the American girl, who, on closer inspection, had green slacks and a red coat and two different kinds of American cigarettes, and lots of money. Themistocles had met her in Hollywood. She paid for the taxi back to St. Germain, and then we filled her full of Pernod, at her expense, and she seemed to get very interested in Schaefer, and he in her, so they left together. Then he came back in about three minutes and complained because she hadn't invited him into the cab. "You're supposed to just *get into* the cab, for God's sake," I said, "not wait until you're invited." "You're right," he said. "I've been getting out of practice."

November 4. . . . Had lunch with Schaefer, who has a long letter from Jimmy. According to some mistake by Themistocles, it turned out when they got to Marseilles that there was no boat sailing for Tangiers on the supposed date of sailing and would be none until a week or so later. It also turned out that a ticket to Tangiers would cost so much that the sum remaining for a month in Tangiers would be so infinitesimal that they decided to give it up and retreat to Aix-en-Provence, where they have entrenched themselves in some small hotel. The theory is that they will stay there a month, at the end of which Jimmy will send off a large chunk of the novel to Frank, who will then send enough money to get to Tangiers. By this time, Gidske also hopes to get some money from Norway. . . .

November 9. . . . Schaefer got a letter from Gidske which says that Jimmy is sick. At first, they thought it was a bite by what Gidske calls "a bedbog," but then it got worse, and he had to go to the hospital. They said it was an inflamed gland, which had to be opened. . . . Jimmy asked Gidske to ask Frank for the Dec. 1 installment, but I don't know whether he will pay. He didn't like the idea of Jimmy's leaving Paris in the first place. Gidske is also cabling some other friends for money. . . . I went to see Themistocles' lady friend, the one in the green slacks, and asked whether she still planned to send money to the stranded people. She said no—Themistocles took her last payment and went on to Tangiers—so I gave her a big sob story about Jimmy being sick and got five thousand francs in cash, which was about all she had, plus a promise to send fifty dollars as soon as she got back to New York the following week. . . .

November 14. . . . Gidske writes now that Jimmy is better, but they still don't know whether he needs another operation. She says they have given up on Tangiers and will stay in Aix, because it's so cheap, and then return to Paris next month. Her English continues to be miraculous. She describes Jimmy's hospital as "croded, dirty, unafficient, and smelling like a hors stable." It is also full of "doctors and nons."

November 18. . . . I got a letter from Jimmy, confirming that they aren't going to Tangiers but will be back in Paris at Christmas. . . . And now it's only the first section of the novel that he hopes to have done by Christmas. . . .

November 19. . . . Another letter from Jimmy, very treacly. "I'm sorry for whatever pain I've caused you. I'm thinking particularly of the last ghastly months in Paris, and I hope I never behave in such a fashion towards you again. I always hate myself for it; get terribly frightened that perhaps you don't want us to be friends any longer, and who in the world could blame you?" What is one supposed to say to that?

November 25. . . . A letter from Gidske, which sounds pretty despairing. Jimmy's "soar" has "reopened," whatever that means. They are coming back to Paris as soon as possible and Jimmy is going to the American Hospital for a complete overhaul. They phoned Frank, and he promised to send 15,000 francs, but the hospital bill there is 13,000, and they are holding Jimmy's passport until it's paid. Then there is a month's hotel bill to pay, and the trip back costs 3,000 apiece. The whole Tangiers expedition sounds like one of the more disastrous crusades. There seems to be no way out except bouncing oneself off the consulate, which Jimmy tried in Marseilles, but they refused. . . .

November 29. . . . Gidske sent me a telegram saying Jimmy would be returning alone at 7:30 A.M. today, so I stayed up all night reading *Moby-Dick* and then walked all the way across Paris in the dawn to the Gare de Lyon to bring home the dying gladiator. And what a sadder and wiser man he seemed to be. Kept saying that I had been right "that awful, awful night" at the Bar du Bac—and which of the many awful nights was that? The one in which I said he might never get a novel written at all. He seems much chastened by his terror in Aix, but I can't help thinking it won't last. As soon as he collects some new admirers, it will all go back to the way it was. . . .

December 3. . . . Nothing is going on. Jimmy seems to have disappeared completely from sight, having moved to a cheaper hotel on the Rue du Bac and never coming out. . . . I am going to hear Kempff play three Mozart piano concertos and then the opening of *La Dame aux Camélias* with Edwige Feuillère as the Dame. . . .

December 6. . . . Saw Jimmy briefly for the first time this week. He is holed up in the Grand Hôtel du Bac in the best and cheapest room he's had in Paris. He is seeing nobody and grinding away at his novel, but so far only twenty pages. It's essentially the same as *Crying Holy*. It ends when the hero is sixteen, so there's no more of the ill-fated attempt to write about the Greenwich Village intelligentsia. And he's thinking of going back to Aix to stay in the apartment of some Americans they met there. . . .

December 7. . . . Jimmy is talking again about writing an essay on the Jewish protest novel for the third issue of *Zero*. I urged him not to. He doesn't really know enough about it. Should work on the novel. . . .

December 10. . . . Jimmy gave me for Christmas a copy of the Henry James Notebooks, inscribed with that marvelous outcry from *The Middle Years*, which I had originally quoted to him: "Our doubt is our passion and our passion is our task. The rest is the madness of art."

People who shut their eyes to reality simply invite their own destruction, and anyone who insists on remaining in a state of innocence long after that innocence is dead turns himself into a monster.

—NOTES OF A NATIVE SON

There is a gap here that I have failed to mention. Throughout all these months, I was pursuing Priscilla Boughton, the girl who was last described as giving the party for *Zero* in the Hôtel de Verneuil. The pursuit began in Paris, and then, when she returned home, it continued by mail. In December of 1949, I decided to go back to New York to persuade her to marry me. Jimmy and Gidske took the bus with me to the Gare St.-Lazare, a dark, cavernous railroad station full of blue-uniformed porters jostling through the crowds with their L-shaped luggage carts. You could see people's breath in the morning cold. I found the boat train for Le Havre and climbed aboard, and Jimmy and Gidske stood on the crowded platform and waved to me as we began creeping away. "Should I look up your mother?" I had said to him. "Sure! Great! Take her out to dinner."

The San Remo, where Jimmy used to make his headquarters during his year in the Village, is a modest trattoria near the corner of MacDougal and Bleecker streets, and I telephoned Mrs. Baldwin to suggest that we all meet there for dinner at seven o'clock, when she finished her day's work. I had some appointments in midtown, but I was all finished by six, so I took the subway down to the Village, found the San Remo, and ordered myself a beer at the bar. It was an ordinary sort of place, with sawdust on the floor and puddles of dark slush tramped in from the street, but it was fairly crowded with young Villagers who all seemed to know each other. I thought I recognized somebody at the other end of the bar, but it didn't much matter, because the people of the Village and the people of St.-Germain-des-Prés were all pretty much the same—looked alike, dressed alike, acted alike. Everybody argued and cadged cigarettes. At about seven, I left the bar and went into the adjoining restaurant to see whether Mrs. Baldwin had arrived, and whether I should reserve a table. Like the bar, it was a plain place, but it was already nearly full of people eating pasta. After looking around and finding no sign of Mrs. Baldwin, I approached the headwaiter and said I was expecting to meet my fiancée and the mother of a friend, a middle-aged Negro lady, and would he please let me know when they arrived?

"Oh, I'm sorry, sir," he said. "We can't do that."

"Can't do what? What do you mean?" I honestly didn't understand.

"We can't serve Negroes in here."

"Why on earth not?"

"It's against the rules. In the bar, okay, but not here."

"You're kidding," I said.

"Come on, now, we don't want any trouble," he said. "You'll just have to go somewhere else."

I looked at him in amazement as he turned his back on me. I was not really angry, perhaps because this had never happened to me before, perhaps because it was not I who was being barred, but I was slightly shaken nonetheless, as though some minor bureaucrat had denied me a passport, denied me the right to exist. I walked out the door and took up a sentry post in the cold darkness outside. Within a few minutes, Priscilla appeared.

"What's the matter?" she asked. "Are they all full?"

"They won't let us eat here," I said. "They say they don't let Negroes eat here."

"Oh, damn them! Who do they think they are? A crummy spaghetti joint!"

"In the bar is all right," I echoed the headwaiter, "but not in the restaurant. They say they don't want any trouble."

"Look, isn't that her?" Priscilla said.

Standing on the corner, looking nervously around her, was a small, dark figure. She looked at us, and at the restaurant, but she didn't seem to know what to do. Priscilla walked over to her and said, "Mrs. Baldwin?"

"Yes, I'm Mrs. Baldwin. You Jimmy's friends?"

"Yes, I'm Priscilla Boughton, and this is Otto Friedrich, and they say they're all full inside, so let's go eat somewhere else."

"That's all right, I don't mind," Mrs. Baldwin said. "I understand."

"Well, where would you like to eat?" Priscilla asked.

Mrs. Baldwin knew a sort of Caribbean place where Jimmy had once worked as a waiter, and so we got into a cab and rode to a dark side street in the West Twenties. Behind the bar of The Calypso sat a large black woman with earrings and a kind of turban on her head. We all stared at one another for a minute, while she seemed to be struggling toward recognition, and then Mrs. Baldwin said, "Don't you remember me? I'm Jimmy Baldwin's mother, and these are two friends of his." The large woman was suddenly full of welcome. She hugged Mrs. Baldwin, shook hands with Priscilla and me, and led us to a table. "*Good* to see you," she said. "How's Jimmy?" "He's fine," I said. "He used to work here, you know," she said. "We all just loved him. How's he getting on?" "Fine," I repeated.

The restaurant tried, by means of lanterns and palms, to look cheerfully Caribbean, but it was bleak and empty. The hostess offered us a choice of two dishes, southern fried chicken or spareribs. I had not eaten spareribs since I was a boy, when we slaughtered our own pigs and ate everything from roast loin to pickled knuckles, and I remembered the fun of gnawing at the rib bones, but these were dry and covered with a thick, sweet sauce, and I decided that I didn't like spareribs any more. Emma Berdis Baldwin, on closer acquaintance, turned out to be an admirable but unapproachable woman. She was small and wiry and tough, with a lined, handsome face and soft, expressive eyes, but all we could find to say was that the spareribs were good, weren't they. We told her about Jimmy, told her that his novel was progressing well, that he had many friends, that everybody thought he was a marvelous writer. She simply sat in silence, listening. Every once in a while, she would say, "That's good to hear, that's good."

At the end of the dinner, when I was beginning to feel that I had performed all the social duties I could, Mrs. Baldwin said softly to Priscilla, "I'd appreciate it a lot if you and Mr. Friedrich would come and have dinner with me, in my house."

"We'd love to," Priscilla said.

"Would you?" she asked me, doubtfully.

"Sure," I said.

The area I am describing, which, in today's gang parlance, would be called "the turf," is bounded by Lenox Avenue on the west, the Harlem River on the east, 135th Street on the north, and 130th Street on the south. We never lived beyond these boundaries; this is where we grew up. . . . When I turn east on 131st Street and Lenox Avenue, there is first a soda-pop joint, then a shoeshine "parlor," then a grocery store, then a dry cleaners', then the houses. All along the street there are people who watched me grow up. . . .

—NOBODY KNOWS MY NAME

Lenox Avenue at dusk, in January, struck me as one of the most forbidding places I had ever seen. The cold had abated, and the gutters were full of dirty slush. The grimy brick buildings stretched away in all directions, neon-lit stores on the ground floors and empty windows overhead. We turned down a trash-littered side street, West 131st Street, looking for the number, stopped next to some overflowing garbage cans, then went into the grim doorway. There was a figure standing just inside who muttered something as we hurried past him and began climbing the dark stairway.

"Come in, come in." Mrs. Baldwin seemed glad to see us as she held open the door on the fifth floor. More than glad, confident. She was at home here, and home was full of her children and neighbors and friends. It was hot and airless, and it smelled of furniture, and somebody was playing the piano. Mrs. Baldwin led us into the living room and stopped the piano playing and introduced us to everyone. One of the two girls on the piano bench was Gloria, Jimmy's older sister, and she smiled and shook hands, and then said, "What'll we play now?" There were three or four teenage girls who had just returned from what they called "a *pro*-grum" at some church in New Jersey, and, having sung all afternoon, they seemed unable to stop.

> *I want to go through, Lord,*
> *I want to go through.*
> *Take me through, Lord,*
> *Take me through.*

Once someone had begun a song, they all began to "harmonize" in the innocent thirds and sixths of the barbershop quartet, and then they added their own touch of innocent blasphemy, syncopating the beat and swaying sensuously as they sang. "And this here's Mister Raspberry," Mrs. Baldwin said, seating us next to a smiling young man on a sofa. Mr. Raspberry inquired who we were and then told us, smiling constantly, that he was a writer too, just like Jimmy. "Yes, sir!" he said. "I write stories and all kinds of things."

For an hour or more, the singing went on, and people drifted in and out, and it got so stuffy that it seemed almost impossible to breathe. I wandered out of the room to look for Mrs. Baldwin and encountered in a corridor a terrifying old lady, dark and withered, with flying white hair. "You Jimmy's friend, ain't you," she said. Yes, I said I was. "Well, I'm his aunt," she said. She took my arm and held it as she glared wildly at me. "Many's the time I whupped him, and you tell him, the next time I see him I gonna whup him again.

You tell him that for me." I said I would tell him that, and she let go of my arm and shuffled past me down the corridor.

> *This may be the last time I pray with you,*
> *This may be the last time, I don't know.*
> *This may be the last time I sing with you,*
> *This may be the last time, I don't know.*

The girls were still singing in the parlor, and I went back to find Priscilla. Next to the piano stood a five-year-old girl, wide-eyed, sucking on a lollipop. "Are you Paula?" I asked. She nodded her head slowly without taking the lollipop out of her mouth. This was the pet sister to whom Jimmy later dedicated *Notes of a Native Son*. "I'm a friend of your brother, Jimmy," I said. "I've heard a lot about you." She stared back at me without saying a word.

"Yes, all of us remember Jimmy," Mr. Raspberry was saying to Priscilla. I had the impression that he had said this several times before.

"Did you find Mrs. Baldwin?" Priscilla asked me. "Did she say anything about dinner?"

"Oh, we're eating any time," Mr. Raspberry said. "Any time."

"Here you are." Mrs. Baldwin suddenly materialized. "You come with me now." To Mr. Raspberry, she added: "Not you."

She led us down the dark corridor where I had met Jimmy's aunt and then into an enormous kitchen–dining room. It was almost like a restaurant. There were about eight tables crammed onto the white-tiled floor, all set for six or eight places, all empty. She led us to one, asked us to sit down, and then brought on a great plate of spareribs, and there we sat, alone except for Mrs. Baldwin. She pulled up a chair to watch us eat.

"There now," she said. "I know Mr. Friedrich likes spareribs, so I hope he likes these."

"Very good," I said, gnawing away at this dish that I had come to hate.

"I know you like spareribs," she repeated.

When that was finished, she carried away the dishes and brought on the second and last course, potato pie—not sweet potato pie, potato pie.

"That's good for you," Mrs. Baldwin said. "Jimmy always liked that."

"Very good," I said. From the distance, the girls were still singing at the piano. Around us, the emptiness of the dining room was a judgment. Mrs. Baldwin did not mean it that way. It just was that way. Everybody would be more comfortable if we ate and left, and so we ate and left. After we had left, all the rest of them could eat.

"It was mighty nice of you to come here," Mrs. Baldwin said at the door. "I appreciated it."

"Thank you," Priscilla said.

"A great pleasure," I said.

"And you'll give Jimmy my love," Mrs. Baldwin said.

"I will," I said.

Down the dark stairway, and at the end, there was a man—the same man?—slouching in the door. We brushed past him, and he cursed at us as we left. Now we are in the street, and we know we can run if we have to. But we don't run. We walk, stared at from every stoop, muttered at by passersby. There is the corner, with neon lights that spell out the word SODA. There is a taxi coming down Lenox Avenue—wave—it stops—and now we can escape from Harlem.

When I got back to Paris the following month, I was feeling very prosperous—I had sold my first novel to Little, Brown, and *Life* had given me an advance to go to Rome to write an article about George Santayana—so I invited Jimmy out to dinner at an elegant restaurant on the boulevard St.-Germain, and there I heard the bizarre story of his arrest. Some friend of Jimmy's, not really a friend but rather a casual acquaintance, had become embroiled in a quarrel with his hotel concierge. Out of some childish desire for revenge, he had stripped the sheets off his bed and stamped out of the hotel.

This all seemed very funny, when he appeared at Jimmy's hotel on the rue du Bac in search of shelter, but then the police arrived at the hotel and arrested him for the theft of the sheets. For good measure, they also arrested Jimmy as a "receiver of stolen goods" (the same sheets) and led both culprits away in handcuffs.

"They kept saying, *'C'est pas grave, c'est pas grave,'* " Jimmy said, "but they locked us in a cell, and they wouldn't tell us when we'd get out."

Habeas corpus was not a concept that greatly concerned the Paris police, particularly in minor cases like this, and that was how Jimmy happened to spend a week in Fresnes, confined in an un-heated cell with five other suspected malefactors. Twice a day, they were given bread, coffee, and a lukewarm concoction known as *"la soupe."* "Silence is really all I remember of those first three days," he later recalled, "silence and the color gray."

After three days—on Christmas Eve—Jimmy was finally carted to the Palais de Justice for a trial, but when the judge learned that he was an American, and that there was no interpreter available, the judge sent him back to Fresnes until after Christmas. It was only because another prisoner got acquitted that day, and offered to de-liver any messages that his incommunicado cellmates wanted to send to the outside world, that Jimmy managed to get word of his plight to Tommy, and Tommy got the charges dropped.

"Write it all down," I said as we sipped our coffee.

"I'm going to, I'm going to," Jimmy said. And he eventually did, calling it "Equal in Paris." "My flight from home was the cruelest trick I had ever played on myself," he wrote, "since it had led me here, down to a lower point than any I could ever in my life have imagined—lower, far, than anything I had seen in . . . Harlem."

A couple of weeks later, I was sitting in some café with Jimmy, I forget which one, and we were talking about something, I forget what, and he suddenly turned on me and said, "There's something you said that I'll never forgive you for."

"Jesus, what now?"

"You told someone that all of Harlem should be bombed and destroyed." He started trembling, and his eyes bulged in fury.

"Yeah, I hated it, I hated everything about it."

"That's very interesting," Jimmy said very formally, "but it so happens that my mother lives there. I'll never forgive you for that."

"For Christ's sake, I didn't mean that your mother was supposed to be bombed—what's the matter with you anyway?—I mean the place itself ought to be wiped out, not the people, the place."

"That's easy to talk about," Jimmy said. "But I grew up there."

"And you like it?"

"No, I hate it."

The people in Harlem know they are living there because white people do not think they are good enough to live anywhere else. No amount of "improvement" can sweeten this fact. Whatever money is now being earmarked to improve this, or any other ghetto, might as well be burnt. A ghetto can be improved in one way only: out of existence.

—NOBODY KNOWS MY NAME

On the afternoon of April 13, 1950, Priscilla and I climbed the marble stairway of the Mairie du VIème Arrondissement, on the southwest corner of the place St.-Sulpice, with Jimmy and Mary following behind as witnesses.

It is not easy to get married in Paris. Once the girl has agreed, you have to confront the French law in all its majesty. Aside from such routine papers as a birth certificate, passport, and *carte de séjour,* you have to provide proof that you do not suffer from tuberculosis or venereal disease.* If any of your documents are in English, they have to be translated by an officially authorized translator. ("Ah," said the old lady whom I had selected from the official list, "you are going to be married on the place St.-Sulpice? How marvelous! You know the finance ministry building that used to be a monastery? That is where Renan lost his faith!"), and the translations must be certified at the local police station. Everything must be stamped by the Foreign Ministry, and the Finance Ministry, and the American embassy. When all the documents are completed, stamped, and paid for—since anybody who stamps anything charges a fee for it—you present them all at the mairie, where a forbidding lady in a blue uniform puts still more stamps on them. Now the banns will be posted for two weeks on the door of the mairie, and only then will Monsieur le Maire perform the ceremony.

We were welcomed at the head of the stairs by the forbidding

---

*At least, these were the regulations in 1950. I have heard that they have been relaxed somewhat in recent years.

lady in blue, who was no longer forbidding. As mistress of ceremonies, she had changed from her blue uniform into a dress of brown velvet, and she led us up another flight of marble stairs to a vast ceremonial room, entirely empty. *"Asseyez-vous,"* she said, "Monsieur le Maire will be with you shortly." Then she left. We all sat numbly on the first row of seats. Next to us, the high narrow windows of the mairie gave onto the sunny place St.-Sulpice, but we were too distracted to notice. The door behind the dais opened, and the lady in brown reappeared with Monsieur le Maire, a frail, gray-haired figure made majestic by the broad, tricolored sash of office that sloped across his chest. He looked at us with some misgivings. Priscilla wore a dark blue dress that she had bought as a wedding gown, but I was dressed in mismatched secondhand corduroys, and neither Jimmy nor Mary, the two witnesses, looked very matrimonial.

"Eh bien, eh bien," the mayor said uncertainly.

"Avancez devant Monsieur le Maire," the lady in brown said to me.

As we stood before him, expecting some French equivalent of the familiar Anglo-American wedding ceremony, the mayor read aloud to us from the relevant sections of the Code Napoléon. It is a splendid document, listing all the duties of the wife to the husband. He alone will decide, among other things, where the couple is to live and how the children are to be educated. When that was done, the mayor asked Priscilla and me whether, having heard the rules of the Code Napoléon, we were ready to accept each other as man and wife. We each said *"Oui,"* and that was that. The civil registry was pushed forward, and we all signed it. Then we were handed the *Livret de famille,* a brown booklet that contained bureaucratic forms for the births and deaths of three spouses and nine children, and we signed that too. Then the lady in brown motioned us forward to accept the compliments of the mayor, and the mayor looked us over again, and then said, *"Eh bien—vous partez bientôt?"* No, we said, we were not planning to leave soon, we were planning to live in Paris. "Ah," said the mayor. *"Eh bien, bonne chance!"*

The rest of that day is very blurred. We went to the Café de la Mairie, the four of us, and to the amazement of the proprietors, we ordered a bottle of champagne. Then we ordered another. Somewhere in the midst of the hilarity, it was agreed that Jimmy and Mary would be the godparents of our first child. Mary promised to knit the infant a pair of "revolutionary mittens," ornamented with tiny hammers and sickles. We wandered down to St.-Germain-des-Prés— to the Café de Flore, I think—and ordered still another bottle of champagne. Then Priscilla and I fell into a taxi and drove to the Gare de Lyon and took a train to Italy for a honeymoon.

Soon after we got back, it became apparent that Monsieur le Maire had been right, and that we were leaving soon. If you live alone in Paris, without responsibilities and without scruples, you can last almost indefinitely, but the economics of married life, no matter how Bohemian, are quite different, and the money goes very fast. In this month or two of accelerating bankruptcy, I saw little of Jimmy, and I never saw him without asking for the money he owed me, an accumulation of borrowed drinks and meals that added up to something on the order of seventy-five dollars. To my surprise, and perhaps to his, I got back every penny of it, a few thousand francs at a time, but it was a painful process for both of us, and it did no good— I was still going bankrupt. At the age of twenty-one, I couldn't get any work in Paris, and so I finally went to Germany and found a job as a sportswriter on *The Stars and Stripes.*

Several of the other people at *Stripes* were also refugees from Paris, and now that we had found a sanctuary, it was customary to drive back to Paris every once in a while. The government work week was five and a half days, which, at *Stripes,* took the form of eleven days' work and three days off. But when the officers'-club life in Darmstadt became totally unbearable, which was fairly common, you could ask permission to work twenty-two days straight in exchange for six days off. At the end of twenty-two days, with your nerves snapping like loose wires, you'd head out onto the autobahn for the west and reach Metz by midnight for late dinner at the Grand Hotel and the first night's sleep back in France.

Coming back to Paris under such circumstances was a fragmentary experience. Lipp's and the Deux Magots still looked the same, with the same portly waiters in their long aprons, but now we were outsiders, tourists, with a car and new clothes, and traveler's checks. We had been outsiders before, of course—always—but living in Paris makes it easy to forget that. And the Quarter was full of new people.

They all looked pretty much the same, with the same beards and long hair and blue jeans, but the faces were unfamiliar. New waves arrived in Paris every month, and old friends kept disappearing. The leftist organization that Mary worked for had been thrown out of the country, and Mary had followed it into exile in Vienna. Gidske was back in Norway, and nobody knew where Themistocles was (actually, the two of them got married in London about a year later). Schaefer had married some American girl, which seemed a good thing, but he and his wife had become total Ouspenskyites, which was not so good. They had bought a farm outside Paris, and there they lived by the mystic regulations on diet and discipline. Jimmy was still around, along with a handful of others, but it takes only a few months for friends to become strangers. You lose track of all the details of what they are doing, and after a while, it doesn't even really matter very much. We'd meet in a café and be glad to see each other, and exchange news, and then there wasn't much more to say, and soon it would be time to get in the car and drive back to Germany.

We all come home, eventually, the expatriates, and we come home with a glum sense of having to buckle down. Europe was great, but it's over now, and so is everything that happened there. Here everything is different. We have to get steady jobs and commute and pay oil bills and take out life insurance. Time is passing, and we must finally confront all those unpleasantnesses that are combined in the term *reality*. I came back in 1954, at the age of twenty-five, with three children, and Jimmy returned two years later, and by now, of course, we were complete strangers.

I got a job on the *New York Daily News,* writing about murder and mayhem, and it seemed very odd to get a telephone call from Jimmy. I don't think I had ever heard his voice on the telephone in Paris. I asked him to meet me at Tim Costello's, a vaguely literary Third Avenue bar (where James Thurber had drawn the murals on the walls), which was then about the best I could afford. I stood at the bar and drank beer for half an hour before Jimmy finally drifted in, bringing a friend. There was no time for more than a sandwich and a few remarks. Jimmy said he wanted to see more of me, and to see Priscilla, and even to see his "godchild," who was then about four, so I invited him out to dinner at the house where we were living, in Massapequa, on the south shore of Long Island. We set a date, and Priscilla cooked a dinner, and then Jimmy called up late that afternoon to say he couldn't make it. The woman scorned, like whom hell hath no fury, is not only the woman rejected in romance but also the woman who has just cooked a dinner for an old friend who telephones to say that he can't come. "Damn him!" Priscilla said. "I don't care if I never see him again."

When I describe the "reality" to which the expatriate inevitably returns, I unconsciously describe the realities of the white middle class. The realities to which Jimmy returned were quite different. The Supreme Court's 1954 decision on school desegregation was by now two years old, the South had pledged resistance, and the civil rights movement was getting under way. These were the days of Montgomery and Little Rock. To me and people like me, these were remote events in which, with the help of our good will, the good blacks of the South would eventually win their way against the wicked rednecks. To Jimmy, these "remote" events were the physical incarnation of every word he had ever said or written. He went south for the first time, to see things happen. He saw the victims being attacked for trying to enter schools or restaurants, for riding a bus or registering to vote, and he got angry in a way that far transcended his old anger about the miseries of a Harlem childhood. He got angry at the sight of schoolchildren being spat upon by shouting mobs, angry at his own fear of being spat upon himself. After all that self-conscious agonizing in Paris, he was finally finding out what it really meant to be black, and one thing that it meant was that the world was divided, and would forever be divided, between white people and colored people. In his best book, *The Fire Next Time,* he put the implications of this perception in the form of an arresting question: "Do I really *want* to be integrated into a burning house?"

More years passed. In about 1960, Jimmy telephoned and asked whether we could have lunch, and I said sure, and we went to the Blue Ribbon, a cluttered old German restaurant off Times Square. It was good to see him again, but we weren't really seeing each other. We exchanged news, but there wasn't much news to exchange. He was writing a lot, and I read about him in the newspapers; I was writing foreign news for *Newsweek,* and nothing else that I did amounted to much. He seemed vaguely surprised to hear that I was writing anything else at all, and not greatly interested. What he wanted, really, was to get in touch with an actor who was a good friend of mine, and who he thought might be useful. Jimmy was in the process of getting his first play staged at the Actors' Studio— *Blues for Mister Charley,* it must have been—and he talked glowingly about "Gadge" and "Lee" and what a great help they were. One was supposed to know immediately who these famous theatrical figures were. That was all part of Jimmy's new world. He seemed very prosperous, and I had four children to support, so when he reached for the bill, I let him pay it.

"Why on earth did you do that?" Priscilla asked later.

"Well, why on earth not?" I said.

I felt—what I felt was that Jimmy was paying me off, settling all scores and all debts outstanding.

And Jimmy's books kept pouring forth: *Go Tell It on the Mountain* had achieved a well-deserved success in 1953; *Notes of a Native Son* an equally well-deserved success in 1955. Then came *Giovanni's Room* (1956), a rather unpleasant attempt to write about white homosexuals, then another excellent collection of magazine articles, *Nobody Knows My Name* (1961), then the rather overblown and sentimental novel *Another Country* (1962), then the powerful sermon *The Fire Next Time* (1963). If this succession of works demonstrated that Jimmy's youthful faith in himself as a novelist was somewhat misplaced, it also demonstrated that as a prophetic polemicist, he had few peers. At a time when the black civil rights movement really had no voice except for the rather simple pieties of Martin Luther King, Jr., Jimmy suddenly became its voice.

He also became, as a consequence, that kind of media icon once known as "a spokesman for his race" and now more generally called "a leader of the black community." Jimmy wisely resisted such designations. "A spokesman assumes that he is speaking for others," he told one interviewer. "I never assumed that I could." Instead, he declared that his purpose was to "bear witness to the truth."

There was an ugly new element, though, in Jimmy's bearing witness, and that was a very open hostility to white people, all of them. "I was forced to admit something I had always hidden from myself . . . that I hated and feared white people," he wrote in the introduction to *Notes of a Native Son*. "This did not mean that I loved black people; on the contrary, I despised them." He went still further in *Blues for Mister Charley*. "I'm going to treat every one of them [whites] as though they were responsible for all the crimes that ever happened in the history of the world—oh, yes!" says the young character named Richard. "They're responsible for all the misery *I've* ever seen, and that's good enough for me. . . . The only way the black man's going to *get* any power is to drive all the white men into the sea."

"You're going to make yourself sick," says his grandmother. "You're going to make yourself sick with hatred."

"No, I'm not," says Richard. "I'm going to make myself well. I'm going to make myself *well* with hatred—what do you think of that?"

The 1960s thought wonderfully well of that. It was a time when a convicted sex offender named Eldridge Cleaver won considerable attention by attacking Jimmy as a self-hating weakling, and declaring that he, Cleaver, was going to tear down the country. Attorney General Robert Kennedy (my college classmate, if I may mention it) summoned Jimmy to Washington to tell the authorities of Camelot what the downtrodden were really thinking. "I and other people have tried to warn the nation," Jimmy declared, warning the nation yet again, "that a day was coming when the young would not speak not only to Bobby Kennedy—they would not speak to Martin Luther King and me." That appeared on the front page of the *Times*. And not too long after that, Jimmy, our Jimmy, appeared on the cover of *Time* magazine.

I kept trying to remember, from time to time, that we had once been good friends. I called up his agent, and got a low, sepulchral voice on the phone.

"Could you tell me how I could get hold of Jimmy Baldwin?" I asked.

"No," said the low, sepulchral voice.

"Does that mean that you don't know or that you can't tell me?"

"Well, let me think. He has gone to Expo to do a television show there, and then he is going to the coast, for a show there, and then to Chicago . . ."

"When will he be back here?"

"People come and go," said the sepulchral voice. "And Thomas Stearns Eliot said they talk of Michelangelo."

"Look, will you please just tell him that I'd like to talk with him?" I said.

"Was this in reference to his possibly writing something for your magazine, or is it just personal?"

"Just personal," I said. No answer ever came.

I have thought a lot about Jimmy over the years, about what he was and what he became, and about the difficulties of maintaining a friendship across time and space and what a sociologist might call a clash of cultures. Friendship is more fragile than we realize, and it breaks like a vase, not in a great explosion but in small, unexplainable cracks that begin to leak. Friendships are more easily lost than made, and as we get older, we make fewer new ones and lose more old ones, and for the most diverse reasons. They marry people one doesn't like, or go into Wall Street, or become tiresome alcoholics, or start preaching anti-Communism, or remain Bohemians after one has passed the age when it is time to stop being Bohemian. Friends are people one discovers on one's path, and likes, and as paths diverge, as they usually do, one finds that there is nothing more to talk about. And all this is worse, more difficult, when one is white and one is black. Can there ever be real friendship, real trust, between the two? I don't think so, and I don't know any substantial evidence to the contrary.

The basic fact is that none of us in Paris ever really knew Jimmy at all, nor did he know us. Not that we were patronizing, not that we congratulated ourselves for liking a black, not that we

represented the "white liberals" who are now so widely criticized. We were not trying to do good works, not trying to "solve
the Negro problem." We were simply innocent ("It is the innocence which constitutes the crime," Jimmy wrote in *The Fire
Next Time*). I, for one, had never before known a black well. And
in our innocence, we really thought that race did not matter very
much.

It is difficult now to imagine such a state of innocence (or ignorance), but there really was a time when television did not exist,
America had the only thermonuclear weapons in the world, people
crossed the Atlantic on steamships, and "the Negro problem" was
largely a matter of minor unpleasantnesses in the remote South. The
South was segregated by law, but that was something that would
eventually be worked out. When we occasionally met a black in the
North, we would treat him politely, if distantly, as a sign that we
didn't care, as long as he behaved himself, what his race was. It
never occurred to us that *he* might care.

In short, we knew very little about Jimmy because we knew very
little about his blackness, but the opposite is just as true: that he
knew very little about whites, that his assumption that knowing
blackness meant knowing whiteness was completely false, that he
could hardly imagine a world in which race was really unimportant,
a minor inconvenience for other people, not a matter worth much
attention, much less emotion, much less anger.

We all divide up the world in different ways, according to our
sense of ourselves, and of what is important. The world can thus be
divided into blacks and whites but also into Jews and Gentiles, Communists and non-Communists, Americans and foreigners, soldiers
and civilians, the blind and the sighted, Catholics and non-Catholics,
Harvard men and non–Harvard men, Armenians and non-Armenians.
Other people's distinctions often seem absurd; only one's own are
important and natural and—

*If one is continually surviving the worst that life can bring, one even-
tually ceases to be controlled by a fear of what life can bring; whatever it
brings must be borne.*

—THE FIRE NEXT TIME

I wrote most of this article twenty years ago, in 1968, but I was never satisfied with it, and so I never made any attempt to get it published. For one thing, it didn't seem to have any ending. Jimmy just drifting off into fifteen years of distant celebrity seemed a rather inconclusive outcome. Then there was a tone of carping and complaint that I didn't much like, as though I were jealous of Jimmy's good fortunes, which I really don't think I was. I disagreed with most of what he said, most of what made him such a hero of the 1960s, but I don't think I am someone who begrudges a friend his success. At least, I hope not. On the contrary, more power to them all, the false prophets just as much as the true.

A couple of years ago, on reading that Jimmy had received the French *légion d'honneur,* I dug out my article again to see if it couldn't be fixed and finished. The *légion d'honneur* for the onetime prisoner of Fresnes, the receiver of stolen sheets! Surely, there was a good ending there. Who else had experienced such a range of official approval and disapproval? "It's a love affair," the newspapers quoted Jimmy as saying about France as a second homeland (he had bought a house in St.-Paul-de-Vence). "This is the place where I grew up, insofar as you can ever say you grow up." But even in quoting such things, I could see that the tone of carping was still there, further soured by a touch of derision.

And I did finally see Jimmy again, in the most absurdly appropriate of places, one of the executive dining rooms on the forty-third floor of the Time-Life Building in Rockefeller Center. The editor in chief, Henry Grunwald, felt that it was some combination of duty and perks to invite eminent figures from the outside world to come and tell the somewhat cloistered editors of *Time* their views of things. These were generally officials from the upper-middle levels of Washington, but Grunwald periodically demanded more diversity, and so his guests could be as diverse as Moshe Dayan and Twiggy.

In July of 1977, for the second time in a decade, all the lights went out in New York. The first time, there had been much stoic fortitude, and the press congratulated the citizenry for behaving almost like the Londoners of the Blitz; the second time, there was widespread looting, and the press took a much darker view of things.

One of *Time*'s black writers (soon to be dismissed) decided that he was hearing too many racist looter jokes in the corridors, and that *Time*'s almost entirely white staff should acquire a new perspective by hearing from that eloquent spokesman of the ghetto, James Baldwin. Grunwald was delighted at the prospect. The invitations to lunch included me, as the editor of several departments of the magazine, plus what few black staffers *Time* then had, three or perhaps four of them.

And Jimmy put on a truly impressive show. There were still strong echoes of what he used to say in Paris, but everything had now been tempered and polished by hundreds of TV talk shows and college lectures, magazine interviews, fund-raising speeches, the whole curriculum of public appearance. He was passionate, witty, rueful, prophetic. He told us why the looters had looted, and why it was our fault. He had, of course, already written all these things at least as well. He had written in *The Fire Next Time* that there had come a moment in his youth when he "could not discover any principled reason for not becoming a criminal," and that this was because he was "icily determined . . . never to make my peace with the ghetto but to die and go to Hell before I would let any white man spit on me." It is one of the odd rules of journalism that journalists are never so impressed by the printed word as by the spoken word, and Jimmy at that lunch, in that melodious voice, could have persuaded his listeners of just about anything.

The thing that stayed in my mind, though, was his grand opening. "Perhaps the best way to explain, the best way to try to tell you what I mean, is to tell you that I have been in your kitchens," he said. "My mother was a cleaning woman, you see, and sometimes, when I was a child, she would take me with her when she went to clean your kitchens. So I have seen your kitchens, you know, but you have never seen mine."

The *Time* staffers sat hushed, impressed, even moved, but I could not help thinking, as I munched on prosciutto down at the far end of the table, "No, Jimmy, that isn't true. I'm the one who has been in your kitchen, eating spareribs and potato pie, and you know nothing about mine." But I knew my place and said nothing like that. I just noticed that Jimmy was one of those word-drunk luncheon

guests—King Norodom Sihanouk of Cambodia was exactly the same—
who talk so volubly that course after course gets served to them,
ignored, and then removed uneaten. When Grunwald finally lit his
cigar and signaled the end of the meal, I took Jimmy out for a
hamburger, and we talked of old times. I put it on my *Time* expense
account.

There was one last encounter. We were going to the opera,
Priscilla and I, and we made a date to meet for dinner at a nearby
restaurant, the Ginger Man. As soon as I arrived, I saw Priscilla
waving from a distant table.

"You'd never guess who's here!" she cried. "Jimmy!"

He was in the middle of being interviewed by a young black
woman. There was also a middle-aged white man who struck me as
the kind of fellow who picked up tabs. Introductions were made,
and drinks ordered, but everything gave way before Jimmy's excited
reunion with Priscilla. She had known him longer than I had, and
she had not seen him for nearly thirty years, and the uneaten dinner
on Long Island now seemed forgotten.

The black woman patiently turned off her tape recorder. Priscilla
apologized for our interruption, and the black woman patiently
smiled. Then the reunion went on. What had happened to the first-
born godchild? (Jimmy had actually met her a few years earlier at
some party for Muhammad Ali. "You spook me," he had said. "Well,
you spook me," she had answered.) The godchild was well, now
working for CBS, and her younger sister was already married. Grand-
children were expected soon.

Jimmy laughed delightedly. Jimmy was courtly. Jimmy said that
the news of the children made him feel old, but it was the old age
of warm reminiscences, a reasonable feeling when one nears sixty.
After twenty minutes or so, though, the reminiscences began to
flicker and die down, like an untended fire, and I mentioned the
implacability of the opera's policies on curtain time. We had planned
to eat at the Ginger Man, but now it seemed more diplomatic to
mention a reservation awaiting us at some other restaurant. Good-
bye, good-bye! Let's keep in touch!

"You're sure you didn't want to join them for dinner?" I said out in the street a few minutes later.

"No," Priscilla said. "But who was that woman interviewing him? I didn't catch her name."

"Alice Walker," I said.

"But she's the one who wrote that new book I've been reading, *The Color Purple,* and it's very good."

"Well, somebody always gets neglected," I said.

"Did you know that James Baldwin died?" one of the *Time* researchers asked.

"No, really? Of what?" I said.

"Stomach cancer, just this morning," she said. "Shouldn't you be the one to write the obituary?"

"Well, maybe I should."

I proposed to the editors what I called "a personal obituary," and they agreed. I began it with the same sentence I used to begin this memoir, but that did not lead anywhere. An obituary, in *Time* or anywhere else, really can't be too personal; it has to include the basic facts of the dead man's life, those and the conventional judgments about what made this life worth an obituary in the first place. The *Times* was no great help. It described Jimmy as "an eloquent voice of the civil rights movement." It reported that "some critics said his language was sometimes too elliptical, his indictments too sweeping," but then it turned to Ralph Ellison to declare that America had "lost one of its most gifted writers," and to Benjamin DeMott to announce that "his work showed a powerful commitment to the right values."

Then came the funeral service at the cavernous Cathedral of St. John the Divine, to which I did not go. I thought about going, I nearly went, but I decided not to. It was destined to be a sort of racial ingathering, a kind of repossession and certification. Jimmy was "not only a writer, an international literary figure," said Amiri Baraka, "he was a man, spirit, voice—old and black and terrible as that first ancestor." Maya Angelou said that he had been a brother, and that "he knew that black women need brothers."

And what did I know? I knew Jimmy for only about two years out of our sixty, and in those two years, he was not making any "commitment to the right values," and he was not being "old and black and terrible as that first ancestor." So what could I use, to write his obituary, except his subsequent writings, and the sheaves of newspaper clippings, the speeches and interviews? As for the overall judgment, I wrote that he had "defined and demonstrated in a new way what it meant to be black, and to be white as well." That was reasonably true, I guess, but it was only an approximation of a public verdict. The Jimmy I remember, as well as I can remember him, is here.

1968/1988

INDEX OF NAMES